Switching Basics
and Intermediate Routing
CCNA 3 Labs and Study Guide

Allan Johnson

W9-AXN-293

Cisco Press

800 East 96th Street
Indianapolis, Indiana 46240 USA

Switching Basics and Intermediate Routing
CCNA 3 Labs and Study Guide

Allan Johnson

Copyright © 2007 Cisco Systems, Inc.

Published by:
Cisco Press
800 East 96th Street
Indianapolis, IN 46240 USA

Printed in the United States of America.

Seventeenth Printing, January 2013

Library of Congress Cataloging-in-Publication Number: 2006920177

ISBN: 1-58713-171-4
ISBN-13: 978-1-58713-171-4

Warning and Disclaimer

This book is designed to provide information about the 640-801 CCNA exam. Every effort has been made to make this book as complete and as accurate as possible, but no warranty or fitness is implied.

The information is provided on an "as is" basis. The authors, Cisco Press, and Cisco Systems, Inc., shall have neither liability nor responsibility to any person or entity with respect to any loss or damages arising from the information contained in this book or from the use of the discs or programs that may accompany it.

The opinions expressed in this book belong to the author and are not necessarily those of Cisco Systems, Inc.

Feedback Information

At Cisco Press, our goal is to create in-depth technical books of the highest quality and value. Each book is crafted with care and precision, undergoing rigorous development that involves the unique expertise of members from the professional technical community.

Readers' feedback is a natural continuation of this process. If you have any comments regarding how we could improve the quality of this book, or otherwise alter it to better suit your needs, you can contact us through e-mail at feedback@ciscopress.com. Please make sure to include the book title and ISBN in your message.

We greatly appreciate your assistance.

Publisher
Paul Boger

Executive Editor
Mary Beth Ray

Cisco Representative
Anthony Wolfenden

Cisco Press Program Manager
Sonia Torres Chavez

Manager, Marketing Communications, Cisco Systems
Scott Miller

Cisco Marketing Program Manager
Edie Quiroz

Executive Editor
Mary Beth Ray

Production Manager
Patrick Kanouse

Development Editor
Andrew Cupp

Senior Project Editor
San Dee Phillips

Copy Editor
Bill McManus

Technical Editor
Bernadette O'Brien

Team Coordinator
Vanessa Williams

Book and Cover Designer
Louisa Adair

CISCO SYSTEMS

Corporate Headquarters
Cisco Systems, Inc.
170 West Tasman Drive
San Jose, CA 95134-1706
USA
www.cisco.com
Tel: 408 526-4000
      800 553-NETS (6387)
Fax: 408 526-4100

European Headquarters
Cisco Systems International BV
Haarlerbergpark
Haarlerbergweg 13-19
1101 CH Amsterdam
The Netherlands
www-europe.cisco.com
Tel: 31 0 20 357 1000
Fax: 31 0 20 357 1100

Americas Headquarters
Cisco Systems, Inc.
170 West Tasman Drive
San Jose, CA 95134-1706
USA
www.cisco.com
Tel: 408 526-7660
Fax: 408 527-0883

Asia Pacific Headquarters
Cisco Systems, Inc.
Capital Tower
168 Robinson Road
#22-01 to #29-01
Singapore 068912
www.cisco.com
Tel: +65 6317 7777
Fax: +65 6317 7799

Cisco Systems has more than 200 offices in the following countries and regions. Addresses, phone numbers, and fax numbers are listed on the
Cisco.com Web site at www.cisco.com/go/offices.

Argentina • Australia • Austria • Belgium • Brazil • Bulgaria • Canada • Chile • China PRC • Colombia • Costa Rica • Croatia • Czech Republic
Denmark • Dubai, UAE • Finland • France • Germany • Greece • Hong Kong SAR • Hungary • India • Indonesia • Ireland • Israel • Italy
Japan • Korea • Luxembourg • Malaysia • Mexico • The Netherlands • New Zealand • Norway • Peru • Philippines • Poland • Portugal
Puerto Rico • Romania • Russia • Saudi Arabia • Scotland • Singapore • Slovakia • Slovenia • South Africa • Spain • Sweden
Switzerland • Taiwan • Thailand • Turkey • Ukraine • United Kingdom • United States • Venezuela • Vietnam • Zimbabwe

Trademark Acknowledgments

All terms mentioned in this book that are known to be trademarks or service marks have been appropriately capitalized. Cisco Press or Cisco Systems, Inc., cannot attest to the accuracy of this information. Use of a term in this book should not be regarded as affecting the validity of any trademark or service mark.

About the Author

Allan Johnson entered the academic world in 1999 after 10 years as a business owner/operator to dedicate his efforts to his passion for teaching. He has an MBA and an M.Ed in occupational training and development. Allan is currently pursuing an MS in information security. He is an information technology instructor at Mary Carroll High School and Del Mar College in Corpus Christi, Texas. Since 2003, Allan has committed much of his time and energy to the CCNA Instructional Support Team providing services for instructors worldwide and creating training materials. He is a familiar voice on the Cisco Networking Academy Community forum, "Ask the Experts" series. He currently holds CCNA and CCAI certifications.

About the Technical Reviewer

Bernadette O'Brien has been teaching in the Cisco Networking Academy since 1998 in Schenectady, New York. Schenectady High School is a Regional Academy for CCNA and a CATC for Sponsored Curriculum, which Bernadette coordinates.

Bernadette received her BS degree from SUNY College at Buffalo and her MS degree in curriculum and instruction from SUNY Albany. She is also CCNA and CCAI certified.

Bernadette, her husband, and two children live in a Victorian village very near the Adirondack Mountains in upstate New York. They enjoy rehabbing their 120-year-old Victorian house, skiing, and hiking.

About the Contributor

Jim Lorenz is a curriculum developer for Cisco Networking Academy Program who co-authored the third editions of the *Lab Companions* for the CCNA courses. He has over 20 years experience in information systems and has held various IT positions in several Fortune 500 companies, including Allied-Signal, Honeywell, and Motorola. Jim has developed and taught computer and networking courses for both public and private institutions for more than 15 years.

Dedications

To my wife Becky, and my daughter Christina. Thank you both for your love and patience.

Acknowledgments

As technical editor, Bernadette O'Brien served admirably as my second pair of eyes, finding and correcting technical inaccuracies as well as grammatical errors that helped make this project a first-class production.

Mary Beth Ray, executive editor, did an outstanding job from beginning to end steering this project through to completion. I can always count on Mary Beth to make the tough decisions.

Andrew Cupp, development editor, has a dedication to perfection that pays dividends in countless, unseen ways. Thank you for providing me much-needed guidance and support. This book could not be a reality without your persistence.

Lastly, I cannot forget to thank all my students—past and present—who have helped me over the years to create engaging and exciting activities and labs. There is no better way to test the effectiveness of an activity than to give it to a team of dedicated students. They excel at finding the obscurest of errors! I could have never done this without all of your support.

Contents at a Glance

Contents

Introduction

Switching Basics and Intermediate Routing CCNA 3 Lab Study Guide is a supplement to your classroom and laboratory experience with the Cisco Networking Academy Program. Specifically, this book covers the third of four courses. To be successful on the exam and achieve your CCNA certification, you should do everything in your power to arm yourself with a variety of tools and training materials to support your learning efforts. This *Lab Study Guide* is just such a collection of tools. Used to its fullest extent, it will help you gain the knowledge as well as practice the skills associated with the content area of the CCNA 3 Switching Basics and Intermediate Routing course. Specifically, this book will help you to work on these main areas of CCNA 3:

- Advanced IP addressing techniques (VLSM)

- Routing protocols: RIPv2, single-area OSPF, and EIGRP

- Switching technologies and LAN design

- Switch configurations: security, STP, VLANs, and VTP

Lab Study Guides similar to this one are also available for the other three courses: *Networking Basics CCNA 1 Lab Study Guide*, *Routers and Routing Basics CCNA 2 Lab Study Guide*, and *WAN Technologies CCNA 4 Lab Study Guide*.

Goals and Methods

The most important goal of this book is to help you pass either the CCNA exam (640-801) or the ICND exam (640-811). Whether you are studying for the full exam or the second part of your CCNA, passing either of these exams means that you not only have the required knowledge of the technologies covered by the exam, but also can plan, design, implement, operate, and troubleshoot these technologies. In other words, these exams are rigorously application-based. In fact, if you view the topics for the CCNA exam at http://www.cisco.com/web/learning/le3/current_exams/640-801.html, you will see the following four categories:

- Planning & Designing

- Implementation & Operation

- Troubleshooting

- Technology

Although Technology is listed last, a CCNA student cannot possibly plan, design, implement, operate, and troubleshoot networks without first fully grasping the technology. So, you need to devote a certain amount of time and effort in the Study Guide section of each chapter learning the concepts and theories before applying them in the Lab Exercises portion.

The Study Guide section of each chapter offers exercises that help you learn the concepts and configurations crucial to your success as a CCNA exam candidate. Each chapter is slightly different and includes some or all of the following types of exercises:

- Vocabulary matching and completion

- Skill building activities and scenarios

- Configuration scenarios

- Concept questions

- Journal entries

- Internet research

Icons Used in This Book

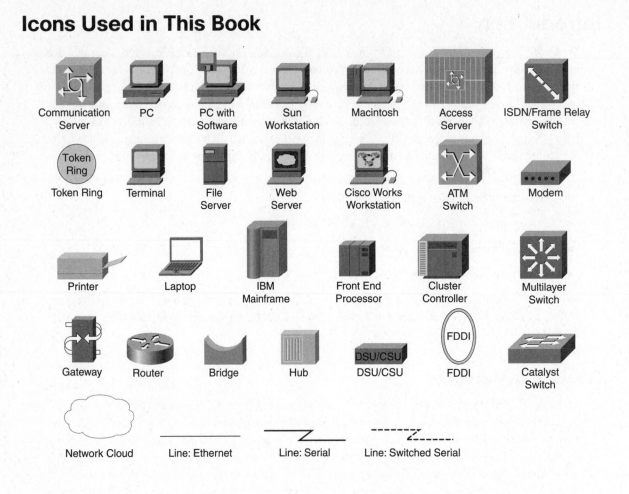

Command Syntax Conventions

The conventions that present command syntax in this book are the same conventions used in the IOS Command Reference. The Command Reference describes these conventions as follows:

- **Bold** indicates commands and keywords that are entered literally as shown. In actual configuration examples and output (not general command syntax), bold indicates commands that are manually input by the user (such as a **show** command).

- *Italic* indicates arguments for which you supply actual values.

- Vertical bars (|) separate alternative, mutually exclusive elements.

- Square brackets ([ ]) indicate optional elements.

- Braces ({ }) indicate a required choice.

- Braces within brackets ([{ }]) indicate a required choice within an optional element.

The Lab Exercises sections include a Command Reference table, all the online Curriculum Labs, and brand-new Comprehensive Labs and Challenge Labs. The Curriculum Labs typically walk you through the configuration tasks step by step. The Comprehensive Labs combine many, if not all, of the configuration tasks of the Curriculum Labs without actually providing you with all the commands. The Challenge Labs take this a step further, often giving you only a general requirement that you must implement fully without the details of each small step. In other words, you must use the knowledge and skills you gained in the Curriculum Labs to successfully complete the Comprehensive and Challenge Labs. In fact, you should not attempt the Comprehensive or Challenge Labs until you have worked through all the Study Guide activities and the Curriculum Labs. When you work through the Comprehensive and Challenge Labs, avoid the temptation to flip back through the Curriculum Labs when you are not sure of a command. Do not try to short-circuit your CCNA training. Study the chapter's topics until you can do the Comprehensive and Challenge Labs without any help. You need a deep understanding of CCNA knowledge and skills to ultimately be successful on the CCNA exam.

How This Book Is Organized

Although you could work through the Study Guides and Lab Exercises in this book in order, the content of knowledge and skills actually flows down three separate paths. The flow chart shown in Figure I-1 graphically displays these paths.

Figure I-1   Paths for Using This Book

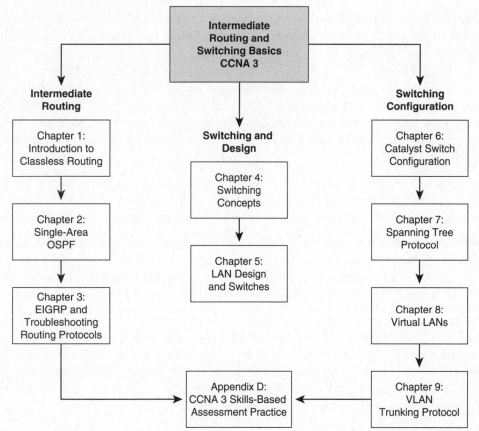

Chapters 1, 2, and 3 belong to the Intermediate Routing path and focus on VLSM and routing configuration. Chapters 4 and 5 belong to the Switching and Design path and focus on switching technologies and LAN design. Chapters 6, 7, 8, and 9 belong to the Switching Configuration path and focus on basic switching protocols and configurations. No path is dependent upon another path. Appendix D provides you with three different CCNA 3 Skills-Based Assessment practice labs.

Work through the Study Guide and Lab Exercises in the sequence in which they are presented. The sequence is designed to take you from a basic understanding of the knowledge topics through the full application and implementation of the skills. Individually, the chapters and appendixes include exercises and labs covering the following knowledge and skills:

- **Chapter 1, "Introduction to Classless Routing"**—Variable-Length Subnet Masking (VLSM) is arguably one of the most challenging skills you must master as a CCNA candidate. Therefore, this chapter spends a great deal of time on this topic. Use the large variety of exercises to solidify your VLSM skills. In the RIPv2 discussion of the Study Guide portion, you compare and contrast RIPv1 and RIPv2 and complete an Internet Research exercise. In the Lab Exercises portion is a Command Reference exercise to help you review all the commands covered in the chapter. The five Curriculum Labs focus your attention on the configuration tasks covered in the chapter. Two additional labs, a Comprehensive Lab and a Challenge Lab, help you review the commands and skills learned in the Curriculum Labs.

- **Chapter 2, "Single-Area OSPF"**—This chapter has plenty of vocabulary exercises to help you get a firm grasp of OSPF terminology. Additional exercises focus on specific concepts and skills. For example, the DR/BDR Election exercise concentrates on this challenging OSPF topic. Concept questions round out your study of the operation of OSPF. In the Lab Exercises portion is a Command Reference exercise to help you review all the commands covered in the chapter. The six Curriculum Labs focus your attention on the configuration tasks covered in the chapter. Two additional labs, a Comprehensive Lab and a Challenge Lab, help you review the commands and skills learned in the Curriculum Labs.

- **Chapter 3, "EIGRP and Troubleshooting Routing Protocols"**—This chapter covers the concepts and configurations of the Cisco-proprietary Enhanced Interior Gateway Routing Protocol (EIGRP). Exercises cover vocabulary and the EIGRP packet types. In the "EIGRP Configuration" section, you work through a comprehensive EIGRP configuration exercise. Finally, you work on your troubleshooting skills in the "Troubleshooting Routing Protocols" section. The Lab Exercises portion has a Command Reference exercise to help you review all the commands covered in the chapter. The two Curriculum Labs focus your attention on the configuration tasks covered in the chapter. Two additional labs, a Comprehensive Lab and a Challenge Lab, help you review the commands and skills learned in the Curriculum Labs.

- **Chapter 4, "Switching Concepts"**—This chapter is in many ways a review of concepts you have already learned in previous course work. Therefore, in addition to some vocabulary exercises, additional exercises concentrate on a few of the more difficult concepts, including CSMA/CD, the MAC address table, collision and broadcast domains, and cabling. There are no Lab Exercises for this chapter.

- **Chapter 5, "LAN Design and Switches"**—This chapter is mostly vocabulary and concepts. The exercises in this chapter ensure that you have a firm grasp of the vocabulary and concepts pertaining to LAN design and the three-layer hierarchical model. There are no Lab Exercises for this chapter.

- **Chapter 6, "Catalyst Switch Configuration"**—This chapter includes some vocabulary exercises and LED switch identification exercises. Most of the Study Guide portion is devoted to a basic switch configuration exercise. In the Lab Exercises section of this chapter, you will find a Command Reference exercise to help you review all the commands covered in the chapter. The ten Curriculum Labs focus your attention on the configuration tasks covered in the chapter. A Challenge Lab will help you review the commands and skills you learned in the Curriculum Labs.

- **Chapter 7, "Spanning Tree Protocol"**—This chapter covers the need for redundancy in today's production networks and explains how the Spanning Tree Protocol (STP) avoids switching loops in a redundant configuration. Study Guide exercises include vocabulary, concept questions, determining the root bridge, and spanning-tree recalculation. Because commands are limited to configuring the root bridge and verifying STP operation, the Lab Exercises are limited to the two online Curriculum Labs. However, STP configuration and verification commands are used in the Comprehensive and Challenge Labs of both Chapter 8 and Chapter 9.

- **Chapter 8, "Virtual LANs"**—This chapter begins the study of VLANs, which are increasingly becoming more prominent in production networks. Exercises focus on vocabulary, concepts, configuration, and troubleshooting. In the Lab Exercises section of this chapter, you will find a Command Reference exercise to help you review all the commands covered in the chapter. The three Curriculum Labs focus your attention on the configuration tasks covered in the chapter. An additional Challenge Lab combines VLAN configuration with port security (Chapter 6) and STP (Chapter 7).

- **Chapter 9, "VLAN Trunking Protocol"**—This chapter rounds out your CCNA study of VLANs with the VLAN Trunking Protocol. Exercises include vocabulary, concept questions, Internet research, and a journal entry. Also included are configuration exercises covering trunk configuration, VTP configuration, and inter-VLAN configuration. In the Lab Exercises section of this chapter, you will find a Command Reference exercise to help you review all the commands covered in the chapter. The four Curriculum Labs focus your attention on the configuration tasks covered in the chapter. Two additional labs, a Comprehensive Lab and a Challenge Lab, help you review the commands and skills learned in the Curriculum Labs as well as reinforce commands from Chapters 6, 7, and 8.

- **Appendix A, "Router Interface Summary Chart"**—This appendix has a table that you can reference for the appropriate IOS interface names to use on Cisco 800, 1600, 1700, 2500, and 2600 series routers.

- **Appendix B, "Erasing and Reloading the Switch"**—Because many of the labs require a clean switch configuration, this appendix includes the procedures you should complete before beginning.

- **Appendix C, "Erasing and Reloading the Router"**—Because many of the labs require a clean router configuration, this appendix includes the procedures you should complete before beginning.

- **Appendix D, "CCNA 3 Skills-Based Assessment Practice"**—This appendix contains three practice labs for the skills-based assessment. The first lab focuses on routing. The second lab focuses on switching. The third lab is comprehensive, including most of the commands and configurations you must master as a CCNA 3 student.

CHAPTER 1

Introduction to Classless Routing

The Study Guide portion of this chapter uses a combination of exercises to test your knowledge on classless routing.

The Lab Exercises portion of this chapter includes all of the online curriculum labs as well as a Comprehensive Lab and a Challenge Lab to ensure that you have mastered the practical, hands-on skills needed about classless routing.

Study Guide

VLSM

Today's networks must be stable yet scalable. Scalability means the initial design of the network must allow for change and growth without any major modifications to the overall design. A key element of good network design is an IP addressing plan that optimizes the use of IP addresses and minimizes the size of routing tables. This is achieved through the use of VLSM, CIDR, and route summarization. These are fundamental concepts and must be incorporated in your CCNA skill set before you move on to the more challenging topics of OSPF and EIGRP, which both incorporate VLSM and scalable network design.

The exercises in this section will help you build your skills in implementing VLSM addressing schemes, determining efficient route summaries, and configuring static and default routing. The exercises are meant to progress logically from establishing the use of terminology in the Vocabulary Exercises through applying your skill in design scenarios and application exercises. If you are new to the topic of VLSM, you should proceed through the exercises in the order presented. However if you are refreshing your skill, try one of the VLSM Addressing Design Scenarios or even Challenge Lab 1-7 to effectively gauge where you are weak. Then, choose additional exercises to reinforce your knowledge and skill.

Vocabulary Exercise: Matching

Match the definition on the left with a term on the right. This exercise is not necessarily a one-to-one matching. Some definitions may be used more than once and some terms may have multiple definitions.

Definition

a. With classful routing, _____ must be avoided because they are not visible across classful network boundaries.

b. does not advertise subnet mask information.

c. describes the combination of multiple contiguous classful network addresses into one advertisement.

d. the policy of advertising routes at the classful boundary.

e. When using a classful routing protocol, it is important that all subnets have the same as mask. This is sometimes referred to as

_____.

f. process of combining multiple subnets into one advertisement with a common prefix length (not necessarily on a classful boundary).

g. advertises subnet mask information.

h. When a router does not have an interface for the destination network, it sends traffic to its

_____.

i. With classless routing protocols, the subnet mask can be different from subnet to subnet. This is called _____.

j. also referred to as CIDR notation, bitmask, and network mask, the number of bits that are shared in common by all addresses in the address space.

k. specified by RFC 1519 to address the critical problems of exhaustion of Class B address space and the growth in size of Internet routing tables.

Term

___ classless inter-domain routing

___ classless routing protocol

___ prefix length

___ discontiguous subnets

___ route aggregation

___ fixed-length subnet masking (FLSM)

___ default route

___ automatic summarization

___ variable-length subnet mask (VLSM)

___ route summarization

___ supernetting

___ classful routing protocol

Vocabulary Exercise: Completion

Complete the paragraphs that follow by filling in appropriate words and phrases.

When using _____ routing protocols such as RIP and _____, you must use _____ _____, which means that all subnets within the same addressing scheme must share the same _____ _____. With these routing protocols, it is also very important to avoid _____, because they perform _____ at classful network boundaries. Subnets must be assigned to networks in sequential order because they are not advertised across the network boundary.

_____ is specified in RFC 1519 as a way to assign addresses by delineating the _____ of the common bits in the network portion of the address space instead of relying on the default subnet masks of Classes A, B, and C.

The implementation of CIDR allows the use of _____ routing protocols such as _____, IS-IS, _____, and BGPv4. These protocols effectively preserve address space and reduce the size of routing tables through the use of _____. These protocols are capable of advertising a collection of classful addresses in one big _____, which is a type of _____ _____ with which multiple address spaces can be combined into one route with a common network prefix.

The process of using routing protocols such as RIP or OSPF is often referred to as dynamic routing. Two other types of routing are available to the network administrator: _____ routing, which is the manual configuration of a network/subnet mask combination, and _____ routing, which is the manual configuration of a gateway of last resort.

Subnetting Review Exercises

Three basic subnetting review exercises follow, which will help you refresh your subnetting skills. You must be able to demonstrate a basic level of competency in subnetting before proceeding into VLSM.

Note: CIDR notation refers to the practice of representing the prefix length of the network portion of an address in "slash" format. For example, the CIDR notation of the Class C default subnet mask 255.255.255.0 is /24.

Class C Subnetting Scenario

Use the address space 192.168.1.0/24 and subnet it to provide enough addresses for 40 hosts.

What are the most bits you can borrow? _____

Assuming subnet 0 and the all-1s subnet are both useable, what is the total number of subnets? _____

What is the total number of useable hosts per subnet? _____

What is the new subnet mask in dotted-decimal notation? _____

What is the new subnet mask in CIDR notation? _____

What is the magic number or subnet multiplier? _____

Fill in the following table for the first ten useable subnets. All rows in the table may not be used.

Subnet No.	Subnet Address	Host Range	Broadcast Address
0			
1			
2			
3			
4			
5			
6			
7			
8			
9			

Class B Subnetting Scenario

Use the address space 172.16.0.0/16 and subnet it to provide 2000 subnets.

How many bits do you need to borrow? _____

Assuming subnet 0 and the all-1s subnet are both useable, what is the total number of subnets?_____

What is the total number of useable hosts per subnet? _____

What is the new subnet mask in dotted-decimal notation? _____

What is the new subnet mask in CIDR notation? _____

What is the magic number or subnet multiplier? _____

Fill in the following table for the first ten useable subnets. Note: All blanks may not be used.

Subnet No.	Subnet Address	Host Range	Broadcast Address
0			
1			
2			
3			
4			
5			
6			
7			
8			
9			

Class A Subnetting Scenario

Use the address space 10.0.0.0/8 and subnet it to provide enough addresses for 30,000 hosts.

What are the most bits you can borrow? _____

Assuming subnet 0 and the all-1s subnet are both useable, what is the total number of subnets? _____

What is the total number of useable hosts per subnet? _____

What is the new subnet mask in dotted-decimal notation? _____

What is the new subnet mask in CIDR notation? _____

What is the magic number or subnet multiplier? _____

Fill in the following table for the first ten useable subnets. Note: All blanks may not be used.

Subnet No.	Subnet Address	Host Range	Broadcast Address
0			
1			
2			
3			
4			
5			
6			
7			
8			
9			

Prefix Length Use Exercises

Use the following exercises to practice converting between dotted-decimal and prefix length representations (CIDR notation) of subnet masks.

Dotted-Decimal to Prefix Length Conversion

Convert the following subnets and subnet masks shown in dotted-decimal format into the equivalent prefix length format.

Example:

192.168.1.0 255.255.255.0; Answer: 192.168.1.0/24

192.168.1.0 255.255.255.128; Answer: _____

192.168.1.128 255.255.255.192; Answer: _____

192.168.1.32 255.255.255.224; Answer: _____

192.168.1.96 255.255.255.248; Answer: _____

192.168.1.48 255.255.255.252; Answer: _____

172.16.128.0 255.255.224.0; Answer: _____

172.16.8.0 255.255.255.128; Answer: _____

172.16.160.0 255.255.254.0; Answer: _____

172.16.80.0 255.255.240.0; Answer: _____

172.16.240.0 255.255.248.0; Answer: _____

172.16.39.0 255.255.255.0; Answer: _____

172.16.224.0 255.255.255.224; Answer: _____

172.16.45.24 255.255.255.248; Answer: _____

172.16.16.16 255.255.255.240; Answer: _____

172.16.200.192 255.255.255.192; Answer: _____

10.0.0.0 255.254.0.0; Answer: _____

10.5.160.32 255.255.255.224; Answer: _____

10.96.128.0 255.255.224.0; Answer: _____

10.64.48.0 255.255.255.240; Answer: _____

10.52.0.0 255.252.0.0; Answer: _____

Prefix Length to Dotted-Decimal Conversion

Convert the following subnets and subnet masks shown in prefix length format into the equivalent dotted-decimal format.

Example:

172.16.0.0/16; Answer: 172.16.0.0 255.255.0.0

192.168.2.240/29; Answer: _____

192.168.2.32/28; Answer: _____

192.168.2.0/25; Answer: _____

192.168.2.240/30; Answer: _____

192.168.2.192/26; Answer: _____

172.20.34.0/25; Answer: _____

172.20.64.0/18; Answer: _____

172.20.224.0/20; Answer: _____

172.20.16.0/23; Answer: _____

172.20.180.0/28; Answer: _____

172.20.36.0/22; Answer: _____

172.20.0.0/19; Answer: _____

172.20.128.0/17; Answer: _____

172.20.144.0/21; Answer: _____

172.20.96.96/27; Answer: _____

10.0.0.0/17; Answer: _____

10.0.154.32/28; Answer: _____

10.224.0.0/13; Answer: _____

10.32.0.0/22; Answer: _____

10.10.0.0/24; Answer: _____

Using Binary Math to AND the Subnet Address

Understanding how a router determines the network or subnet address for a given IP address is a fundamental skill to implementing VLSM and interpreting routing tables.

In the following exercises, use binary math to "AND" the host IP address and subnet mask to determine the subnet address. After completing the binary math, write the subnet address in dotted-decimal format.

In binary math, the AND operation is as follows:

1 AND 1 = 1; all other possibilities equal 0

Example:

192.168.1.67/28

IP address	11000000.10101000.00000001.01000011
Subnet mask	11111111.11111111.11111111.11110000
Subnet address	11000000.10101000.00000001.01000000
Dotted-decimal	192.168.1.64

1. 192.168.18.237/27

   IP address   _____

   Subnet mask   _____

   Subnet address   _____

   Dotted-decimal   _____

2. 192.168.35.142/29

   IP address   _____

   Subnet mask   _____

   Subnet address   _____

   Dotted-decimal   _____

3. 172.28.23.54/21

   IP address   _____

   Subnet mask   _____

   Subnet address   _____

   Dotted-decimal   _____

4. 172.31.32.69/25

   IP address   _____

   Subnet mask   _____

   Subnet address   _____

   Dotted-decimal   _____

5. 10.64.150.197/18

IP address
_____

Subnet mask
_____

Subnet address
_____

Dotted-decimal
_____

VLSM Subnetting a Subnet Exercises

Note: Now is a good time to complete Curriculum Lab 1-1: Calculating VLSM Subnets (1.1.4), which walks you through a VLSM addressing scenario.

VLSM is simply "subnetting a subnet." In the following exercises, use your subnetting skills to further subnet a given subnet. If it helps you, draw a topology that represents the requirement you are given.

Example:

Use the subnet 192.168.1.64/27 and further subnet this address to provide four additional subnets with at least six hosts per subnet. List all four subnets in network address/prefix format.

Step 1.   Determine how many host bits you have available in the given subnet. For subnet 192.168.1.64/27, you have a total of 5 host bits.

Step 2.   Determine how many host bits you can borrow to make an additional four subnets with at least six hosts per subnet. Borrowing an additional 2 bits will make four subnets ($2^2 = 4$). Because there are 3 host bits left after borrowing, each subnet will have exactly six host addresses ($2^3 - 2 = 6$).

Step 3.   Determine the new prefix and list the new subnets. Because you borrowed 2 bits, the new prefix is /29. You start with the first address 192.168.1.64 and list the four subnets.

Subnet No.	Network Address/Prefix
0	192.168.1.64/29
1	192.168.1.72/29
2	192.168.1.80/29
3	192.168.1.88/29

1. Use the subnet 192.168.1.128/25 and further subnet this address to provide eight additional subnets with at least ten hosts per subnet. List the first five subnets in network address/prefix format. What would be the last subnet?

_____

Subnet No.	Network Address/Prefix
0	
1	
2	
3	
4	

2. Use the subnet 172.16.32.0/19 and further subnet this address to provide eight additional subnets with at least 1000 hosts per subnet. List the first five subnets in network address/prefix format. What would be the last subnet?

_____

Subnet No.	Network Address/Prefix
0	
1	
2	
3	
4	

3. Use subnet 2 from the last question and further subnet this address to provide eight additional subnets with at least 100 hosts per subnet. List the first five subnets in network address/prefix format. What would be the last subnet?

_____

Subnet No.	Network Address/Prefix
0	
1	
2	
3	
4	

4. Use subnet 4 from the last question and further subnet this address to provide eight additional subnets with at least ten hosts per subnet. List the first five subnets in network address/prefix format. What would be the last subnet?

_____

Subnet No.	Network Address/Prefix
0	
1	
2	
3	
4	

5. Use subnet 0 from the last question and further subnet this address to provide four additional subnets to be used for point-to-point links. List all four subnets in network address/prefix format.

Subnet No.	Network Address/Prefix
0	
1	
2	
3	

6. Use the subnet 10.1.0.0/16 and further subnet this address to provide 30 additional subnets with at least 2000 hosts per subnet. List the first five subnets in network address/prefix format. What would be the last subnet?

Subnet No.	Network Address/Prefix
0	
1	
2	
3	
4	

7. Use subnet 4 from the last question and further subnet this address to provide 30 additional subnets with at least 60 hosts per subnet. List the first five subnets in network address/prefix format. What would be the last subnet?

Subnet No.	Network Address/Prefix
0	
1	
2	
3	
4	

8. Use subnet 1 from the last question and further subnet this address to provide 16 additional subnets to be used for point-to-point links. List the first 5 subnets in network address/prefix format. What would be the last subnet?

Subnet No.	Network Address/Prefix
0	
1	
2	
3	
4	

VLSM Addressing Design Exercises

In the following VLSM Addressing Design Exercises, you apply your VLSM addressing skills to a three router topology. Each exercise is progressively more difficult than the last. There may be more than one correct answer in some situations. However, you should always practice good addressing design by assigning your subnets contiguously. This allows the summary of a group of subnets into one aggregate route, thus decreasing the size of routing tables.

VLSM Addressing Design Exercise 1

Assume that 4 bits were borrowed from the host portion of 192.168.1.0/24. You are *not* using VLSM. Starting with subnet 0, label Figure 1-1 contiguously with subnets. Start with the LAN on RTA and proceed clockwise.

Figure 1-1   Addressing Design Exercise 1 Topology: Subnets

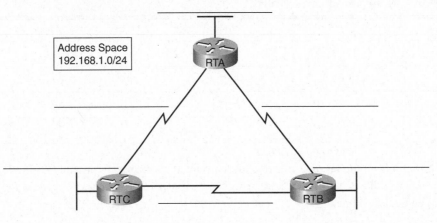

How many *total* valid host addresses will be wasted on the WAN links?

_____

_____

Now, come up with a better addressing scheme using VLSM. Start with the same 4 bits borrowed from the host portion of 192.168.1.0/24. Label each of the LANs with a subnet. Then, subnet the next available subnet to provide WAN subnets without wasting any host addresses. Label Figure 1-2 with the subnets.

Figure 1-2   Addressing Design Exercise 1 Topology: VLSM Subnets

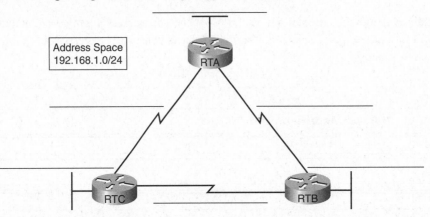

List the address space that is still available for future expansion.

___

The topology shown in Figure 1-3 has LAN subnets already assigned out of the 192.168.1.0/24 address space. Using VLSM, create and label the WANs with subnets from the remaining address space.

Figure 1-3   Addressing Design Exercise 1 Topology: WAN Subnets

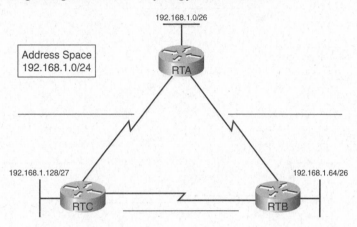

List the address space that is still available for future expansion.

___

___

VLSM Addressing Design Exercise 2

Your address space is 192.168.1.192/26. Each LAN needs to support ten hosts. Use VLSM to create a contiguous IP addressing scheme. Label Figure 1-4 with your addressing scheme. Don't forget the WAN links.

Figure 1-4   Addressing Design Exercise 2 Topology

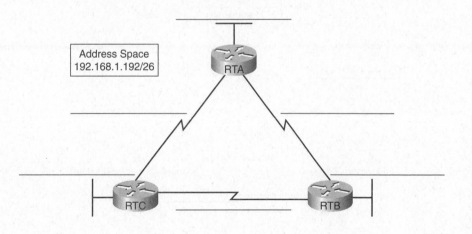

List the address space that is still available for future expansion.

___

VLSM Addressing Design Exercise 3

Your address space is 192.168.6.0/23. The number of hosts needed for each LAN is shown in Figure 1-5. Use VLSM to create a contiguous IP addressing scheme. Label Figure 1-5 with your addressing scheme. Don't forget the WAN links.

Figure 1-5   Addressing Design Exercise 3 Topology

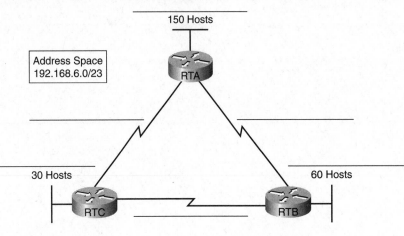

List the address space that is still available for future expansion.

VLSM Addressing Design Exercise 4

Your address space is 10.10.96.0/21. The number of hosts needed for each LAN is shown in Figure 1-6. Use VLSM to create a contiguous IP addressing scheme. Label Figure 1-6 with your addressing scheme. Don't forget the WAN links.

Figure 1-6   Addressing Design Exercise 4 Topology

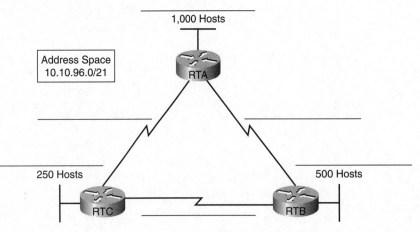

List the address space that is still available for future expansion.

VLSM Addressing Design Scenarios

The following VLSM Addressing Design Scenarios will build upon your addressing design skills. In these scenarios, you will fully document your network design, including IP addresses for interfaces and hosts.

VLSM Addressing Design Scenario 1

Complete Addressing Design Scenario 1 using the following list of requirements:

- Address space: 192.168.1.0/25.

- RTA LAN, 60 hosts; RTB LAN, 30 hosts; RTC LAN, 10 hosts.

- Using good VLSM design practices, contiguously assign subnets to the topology shown in Figure 1-7.

- Fill in the table with all necessary IP address configuration information for all devices. Use dotted-decimal format for the subnet mask.

- List the address space that is still available for future expansion.

Figure 1-7   Addressing Design Scenario 1 Topology

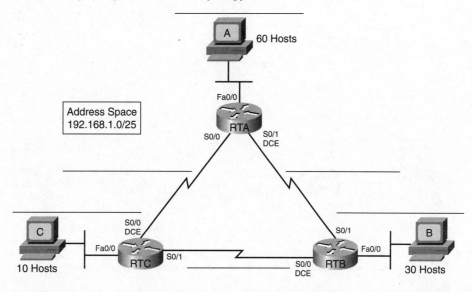

Device	Interface	IP Address	Subnet Mask	Default Gateway
RTA	Fa0/0			
	S0/1			
	S0/0			
RTB	Fa0/0			
	S0/1			
	S0/0			
RTC	Fa0/0			
	S0/1			
	S0/0			
Host A				
Host B				
Host C				

VLSM Addressing Design Scenario 2

Complete Addressing Design Scenario 2 using the following list of requirements:

- Address space: 192.168.18.0/23.

- RTA LAN, 250 hosts; RTB LAN, 100 hosts; RTC LAN, 60 hosts.

- Using good VLSM design practices, contiguously assign subnets to the topology shown in Figure 1-8.

- Fill in the table with all necessary IP address configuration information for all devices. Use dotted-decimal format for the subnet mask.

- List the address space that is still available for future expansion.

Figure 1-8   Addressing Design Scenario 2 Topology

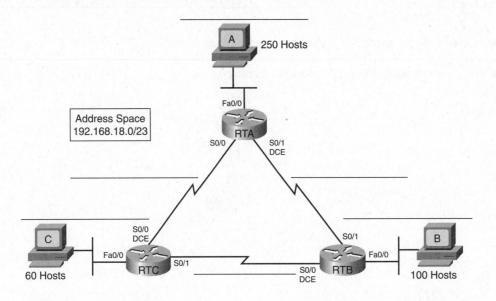

Device	Interface	IP Address	Subnet Mask	Default Gateway
RTA	Fa0/0			
	S0/1			
	S0/0			
RTB	Fa0/0			
	S0/1			
	S0/0			
RTC	Fa0/0			
	S0/1			
	S0/0			
Host A				
Host B				
Host C				

VLSM Addressing Design Scenario 3

Complete Addressing Design Scenario 3 using the following list of requirements:

- Address space: 172.16.0.0/22.
- RTA LAN, 500 hosts; RTB LAN, 250 hosts; RTC LAN, 100 hosts.
- Using good VLSM design practices, contiguously assign subnets to the topology shown in Figure 1-9.
- Fill in the table with all necessary IP address configuration information for all devices. Use dotted-decimal format for the subnet mask.
- List the address space that is still available for future expansion.

Figure 1-9   Addressing Design Scenario 3 Topology

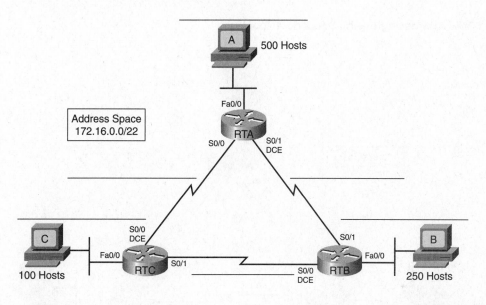

Device	Interface	IP Address	Subnet Mask	Default Gateway
RTA	Fa0/0			
	S0/1			
	S0/0			
RTB	Fa0/0			
	S0/1			
	S0/0			
RTC	Fa0/0			
	S0/1			
	S0/0			
Host A				
Host B				
Host C				

VLSM Addressing Design Scenario 4

Complete Addressing Design Scenario 4 using the following list of requirements:

- Address space: 172.24.0.0/21.

- RTA LAN, 1000 hosts; RTB LAN, 500 hosts; RTC LAN, 250 hosts.

- Using good VLSM design practices, contiguously assign subnets to the topology shown in Figure 1-10.

- Fill in the table with all necessary IP address configuration information for all devices. Use dotted-decimal format for the subnet mask.

- List the address space that is still available for future expansion.

Figure 1-10   Addressing Design Scenario 4 Topology

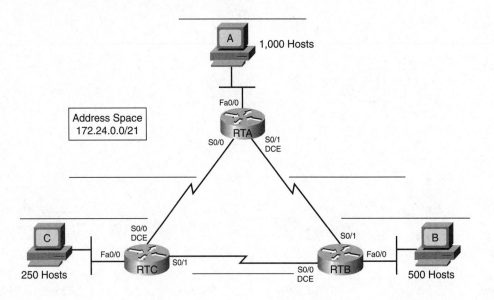

Device	Interface	IP Address	Subnet Mask	Default Gateway
RTA	Fa0/0			
	S0/1			
	S0/0			
RTB	Fa0/0			
	S0/1			
	S0/0			
RTC	Fa0/0			
	S0/1			
	S0/0			
Host A				
Host B				
Host C				

VLSM Addressing Design Scenario 5

Complete Addressing Design Scenario 5 using the following list of requirements:

- Address space: 10.8.64.0/18.

- RTA LAN, 6000 hosts; RTB LAN, 3000 hosts; RTC LAN, 1000 hosts.

- Using good VLSM design practices, contiguously assign subnets to the topology shown in Figure 1-11.

- Fill in the table with all necessary IP address configuration information for all devices. Use dotted-decimal format for the subnet mask.

- List the address space that is still available for future expansion.

Figure 1-11   Addressing Design Scenario 5 Topology

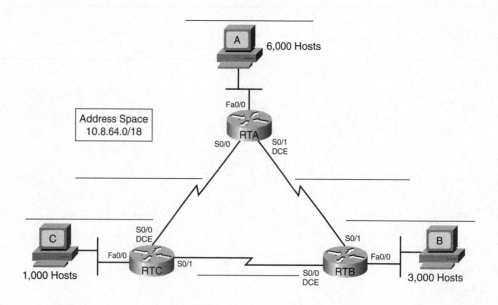

Device	Interface	IP Address	Subnet Mask	Default Gateway
RTA	Fa0/0			
	S0/1			
	S0/0			
RTB	Fa0/0			
	S0/1			
	S0/0			
RTC	Fa0/0			
	S0/1			
	S0/0			
Host A				
Host B				
Host C				

VLSM Addressing Design Scenario 6

Complete Addressing Design Scenario 6 using the following list of requirements:

- Address space: 10.0.0.0/15.

- RTA LAN, 65,000 hosts; RTB LAN, 30,000 hosts; RTC LAN, 8000 hosts.

- Using good VLSM design practices, contiguously assign subnets to the topology shown in Figure 1-12.

- Fill in the table with all necessary IP address configuration information for all devices. Use dotted-decimal format for the subnet mask.

- List the address space that is still available for future expansion.

Figure 1-12   Addressing Design Scenario 6 Topology

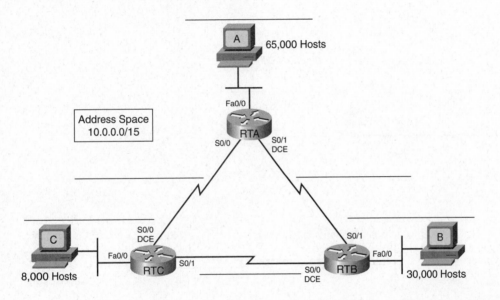

Device	Interface	IP Address	Subnet Mask	Default Gateway
RTA	Fa0/0			
	S0/1			
	S0/0			
RTB	Fa0/0			
	S0/1			
	S0/0			
RTC	Fa0/0			
	S0/1			
	S0/0			
Host A				
Host B				
Host C				

Summary Route Exercises

Use the following exercises to practice determining the summary route for a collection of subnets.

The following is an example with the answer:

Referring to Figure 1-13, what summary route would R1 send to BBR (Backbone Router) for the four networks? Write your answer in the space provided.

Figure 1-13   Summary Route Example

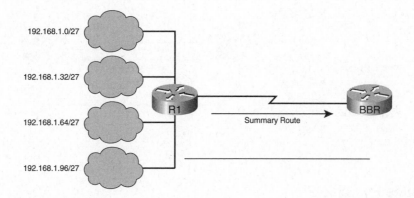

Step 1.   Find the number of highest-order bits that match in all the addresses, convert the addresses to binary format, and align them in a list.

To make sure that you are including the entire address range from the lowest to the highest network address, find the lowest IP address, which is the network address 192.168.1.0 in the example. Then, find the highest IP address, which is 192.168.1.127, or the last address in the highest network, 192.168.1.96.

Write the lowest and highest IP addresses in binary:

192.168.1.0:   11000000.10101000.00000001.00000000

192.168.1.127:   11000000.10101000.00000001.01111111

Step 2.   Locate where the common pattern of digits ends. The common bits are shaded in the following example.

First IP   192.168.1.0   11000000.10101000.00000001.00000000

Last IP   192.168.1.127   11000000.10101000.00000001.01111111

Step 3.   Count the number of common bits. This number is the prefix length of the summary route. It is represented at the end of the first IP address in the block and preceded by a slash.

In this example, counting from left to right, you have 25 common bits. Your first address in the address block is 192.168.1.0. Therefore, your summary route is 192.168.1.0/25.

Summary Route Exercise 1

Referring to Figure 1-14, what summary route would R1 send to BBR for the four networks? Write your answer in the space provided.

Figure 1-14   Summary Route Exercise 1

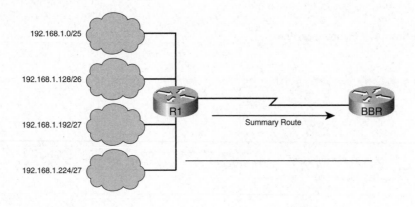

Summary Route Exercise 2

Referring to Figure 1-15, what summary route would R1 send to BBR for the four networks? Write your answer in the space provided.

Figure 1-15   Summary Route Exercise 2

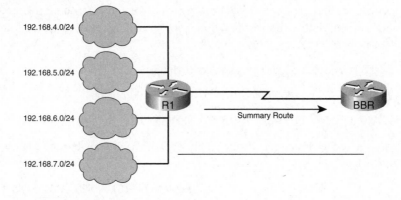

Summary Route Exercise 3

Referring to Figure 1-16, what summary route would R1 send to BBR for the four networks? Write your answer in the space provided.

Figure 1-16   Summary Route Exercise 3

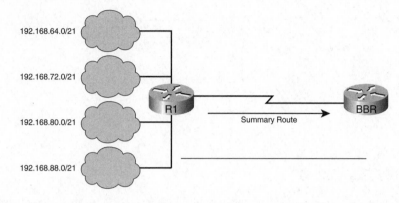

Summary Route Exercise 4

Referring to Figure 1-17, what summary route would R1 send to BBR for the four networks? Write your answer in the space provided.

Figure 1-17   Summary Route Exercise 4

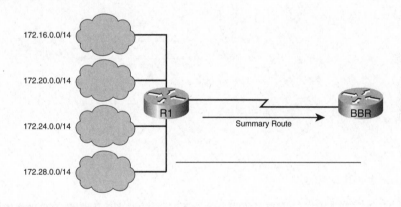

Summary Route Exercise 5

Referring to Figure 1-18, what summary route would R1 send to BBR for the four networks? Write your answer in the space provided.

Figure 1-18   Summary Route Exercise 5

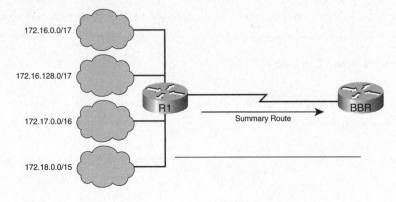

Summary Route Exercise 6

Referring to Figure 1-19, what summary route would R1 send to BBR for the four networks? Write your answer in the space provided.

Figure 1-19   Summary Route Exercise 6

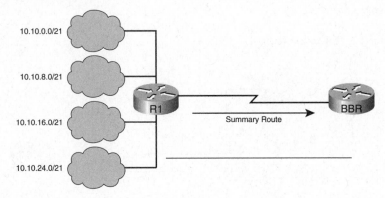

Summary Route Exercise 7

Referring to Figure 1-20, what summary route would R1 send to BBR for the four networks? Write your answer in the space provided.

Figure 1-20   Summary Route Exercise 7

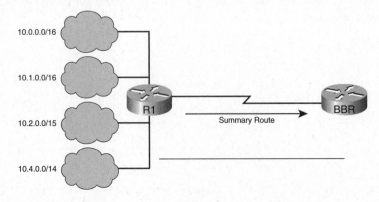

Default and Static Routing Scenario

In Figure 1-21, both static and default routing are used between RTA and ISP to route traffic. First, determine the summary route that would summarize all of the subnets from the 10.0.0.0 address space. Then, record the commands that would be configured on RTA and ISP to provide full connectivity. (Hint: RTA will use a default route and ISP will use a static route.)

Figure 1-21   Default and Static Routing Scenario

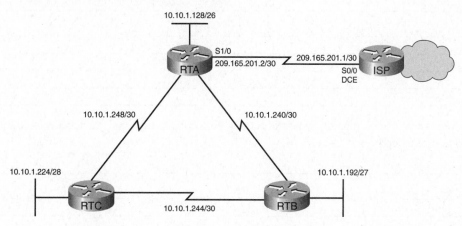

Concept Questions

List at least three reasons why you should use VLSM when designing your addressing scheme.

- _____

- _____

- _____

Why is VLSM described as "subnetting a subnet"?

_____

_____

_____

_____

_____

Why was VLSM not used in CCNA 1 and CCNA 2?

_____

_____

- _____

_____

_____

- _____

_____

_____

What is the difference between CIDR and supernetting or router summarization?

_____

_____

_____

_____

_____

_____

_____

_____

_____

_____

_____

List the two ways a router running a classful routing protocol can calculate the network portion of routes received in routing updates.

_____

■ _____

_____

■ _____

_____

Explain three ways a router can learn paths to destination networks.

_____

■ _____

_____

■ _____

_____

_____

_____

■ _____

_____

Explain the effect of the command **ip classless** on both classful and classless routing protocols.

_____

_____

_____

_____

_____

List the two classful routing protocols and explain the most serious limitation of these two protocols.

_____

_____

_____

_____

Which classless routing protocols automatically summarize at the classful boundary? Why do these protocols operate in a classful manner? What command will turn off automatic summarization and with which IOS versions must you enter the command?

_____

_____

_____

_____

_____

_____

_____

VLSM Case Study

You are the new network administrator for Mom and Pop's Stop & Shop, a multibranch convenience store corporation. The previous network administrator used the 192.168.1.0/24 private network exclusively to communicate between branch locations and corporate headquarters. The current topology and addressing scheme is shown in Figure 1-22.

Mom and Pop's Stop & Shop plans to add two new locations this year. With the current addressing scheme, how many subnets are left to provide address space for the new locations? As the new network administrator, what plan would you have for adding additional address space when needed? What routing protocol would you use?

Figure 1-22   Mom and Pop's Stop & Shop Network Topology

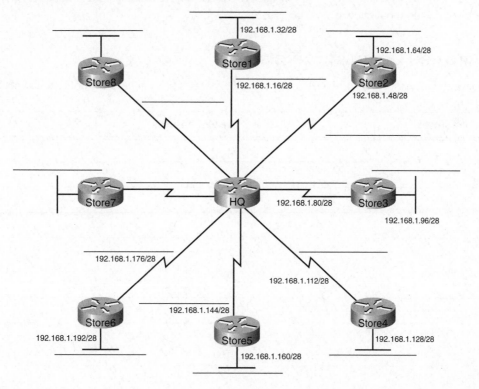

_____

_____

_____

_____

_____

_____

_____

_____
_____
_____
_____
_____
_____
_____
_____
_____
_____
_____
_____
_____
_____
_____
_____

RIP Version 2

RIP was designed to work as a simple Interior Gateway Protocol (IGP) within small and moderate-sized autonomous systems. The first version of RIP did not support VLSM, but rather simply advertised the classful network to RIP neighbors. However, the original RIP specification (RFC 1058) provided several empty fields in the RIP update that are now used by RIP version 2 (RFC 2453). In the following two exercises, you will compare and contrast RIPv1 and RIPv2. Then, you will complete a research exercise to discover more details about the two versions of RIP.

Compare and Contrast Exercise

Compare and contrast RIPv1 and RIPv2 by listing the features of each protocol in the following table.

RIPv1 Features	RIPv2 Features

From your preceding list of features, what are the four improvements added to RIPv2?

_____

_____

_____

_____

Internet Research

RIP is an open standard, which means the specifications for the format of RIP messages is not proprietary and can be implemented by any vendor or software developer. When you are not sure about an open standard such as RIP or OSPF, you can always refer to the original Request For Comments (RFC) for that standard. For this research exercise, use the Internet to find the RFC for RIPv2 and answer the following questions.

_____

_____

_____

_____

_____

_____

_____

_____

What Layer 4 protocol does RIP use and what is its port number?

_____

How many routing updates can a RIP update contain?

_____

RIPv1 and RIPv2 both use the same header information. RIPv2 uses empty fields in the 20-byte RIPv1 route entry. Fill in the names of the fields for both the RIPv1 and RIPv2 route entries in Figure 1-23 and Figure 1-24, respectively. (Hint: Look for phrases "message format" and "protocol extensions.")

Figure 1-23   RIPv1 Header and Route Entry

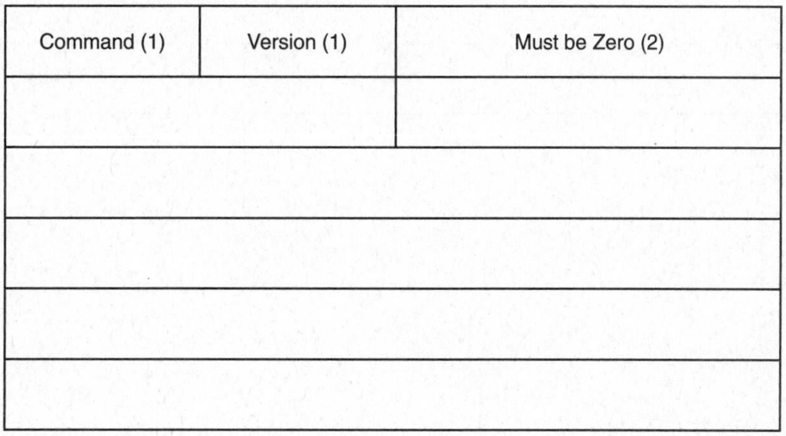

Command (1)	Version (1)	Must be Zero (2)

Figure 1-24   RIPv2 Header and Route Entry

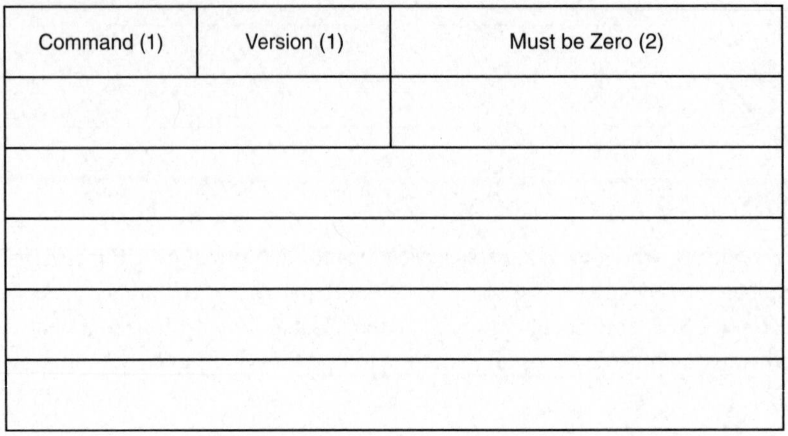

Notice that authentication is not listed in any of the fields. Briefly explain how RIPv2 allows authentica-

Command (1)	Version (1)	Must be Zero (2)

tion of messages.

_____

_____

_____

_____

_____

_____

_____

Briefly explain the use of the fields Route Tag and Next Hop.

_____

_____

_____

_____

_____

_____

_____

_____

Lab Exercises

Command Reference

In the table that follows, record the command, including the correct router prompt, that fits the description.

Command	Description
	Causes a classful routing protocol to evaluate all packets using the longest-match criterion. As a last resort, the router will use the default route rather than discard traffic bound for unknown subnets of a known classful network.
	Allows the use of the all-0 subnets; on by default in Cisco IOS Software Release 12.0 and later.
	Turns off the RIP routing process.
	Turns on Version 2 of the routing process.
	Configures the network number of the directly connect ed classful network you want to advertise.
	RIPv2 summarizes networks at the classful boundary. This command turns off autosummarization.
	Displays all RIP activity in real time.
	Displays contents of the RIP database.

Curriculum Lab 1-1: Calculating VLSM Subnets (1.1.4)

Figure 1-25   Topology for Lab 1-1

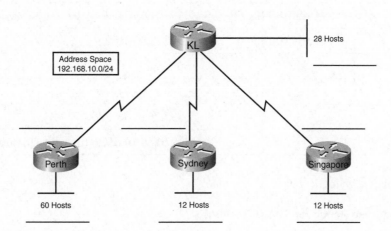

Objective

Use variable-length subnet masking (VLSM) to support more efficient use of the assigned IP address and to reduce the amount of routing information at the top level.

Background/Preparation

A Class C address of 192.168.10.0/24 has been allocated.

Perth, Sydney, and Singapore have a WAN connection to Kuala Lumpur. The host requirements are as follows:

- Perth requires 60 hosts.
- Kuala Lumpur requires 28 hosts.
- Sydney and Singapore each require 12 hosts.

To calculate VLSM subnets and the respective hosts, allocate the largest requirements first from the address range. Requirements levels should be listed from the largest to the smallest.

In this example, Perth requires 60 hosts. Use 6 bits, because $2^6 - 2 = 62$ usable host addresses. Thus, 2 bits will be used from the fourth octet to represent the extended network prefix of /26, and the remaining 6 bits will be used for host addresses.

Task 1: Divide the Allocated Addresses into Four Equal-Sized Address Blocks

Step 1. Divide the allocated address of 192.168.10.0/24 into four equal-sized address blocks. Because $4 = 2^2$, 2 bits are required to identify each of the four subnets.

Step 2. Take subnet 0 (192.168.10.0/26) and identify each of its hosts. Table 1-1 documents the allocated addresses, subnetworks, and usable hosts.

Table 1-1   Usable Hosts for 192.168.10.0/24

Allocated Address	Subnetworks	62 Usable Hosts/Subnetworks (Subnet 0)
192.168.10.0/24	**192.168.10.0/26**	**192.168.10.0/26 (network address)**
	192.168.10.64/26	192.168.10.1/26
	192.168.10.128/26	192.168.10.2/26
	192.168.10.192/26	192.168.10.3/26
		through
		192.168.10.61/26
		192.168.10.62/26
		192.168.10.63/26 (broadcast address)

Table 1-2 lists the range for the /26 mask.

Table 1-2   IP Address Range for 192.168.10.0/26

Perth	Range of Addresses in the Last Octet
192.168.10.0/26	From 0 to 63. Sixty hosts required.
	Hosts 0 and 63 cannot be used because they are the network and broadcast addresses for their subnet.

Task 2: Allocate the Next Level After All the Requirements Are Met for the Higher Level(s)

Kuala Lumpur requires 28 hosts. The next available address after 192.168.10.63/26 is 192.168.10.64/26. Note from Table 1-2 that this is subnet 1. Because 28 hosts are required, $2^5 - 2 = 30$ usable network addresses. Thus, 5 bits will be required to represent the hosts, and 3 bits will be used to represent the extended network prefix of /27. Applying VLSM on address 192.168.10.64/27 gives the results in Table 1-3.

Table 1-3   Usable Hosts for 192.168.10.64/26

Subnetwork 1	Sub-Subnetworks	30 Usable Hosts
		192.168.10.64/27 (network address)
192.168.10.64/26	**192.168.10.64/27**	192.168.10.65/27
	192.168.10.96/27	192.168.10.66/27
	192.168.10.128/27	192.168.10.67/26
	192.168.10.192/27	through
		192.168.10.93/27
		192.168.10.94/27
		192.168.10.95/27 (broadcast address)

Table 1-4 lists the range for the /27 mask.

Table 1-4   IP Address Range for 192.168.10.64/27

Kuala Lumpur	Range of Addresses in the Last Octet
192.168.10.64/27	From 64 to 95. 28 hosts required. Hosts 64 and 95 cannot be used because they are the network and broadcast addresses for their subnet. Thirty usable addresses are available in this range for the hosts.

Task 3: Allocate Address Space for Sydney

Sydney and Singapore require 12 hosts each. The next available address starts from 192.168.10.96/27. Note from Table 1-2 that this is the next subnet available. Because 12 hosts are required, $2^4 - 2 = 14$ usable addresses. Thus, 4 bits are required to represent the hosts, and 4 bits are required for the extended network prefix of /28. Applying VLSM on address 192.168.10.96/27 gives the results in Table 1-5.

Table 1-5   Usable Hosts for 192.168.10.96/27

Subnetwork 2	Sub-Subnetworks	14 Usable Hosts
192.168.10.96/27	**192.168.10.96/28**	**192.168.10.96/28 (network address)**
	192.168.10.112/28	192.168.10.97/28
	192.168.10.128/28	192.168.10.98/28
	192.168.10.224/28	192.168.10.99/28
	192.168.10.240/28	through
		192.168.10.109/28
		192.168.10.110/28
		192.168.10.111/28 (broadcast address)

Table 1-6 lists the range for the /28 mask.

Table 1-6   IP Address Range for 192.168.10.96/28

Sydney	Range of Addresses in the Last Octet
192.168.10.96/28	From 96 to 111. Twelve hosts required. Hosts 96 and 111 cannot be used because they are network and broadcast addresses for their subnet. Fourteen usable addresses are available in this range for the hosts.

Task 4: Allocate Address Space for Singapore

Because Singapore also requires 12 hosts, the next set of host addresses in Table 1-7 can be derived from the next available subnet (192.168.10.112/28).

Table 1-7   Singapore Host Addresses

Sub-Subnetworks	14 Usable Hosts
192.168.10.96/28	**192.168.10.112/28 (network address)**
192.168.10.112/28	192.168.10.113/28
192.168.10.128/28	192.168.10.114/28
192.168.10.224/28	192.168.10.115/28
	through
192.168.10.240/28	192.168.10.125/28
	192.168.10.126/28
	192.168.10.127/28 (broadcast address)

Table 1-8 lists the range for the /28 mask.

Table 1-8   IP Address Range for 192.168.10.112/28

Singapore	Range of Addresses in the Last Octet
192.168.10.112/28	From 112 to 127. Twelve hosts required. Hosts 112 and 127 cannot be used because they are network and broadcast addresses for their subnet. Fourteen usable addresses are available in this range for the hosts.

Task 5: Allocate Address Space for WAN Links

Now allocate addresses for the WAN links. Remember that each WAN link requires two IP addresses. The next available subnet is 192.168.10.128/28. Because two network addresses are required for each WAN link, $2^2 - 2 = 2$ usable addresses. Thus, 2 bits are required to represent the links, and 6 bits are required for the extended network prefix of /30. Applying VLSM on 192.168.10.128/28 gives the results in Table 1-9.

Table 1-9   Usable Hosts After Applying VLSM on 192.168.10.112/28

Sub-Subnetworks	14 Usable Hosts
192.168.10.128/30	**192.168.10.128/30 (network address)**
	192.168.10.129/30
	192.168.10.130/30
	192.168.10.31/30 (broadcast address)
192.168.10.132/30	**192.168.10.132/30 (network address)**
	192.168.10.133/30
	192.168.10.134/30
	192.168.10.135/30 (broadcast address)
192.168.10.136/30	**192.168.10.136/30 (network address)**
	192.168.10.137/30
	192.168.10.138/30
	192.168.10.139/30 (broadcast address)

The available addresses for the WAN links can be taken from the available addresses in each of the /30 subnets.

Curriculum Lab 1-2: Review of Basic Router Configuration with RIP (1.2.3)

Figure 1-26   Topology for Lab 1-2

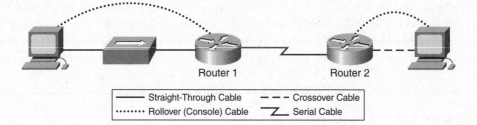

Table 1-10   Lab Equipment Configuration

Router Designation	Router Name	Fast Ethernet 0 Address	Interface Type	Serial 0 Address
Router 1	GAD	172.16.0.1	DCE	172.17.0.1
Router 2	BHM	172.18.0.1	DTE	172.17.0.2

The enable secret password for both routers is **class**.

The enable, VTY, and console password for both routers is **cisco**.

The subnet mask for both interfaces on both routers is 255.255.0.0.

Objectives

- Cable and configure workstations and routers.

- Set up an IP addressing scheme by using Class B networks.

- Configure RIP on routers.

Background/Preparation

Cable a network that is similar to the one in Figure 1-26. You can use any router that meets the interface requirements in Figure 1-26 (that is, 800, 1600, 1700, 2500, and 2600 routers or a combination). Refer to the information in Appendix A, "Router Interface Summary Chart," to correctly specify the interface identifiers based on the equipment in your lab. The 1721 series routers produced the configuration output in this lab. Another router might produce slightly different output. You should execute the following steps on each router unless you are specifically instructed otherwise.

Implement the procedure documented in Appendix C, "Erasing and Reloading the Router," before you continue with this lab.

General Configuration Tips

- Use the question mark (**?**) and arrow keys to help to enter commands.

- Each command mode restricts the set of available commands. If you have difficulty entering a command, check the prompt and then enter **?** for a list of available commands. The problem might be a wrong command mode or wrong syntax.

- To disable a feature, enter the keyword **no** before the command; for example, **no ip routing**.

- Save the configuration changes to nonvolatile RAM (NVRAM) so that the changes are not lost if there is a system reload or power outage.

Table 1-11 lists the router command modes for this and other labs in the chapter.

Table 1-11   Router Command Modes

Command Mode	Access Method	Router Prompt Displayed	Exit Method
User EXEC	Log in.	Router>	Use the **logout** command.
Privileged EXEC	From user EXEC mode, enter the **enable** command.	Router#	To exit to user EXEC mode, use the **disable**, **exit**, or **logout** command.

Continued

Table 1-11   Continued

Command Mode	Access Method	Router Prompt Displayed	Exit Method
Global configuration	From privileged EXEC mode, enter the **configure terminal** command.	Router(config)#	To exit to privileged EXEC mode, use the **exit** or **end** command, or press **Ctrl-Z**.
Interface configuration	From global configuration mode, enter the **interface** *type number* command, such as **interface serial 0**.	Router(config-if)#	To exit to global configuration mode, use the **exit** command.

Task 1: Basic Router Configuration

Connect one end of a rollover cable to the console port on the router and connect the other end to the PC with a DB-9 or DB-25 adapter to a COM port. You should do this prior to powering on any devices.

Task 2: Start the HyperTerminal Program

Step 1.   Turn on the computer and router.

Step 2.   From the Windows taskbar, locate the HyperTerminal program by choosing **Start > Programs > Accessories > Communications > HyperTerminal**.

Task 3: Name the HyperTerminal Session

In the Connection Description dialog box, enter a name in the Name field and click **OK** (see Figure 1-27).

Figure 1-27   HyperTerminal Connection Description Dialog Box

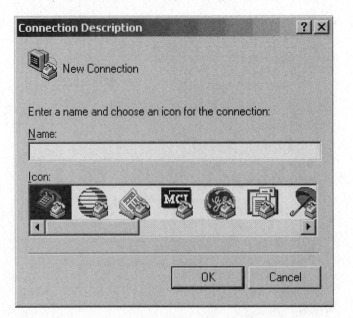

Task 4: Specify the Computer's Connecting Interface

In the Connect To dialog box, select **COM1** from the Connect Using drop-down list and click **OK** (see Figure 1-28).

Figure 1-28   HyperTerminal Connect To Dialog Box

Task 5: Specify the Interface Connection Properties

Step 1.   In the COM1 Properties dialog box, use the drop-down arrows to select the following (see Figure 1-29):

Bits per second = **9600**

Data bits = **8**

Parity = **None**

Stop bits = **1**

Flow control = **None**

Step 2.   Click **OK**.

Figure 1-29   HyperTerminal Interface Connection Property Settings

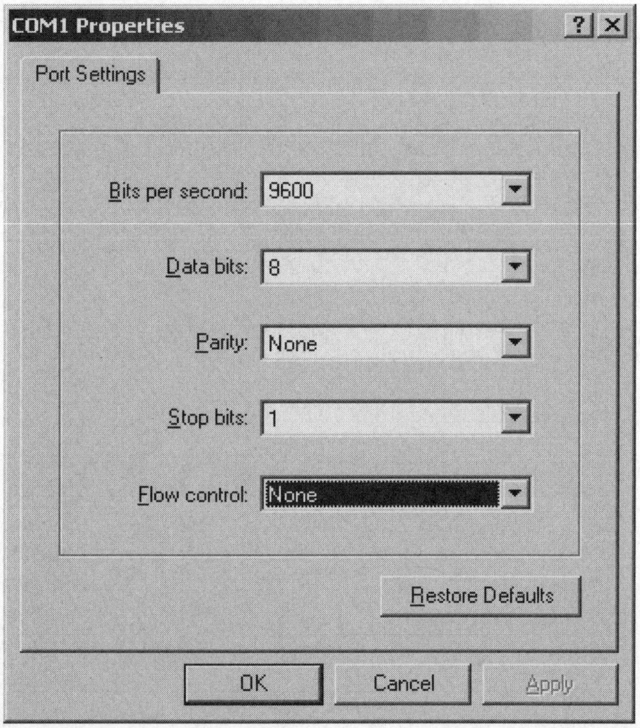

Step 3.   When the HyperTerminal session window opens (see Figure 1-30), turn on the router. If the router is already on, press the **Enter** key. The router should respond.

Figure 1-30   HyperTerminal Session Window

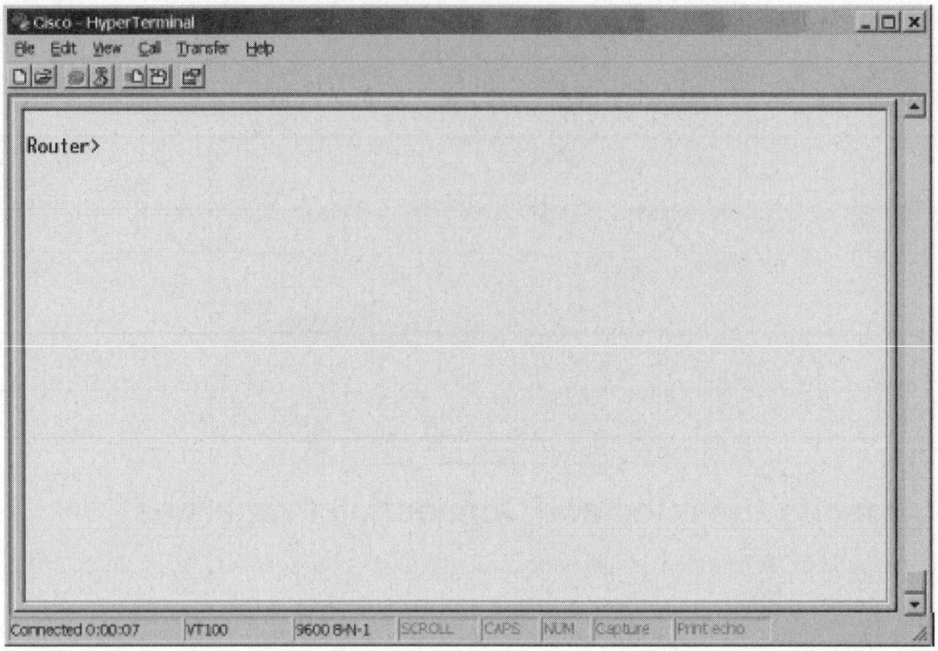

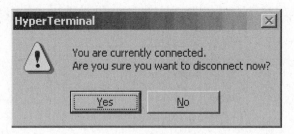

If the router responds, the connection has been successfully completed.

Task 6: Close the Session

Step 1.   To end the console session from a HyperTerminal session, choose **File > Exit**.

Step 2.   When the HyperTerminal disconnect warning dialog box appears, click **Yes** (see Figure 1-31).

Figure 1-31   Closing a HyperTerminal Session

Step 3.   The computer asks if you want to save the session (see Figure 1-32). Click **Yes**.

Figure 1-32   Saving a HyperTerminal Session

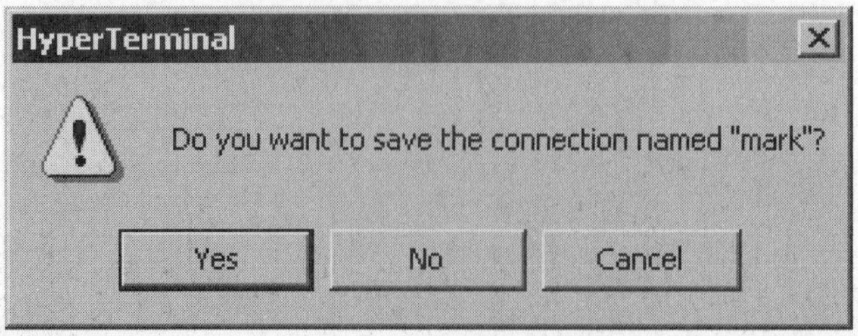

Task 7: Reopen the HyperTerminal Connection

Step 1.   In the Connection Description dialog box (refer to Figure 1-27), click **Cancel**.

Step 2.   To open the saved console session from HyperTerminal, choose **File > Open**. The saved session will appear. By double-clicking on the name, the connection opens without reconfiguring it each time.

Task 8: Configure Hostname and Passwords on Router GAD

Enter **enable** at the user mode prompt and enter the rest of the commands in the following code.

```
Router>enable
Router#configure terminal
Router(config)#hostname GAD
GAD(config)#enable password cisco
GAD(config)#enable secret class
GAD(config)#line console 0
GAD(config-line)#password cisco
GAD(config-line)#login
GAD(config-line)#line vty 0 4
GAD(config-line)#password cisco
GAD(config-line)#login
GAD(config-line)#exit
GAD(config)#
```

Task 9: Configure Interface Serial 0 on Router GAD

From global configuration mode, configure interface serial 0 (refer to Appendix A) on router GAD.

```
GAD(config)#interface serial 0
GAD(config-if)#ip address 172.17.0.1 255.255.0.0
GAD(config-if)#clock rate 64000
GAD(config-if)#no shutdown
GAD(config-if)#exit
```

Task 10: Configure the Fast Ethernet 0 Interface on Router GAD

```
GAD(config)#interface fastethernet 0
GAD(config-if)#ip address 172.16.0.1 255.255.0.0
GAD(config-if)#no shutdown
GAD(config-if)#exit
```

Task 11: Configure the IP Host Statements on Router GAD

```
GAD(config)#ip host BHM 172.18.0.1 172.17.0.1
```

Task 12: Configure RIP Routing on Router GAD

```
GAD(config)#router rip
GAD(config-router)#network 172.16.0.0
```

```
GAD(config-router)#network 172.17.0.0
GAD(config-router)#exit
GAD(config)#exit
```

Task 13: Save the GAD Router Configuration

```
GAD#copy running-config startup-config
Destination filename [startup-config]?[Enter]
```

Task 14: Configure Hostname and Passwords on Router BHM

Enter **enable** at the user mode prompt and enter the rest of the commands in the following code.

```
Router>enable
Router#configure terminal
Router(config)#hostname BHM
BHM(config)#enable password cisco
BHM(config)#enable secret class
BHM(config)#line console 0
BHM(config-line)#password cisco
BHM(config-line)#login
BHM(config-line)#line vty 0 4
BHM(config-line)#password cisco
BHM(config-line)#login
BHM(config-line)#exit
BHM(config)#
```

Task 15: Configure Interface Serial 0 on Router BHM

From global configuration mode, configure interface serial 0 (refer to Appendix A) on router BHM.

```
BHM(config)#interface serial 0
BHM(config-if)#ip address 172.17.0.2 255.255.0.0
BHM(config-if)#no shutdown
BHM(config-if)#exit
```

Task 16: Configure the Fast Ethernet 0 Interface on Router BHM

```
BHM(config)#interface fastethernet 0
BHM(config-if)#ip address 172.18.0.1 255.255.0.0
BHM(config-if)#no shutdown
BHM(config-if)#exit
```

Task 17: Configure the IP Host Statements on Router BHM

```
BHM(config)#ip host GAD 172.16.0.1 172.17.0.1
```

Task 18: Configure RIP Routing on Router BHM

```
BHM(config)#router rip
BHM(config-router)#network 172.18.0.0
BHM(config-router)#network 172.17.0.0
BHM(config-router)#exit
BHM(config)#exit
```

Task 19: Save the BHM Router Configuration

```
BHM# copy running-config startup-config
Destination filename [startup-config]?[Enter]
```

Task 20: Configure the Hosts

Using the following information, configure the hosts with the proper IP address, subnet mask, and default gateway:

Host connected to router GAD

IP address: 172.16.0.2

Subnet mask: 255.255.0.0

Default gateway: 172.16.0.1

Host connected to router BHM

IP address: 172.18.0.2

Subnet mask: 255.255.0.0

Default gateway: 172.18.0.1

Task 21: Verify the Internetwork Is Functioning by Pinging the Fast Ethernet Interface of the Other Router

Step 1.   From the host that is attached to GAD, ping the BHM router Fast Ethernet interface. Was the ping successful? _____

Step 2.   From the host that is attached to BHM, ping the GAD router Fast Ethernet interface. Was the ping successful? _____

Step 3.   If the answer is no for either question, troubleshoot the router configurations to find the error. Then, do the pings again until the answer to both questions is yes. Finally, ping all interfaces in the network.

Task 22: Show the Routing Tables for Each Router

Step 1.   From enable (privileged EXEC) mode, examine the routing table entries by using the **show ip route** command on each router.

What are the entries in the GAD routing table?

_____

_____

What are the entries in the BHM routing table?

_____

_____

Step 2.   Upon completion of the previous step, log off (by typing **exit**) and turn the router off. Then, remove and store the cables and adapter.

Curriculum Lab 1-3: Converting RIPv1 to RIPv2 (1.2.4)

Figure 1-33   Topology for Lab 1-3

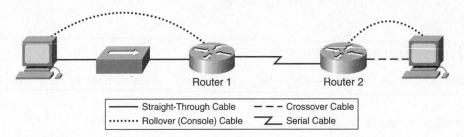

| Straight-Through Cable | Crossover Cable |
| Rollover (Console) Cable | Serial Cable |

Table 1-12   Lab Equipment Configuration

Router Designation	Router Name	Fast Ethernet 0 Address	Interface Type	Serial 0 Address
Router 1	GAD	172.16.0.1	DCE	172.17.0.1
Router 2	BHM	172.18.0.1	DTE	172.17.0.2

The enable secret password for both routers is **class**.

The enable, VTY, and console password for both routers is **cisco**.

The subnet mask for both interfaces on both routers is 255.255.0.0.

Objectives

- Configure RIP Version 1 on routers.

- Convert to RIP Version 2 on routers.

Background/Preparation

Cable a network similar to the one in Figure 1-33. You can use any router that meets the interface requirements in Figure 1-33 (that is, 800, 1600, 1700, 2500, and 2600 routers or a combination). Refer to the information in Appendix A to correctly specify the interface identifiers based on the equipment in your lab. The 1721 series routers produced the configuration output in this lab. Another router might produce slightly different output. You should execute the following steps on each router unless you are specifically instructed otherwise.

Start a HyperTerminal session.

Implement the procedure documented in Appendix C on all routers before you continue with this lab.

Task 1: Configure the Routers

On the routers, configure the hostnames, console, virtual terminal, and enable passwords. Next, configure the serial (IP address and clock rate) and Fast Ethernet (IP address) interfaces. Finally, configure

IP hostnames. If you have problems performing the basic configuration, refer to Lab 1-2, "Review of Basic Router Configuration with RIP." You can also configure optional interface descriptions and message of the day banners. Be sure to save the configurations you just created.

Task 2: Configure the Routing Protocol on Router GAD

Go to the proper command mode and configure RIP routing on the GAD router according to Table 1-12.

Task 3: Save the GAD Router Configuration

Any time that changes are correctly made to the running configuration, you should save them to the startup configuration. Otherwise, if the router is reloaded or power cycled, the changes that are not in the startup configuration are lost.

Task 4: Configure the Routing Protocol on Router BHM

Go to the proper command mode and configure RIP routing on the BHM router according to Table 1-12.

Task 5: Save the BHM Router Configuration

Task 6: Configure the Hosts

Configure the hosts with proper IP addresses, subnet masks, and default gateways. Document your choices here:

Task 7: Verify that the Internetwork Is Functioning

Step 1.   From each router, ping the other router's Fast Ethernet interface.

Step 2.   From the host that is attached to GAD, ping the other host that is attached to the BHM router. Was the ping successful? _____

Step 3.   From the host that is attached to BHM, ping the other host that is attached to the GAD router. Was the ping successful? _____

Step 4.   If the answer is no for either question, troubleshoot the router configurations to find the error. Then, do the pings again until the answer to both questions is yes.

Task 8: Enable RIPv2 Routing

Enable version 2 of the RIP routing protocol on both the GAD and BHM routers.

```
GAD(config)#router rip
GAD(config-router)#version 2
GAD(config-router)#exit
GAD(config)#exit
```

```
BHM(config)#router rip
BHM(config-router)#version 2
BHM(config-router)#exit
BHM(config)#exit
```

Task 9: Ping All Interfaces on the Network from Each Host

Step 1.   Could you still ping all of the interfaces on the network from each host? ____

Step 2.   If not, troubleshoot the network and ping again.

Step 3.   Upon completion of the previous steps, log off (by typing **exit**) and turn the router off. Then, remove and store the cables and adapter.

Curriculum Lab 1-4: Verifying RIPv2 Configuration (1.2.5)

Figure 1-34   Topology for Lab 1-4

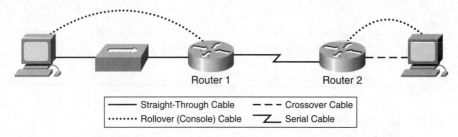

Router 1   Router 2

———— Straight-Through Cable   – – – Crossover Cable
·········· Rollover (Console) Cable   ⌐Z⌐ Serial Cable

Table 1-13   Lab Equipment Configuration

Router Designation	Router Name	Fast Ethernet 0 Address	Interface Type	Serial 0 Address
Router 1	GAD	172.16.0.1	DCE	172.17.1.1
Router 2	BHM	172.18.0.1	DTE	172.17.1.2

The enable secret password for both routers is **class**.

The enable, VTY, and console password for both routers is **cisco**.

The subnet mask for both interfaces on both routers is 255.255.0.0.

Objectives

- Configure RIPv1 and RIPv2 on routers.

- Use **show** commands to verify RIPv2 operation.

`Background/Preparation`

Cable a network that is similar to the one in Figure 1-34. You can use any router that meets the interface requirements in Figure 1-34 (that is, 800, 1600, 1700, 2500, and 2600 routers or a combination). Refer to the information in Appendix A to correctly specify the interface identifiers based on the equipment in your lab. The 1721 series routers produced the configuration output in this lab. Another router might produce slightly different output. You should execute the following steps on each router unless you are specifically instructed otherwise.

Start a HyperTerminal session.

Implement the procedure documented in Appendix C on all routers before continuing with this lab.

Task 1: Configure the Routers

On the routers, configure the hostnames, console, virtual terminal, and enable passwords. Next, configure the serial (IP address and clock rate) and Fast Ethernet (IP address) interfaces. Finally, configure

IP hostnames. If you have problems performing the basic configuration, refer to Lab 1-2, "Review of Basic Router Configuration with RIP." You can also configure optional interface descriptions and message of the day banners. Be sure to save the configurations you just created.

Task 2: Configure the Routing Protocol on Router Gadsden

Go to the correct command mode and configure RIP routing on the GAD router according to Table 1-13.

Task 3: Save the Gadsden Router Configuration

Any time that changes are correctly made to the running configuration, you should save them to the startup configuration. Otherwise, if you reload or power cycle the router, you will lose the changes that are not in the startup configuration.

Task 4: Configure the Routing Protocol on Router BHM

Go to the correct command mode and configure RIP routing on the BHM router according to Table 1-13.

Task 5: Save the BHM Router Configuration

Enter the command **copy run start** to save the current running configuration to NVRAM.

Task 6: Configure the Hosts

Configure the hosts with proper IP addresses, subnet masks, and default gateways. Document your choices here:

_____

_____

_____

_____

_____

_____

_____

_____

Task 7: Verify that the Internetwork Is Functioning

Step 1.   From each router, ping the other router's Fast Ethernet interface.

Step 2.   From the host that is attached to GAD, ping the other host that is attached to the BHM router. Was the ping successful? _____

Step 3.   From the host that is attached to BHM, ping the other host that is attached to the GAD router. Was the ping successful? _____

Step 4.   If the answer is no for either question, troubleshoot the router configurations to find the error. Then, do the pings again until the answer to both questions is yes.

Task 8: Show the Routing Tables for Each Router

From enable (privileged EXEC) mode, examine the routing table entries by using the **show ip route** command on each router.

What are the entries in the GAD routing table?

_____

_____

_____

What are the entries in the BHM routing table?

_____

_____

_____

Task 9: Enable RIPv2 Routing

Enable Version 2 of the RIP routing protocol on the GAD and BHM routers.

```
GAD(config)#router rip
GAD(config-router)#version 2
GAD(config-router)#exit
GAD(config)#exit

BHM(config)#router rip
BHM(config-router)#version 2
BHM(config-router)#exit
BHM(config)#exit
```

Task 10: Show the Routing Tables

Show the routing tables on both routers again.

Have they changed now that RIPv2 is being used instead of RIPv1? _____

What is the difference between RIPv2 and RIPv1?

_____

What must you do to see a difference between RIPv2 and RIPv1?

_____

Task 11: Change the Fast Ethernet IP Subnet Mask on Router GAD

Change the subnet mask on router GAD from a Class B (255.255.0.0) to a Class C (255.255.255.0). Use the same IP address.

```
GAD(config)#interface fastethernet 0
GAD(config-if)#ip address 172.16.0.1 255.255.255.0
GAD(config-if)#exit
```

How does this change affect the address for the Fast Ethernet interface?

_____

Task 12: Show the GAD Routing Table

Show the GAD routing table.

Has the output changed now that you have added a subnetted IP address? _____

How has it changed?

_____

Task 13: Show the BHM Routing Table

Show the BHM routing table.

Has the output changed now that you have added a subnetted IP address? _____

Task 14: Change the Network Addressing Scheme

Change the addressing scheme of the network to a single Class B network with a Class C subnet (8 bits of subnetting).

On the BHM router:

```
BHM(config)#interface serial 0
BHM(config-if)#ip address 172.16.1.2 255.255.255.0
BHM(config-if)#exit
BHM(config)#interface fastethernet 0
BHM(config-if)#ip address 172.16.3.1 255.255.255.0
BHM(config-if)#exit
BHM(config)#exit
```

On the GAD router:

```
GAD(config)#interface serial 0
GAD(config-if)#ip address 172.16.1.1 255.255.255.0
GAD(config-if)#exit
```

Task 15: Show the Routing Table for Router GAD

Show the GAD routing table.

Has the output changed now that you have added a subnetted IP address? _____

How has it changed?

_____
_____

Task 16: Show the Routing Table for Router BHM

Show the BHM routing table.

Has the output changed now that you have added a subnetted IP address? _____

Task 17: Change the Host Configurations

Change the host configuration to reflect the new IP addressing scheme of the network.

Task 18: Ping All Interfaces on the Network from Each Host

Step 1.   Could you still ping all of the interfaces on the network from each host? _____

Step 2.   If not, troubleshoot the network and ping again.

Task 19: Use show ip route to See Different Routes by Type

Step 1.   Enter **show ip route connected** on the GAD router.

What networks are displayed?

_____

_____

_____

What interface is directly connected?

_____

_____

Step 2.   Enter **show ip route rip**.

Step 3.   List the routes in the routing table.

What is the administrative distance? _____

Step 4.   Enter **show ip route connected** on the BHM router.

What networks are displayed?

_____

_____

_____

What interface is directly connected?

_____

_____

Step 5.   Enter **show ip route rip**.

Step 6.   List the routes in the routing table

_____

_____

Task 20: Use the show ip protocol Command

Enter the **show ip protocol** command on the GAD router.

When will the routes be flushed? _____

What is the default distance listed for RIP? _____

Task 21: Remove the Version 2 Option for RIP

Remove the version 2 option on the RIP configuration for both routers.

Task 22: Show the Routing Table for Router GAD

Show the GAD routing table.

Has the output changed now that RIPv2 has been removed? ____

Task 23: Show the Routing Table for Router BHM

Step 1.   Show the BHM routing table.

Has the output changed now that RIPv2 has been removed? ____

Step 2.   Upon completion of the previous step, log off (by typing **exit**) and turn the router off. Then, remove and store the cables and adapter.

Curriculum Lab 1-5: Troubleshooting RIPv2 Using debug (1.2.6)

Figure 1-35   Topology for Lab 1-5

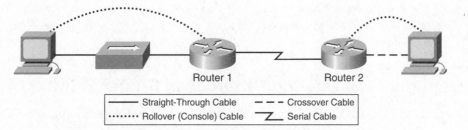

```
                                    Router 1            Router 2
            ——— Straight-Through Cable    – – – Crossover Cable
            ......... Rollover (Console) Cable    ⎓ Serial Cable
```

Table 1-14   Lab Equipment Configuration

Router Designation	Serial 0 Address	Router Name	Fast Ethernet 0 Address	Interface Type
Router 1	GAD	172.16.0.1	DCE	172.17.1.1
Router 2	BHM	172.18.0.1	DTE	172.17.1.2

The enable secret password for both routers is **class**.

The enable, VTY, and console password for both routers is **cisco**.

The subnet mask for both interfaces on both routers is 255.255.0.0.

Objectives

- Configure RIP Version 2 on both routers.

- Use **debug** commands to verify proper RIP operation and analyze data that is transmitted between routers.

Background/Preparation

Cable a network that is similar to the one in Figure 1-35. You can use any router that meets the interface requirements in Figure 1-35 (that is, 800, 1600, 1700, 2500, and 2600 routers or a combination). Refer to the information in Appendix A to correctly specify the interface identifiers based on the equipment in your lab. The 1721 series routers produced the configuration output in this lab. Another router might produce slightly different output. You should execute the following steps on each router unless you are specifically instructed otherwise.

Start a HyperTerminal session.

Implement the procedure documented in Appendix C on all routers before you continue with this lab.

Task 1: Configure the Routers

On the routers, configure the hostnames, console, virtual terminal, and enable passwords. Next, configure the serial (IP address and clock rate) and Fast Ethernet (IP address) interfaces. Finally, configure IP hostnames. If you have problems performing the basic configuration, refer to Lab 1-2, "Review of Basic Router Configuration with RIP." You can also configure optional interface descriptions and message of the day banners. Be sure to save the configurations you just created.

Task 2: Configure the Routing Protocol on Router GAD

Go to the proper command mode and configure RIP routing on the GAD router according to Table 1-14.

Task 3: Save the GAD Router Configuration

Anytime that changes are correctly made to the running configuration, you should save them to the startup configuration. Otherwise, if you reload or power cycle the router, you will lose the changes that are not in the startup configuration.

Task 4: Configure the Routing Protocol on Router BHM

Go to the proper command mode and configure RIP routing on the BHM router according to Table 1-14.

Task 5: Save the BHM Router Configuration

Enter the command **copy run start** to save the current running configuration to NVRAM.

Task 6: Configure the Hosts

Configure the hosts with proper IP addresses, subnet masks, and default gateways. Document your choices here:

Task 7: Verify the Internetwork Is Functioning

Step 1.   From each router, ping the other router's Fast Ethernet interface.

Step 2.   From the host that is attached to GAD, ping the other host that is attached to the BHM router. Was the ping successful? _____

Step 3.   From the host that is attached to BHM, ping the other host that is attached to the GAD router. Was the ping successful? _____

Step 4.   If the answer is no for either question, troubleshoot the router configurations to find the error. Then, do the pings again until the answer to both questions is yes.

Task 8: Show the debug ip Command Options

At the privileged EXEC mode prompt, type **debug ip ?**.

Which routing protocols have **debug** commands?

_____

Task 9: Show the debug ip rip Command Options

At the privileged EXEC mode prompt, type **debug ip rip ?**.

How many options are available for **debug ip rip ?** _____

Task 10: Show the RIP Routing Updates

Step 1.   From enable (privileged EXEC) mode, examine the routing table entries by using the **debug ip rip** command on each router.

What three operations that take place are listed in the RIP debug statements?

_____

Step 2.   Turn off debugging by typing either **no debug ip rip** or **undebug all**.

Task 11: Enable RIPv2 Routing on Router GAD Only

Enable version 2 of the RIP routing protocol on the GAD router only.

Task 12: Restart the Debug Function on Router GAD

Does a problem occur now that RIPv2 is configured on the GAD router? _____

If so, what is the problem?

_____

_____

Task 13: Clear the Routing Table

Step 1.   Instead of waiting for the routes to time out, type **clear ip route ***. Then type **show ip route**.

What has happened to the routing table?

_____

Will the routing table be updated to include RIP routes if the debug output says the update is ignored? _____

Step 2.   Turn off debugging by typing either **no debug ip rip** or **undebug all**.

Task 14: Start the Debug RIP Function

Start the debug RIP function on the BHM router again by typing **debug ip rip**.

Does a problem occur now that the GAD router is configured with RIPv2? _____

If so, what is the problem?

_____

_____

_____

Task 15: Clear the Routing Table

Step 1.   Instead of waiting for the routes to time out, type **clear ip route ***. Then type **show ip route**.

What has happened to the routing table?

_____

Will the routing table be updated to include RIP routes if the update is from RIPv2? _____

Step 2.   Turn off debugging by typing either **no debug ip rip** or **undebug all**.

Task 16: Enable RIPv2 Routing on Router BHM

Enable RIPv2 on the BHM router.

Task 17: Use the Debug Function to See Packet Traffic on a Router

Use the debug function to see packet traffic on the BHM router by typing **debug ip packet** at the privileged EXEC mode prompt.

When a RIP update is sent, how many source addresses are used? _____

Why are multiple source addresses used?

_____

What is the source address that is used?

_____

Why is this address used?

_____

Task 18: Start the debug ip rip database Function on Router BHM

Step 1.   Start the RIP database debugging by typing **debug ip rip database**. Then, clear the routing table by typing **clear ip route ***.

Are the old routes in the table deleted? _____

Are new routes added back into the table? _____

What does the last entry in the debug output say?

_____

Step 2.   Turn off debugging by typing either **no debug ip rip** or **undebug all**.

Task 19: Use the Debug Function to See Routing Updates

Step 1.   Use the debug function to see routing updates by typing **debug ip rip events** in privileged EXEC mode on the BHM router.

What interfaces are the routing updates sent on?

_____

How many routes are in the routing updates that are being sent? _____

Step 2. Upon completion of the previous steps, log off (by typing **exit**) and turn the router off. Then, remove and store the cables and adapter.

Comprehensive Lab 1-6: Default Routing and RIPv2

Figure 1-36   Default Routing and RIPv2 Topology

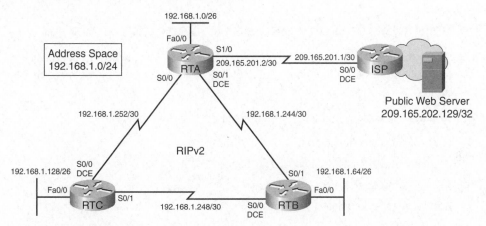

Table 1-15   Addressing Scheme

Device	Interface	IP Address	Subnet Mask
ISP	S0/0	209.165.201.1	255.255.255.252
	Lo0/0	209.165.202.129	255.255.255.252
RTA	Fa0/0	192.168.1.1	255.255.255.192
	S1/0	209.165.201.2	255.255.255.252
	S0/1	192.168.1.245	255.255.255.252
	S0/0	192.168.1.254	255.255.255.252
RTB	S0/1	192.168.1.246	255.255.255.192
	Fa0/0	192.168.1.65	255.255.255.192
	S0/0	192.168.1.249	255.255.255.252
RTC	S0/1	192.168.1.250	255.255.255.252
	Fa0/0	192.168.1.129	255.255.255.192
	S0/0	192.168.1.253	255.255.255.252

Objectives

■ Review basic router configurations.

■ Configure RIPv2.

■ Configure static and default routing.

■ Verify connectivity and troubleshoot problems.

Equipment

The topology shown in Figure 1-36 is using 2600 series routers. This lab can be done with any combination of 1700, 2500, and 2600 series routers. If a router with three serial interfaces is not available, you can use a router with two Ethernet interfaces and attach the ISP router through the Ethernet interfaces. If a router with four interfaces is not available, you can simulate the LAN off of RTA with a loopback instead of using the Ethernet interface.

NetLab Compatibility Notes

Most of this lab can be completed on a standard NetLab three router pod. To simulate the ISP connection, simply configure a loopback address. However, you will not be able to test connectivity to the Public Web Server.

Task 1: Cable the Topology and Basic Configurations

Step 1.   Cable the topology as shown in Figure 1-36. If DCE/DTE connections and interfaces are different from those shown in Figure 1-36 and Table 1-15, relabel the figure to match your connections.

Step 2.   Configure the routers with basic router configurations, including:

- Hostnames and host tables
- Enable secret password and MOTD banner
- Line configurations
- IOS-specific commands (e.g. **ip subnet-zero** with IOS versions prior to 12)

Task 2: Configure Interfaces and Enable RIPv2

Step 1.   Use Table 1-15 and the topology shown in Figure 1-37 to configure each router with the correct interface addresses.

Step 2.   If you are not using a router with four interfaces for RTA, you need to simulate ISP. To simulate an ISP connection, use the following configuration on RTA:

```
RTA(config)#interface Loopback0
RTA(config-if)#description Simulated Link to ISP
RTA(config-if)#ip address 209.165.201.2 255.255.255.252
```

Step 3.   Configuring RIPv2 requires adding the **version 2** command after entering RIP routing configuration mode. With RIPv2, **auto-summary** is enabled by default, so you need to add the **no auto-summary** command. All connected networks participating in RIP are defined with the **network** command in the form of classful networks. In this case, you only need to add the 192.168.1.0 network. *Do not* configure the ISP link as part of RIP.

Task 3: Verify Connectivity

Step 1.   You should now have full connectivity between RTA, RTB, and RTC. Issue the **show ip route** command to verify full convergence.

Routing table on RTA:

```
RTA#show ip route
Codes: C - connected, S - static, I - IGRP, R - RIP, M - mobile, B - BGP
        D - EIGRP, EX - EIGRP external, O - OSPF, IA - OSPF inter area
        N1 - OSPF NSSA external type 1, N2 - OSPF NSSA external type 2
        E1 - OSPF external type 1, E2 - OSPF external type 2, E - EGP
```

```
              i - IS-IS, L1 - IS-IS level-1, L2 - IS-IS level-2, ia - IS-IS inter
       area
              * - candidate default, U - per-user static route, o - ODR
              P - periodic downloaded static route

       Gateway of last resort is not set

            209.165.201.0/30 is subnetted, 1 subnets
       C       209.165.201.0 is directly connected, Serial1/0
            192.168.1.0/24 is variably subnetted, 6 subnets, 2 masks
       R       192.168.1.64/26 [120/1] via 192.168.1.246, 00:00:25, Serial0/1
       C       192.168.1.0/26 is directly connected, FastEthernet0/0
       R       192.168.1.248/30 [120/1] via 192.168.1.246, 00:00:25, Serial0/1
                              [120/1] via 192.168.1.253, 00:00:04, Serial0/0
       C       192.168.1.252/30 is directly connected, Serial0/0
       C       192.168.1.244/30 is directly connected, Serial0/1
       R       192.168.1.128/26 [120/1] via 192.168.1.253, 00:00:06, Serial0/0
```

Step 2.   Notice that RTA has four connected routes (including the connected route to ISP) and three RIP routes. RTB and RTC should both have three connected routes and three RIP routes.

Step 3.   Pings sourced from any router to a LAN interface on another router should succeed. Make sure each router can ping the LAN interfaces of the other two routers. RTA pings to RTB and RTC LAN interfaces are shown here:

```
RTA#ping 192.168.1.65

Type escape sequence to abort.
Sending 5, 100-byte ICMP Echos to 192.168.1.65, timeout is 2 seconds:
!!!!!
Success rate is 100 percent (5/5), round-trip min/avg/max = 28/28/32 ms
RTA#ping 192.168.1.129

Type escape sequence to abort.
Sending 5, 100-byte ICMP Echos to 192.168.1.129, timeout is 2 seconds:
!!!!!
Success rate is 100 percent (5/5), round-trip min/avg/max = 28/29/32 ms
```

Task 4: Add ISP Router

Step 1.   If you are not simulating the ISP router, configure ISP with the following script:

```
Router(config)#hostname ISP
ISP(config)#enable secret class
ISP(config)#no ip domain-lookup
ISP(config)#ip host RTA 209.165.201.1
ISP(config)#interface Loopback0
ISP(config-if)#description Public Web Server
ISP(config-if)#ip address 209.165.202.129 255.255.255.255
ISP(config-if)#interface Serial0
ISP(config-if)#description Link to RTA
ISP(config-if)#ip address 209.165.201.1 255.255.255.252
ISP(config-if)#clockrate 64000
ISP(config-if)#no shutdown
ISP(config-if)#exit
```

```
ISP(config)#banner motd &
***********************************
  !!!AUTHORIZED ACCESS ONLY!!!
***********************************
&
ISP(config)#line con 0
ISP(config-line)#exec-timeout 30 0
ISP(config-line)#password cisco
ISP(config-line)#logging synchronous
ISP(config-line)#login
ISP(config-line)#line aux 0
ISP(config-line)#exec-timeout 30 0
ISP(config-line)#password cisco
ISP(config-line)#logging synchronous
ISP(config-line)#login
ISP(config-line)#line vty 0 4
ISP(config-line)#exec-timeout 30 0
ISP(config-line)#password cisco
ISP(config-line)#logging synchronous
ISP(config-line)#login
ISP(config-line)#end
ISP#copy run start
```

Step 2.   Verify that ISP can now ping the 209.165.201.2 interface on RTA.

```
ISP#ping RTA

Type escape sequence to abort.
Sending 5, 100-byte ICMP Echos to 209.165.201.2, timeout is 2 seconds:
!!!!!
Success rate is 100 percent (5/5), round-trip min/avg/max = 28/29/32 ms
```

RTA will not be able to ping the Public Web Server and ISP will not be able to ping beyond the 209.165.201.2 interface of RTA. Why?

_____

_____

_____

_____

_____

_____

Task 5: Configure Static and Default Routing

Step 1.   For ISP to be able to send Echo replies back to hosts belonging to the 192.168.1.0/24 address space, it must have a route. Use the following command on ISP to configure a static route pointing to the 192.168.1.0/24 address space:

```
ISP(config)#ip route 192.168.1.0 255.255.255.0 209.165.201.2
```

Step 2.   Now ISP can route back to any host belonging to 192.168.1.0/24. However, RTA, RTB, and RTC do not yet have a route for any address space other than 192.168.1.0/24. Because ISP represents the connection to the rest of the world, you need to configure default routing. A router without a more specific route in the routing table will send traffic to the default route. Use the following command on RTA to configure a default route:

```
RTA(config)#ip route 0.0.0.0 0.0.0.0 209.165.201.1
```

Step 3.   If you are simulating ISP, use the following command to configure a default route:

RTA(config)#**ip route 0.0.0.0 0.0.0.0 Loopback0**

Step 4.   Now RTA should be able to ping the Public Web Server. However, RTB and RTC still cannot ping outside the 192.168.1.0/24 address space. The reason is that RTA does not advertise the default route unless specifically configured to do so. Use the following command with RIP to propagate a default route to RTB and RTC in the RIP updates:

RTA(config)#**router rip**
RTA(config-router)#**default-information originate**

Note: With RIP routing, depending on the platform and IOS version, you may need to reload the router that is propagating the default route before the default route will be sent in routing updates.

Task 6: Verify Connectivity and Capture Scripts

Step 1.   Verify that all routers now have a default route and can ping the Public Web Server.

Note: If you are simulating ISP, test by pinging the loopback interface, 209.165.201.2 on RTA.

```
RTA>show ip route
Codes: C - connected, S - static, I - IGRP, R - RIP, M - mobile, B - BGP
       D - EIGRP, EX - EIGRP external, O - OSPF, IA - OSPF inter area
       N1 - OSPF NSSA external type 1, N2 - OSPF NSSA external type 2
       E1 - OSPF external type 1, E2 - OSPF external type 2, E - EGP
       i - IS-IS, L1 - IS-IS level-1, L2 - IS-IS level-2, ia - IS-IS inter
area
       * - candidate default, U - per-user static route, o - ODR
       P - periodic downloaded static route

Gateway of last resort is 209.165.201.1 to network 0.0.0.0

     209.165.201.0/30 is subnetted, 1 subnets
C       209.165.201.0 is directly connected, Serial1/0
     192.168.1.0/24 is variably subnetted, 6 subnets, 2 masks
R       192.168.1.64/26 [120/1] via 192.168.1.246, 00:00:15, Serial0/1
C       192.168.1.0/26 is directly connected, FastEthernet0/0
R       192.168.1.248/30 [120/1] via 192.168.1.253, 00:00:15, Serial0/0
                         [120/1] via 192.168.1.246, 00:00:15, Serial0/1
C       192.168.1.252/30 is directly connected, Serial0/0
C       192.168.1.244/30 is directly connected, Serial0/1
R       192.168.1.128/26 [120/1] via 192.168.1.253, 00:00:16, Serial0/0
S*   0.0.0.0/0 [1/0] via 209.165.201.1

RTA>ping WEB

Type escape sequence to abort.
Sending 5, 100-byte ICMP Echos to 209.165.202.129, timeout is 2 seconds:
!!!!!
Success rate is 100 percent (5/5), round-trip min/avg/max = 32/38/56 ms
```

```
RTB>show ip route
Codes: C - connected, S - static, I - IGRP, R - RIP, M - mobile, B - BGP
       D - EIGRP, EX - EIGRP external, O - OSPF, IA - OSPF inter area
       N1 - OSPF NSSA external type 1, N2 - OSPF NSSA external type 2
       E1 - OSPF external type 1, E2 - OSPF external type 2, E - EGP
       i - IS-IS, L1 - IS-IS level-1, L2 - IS-IS level-2, ia - IS-IS inter
area
       * - candidate default, U - per-user static route, o - ODR
       P - periodic downloaded static route

Gateway of last resort is 192.168.1.245 to network 0.0.0.0

     192.168.1.0/24 is variably subnetted, 6 subnets, 2 masks
C       192.168.1.64/26 is directly connected, FastEthernet0/0
R       192.168.1.0/26 [120/1] via 192.168.1.245, 00:00:13, Serial0/1
C       192.168.1.248/30 is directly connected, Serial0/0
R       192.168.1.252/30 [120/1] via 192.168.1.250, 00:00:04, Serial0/0
                        [120/1] via 192.168.1.245, 00:00:13, Serial0/1
C       192.168.1.244/30 is directly connected, Serial0/1
R       192.168.1.128/26 [120/1] via 192.168.1.250, 00:00:04, Serial0/0
R*   0.0.0.0/0 [120/1] via 192.168.1.245, 00:00:13, Serial0/1


RTB>ping WEB


Type escape sequence to abort.
Sending 5, 100-byte ICMP Echos to 209.165.202.129, timeout is 2 seconds:
!!!!!
Success rate is 100 percent (5/5), round-trip min/avg/max = 32/38/56 ms



RTC>show ip route
Codes: C - connected, S - static, I - IGRP, R - RIP, M - mobile, B - BGP
       D - EIGRP, EX - EIGRP external, O - OSPF, IA - OSPF inter area
       N1 - OSPF NSSA external type 1, N2 - OSPF NSSA external type 2
       E1 - OSPF external type 1, E2 - OSPF external type 2, E - EGP
       i - IS-IS, L1 - IS-IS level-1, L2 - IS-IS level-2, ia - IS-IS inter
area
       * - candidate default, U - per-user static route, o - ODR
       P - periodic downloaded static route

Gateway of last resort is 192.168.1.254 to network 0.0.0.0

     192.168.1.0/24 is variably subnetted, 6 subnets, 2 masks
R       192.168.1.64/26 [120/1] via 192.168.1.249, 00:00:24, Serial0/1
R       192.168.1.0/26 [120/1] via 192.168.1.254, 00:00:04, Serial0/0
C       192.168.1.248/30 is directly connected, Serial0/1
C       192.168.1.252/30 is directly connected, Serial0/0
R       192.168.1.244/30 [120/1] via 192.168.1.249, 00:00:24, Serial0/1
                        [120/1] via 192.168.1.254, 00:00:04, Serial0/0
C       192.168.1.128/26 is directly connected, FastEthernet0/0
R*   0.0.0.0/0 [120/1] via 192.168.1.254, 00:00:04, Serial0/0


RTC>ping WEB
```

```
Type escape sequence to abort.
Sending 5, 100-byte ICMP Echos to 209.165.202.129, timeout is 2 seconds:
!!!!!
Success rate is 100 percent (5/5), round-trip min/avg/max = 32/38/56 ms
```

Step 2.   Troubleshoot, if necessary, to obtain output similar to the preceding output.

Step 3.   When finished, capture your scripts for your records and erase/reload the routers.

Challenge Lab 1-7: VLSM Design, RIPv2, and Default Routing

Figure 1-37   VLSM Design, RIPv2, and Default Routing Topology

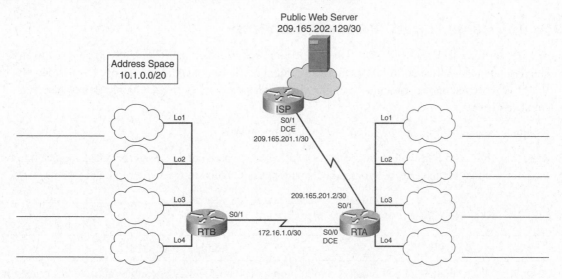

Table 1-16   Addressing Scheme

Device	Interface	IP Address	Subnet Mask
ISP	S0/0	209.165.201.1	255.255.255.252
	Lo0/0	209.165.202.129	255.255.255.252
RTA	S0/1	209.165.201.2	255.255.255.252
	S0/0	172.16.1.1	255.255.255.252
	Lo1		
	Lo2		
	Lo3		
	Lo4		
RTB	S0/1	172.16.1.2	255.255.255.252
	Lo1		
	Lo2		
	Lo3		
	Lo4		

Objectives

- Design a scalable addressing scheme.

- Configure routers with basic configurations using your addressing scheme.

- Configure dynamic, static, and default routing.

- Verify connectivity and troubleshoot problems.

Equipment

The topology shown in Figure 1-37 uses 2600 series routers. This lab can be done with any combination of 1700, 2500, and 2600 series routers.

NetLab Compatibility Notes

This lab can be completed on a standard NetLab three router pod.

Task 1: Design the Addressing Scheme

You are given the address space, 10.1.0.0/20. The loopback interfaces on RTA and RTB are used to simulate different areas of the network. Although each loopback interface could be one LAN or a group of LANs summarized in one routing update, this discussion simply refers to each loopback interface as a simulated LAN.

Design an addressing scheme by following these requirements:

Step 1.   RTA and RTB will share the 10.1.0.0/20 address space equally. Split the address space into two equal subnets. Record your subnets with prefix notation in the space provided.

Address space for RTB	Address space for RTA

Step 2.   Each simulated LAN requires a minimum of 100 host addresses. Subnet the address space for both RTA and RTB, maximizing the total number of subnets while still providing enough host addresses for each simulated LAN. You will use the first four subnets in each address space. Record your subnets with prefix notation in the space provided.

Subnets for RTA LANs	Subnets for RTB LANs
Lo1	Lo1
Lo2	Lo1
Lo3	Lo1
Lo4	Lo1

Step 3.   Now label the topology with your subnets and finish filling in the addressing table. Make sure you record the subnet masks in dotted-decimal format.

Step 4.   If required, obtain your instructor's approval before proceeding.

Instructor Initials _____

Task 2: Cable the Topology and Basic Configurations

Step 1.   Cable the topology as shown in Figure 1-37.

Step 2.   Configure the routers with basic router configurations, including

- Hostnames and host tables

- Enable secret password and MOTD banner

- Line configurations

- IOS-specific commands (that is, **ip subnet-zero** with IOS versions prior to 12)

Task 3: Configure the Interfaces and Enable RIPv2

Step 1.   Configure all interfaces, including the loopbacks, according to your addressing scheme.

Step 2.   Configure RIPv2 on RTA and RTB. Make sure to add the 172.16.0.0 network to RIP configuration on both RTA and RTB. Do not configure RIP on ISP. Do not add the 209.165.201.0/30 network to the RIP configuration on RTA.

Task 4: Configure Static and Default Routing

Step 1.   ISP needs two static routes: one pointing to the 10.1.0.0/20 address space and one pointing to the 172.16.1.0/30 address space. Configure ISP with these static routes.

Step 2.   RTA needs a default route point to ISP. Configure RTA with a default route.

Step 3.   RTA needs to send RTB the default router. Configure RTA to originate default information within the RIP routing process. Refer to Lab 1-6, if you need help.

Note: With RIP routing, you must reload the router that is propagating the default route before the default route will be sent in routing updates.

Task 5: Verify Connectivity

Step 1.   Verify that all routers now have a default route and can ping the Public Web Server. The routing tables should have all the routes shown in the following output:

Routing Table for ISP:

```
        Gateway of last resort is not set

        172.16.0.0/30 is subnetted, 1 subnets
S          172.16.1.0 [1/0] via 209.165.201.2
        209.165.201.0/30 is subnetted, 1 subnets
C          209.165.201.0 is directly connected, Serial0/1
        209.165.202.0/32 is subnetted, 1 subnets
C          209.165.202.129 is directly connected, Loopback0
        10.0.0.0/20 is subnetted, 1 subnets
S          10.1.0.0 [1/0] via 209.165.201.2
```

Routing Table for RTA:

```
        Gateway of last resort is 209.165.201.1 to network 0.0.0.0

        172.16.0.0/30 is subnetted, 1 subnets
C          172.16.1.0 is directly connected, Serial0/0
        209.165.201.0/30 is subnetted, 1 subnets
C          209.165.201.0 is directly connected, Serial0/1
        10.0.0.0/25 is subnetted, 8 subnets
R          10.1.9.0 [120/1] via 172.16.1.2, 00:00:26, Serial0/0
R          10.1.8.0 [120/1] via 172.16.1.2, 00:00:26, Serial0/0
```

```
C        10.1.1.0 is directly connected, Loopback3
C        10.1.0.0 is directly connected, Loopback1
R        10.1.9.128 [120/1] via 172.16.1.2, 00:00:27, Serial0/0
R        10.1.8.128 [120/1] via 172.16.1.2, 00:00:27, Serial0/0
C        10.1.1.128 is directly connected, Loopback4
C        10.1.0.128 is directly connected, Loopback2
S*    0.0.0.0/0 [1/0] via 209.165.201.1
```

Routing Table for RTB:
```
     Gateway of last resort is 172.16.1.1 to network 0.0.0.0


     172.16.0.0/30 is subnetted, 1 subnets
C        172.16.1.0 is directly connected, Serial0/1
     10.0.0.0/25 is subnetted, 8 subnets
C        10.1.9.0 is directly connected, Loopback3
C        10.1.8.0 is directly connected, Loopback1
R        10.1.1.0 [120/1] via 172.16.1.1, 00:00:20, Serial0/1
R        10.1.0.0 [120/1] via 172.16.1.1, 00:00:20, Serial0/1
C        10.1.9.128 is directly connected, Loopback4
C        10.1.8.128 is directly connected, Loopback2
R        10.1.1.128 [120/1] via 172.16.1.1, 00:00:21, Serial0/1
R        10.1.0.128 [120/1] via 172.16.1.1, 00:00:21, Serial0/1
R*    0.0.0.0/0 [120/1] via 172.16.1.1, 00:00:21, Serial0/1
```

Step 2.   Troubleshoot, if necessary, to obtain output similar to the preceding output.

Step 3.   Once finished, capture your scripts for your records and erase/reload the routers.

Task 6: Challenge

Looking forward to your studies of EIGRP, you will learn that it is possible to reduce the size of the routing tables on RTA and RTB by configuring EIGRP to summarize the simulated LANs into one route.

What summary route would you configure on RTB to send to RTA? Record the summary route with the correct prefix length here:

_____

What summary route would you configure on RTA to send to RTB? Record the summary route with the correct prefix length here:

_____

What interface would send the summary on RTB?

_____

What interface would send the summary on RTA?

_____

Now use the Cisco IOS help facility to discover a command you can use to configure a summary route. To get you started on RTA, enter interface configuration mode for the interface attached to RTB. Then enter **ip ?**. Can you find an **ip** command that looks like a summary route? Continue to use the help facility to discover all the parameters and configure your summary route.

Now verify that RTB has received the new summary route as highlighted in the following output. All the routes may be listed, including the /25 routes, because RIP has not yet timed out these routes. You can either wait for the /25 routes to be flushed or simply refresh the routing table by using the **clear ip route *** command.

```
RTB#show ip route
Codes: C - connected, S - static, I - IGRP, R - RIP, M - mobile, B - BGP
       D - EIGRP, EX - EIGRP external, O - OSPF, IA - OSPF inter area
       N1 - OSPF NSSA external type 1, N2 - OSPF NSSA external type 2
       E1 - OSPF external type 1, E2 - OSPF external type 2, E - EGP
       i - IS-IS, L1 - IS-IS level-1, L2 - IS-IS level-2, ia - IS-IS inter area
       * - candidate default, U - per-user static route, o - ODR
       P - periodic downloaded static route

Gateway of last resort is 172.16.1.1 to network 0.0.0.0

     172.16.0.0/30 is subnetted, 1 subnets
C       172.16.1.0 is directly connected, Serial0/1
     10.0.0.0/8 is variably subnetted, 9 subnets, 2 masks
C       10.1.9.0/25 is directly connected, Loopback3
C       10.1.8.0/25 is directly connected, Loopback1
R       10.1.1.0/25 [120/1] via 172.16.1.1, 00:00:55, Serial0/1
R       10.1.0.0/21 [120/1] via 172.16.1.1, 00:00:28, Serial0/1
R       10.1.0.0/25 [120/1] via 172.16.1.1, 00:00:55, Serial0/1
C       10.1.9.128/25 is directly connected, Loopback4
C       10.1.8.128/25 is directly connected, Loopback2
R       10.1.1.128/25 [120/1] via 172.16.1.1, 00:00:55, Serial0/1
R       10.1.0.128/25 [120/1] via 172.16.1.1, 00:00:55, Serial0/1
R*   0.0.0.0/0 [120/1] via 172.16.1.1, 00:00:28, Serial0/1

RTB#clear ip route *

RTB#show ip route
Codes: C - connected, S - static, I - IGRP, R - RIP, M - mobile, B - BGP
       D - EIGRP, EX - EIGRP external, O - OSPF, IA - OSPF inter area
       N1 - OSPF NSSA external type 1, N2 - OSPF NSSA external type 2
       E1 - OSPF external type 1, E2 - OSPF external type 2, E - EGP
       i - IS-IS, L1 - IS-IS level-1, L2 - IS-IS level-2, ia - IS-IS inter area
       * - candidate default, U - per-user static route, o - ODR
       P - periodic downloaded static route

Gateway of last resort is 172.16.1.1 to network 0.0.0.0

     172.16.0.0/30 is subnetted, 1 subnets
C       172.16.1.0 is directly connected, Serial0/1
     10.0.0.0/8 is variably subnetted, 5 subnets, 2 masks
C       10.1.9.0/25 is directly connected, Loopback3
C       10.1.8.0/25 is directly connected, Loopback1
R       10.1.0.0/21 [120/1] via 172.16.1.1, 00:00:03, Serial0/1
C       10.1.9.128/25 is directly connected, Loopback4
C       10.1.8.128/25 is directly connected, Loopback2
R*   0.0.0.0/0 [120/1] via 172.16.1.1, 00:00:03, Serial0/1
```

Now configure RTB to summarize the simulated LANs in RIP routing updates sent to RTA. What is the command, including router prompt?

_____

Clear the routing table on RTA and verify that RTA lists only the summary route for RTB. Test the route by pinging the loopback interfaces on RTB.

```
RTA#show ip route
Codes: C - connected, S - static, I - IGRP, R - RIP, M - mobile, B - BGP
       D - EIGRP, EX - EIGRP external, O - OSPF, IA - OSPF inter area
       N1 - OSPF NSSA external type 1, N2 - OSPF NSSA external type 2
       E1 - OSPF external type 1, E2 - OSPF external type 2, E - EGP
       i - IS-IS, L1 - IS-IS level-1, L2 - IS-IS level-2, ia - IS-IS inter area
       * - candidate default, U - per-user static route, o - ODR
       P - periodic downloaded static route


Gateway of last resort is 209.165.201.1 to network 0.0.0.0


     172.16.0.0/30 is subnetted, 1 subnets
C       172.16.1.0 is directly connected, Serial0/0
     209.165.201.0/30 is subnetted, 1 subnets
C       209.165.201.0 is directly connected, Serial0/1
     10.0.0.0/8 is variably subnetted, 5 subnets, 2 masks
R       10.1.8.0/21 [120/1] via 172.16.1.2, 00:00:05, Serial0/0
C       10.1.1.0/25 is directly connected, Loopback3
C       10.1.0.0/25 is directly connected, Loopback1
C       10.1.1.128/25 is directly connected, Loopback4
C       10.1.0.128/25 is directly connected, Loopback2
S*   0.0.0.0/0 [1/0] via 209.165.201.1
RTA#ping 10.1.8.1


Type escape sequence to abort.
Sending 5, 100-byte ICMP Echos to 10.1.8.1, timeout is 2 seconds:
!!!!!
Success rate is 100 percent (5/5), round-trip min/avg/max = 28/28/28 ms
RTA#ping 10.1.8.129


Type escape sequence to abort.
Sending 5, 100-byte ICMP Echos to 10.1.8.129, timeout is 2 seconds:
!!!!!
Success rate is 100 percent (5/5), round-trip min/avg/max = 28/28/32 ms
RTA#ping 10.1.9.129
```

```
Type escape sequence to abort.
Sending 5, 100-byte ICMP Echos to 10.1.9.129, timeout is 2 seconds:
!!!!!
Success rate is 100 percent (5/5), round-trip min/avg/max = 28/28/28 ms
RTA#ping 10.1.9.1

Type escape sequence to abort.
Sending 5, 100-byte ICMP Echos to 10.1.9.1, timeout is 2 seconds:
!!!!!
Success rate is 100 percent (5/5), round-trip min/avg/max = 28/29/32 ms
```

CHAPTER 2

Single-Area OSPF

The Study Guide portion of this chapter uses a combination of matching, fill in the blank, open-ended questions, and unique custom exercises to test your knowledge on the theory of link-state routing protocols, single-area OSPF concepts, and single-area OSPF configuration.

The Lab Exercises portion of this chapter includes all the online curriculum labs as well as a comprehensive lab and a challenge lab to ensure that you have mastered the practical, hands-on skills needed about single-area OSPF.

Study Guide

Link-State Routing Overview

In this section of the Study Guide, you complete exercises that solidify your knowledge of the features, benefits, and limitations of link-state routing protocols. You also work on your OSPF vocabulary. The following exercises build on each other and are best done in sequence.

Vocabulary Exercise: Matching

Match the definition on the left with a term on the right. This exercise is not necessarily a one-to-one matching. Some definitions may be used more than once and some terms may have multiple definitions. Finally, some terms may not be used at all.

Definition

a. A collection of networks under a common administration that share a common routing strategy

b. Link-state routing protocol

c. Attaches to multiple areas, maintains separate link-state databases for each area it is connected to, and routes traffic destined for or arriving from other areas

d. Describes the details of OSPF link-state concepts and operations

e. A listing of links used by the SPF algorithm to calculate the best paths through the network and build the SPF tree

f. A group of contiguous subnets that is a logical subdivision of an autonomous system

g. Flooded throughout an area when a failure occurs in the network, such as when a neighbor becomes unreachable

h. An open-standard, link-state routing protocol designed to address the limitations of RIP

i. Calculates and maintains a complex database of topology information

j. Within each autonomous system, a contiguous transition area through which all other areas communicate

k. Connects to an external routing domain that uses a different routing policy

l. The part of the network through which multiple OSPF areas connect

m. When this is not equal, the router with the highest will be the DR regardless of router ID values

j. The Router ID for an OSPF router if no loopbacks are configured

Term

____ link-state database

____ Intermediate System-to-Intermediate System (IS-IS)

____ area

____ link-state advertisements

____ highest IP address

____ Open Shortest Path First (OSPF)

____ router priority

____ area 0

____ RFC 2328

____ Shortest Path First algorithm

____ autonomous system

____ Area Border Router (ABR)

____ topological database

____ the backbone

____ Autonomous System Boundary Router (ASBR)

_____lowest IP address

____ Dijkstra

Vocabulary Exercise: Completion

Complete the paragraphs that follow by filling in appropriate words and phrases.

_____ and _____ protocols are classified as link-state routing protocols. RFC _____ describes OSPF link-state concepts and operations. Link-state routing protocols were designed to overcome the limitations of _____ routing protocols. When a failure occurs in the network, such as when a neighbor becomes unreachable, link-state protocols flood _____ (acronym) using a special _____ address throughout an area. A _____ is the same as an interface on a router. The state of the _____ is a description of an interface and the relationship to its neighboring routers. The collection of _____ forms a _____ database, sometimes called a topological database.

Link-state routers find the best paths to destinations by applying the _____ algorithm against the link-state database to build the shortest-path first (SPF) tree, with the _____ router as the root. The best paths are then selected from the SPF tree and placed in the _____

An _____ consists of a collection of networks under a common administration that share a common routing strategy. The _____ area is the transition point between areas in an AS because all other areas communicate through it.

Compare and Contrast Exercise

In the following table, list the benefits and limitations of link-state routing protocols. You should have at least four entries for each side of the table.

Benefits	Limitations

Concept Questions

What two names refer to the same algorithm used by all link-state routing protocols?

_____

_____

_____

What is the difference between the way link-state routing protocols view the network and the way distance vector routing protocols view the network?

_____

_____

_____

_____

_____

_____

Journal Entry

Describe a network implementation where a distance vector routing protocol would be preferred over a link-state routing protocol.

_____

_____

_____

_____

_____

_____

_____

_____

_____

Single-Area OSPF Concepts

One of the main limitations of OSPF is its sheer complexity. Although you are only responsible for understanding single-area OSPF concepts and configurations, it is still the most complex routing protocol you will use at the CCNA level. The exercises in the section focus on the conceptual framework of OSPF. It is important to have a good grasp of these concepts before proceeding into the configuration of OSPF. The following exercises build on each other and are best done in sequence.

Vocabulary Exercise: Completion

Complete the paragraphs that follow by filling in appropriate words and phrases.

OSPF is a routing protocol developed for IP networks by the OSPF working group of the
_____ OSPF has two primary characteristics. The first is that the protocol is an
open _____ which means that its specification is in the public domain, described in RFC
2328. The second principal characteristic is that OSPF is based on the _____ algorithm.

OSPF is a _____ routing protocol, whereas _____ and _____ are distance vector routing protocols. Routers that are running distance vector algorithms send all or a portion of their _____ in routing-update messages to their neighbors.

The term *link* simply refers to the _____ on a router and its relationship to its neighboring _____ The collection all of these states forms the link-state database, which is an overall picture of networks in relation to routers.

The ability of OSPF to separate a large internetwork into multiple _____ is also referred to as hierarchical routing. Routing still occurs between _____ but recalculating databases can be isolated to the _____ where the change occurred.

The SPF algorithm is used to calculate the _____ of links. The OSPF _____ of an interface is inversely proportional to the _____ of that interface, so a higher _____ indicates a lower _____ The default formula used to calculate OSPF _____ is

_____

The SPF algorithm calculates a _____ topology using the _____ as the starting point and examining, in turn, information it has about adjacent nodes.

Build the SPF Loop-Free Topology

A physical topology is shown in Figure 2-1. All seven routers are running OSPF in the same single area network. The OSPF cost value has been simplified for this exercise. Each link is labeled with its cost. Each router will use the SPF algorithm to construct a loop-free topology with the local router as the root. In the space provided or on a separate sheet of paper, draw the logical spanning-tree topology for each router. (Hint: Use a pencil. You will make mistakes.)

Figure 2-1   Build the SPF Loop-Free Topology

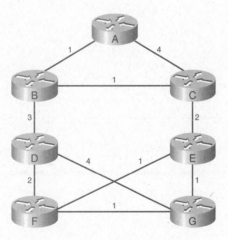

Example: The following describes how you would draw the spanning-tree topology in Figure 2-1a showing Router A as the local or root router. Start by drawing router A at the top. Router A can send traffic to both router B and router C. You can see that router A will always send traffic destined for router B directly to router B, so draw router B and connect it to router A. Label the link with the cost, which is 1. But will router A send traffic destined for router C directly to router C? No. The cost of 4 is too high compared to the path through router B, which has a cumulative cost of only 2. So, attach router C to router B and label the link with its cost. Now, how would router A send traffic to router D? It would send it to router B, which would forward the traffic directly to router D because the cumulative cost of 4 is lower than the cumulative cost to forward the traffic to router C. So, attach router D to router B and label the link with its cost. Now router B has three routers attached to it. Continue adding routers. Router E would receive traffic from router A via router C. Both router F and router G would receive traffic from router A via router E.

Figure 2-1a   Loop-free Topology for Router A

Figure 2-1b   Loop-free Topology for Router B

Figure 2-1c   Loop-free Topology for Router C

Figure 2-1d   Loop-free Topology for Router D

Figure 2-1e   Loop-free Topology for Router E

Figure 2-1f   Loop-free Topology for Router F

Figure 2-1g   Loop-free Topology for Router G

Concept Questions

What is the formula Cisco IOS uses to calculate the cost metric for OSPF?

_____

What is the OSPF cost of a T1 link?

_____

What is the OSPF cost of a Fast Ethernet link?

_____

What is the OSPF cost of a 56-kps dialup link?

_____

The routers within an OSPF area have converged. What can you safely assume about the link-state data-bases of all the routers within the area?

_____

_____

_____

Name at least three advantages of OSPF that relate to its hierarchical routing characteristic.

_____

■ _____

■ _____

■ _____

Single-Area OSPF Configuration

Now that you have a good understanding of how OSPF works, it is time to learn the configuration com-mands that you use in a single-area OSPF network. The first exercise in this section takes you step-by-step through an OSPF configuration. The second exercise focuses on a topic that often causes problems for stu-dents: the DR/BDR election. The final exercise is a journal entry. These exercises build on each other and are best done in sequence.

Learn the OSPF Commands Exercise

1. Document the command syntax, including router prompt, to configure the OSPF routing process.

    _____

2. The value for *process-id* can be any number between __ and _____

3. True or False: All routers in an area must have the same *process-id*.

    _____

    _____

4. The command syntax, including router prompt, for adding network statements to the OSPF routing process is

    _____

5. For single area OSPF configurations, the *area-id* should always be __

6. The *wildcard-mask* argument works the same way as wildcard masks in access control list statements. List the corresponding wildcard mask for each of the following subnet masks:

    255.255.255.0   _____

    255.255.255.128 _____

    255.255.255.192 _____

    255.255.255.240 _____

    255.255.0.0   _____

    255.255.252.0   _____

    255.255.240.0   _____

    255.0.0.0   _____

    255.224.0.0   _____

    255.248.0.0   _____

7. Refer to Figure 2-2. In the space provided, document the correct commands, including router prompt, to configure RTA to advertise all directly connected networks in OSPF.

Figure 2-2   RTA OSPF Configuration

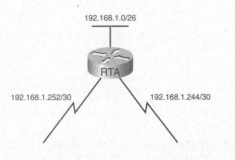

_____

_____

_____

_____

8. OSPF routers that share a common link become _____ on that link. In Figure 2-3, RTB and RTC are _____ of RTA, but not of each other. These routers send each other OSPF _____ packets to establish adjacency. These packets also act as _____ so that each router knows that adjacent routers are still functional.

Figure 2-3   Establishing OSPF Adjacency

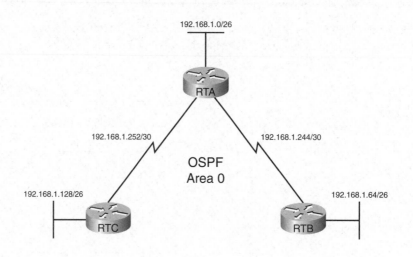

9. Using Figure 2-3, document the correct commands, including router prompt, to configure RTB and RTC to advertise all directly connected networks in OSPF.

_____

_____

_____

_____

_____

_____

_____

_____

_____

Note: Now is a good time to complete Curriculum Lab 2-1: Configuring the OSPF Routing Process (2.3.1).

10. On _____ networks (networks supporting more than two routers) such as _____ and Frame-Relay networks, the Hello protocol elects a _____ and a _____ Among other things, the _____is

responsible for generating LSAs for the entire multiaccess network, which reduces both routing-update traffic and management of _____ synchronization.

11. The DR/BDR election is based on OSPF _____ and OSPF _____ By default, all OSPF routers have a _____ of ___ If all OSPF routers have the same _____ the highest _____ determines the DR and BDR.

12. Unless a loopback interface is configured, the _____ IP address on an active interface at the moment of OSPF process startup is used as the _____

13. In Figure 2-4, label each router with its router ID. Assume that all routers came up simultaneously and that all interfaces are active.

Figure 2-4   Determine the Router ID

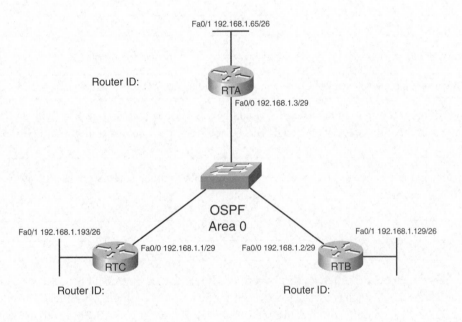

14. In Figure 2-4, which router would be the DR? _____ BDR? _____

15. You can override the Router ID that OSPF chooses by configuring an IP address on a _____ inter-face. This will provide stability to your OSPF network, because _____ interfaces do not become inactive.

16. The syntax for configuring a loopback interface with an IP address is

_____

_____

17. Assume that network policy has determined that RTA is best suited to be the DR. In addition, the poli-cy states that all OSPF routers will be configured with a loopback interface, as follows, to provide sta-bility to OSPF:

   ■ 10.0.0.3/32 for RTA

   ■ 10.0.0.2/32 for RTB

   ■ 10.0.0.1/32 for RTC

18. Document the correct commands, including router prompt, to configure loopback interfaces on each router.

_____

_____

_____

_____

_____

_____

19. With loopback interfaces now configured on each router, what must you do to change which router is DR?

_____

_____

_____

_____

_____

Note: Now is a good time to complete Curriculum Lab 2-2: Configuring OSPF with Loopback Addresses (2.3.2).

20. In addition to configuring loopbacks, it would be a good idea to configure RTA with an OSPF priority that ensures that it always wins the DR/BDR election. The syntax for configuring OSPF priority is

_____

21. Document the commands you would configure on RTA to make sure its priority always wins the DR/BDR election.

_____

_____

_____

22. In Figure 2-5, note the differences in bandwidth. If OSPF uses the default bandwidth on the serial interfaces to calculate the cost, RTB will send traffic destined for the LAN on RTC directly to RTC, and RTC will send traffic destined for the LAN on RTB directly to RTB. However, the path through RTA is faster. There are two ways to force RTB and RTC to send traffic to RTA. Explain the two different ways to configure the correct cost. In what situations would one be better than the other?

Figure 2-5   Configure OSPF Cost Metric

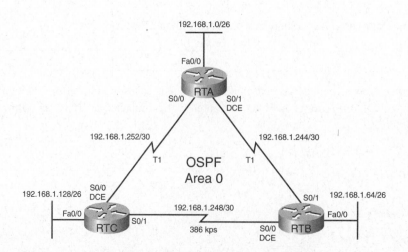

_____

_____

_____

_____

_____

_____

_____

23. RTB and RTC are both Cisco 2600 series routers. The default bandwidth on serial interfaces for 2600 routers is 1544 kbps (T1). What command would you enter to verify the default or configured bandwidth on an interface? _____ _____ Referring to Figure 2-5, document the commands needed to configure the bandwidth correctly so that OSPF uses an accurate cost metric.

_____

_____

_____

_____

Note: Now is a good time to complete Curriculum Lab 2-3: Modifying OSPF Cost Metric (2.3.3).

24. By default, a router trusts that information arriving from another router is "believable." However, to avoid malicious or inadvertent misinformation, you should configure authentication. The Cisco IOS has two methods for authenticating OSPF routing updates: simple authentication and encrypted authentication. With simple authentication, passwords are sent in clear text, affording no protection from sniffer programs. Document the command syntax, including router prompt, to configure simple authentication (two commands).

_____

_____

_____

_____

25. You should use encrypted authentication whenever possible. Document the command syntax, including router prompt, to configure encrypted authentication (two commands).

_____

_____

_____

_____

26. Document the commands necessary to configure encrypted authentication of OSPF routing updates for the routers in Figure 2-5. Because the commands are the same for all three routers, it is only necessary that you document the commands for RTA. Use "allrouters" as the key.

_____

_____

_____

_____

_____

Note: Now is a good time to complete Curriculum Lab 2-4: Configuring OSPF Authentication (2.3.4).

27. The DR, BDR, and every other router in an OSPF network sends out Hellos using _____ as the destination address. If a DRother (a router that is not the DR) needs to send an LSA, it will send it using _____ as the destination address. The DR and the BDR will receive LSAs at this address.

28. Complete the following table by listing the four types of OSPF networks and whether they have a DR/BDR election.

Network Type Election?	Characteristics	DR/BDR
	Ethernet, Token Ring, or FDDI	
	Frame Relay, X.25, SMDS	
	PPP, HDLC	
-	Configured by an administrator	

29. OSPF routers must use matching _____ intervals and _____ intervals on the same link. These are used to time the exchange of link-state information as well as to determine when a link is down.

30. On broadcast OSPF networks, the default _____ interval is ____ seconds and the default _____ interval is ___ seconds. On nonbroadcast networks, the default _____ interval is _____ seconds and the default _____ interval is ____ seconds.

31. These default interval values result in efficient OSPF operation and seldom need to be modified. However, you can change them. Document the command syntax, including router prompt, to change these values.

_____

_____

32. Again, refer to Figure 2-5. Assuming that the current intervals are 10 and 40, document the commands necessary to change these intervals on the link between RTB and RTC to a value four times greater than the current value.

_____

_____

_____

_____

_____

_____

_____

Note: Now is a good time to complete Curriculum Lab 2-5: Configuring OSPF Timers (2.3.5).

33. Refer to Figure 2-6 for the remaining questions in this section. RTA is your gateway router because it provides access outside the area. In OSPF terminology, RTA is called the _____ _____ because it connects to an external routing domain that uses a different routing policy.

Figure 2-6   Propagating a Default Route

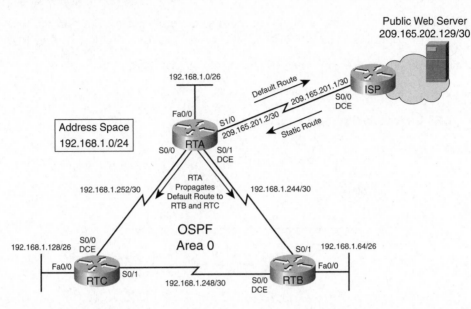

34. Each routing protocol handles the propagation of default routing information a little differently. For OSPF, the gateway router must be configured with two commands. First, RTA needs a static default route (also known as the "quad-zero" route) pointing to ISP. Document the command syntax to configure a static default route on RTA.

35. Using the *interface* argument, document the command necessary to configure RTA with a static default route pointing to ISP.

36. At this point, RTA can send pings to ISP, and ISP will respond as long as the pings are sourced from the serial 1/0 interface on RTA. However, any ping coming from the 192.168.1.0/24 address space will be discarded by ISP. Why?

37. Document the command syntax used to configure a static route.

38. Using the *next-hop-address* argument, document the command necessary to configure ISP with a static route pointing to the 192.168.1.0/24 address space.

39. At this point, any host on the LAN attached to RTA will be able to access ISP and ping the Public Web Server at 209.165.202.129. However, RTB and RTC still cannot ping outside the 192.168.1.0/24 address space. Why?

40. Document the command that needs to be configured on RTA to fix this problem.

Note: Now is a good time to complete Curriculum Lab 2-6: Propagating Default Routes in an OSPF Domain (2.3.6).

DR/BDR Election Exercise

In the following exercises, assume that all routers are simultaneously booted. Determine the network type, if applicable, and label which router is elected as the DR and which router is elected as the BDR.

Hint: Remember, if priority is equal, router ID determines DR and BDR.

Refer to Figure 2-7 and answer the following questions:

Figure 2-7   DR/BDR Election Exercise 1 Topology

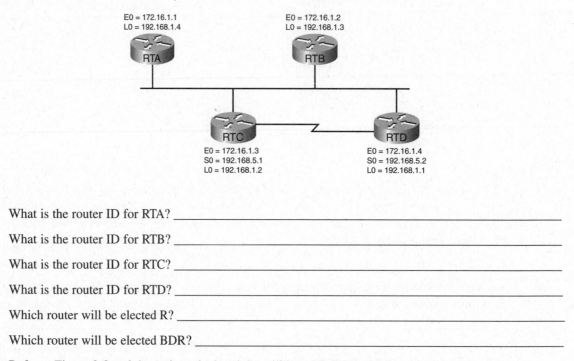

What is the router ID for RTA? _____

What is the router ID for RTB? _____

What is the router ID for RTC? _____

What is the router ID for RTD? _____

Which router will be elected R? _____

Which router will be elected BDR? _____

Refer to Figure 2-8 and determine whether there will be a DR/BDR election. If applicable, designate which router is DR and which router is BDR.

Figure 2-8   DR/BDR Election Exercise 2 Topology

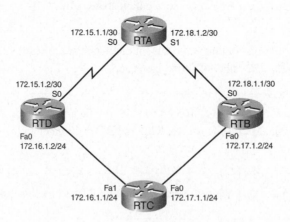

Network	DR/BDR Election?	Which Router Is the DR?	Which Router Is the BDR?
172.15.1.0/30			
172.16.1.0/24			
172.17.1.0/24			
172.18.1.0/30			

Refer to Figure 2-9 and answer the following questions:

Figure 2-9   DR/BDR Election Exercise 3 Topology

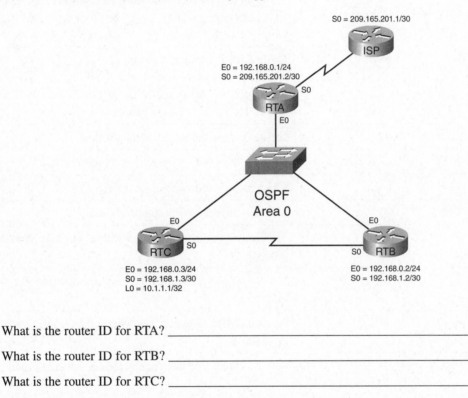

What is the router ID for RTA? _____

What is the router ID for RTB? _____

What is the router ID for RTC? _____

Which router is DR for the 192.168.0.0/24 network? _____

Which router is BDR for the 192.168.0.0/24 network? _____

Assuming a priority of zero on RTA, which router is DR for the 192.168.1.0/24 network? _____

What will happen if another router, RTD, joins the 192.168.1.0/24 network with a router ID of 209.165.201.9?

_____

Journal Entry

In a simple three-router topology, it may not be necessary to run OSPF as your routing protocol. Under what circumstances would you choose to use OSPF instead of RIPv2?

_____
_____
_____
_____

Lab Exercises

Command Reference

In the table that follows, record the command, including the correct router prompt, that fits the description. Fill in any blanks with the appropriate missing information.

Command	Description
	Turns on OSPF process number 123. The process ID is any value between ___ and _____ The process ID *does not equal* the OSPF area.
	OSPF advertises interfaces, not networks. Uses the wildcard mask to determine which interfaces to advertise. The command shown reads: any interface with an address of 172.16.10.x is to be put into area 0.
	Creates the virtual interface loopback 0.
	Changes the OSPF priority for an interface to 50.
	Changes the bandwidth of an interface to 128 kbps.
	Changes the cost to a value of 1564.
	Turns on simple authentication within the OSPF routing process.
	Sets the simple authentication key (password) to fred on an interface.
	Turns on MD5 authentication within the OSPF routing process.
	Sets 1 as the *key-id* and fred as the *key* on an interface.
	Changes the Hello Interval timer to 20 seconds.
	Changes the Dead Interval timer to 80 seconds.
	Creates a static default route pointing out the serial 0/0 interface. This route will have an administrative distance of
	Creates a static default route pointing to the next-hop IP address of 192.168.1.1. This route will have an administrative distance of
	Sets the default route to be propagated to all OSPF routers.
	Displays parameters for all routing protocols running on the router.

Command	Description
	Displays complete IP routing table.
	Displays basic OSPF information for all OSPF processes running on the router.
	Displays OSPF information as it relates to all interfaces.
	List all the OSPF neighbors and their states.
	Displays a detailed list of neighbors.
	Clears entire routing table, forcing it to rebuild.
	Resets OSPF counters.
	Resets *entire* OSPF process, forcing OSPF to re-create neighbors, the database, and the routing table.
	Displays *all* OSPF events.
	Displays the various OSPF states as neighbors form adjacencies as well as the DR and BDR election between adjacent routers.
	Displays OSPF packets as they are sent and received.

Curriculum Lab 2-1: Configuring the OSPF Routing Process (2.3.1)

Figure 2-10   Topology for Lab 2-1

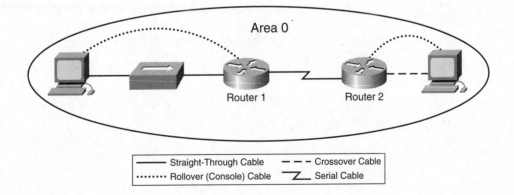

Table 2-1   Lab Equipment Configuration

Router Designation	Router Name	Routing Protocol	Network Statements
Router 1	BERLIN	OSPF	192.168.1.128
			192.168.15.0
Router 2	ROME	OSPF	192.168.15.0
			192.168.0.0

The enable secret password for both routers is **class**.

The enable, VTY, and console password for both routers is **cisco**.

Table 2-2   Lab Equipment Interface/IP Address Configurations

Router Designation	IP Host Table Entry	Fast Ethernet 0 Address/Subnet Mask	Interface Type Serial 0	Serial 0 Address/ Subnet Mask
Router 1	ROME	192.168.1.129/26	DCE	192.168.15.1/30
Router 2	BERLIN	192.168.0.1/24	DTE	192.168.15.2/30

The interface type and address/subnet mask for the serial 1 interface on both routers is not applicable for this lab.

The "IP Host Table Entry" column contents indicate the names of the other routers in the IP host table.

Objectives

- Set up an IP addressing scheme for OSPF area 0.

- Configure and verify OSPF routing.

Background/Preparation

Cable a network that is similar to the one in Figure 2-10. You can use any router that meets the interface requirements in Figure 2-10 (that is, 800, 1600, 1700, 2500, and 2600 routers or a combination). Refer to the information in Appendix A, "Router Interface Summary Chart," to correctly specify the interface identifiers based on the equipment in your lab. The 1721 series routers produced the configuration output in this lab. Another router might produce slightly different output. You should execute the following steps on each router unless you are specifically instructed otherwise. Start a HyperTerminal session.

Implement the procedure documented in Appendix C, "Erasing and Reloading the Router," before you continue with this lab.

Task 1: Configure the Routers

On the routers, enter global configuration mode and configure the hostname as shown in Table 2-1. Then, configure the console, virtual terminal, and enable passwords. Next, configure the interfaces according to Table 2-2. Finally, configure the IP hostnames. Do not configure the routing protocol until you are specifically told to. If you have problems configuring the router basics, refer to Lab 1-2, "Review of Basic Router Configuring with RIP."

Note: You may need to add the command **ip subnet-zero** because of the use of the ZERO subnet with VLSM on the 192.168.1.0/30 and 192.168.1.128/26 networks.

Task 2: Save the Configuration Information from Privileged EXEC Command Mode

```
BERLIN#copy running-config startup-config
Destination filename [startup-config]? [Enter]
```

Why save the running configuration to the startup configuration?

_____

Task 3: Configure the Hosts

Step 1. Configure the hosts with the proper IP address, subnet mask, and default gateway.

Step 2. Each workstation should be able to ping the attached router. Troubleshoot as necessary. Hint: Remember to assign a specific IP address and default gateway to the workstation. If you are running Windows 98, check using **Start > Run > winipcfg**. If you are running Windows 2000, check using **ipconfig** in a DOS window.

Step 3. At this point, the workstations will not be able to communicate with each other. The following tasks will demonstrate the process that is required to get communication working while using OSPF as the routing protocol.

Task 4: View the Router's Configuration and Interface Information

Step 1. At the privileged EXEC mode prompt, type the following:

```
BERLIN#show running-config
```

Step 2. Using the **show ip interface brief** command, check the status of each interface.

What is the state of the interfaces on each router?

BERLIN:

Fast Ethernet 0: _____

Serial 0: _____

Serial 1: _____

ROME:

Fast Ethernet 0: _____

Serial 0: _____

Serial 1: _____

Step 3. Ping from one of the connected serial interfaces to the other.

Was the ping successful? _____

Step 4. If the ping was not successful, troubleshoot the router configuration until the ping is successful.

Task 5: Configure OSPF Routing on Router BERLIN

Step 1.   Configure an OSPF routing process on router BERLIN. Use OSPF process number 1 and ensure that all networks are in area 0.

```
BERLIN(config)#router ospf 1
BERLIN(config-router)#network 192.168.1.128 0.0.0.63 area 0
BERLIN(config-router)#network 192.168.15.0 0.0.0.3 area 0
BERLIN(config-router)#end
```

Step 2.   Examine the routers that are running configuration files.

Did the IOS version automatically add any lines under router OSPF 1? _____

If so, what did it add? _____

Step 3.   If there were no changes to the running configuration, type the following commands:

```
BERLIN(config)#router ospf 1
BERLIN(config-router)#log-adjacency-changes
BERLIN(config-router)#end
```

Step 4.   Show the routing table for the BERLIN router.

```
BERLIN#show ip route
```

Do entries exist in the routing table? _____

Why?

_____

Task 6: Configure OSPF Routing on Router ROME

Step 1.   Configure an OSPF routing process on router ROME. Use OSPF process number 1 and ensure that all networks are in area 0.

```
ROME(config)#router ospf 1
ROME(config-router)#network 192.168.0.0 0.0.0.255 area 0
ROME(config-router)#network 192.168.15.0 0.0.0.3 area 0
ROME(config-router)#end
```

Step 2.   Examine the ROME router running configuration files.

Did the IOS version automatically add lines under router OSPF 1? _____

If so, what did it add? _____

Step 3.   If there were no changes to the running configuration, type the following commands:

```
ROME(config)#router ospf 1
ROME(config-router)#log-adjacency-changes
ROME(config-router)#end
```

Step 4.   Show the routing table for the ROME router.

```
ROME#show ip route
```

Are there OSPF entries in the routing table now? _____

What is the metric value of the OSPF route?

_____

What is the VIA address in the OSPF route? _____

Are routes to all networks shown in the routing table? _____

What does the O mean in the first column of the routing table?

_____

Task 7: Test Network Connectivity

Ping the BERLIN host from the ROME host. Was it successful? _____

If not, troubleshoot as necessary.

After you complete the previous steps, log off (by typing **exit**) and turn the router off. Then, remove and store the cables and adapter.

Curriculum Lab 2-2: Configuring OSPF with Loopback Addresses (2.3.2)

Figure 2-11   Topology for Lab 2-2

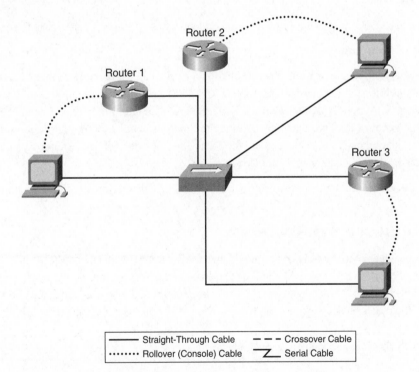

| ——— Straight-Through Cable | – – – Crossover Cable |
| · · · · · · · Rollover (Console) Cable | ⏚ Serial Cable |

Table 2-3   Lab Equipment Configuration: Part I

Router Designation	Router Name	Routing Protocol	OSPF Routing ID	Network Statements
Router 1	London	OSPF	1	192.168.1.0
Router 2	Ottawa	OSPF	1	192.168.1.0
Router 3	Brasilia	OSPF	1	192.168.1.0

The enable secret password for all routers is **class**.

The enable, VTY, and console passwords for each router is **cisco**.

Table 2-4   Lab Equipment Configuration: Part II

Router Designation	IP Host Table Entry	Fast Ethernet 0 Address/Subnet Mask	Loopback Interface/ Subnet Mask
Router 1	Ottawa Brasilia	192.168.1.1/24	192.168.31.11/32
Router 2	London Brasilia	192.168.1.2/24	192.168.31.22/32
Router 3	London Ottawa	192.168.1.3/24	192.168.31.33/32

The "IP Host Table Entry" column contents indicate the names of the other routers in the IP host table.

Objectives

- Configure routers with a Class C IP addressing scheme.

- Observe the election process for designated routers (DR) and backup designated routers (BDR) on the multiaccess network.

- Configure loopback addresses for OSPF stability.

- Assign each OSPF interface a priority to force the election of a specific router as DR.

Background/Preparation

Cable a network that is similar to the one in Figure 2-11. You can use any router that meets the interface requirements in Figure 2-11 (that is, 800, 1600, 1700, 2500, and 2600 routers or a combination). Refer to the information in Appendix A to correctly specify the interface identifiers based on the equipment in your lab. The 1721 series routers produced the configuration output in this lab. Another router might produce slightly different output. You should execute the following steps on each router unless you are specifically instructed otherwise. Start a HyperTerminal session.

Implement the procedure documented in Appendix C on all routers before continuing with this lab.

Task 1: Configure the Routers

On the routers, enter global configuration mode and configure the hostname as shown in Table 2-3. Then, configure the console, virtual terminal, and enable passwords. Next, configure the interfaces and the IP hostnames according to the Lab Equipment Configuration tables, Tables 2-3 and 2-4. If you have problems configuring the router basics, refer to Lab 1-2, "Review of Basic Router Configuring with RIP."

Note: Do not configure loopback interfaces and routing protocols yet.

Task 2: Save the Configuration Information for All the Routers

Why should you save the running configuration to the startup configuration?

Task 3: Configure the Hosts

Step 1.   Configure the hosts with the proper IP address, subnet mask, and default gateway.

Step 2.   Each workstation should be able to ping all the attached routers, because they are all part of the same subnetwork. Troubleshoot as necessary. Hint: Remember to assign a specific IP address and default gateway to the workstation. If you are running Windows 98, check using **Start > Run > winipcfg**. If you are running Windows 2000, check using **ipconfig** in a DOS window.

Step 3.   At this point, the workstations will not be able to communicate with each other. The following tasks demonstrate the process required to get communication working by using OSPF as the routing protocol.

Task 4: View the Router's Configuration and Interface Information

Step 1.   At the privileged EXEC mode prompt, type **show running-config**.

Step 2.   Using the **show ip interface brief** command, check the status of each interface.

What is the state of the interfaces on each router?

London:

- Fast Ethernet 0: _____

- Serial 0: _____

- Serial 1: _____

Ottawa:

- Fast Ethernet 0: _____

- Serial 0: _____

- Serial 1: _____

Brasilia:

- Fast Ethernet 0: _____

- Serial 0: _____

- Serial 1: _____

Task 5: Verify Connectivity of the Routers

Ping all the connected Fast Ethernet interfaces from each other.

Were the pings successful? _____

If the pings were not successful, troubleshoot the router configuration until the ping is successful.

Task 6: Configure OSPF Routing on Router London

Step 1.   Configure an OSPF routing process on router London. Use OSPF process number 1 and ensure that all networks are in area 0.

```
London(config)#router ospf 1
London(config-router)#network 192.168.1.0 0.0.0.255 area 0
London(config-router)#end
```

Step 2.   Examine the London router running the configuration file.

Did the IOS version automatically add lines under router OSPF 1? _____

Step 3.   If there were no changes to the running configuration, type the following commands:

```
London(config)#router ospf 1
London(config-router)#log-adjacency-changes
London(config-router)#end
```

Step 4.   Show the routing table for the London router:

```
London#show ip route
```

Are entries in the routing table? _____

Why?

_____

Task 7: Configure OSPF Routing on Router Ottawa

Step 1.   Configure an OSPF routing process on router Ottawa. Use OSPF process number 1 and ensure that all networks are in area 0.

```
Ottawa(config)#router ospf 1
Ottawa(config-router)#network 192.168.1.0 0.0.0.255 area 0
Ottawa(config-router)#end
```

Step 2.   Examine the Ottawa router running configuration files.

Did the IOS version automatically add lines under router OSPF 1? _____

Step 3.   If no changes were made to the running configuration, type the following commands:

```
Ottawa(config)#router ospf 1
Ottawa(config-router)#log-adjacency-changes
Ottawa(config-router)#end
```

Task 8: Configure OSPF Routing on Router Brasilia

Step 1.   Configure an OSPF routing process on router Brasilia. Use OSPF process number 1 and ensure that all networks are in area 0.

```
Brasilia(config)#router ospf 1
Brasilia(config-router)#network 192.168.1.0 0.0.0.255 area 0
Brasilia(config-router)#end
```

Step 2.   Examine the Brasilia router running configuration files.

Did the IOS version automatically add lines under router OSPF 1? _____

What did it add? _____

Step 3.   If there were no changes to the running configuration, type the following commands:

```
Brasilia(config)#router ospf 1
Brasilia(config-router)#log-adjacency-changes
Brasilia(config-router)#end
```

Task 9: Test Network Connectivity

Ping the Brasilia router from the London router. Was it successful? _____

If not, troubleshoot as necessary.

Task 10: Show OSPF Adjacencies

Type the command **show ip ospf neighbor** on all routers to verify that the OSPF routing has formed adjacencies.

Is there a designated router identified? _____

Is there a backup designated router? _____

Type the command **show ip ospf neighbor detail** for more information.

What is the neighbor priority of 192.168.1.1 from router Brasilia? _____

What interface is identified as being part of area 0? _____

Task 11: Configure the Loopback Interfaces

Configure the loopback interface on each router to allow for an interface that will not go down due to network change or failure. You can accomplish this by typing **interface loopback #** at the global configuration mode prompt, where the # represents the number of the loopback interface from 0 to 2,147,483,647.

```
London(config)#interface loopback 0
London(config-if)#ip address 192.168.31.11 255.255.255.255
London(config-router)#end

Ottawa(config)#interface loopback 0
Ottawa(config-if)#ip address 192.168.31.22 255.255.255.255
Ottawa(config-router)#end

Brasilia(config)#interface loopback 0
Brasilia(config-if)#ip address 192.168.31.33 255.255.255.255
Brasilia(config-router)#end
```

Task 12: Save the Configuration Information for All the Routers

After you save the configurations on all the routers, power them down and back up again.

Task 13: Show OSPF Adjacencies

Step 1.   Type the command **show ip ospf neighbor** on all routers to verify that the OSPF routing has formed adjacencies.

Is a designated router identified? _____

What are the Router ID and link address of the DR?

_____

Is there a backup designated router? _____

What are the Router ID and link address of the BDR?

_____

What is the third router referred to as? _____

What is that router's ID and link address?

_____

Step 2.   Type the command **show ip ospf neighbor detail** for more information.

What is the neighbor priority of 192.168.1.1 from router Brasilia? _____

Which interface is identified as being part of area 0? _____

Task 14: Verify OSPF Interface Configuration

Type **show ip ospf interface fastethernet 0** on the London router.

What is the OSPF state of the interface? _____

What is the default priority of the interface? _____

What is the network type of the interface? _____

Task 15: Configure London to Always Be the DR

Step 1.   To ensure that the London router always becomes the DR for this multiaccess segment, you
must set the OSPF priority. London is the most powerful router in the network, so it is best
suited to become the DR. Giving London's loopback a higher IP address is not advised because
the numbering system has advantages for troubleshooting. Also, London is not to act as the DR
for all segments to which it might belong.

Step 2.   Set the priority of the interface to 50 on the London router only.

```
London(config)#interface fastethernet 0/0
London(config-if)#ip ospf priority  50
London(config-router)#end
```

Step 3.   Display the priority for interface FastEthernet 0/0.

```
London#show ip ospf interface fastethernet 0/0
```

Task 16: Watch the Election Process

To watch the OSPF election process, restart all the routers. As soon as the router prompt is available, type
the following:

```
Ottawa>enable
Ottawa#debug ip ospf events
```

Which router was elected DR? _____

Which router was elected BDR? _____

Why?

_____

To turn off all debugging, type **undebug all**.

Task 17: Show OSPF Adjacencies

Type the command **show ip ospf neighbor** on the Ottawa router to verify that the OSPF routing has formed adjacencies.

What is the priority of the DR? _____

After you complete the previous steps, log off (by typing **exit**) and turn the router off. Then, remove and store the cables and adapter.

Curriculum Lab 2-3: Modifying OSPF Cost Metric (2.3.3)

Figure 2-12   Topology for Lab 2-3

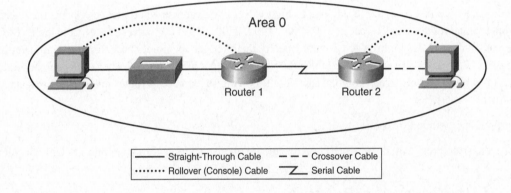

Table 2-5   Lab Equipment Configuration: Part I

Router Designation	Router Name	Routing Protocol	Network Statements
Router 1	Cairo	OSPF	192.168.1.0
Router 2	Moscow	OSPF	192.168.1.0 192.168.0.0

The enable secret password for both routers is **class**.

The enable, VTY, and console password for both routers is **cisco**.

Table 2-6   Lab Equipment Configuration: Part II

Router Designation	IP Host Table Entry	Fast Ethernet 0 Address/Subnet Mask	Interface Type Serial 0	Serial 0 Address/ Subnet Mask
Router 1	Moscow	192.168.1.129/26	DCE	192.168.1.1/30
Router 2	Cairo	192.168.0.1/24	DTE	192.168.1.2/30

The interface type and address/subnet mask for the serial 1 interface on both routers are not applicable for this lab.

The "IP Host Table Entry" column contents indicate the names of the other routers in the IP host table.

Objectives

- Set up an IP addressing scheme for the OSPF area.

- Configure and verify OSPF routing.

- Modify the OSPF cost metric on an interface.

Background/Preparation

Cable a network that is similar to the one in Figure 2-12. You can use any router that meets the interface requirements in Figure 2-12 (that is, 800, 1600, 1700, 2500, and 2600 routers or a combination). Refer to the information in Appendix A to correctly specify the interface identifiers based on the equipment in your lab. The 1721 series routers produced the configuration output in this lab. Another router might produce slightly different output. You should execute the following steps on each router unless you are specifically instructed otherwise.

Start a HyperTerminal session.

Implement the procedure documented in Appendix C on all routers before you continue with this lab.

Task 1: Configure the Routers

On the routers, enter the global configuration mode and configure the hostname, console, virtual terminal, and enable passwords. Next, configure the interfaces and IP hostnames according to the Lab Equipment Configuration tables, Tables 2-5 and 2-6. If you have problems configuring the router basics, refer to Lab 1-2, "Review of Basic Router Configuring with RIP."

Note: You may need to add the command **ip subnet-zero** because of the use of the ZERO subnet with VLSM on the 192.168.1.0/30 and 192.168.1.128/26 networks.

Note: Do not configure the routing protocol until you are specifically told to.

Task 2: Save the Configuration Information from Privileged EXEC Command Mode

```
Cairo#copy running-config startup-config
Destination filename [startup-config]?[Enter]
Moscow#copy running-config startup-config
Destination filename [startup-config]?[Enter]
```

Why should you save the running configuration to the startup configuration?

Task 3: Configure the Hosts

Step 1.   Configure the hosts with the proper IP address, subnet mask, and default gateway.

Default gateway: 192.168.0.1

Step 2.   Each workstation should be able to ping the attached router. Troubleshoot as necessary. Hint: Remember to assign a specific IP address and default gateway to the workstation. If you are running Windows 98, check using **Start > Run > winipcfg**. If you are running Windows 2000, check using **ipconfig** in a DOS window.

Step 3.   At this point, the workstations will not be able to communicate with each other. The following tasks demonstrate the process that is required to get communication working while using OSPF as the routing protocol.

Task 4: View the Router's Configuration and Interface Information

Step 1.   At the privileged EXEC mode prompt, type the following:

```
Cairo#show running-config
```

Step 2.   Using the **show ip interface brief** command, check the status of each interface.

What is the state of the interfaces on each router?

Cairo:

- Fast Ethernet 0: _____

- Serial 0: _____

Moscow:

- Fast Ethernet 0: _____

- Serial 0: _____

Step 3.   Ping from one of the connected router serial interfaces to the other.

Was the ping successful? _____

If the ping was not successful, troubleshoot the router configuration until the ping is successful.

Task 5: Configure OSPF Routing on Router Cairo

Step 1.   Configure OSPF routing on each router. Use OSPF process number 1 and ensure that all networks are in area 0.

```
Cairo(config)#router ospf 1
Cairo(config-router)#network 192.168.1.128 0.0.0.63 area 0
Cairo(config-router)#network 192.168.1.0 0.0.0.3 area 0
Cairo(config-router)#end
```

Step 2.   Examine the running configuration file.

Did the IOS version automatically add lines under router OSPF 1? _____

What did it add? _____

Step 3.   If there were no changes to the running configuration, type the following commands:

```
Cairo(config)#router ospf 1
Cairo(config-router)#log-adjacency-changes
Cairo(config-router)#end
```

Step 4.   Show the routing table for the Cairo router.

```
Cairo#show ip route
```

Do entries exist in the routing table? _____

Why?

_____

Task 6: Configure OSPF Routing on the Moscow Router

Step 1.   Configure OSPF routing on each router. Use OSPF process number 1 and ensure that all networks are in area 0.

```
Moscow(config)#router ospf 1
Moscow(config-router)#network 192.168.0 .0 0.0.0.255 area 0
Moscow(config-router)#network 192.168.1.0 0.0.0.3 area 0
Moscow(config-router)#end
```

Step 2.   Examine the running configuration file.

Did the IOS version automatically add lines under router OSPF 1? _____

Step 3.   If there were no changes to the running configuration, type the following commands:

```
Moscow(config)#router ospf 1
Moscow(config-router)#log-adjacency-changes
Moscow(config-router)#end
```

Task 7: Show the Routing Table Entries

Show the routing table entries for the Cairo router.

```
Cairo#show ip route
```

Does the routing table have OSPF entries now? _____

What is the metric value of the OSPF route?_____

What is the VIA address in the OSPF route? _____

Are routes to all networks shown in the routing table? _____

What does the O mean in the first column of the routing table?

_____

Task 8: Test Network Connectivity

Ping the Cairo host from the Moscow host. Was it successful? _____

If not, troubleshoot as necessary.

Task 9: Look at the OSPF Cost on the Cairo Router Interfaces

Show the properties of the Cairo router serial and Fast Ethernet interfaces by using the **show interfaces** command.

What is the default bandwidth of the interfaces?

- Serial interface: _____

- Fast Ethernet interface: _____

Calculate the OSPF cost.

- Serial interface: _____

- Fast Ethernet interface:

Table 2-7   OSPF Cost Calculations for Common Link Types

Link Bandwidth	Default OSPF Cost
56 kbps	1785
T1	64
10-Mbps Ethernet	10
16-Mbps Token Ring	6
FDDI/Fast Ethernet	1

Task 10: Record the OSPF Cost of the Serial and Fast Ethernet Interfaces

Using the **show ip ospf interface** command, record the OSPF cost of the serial and Fast Ethernet interfaces:

- OSPF cost of serial interface: _____

- OSPF cost of Ethernet interface: _____

Do these agree with the calculations? _____

The clock rate set for the interface should have been 64,000. This is what has been used as a default to this point and specified in Lab 1-2, "Review of Basic Router Configuring with RIP." Therefore, to calculate the cost of this bandwidth, you need to divide 10^8 by 64,000.

Task 11: Manually Set the Cost on the Serial Interface

On the serial interface of the Cairo router, set the OSPF cost to 1562 by typing **ip ospf cost 1562** at the serial interface configuration mode prompt.

_____

_____

_____

Task 12: Verify Cost

Note that it is essential that all connected links agree about the cost for consistent calculation of the SPF in an area.

Step 1.   Verify that the interface OSPF cost was successfully modified.

_____

Step 2.   Reverse the effect of this command by entering the command **no ip ospf cost** in interface configuration mode.

Step 3.   Verify that the default cost for the interface has returned.

Step 4.   Enter the command **bandwidth 2000** at the serial 0 interface configuration mode prompt.

Record the new OSPF cost of the serial interface. _____

Can the OSPF cost of an Ethernet interface be modified in this way? _____

You can set the speed on an Ethernet interface. Will this affect the OSPF cost of that interface?

_____

Step 5.   Verify or explain the previous answer.

Step 6.   Reset the bandwidth on the serial interface by using **no bandwidth 2000** at the serial 0 interface configuration mode prompt.

After you complete the previous steps, log off (by typing **exit**) and turn the router off. Then, remove and store the cables and adapter.

Curriculum Lab 2-4: Configuring OSPF Authentication (2.3.4)

Figure 2-13   Topology for Lab 2-4

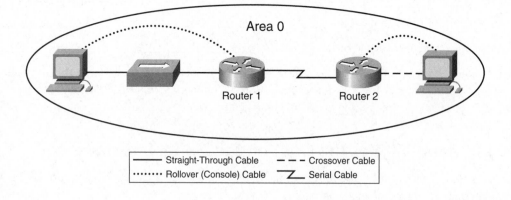

Table 2-8   Lab Equipment Configuration: Part I

Router Designation	Router Name	Routing Protocol	Network Statements
Router 1	Dublin	OSPF	192.168.1.0
Router 2	Washington	OSPF	192.168.1.0 192.168.0.0

The enable secret password for both routers is **class**.

The enable, VTY, and console password for both routers is **cisco**.

Table 2-9   Lab Equipment Configuration: Part II

Router Designation	IP Host Table Entry	Fast Ethernet 0 Address/Subnet Mask	Inter-face Type Serial 0	Serial 0 Address/ Subnet Mask	Loopback 0 Address/ Subnet Mask
Router 1	Washington	192.168.1.129/26	DCE	192.168.1.1/30	192.168.31.11/32
Router 2	Dublin	192.168.0.1/24	DTE	192.168.1.2/30	192.168.31.22/32

The interface type and address/subnet mask for the serial 1 interface on both routers is not applicable for this lab.

The "IP Host Table Entry" column contents indicate the names of the other routers in the IP host table.

Objectives

- Set up an IP addressing scheme for the OSPF area.

- Configure and verify OSPF routing.

- Introduce OSPF authentication into the area.

Background/Preparation

Cable a network that is similar to the one in Figure 2-13. You can use any router that meets the interface requirements in Figure 2-13 (that is, 800, 1600, 1700, 2500, and 2600 routers or a combination). Refer to the information in Appendix A to correctly specify the interface identifiers based on the equipment in your lab. The 1721 series routers produced the configuration output in this lab. Another router might produce slightly different output. You should execute the following steps on each router unless you are specifically instructed otherwise.

Start a HyperTerminal session.

Implement the procedure documented in Appendix C on all routers before you continue with this lab.

Task 1: Configure the Routers

On the routers, enter global configuration mode and configure the hostname, console, virtual terminal, and enable passwords. Next, configure the interfaces and IP hostnames according to the Lab Equipment Configuration tables, Tables 2-8 and 2-9. If you have problems configuring the router basics, refer to Lab 1-2, "Review of Basic Router Configuring with RIP."

Note: You may need to add the command **ip subnet-zero** because of the use of the ZERO subnet with VLSM on the 192.168.1.0/30 and 192.168.1.128/26 networks.

Note: Do not configure the routing protocol until you are specifically told to.

Task 2: Save the Configuration Information from Privileged EXEC Command Mode

```
Dublin#copy running-config startup-config
Destination filename [startup-config]? [Enter]


Washington#copy running-config startup-config
Destination filename [startup-config]? [Enter]
```

Why should you save the running configuration to the startup configuration?

_____

Task 3: Configure the Hosts

Step 1.   Configure the hosts with the proper IP address, subnet mask, and default gateway.

Step 2.   Each workstation should be able to ping the attached router. Troubleshoot as necessary. Hint: Remember to assign a specific IP address and default gateway to the workstation. If you are running Windows 98, check using **Start > Run > winipcfg**. If you are running Windows 2000, check using **ipconfig** in a DOS window.

Step 3.   At this point, the workstations will not be able to communicate with each other. The following tasks demonstrate the process required to get communication working by using OSPF as the routing protocol.

Task 4: Verify Connectivity

Ping from one of the connected router serial interfaces to the other.

Was the ping successful? _____

If the ping was not successful, troubleshoot the router's configurations until the ping is successful.

Task 5: Configure OSPF Routing on Both Routers

Step 1.   Configure OSPF routing on each router. Use OSPF process number 1 and ensure that all networks are in area 0. Refer to Lab 2-2, "Configuring OSPF with Loopback Addresses," for a review on configuring OSPF routing.

Step 2.   Examine the Dublin router running the configuration file. Did the IOS version automatically add lines under router OSPF 1? _____

Step 3.   Show the routing table for the Dublin router.

```
Dublin#show ip route
```

Do entries exist in the routing table? _____

Why?

_____

Task 6: Test Network Connectivity

Ping the Dublin host from the Washington host. Was it successful? _____

If not, troubleshoot as necessary.

Task 7: Set Up OSPF Authentication

OSPF authentication is being established on the routers in the network. First, introduce authentication only on the Dublin router.

In interface configuration mode on serial 0, enter the command **ip ospf message-digest-key 1 md5 7 asecret**.

```
Dublin(config)#interface Serial 0
Dublin(config-if)#ip ospf message-digest-key 1 md5 ?
<0-7> Encryption type (0 for not yet encrypted, 7 for proprietary)
Dublin(config-if)#ip ospf message-digest-key 1 md5 7 ?
LINE The OSPF password (key)
Dublin(config-if)#ip ospf message-digest-key 1 md5 7 asecret
```

What is the OSPF password that is being used for MD5 authentication? _____

What encryption type is being used? _____

Task 8: Enable OSPF Authentication in this Area, Area 0

```
Dublin(config-if)#router ospf 1
Dublin(config-router)#area 0 authentication
```

Step 1. Wait for a few seconds. Does the router generate output? _____

Step 2. Enter the command **show ip ospf neighbor**.

Are there OSPF neighbors? _____

Step 3. Examine the routing table by entering **show ip route**.

Are there OSPF routes in the Dublin router routing table? _____

Can the Dublin host ping the Washington host? _____

Step 4. Enter configuration commands, one per line. End with **Ctrl-Z**.

```
Washington#configure terminal
Washington(config)#interface serial 0
Washington(config-if)#ip ospf message-digest-key 1 md5 7 asecret
Washington(config-if)#router ospf 1
Washington(config-router)#area 0 authentication
```

Step 5. Verify that there is an OSPF neighbor by entering the **show ip ospf neighbor** command.

Step 6. Show the routing table by typing **show ip route**.

Step 7. Ping the Washington host from Dublin. If it is not successful, troubleshoot as necessary.

After you complete the previous steps, log off (by typing **exit**) and turn the router off. Then, remove and store the cables and adapter.

Curriculum Lab 2-5: Configuring OSPF Timers (2.3.5)

Figure 2-14   Topology for Lab 2-5

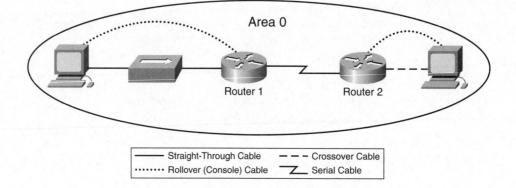

Table 2-10   Lab Equipment Configuration: Part I

Router Designation	Router Name	Routing Protocol	Network Statements
Router 1	Sydney	OSPF	192.168.1.0
Router 2	Rome	OSPF	192.168.1.0 192.168.0.0

The enable secret password for both routers is **class**.

The enable, VTY, and console password for both routers is **cisco**.

Table 2-11   Lab Equipment Configuration: Part II

Router Designation	IP Host Table Entry	Fast Ethernet 0 Address/Subnet Mask	Inter-face Type Serial 0	Serial 0 Address/ Subnet Mask	Loopback 0 Address/ Subnet Mask
Router 1	Rome	192.168.1.129/26	DCE	192.168.1.1/30	192.168.31.11/32
Router 2	Sydney	192.168.0.1/24	DTE	192.168.1.2/30	192.168.31.22/32

The interface type and address/subnet mask for the serial 1 interface on both routers is not applicable for this lab.

The "IP Host Table Entry" column contents indicate the names of the other routers in the IP host table.

Objectives

- Set up an IP addressing scheme for the OSPF area.

- Configure and verify OSPF routing.

- Modify OSPF interface timers to adjust efficiency of the network.

Background/Preparation

Cable a network that is similar to the one in Figure 2-14. You can use any router that meets the interface requirements in Figure 2-14 (that is, 800, 1600, 1700, 2500, and 2600 routers or a combination). Refer to the information in Appendix A to correctly specify the interface identifiers based on the equipment in your lab. The 1721 series routers produced the configuration output in this lab. Another router might produce slightly different output. You should execute the following steps on each router unless you are specifically instructed otherwise. Start a HyperTerminal session.

Implement the procedure documented in Appendix C on all routers before you continue with this lab.

Task 1: Configure the Routers

On the routers, enter global configuration mode and configure the hostname, console, virtual terminal, and enable passwords. Next, configure the interfaces and IP hostnames according to the Lab Equipment Configuration tables, Tables 2-10 and 2-11. If you have problems configuring the router basics, refer to Lab 1-2, "Review of Basic Router Configuring with RIP."

Note: You may need to add the command **ip subnet-zero** because of the use of the ZERO subnet with VLSM on the 192.168.1.0/30 and 192.168.1.128/26 networks.

Note: Do not configure the routing protocol until you are specifically told to.

Task 2: Save the Configuration Information from Privileged EXEC Command Mode

```
Sydney#copy running-config startup-config
Destination filename [startup-config]? [Enter]
```

```
Rome#copy running-config startup-config
Destination filename [startup-config]? [Enter]
```

Why should you save the running configuration to the startup configuration?

Task 3: Configure the Hosts

Step 1.   Configure the hosts with the proper IP address, subnet mask, and default gateway.

Step 2.   Each workstation should be able to ping the attached router. Troubleshoot as necessary. Hint: Remember to assign a specific IP address and default gateway to the workstation. If you are running Windows 98, check using **Start > Run > winipcfg**. If you are running Windows 2000, check using **ipconfig** in a DOS window.

Step 3.   At this point, the workstations will not be able to communicate with each other. The following tasks demonstrate the process that is required to get communication working by using OSPF as the routing protocol.

Task 4: Verify Connectivity

Ping from one of the connected serial interfaces to the other.

Was the ping successful? _____

If the ping was not successful, troubleshoot the router configurations until the ping is successful.

Task 5: Configure OSPF Routing on both Routers

Step 1.   Configure OSPF routing on each router. Use OSPF process number 1 and ensure that all networks are in area 0. Refer to Lab 2-2, "Configuring OSPF with Loopback Interfaces," for a review on configuring OSPF routing.

Did the IOS version automatically add lines under router OSPF 1? _____

Step 2.   Show the routing table for the Sydney router.

Sydney#**show ip route**

Do entries exist in the routing table? _____

Task 6: Test Network Connectivity

Ping the Sydney host from the Rome host. Was it successful? _____

If not, troubleshoot as necessary.

Task 7: Observe OSPF Traffic

Step 1.   At privileged EXEC mode, type the command **debug ip ospf events** and observe the output.

How frequently are Hello messages sent? _____

Where are Hello messages coming from?

_____

_____

Step 2.   Turn off debugging by typing **no debug ip ospf events** or **undebug all**.

Task 8: Show Interface Timer Information

Show the hello and dead interval timers on the Sydney router Ethernet and serial interfaces by entering the command **show ip ospf interface** in privileged EXEC mode.

Record the Hello and Dead interval timers for these interfaces:

- Hello interval: _____
- Dead interval: _____

What is the purpose of the dead interval?

_____

_____

Task 9: Modify the OSPF Timers

Step 1.   Modify the Hello and Dead interval timers to smaller values to try to improve performance. On the Sydney router only, enter the commands **ip ospf hello-interval 5** and **ip ospf dead-interval 20** for interface serial 0.

```
Sydney(config)#interface Serial 0
Sydney(config-if)#ip ospf hello-interval 5
Sydney(config-if)#ip ospf dead-interval 20
```

Step 2.   Wait for a minute and then enter the command **show ip ospf neighbor**.

Do OSPF neighbors exist? _____

Task 10: Examine the Routing Table

Examine the Sydney router routing table by entering **show ip route**.

Do OSPF routes exist in the table? _____

Can the Sydney host ping the Rome host? _____

Task 11: Look at the OSPF Data Transmissions

Enter the command **debug ip ospf events** in privileged EXEC mode.

Is there an issue that is identified?_____

If there is, what is the issue?

_____

Task 12: Check the Rome Router Routing Table Status

On the Rome router, check the routing table by typing **show ip route**.

Do OSPF routes exist in the table? _____

Task 13: Set the Rome Router Interval Timers

Step 1.   Match the timer values on the Rome serial link with the Sydney router.

```
Rome(config)#interface serial 0
Rome(config-if)#ip ospf hello-interval 5
Rome(config-if)#ip ospf dead-interval 20
```

Step 2.   Verify the OSPF neighbor by entering the **show ip ospf neighbor** command.

Step 3.   Show the routing table by typing **show ip route**.

Do OSPF routes exist in the table? _____

Step 4.   Ping the Rome host from Sydney. If this is not successful, troubleshoot the configurations.

Task 14: Reset the Router's Interval Timers to the Default Values

Use the **no** form of the **ip ospf hello-interval** and the **ip ospf dead-interval** to reset the OSPF timers back to their default values.

Task 15: Verify that the Interval Timers Are Returned to the Default Values

Use the **show ip ospf interface** command to verify that the timers are reset to their default values.

Are the values back to the default? _____

If not, repeat Task 14 and verify again.

After you complete the previous steps, log off (by typing **exit**) and turn the router off. Then, remove and store the cables and adapter.

Curriculum Lab 2-6: Propagating Default Routes in an OSPF Domain (2.3.6)

Figure 2-15   Topology for Lab 2-6

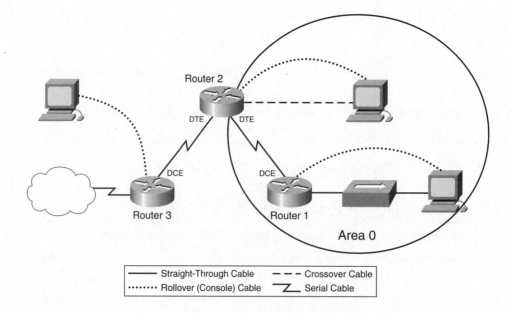

Table 2-12   Lab Equipment Configuration: Part I

Router Designation	Router Name	Routing Protocol	Network Statements	Loopback 0	Address/ Subnet Mask
Router 1	Tokyo	OSPF	192.168.1.0	192.168.31.11/32	
Router 2	Madrid	OSPF	192.168.1.0	192.168.0.0	192.168.31.22/32

The enable secret password for all routers is **class**.

The enable, VTY, and console passwords for each router is **cisco**.

Table 2-13   Lab Equipment Configuration: Part II

Router Designation	IP Host Table Entry	Fast Ethernet 0 Address/Subnet Mask	Interface Type Serial 0	Serial 0 Address/ Subnet Mask	Inter-face Type Serial 1	Serial 1 Address/ Subnet Mask
Router 1	Madrid	192.168.1.129/26	DCE	192.168.1.1/30	N/A	N/A
Router 2	Tokyo	192.168.0.1/24	DTE	192.168.1.2/30	DTE	200.20.20.2/30

The "IP Host Table Entry" column contents indicate the names of the other routers in the IP host table.

Objectives

- Set up an IP addressing scheme for the OSPF area.

- Configure and verify OSPF routing.

- Configure the OSPF network so that all hosts in an OSPF area can connect to outside networks.

Background/Preparation

Cable a network that is similar to the one in Figure 2-15. You can use any router that meets the interface requirements in Figure 2-15 (that is, 800, 1600, 1700, 2500, and 2600 routers or a combination). Refer to the information in Appendix A to correctly specify the interface identifiers based on the equipment in your lab. The 1721 series routers produced the configuration output in this lab. Another router might produce slightly different output. You should execute the following steps on each router unless you are specifically instructed otherwise. Start a HyperTerminal session.

Implement the procedure documented in Appendix C on all routers before you continue with this lab.

Task 1: Configure the ISP Router

Normally, the ISP would configure the ISP router (Router 3). For the purpose of this lab, after you erase the old configuration, configure the ISP router (Router 3) by typing the following:

```
Router>enable
Router#configure terminal
Router(config)#hostname ISP
ISP(config)#line vty 0 4
ISP(config-line)#password cisco
ISP(config-line)#login
ISP(config-line)#interface serial 1
ISP(config-if)#ip address 200.20.20.1 255.255.255.252
ISP(config-if)#clock rate 64000
ISP(config-if)#no shutdown
```

```
ISP(config-if)#interface loopback 0
ISP(config-if)#ip address 138.25.6.33 255.255.255.255
ISP(config-if)#exit
ISP(config)#ip route 192.168.1.0 255.255.255.0 200.20.20.2
ISP(config)#ip route 192.168.0.0 255.255.255.0 200.20.20.2
ISP(config)#end
ISP#copy running-config startup-config
Destination filename [startup-config]? [Enter]
Building configuration...
[OK]
ISP#
```

Task 2: Configure the Area 0 OSPF Routers

On the routers, enter global configuration mode and configure the hostname, console, virtual terminal, and enable passwords. Next, configure the interfaces and IP hostnames according to the Lab Equipment Configuration tables, Tables 2-12 and 2-13. If you have problems configuring the router basics, refer to Lab 1-2, "Review of Basic Router Configuring with RIP."

Note: Do not configure the routing protocol until you are specifically told to.

Task 3: Save the Configuration Information from Privileged EXEC Command Mode

```
Tokyo#copy running-config startup-config
Destination filename [startup-config]? [Enter]


Madrid#copy running-config startup-config
Destination filename [startup-config]? [Enter]
```

Why should you save the running configuration to the startup configuration?

Task 4: Configure the Hosts

Step 1.   Configure the hosts with the proper IP address, subnet mask, and default gateway.

Step 2.   Each workstation should be able to ping the attached router. Troubleshoot as necessary. Hint: Remember to assign a specific IP address and default gateway to the workstation. If you are running Windows 98, check using **Start > Run > winipcfg**. If you are running Windows 2000, check using **ipconfig** in a DOS window.

Step 3.   At this point, the workstations will not be able to communicate with each other. The following tasks demonstrate the process that is required to get communication working by using OSPF as the routing protocol.

Task 5: Verify Connectivity

Ping from the Madrid router to both the Tokyo and ISP routers.

Were the pings successful? _____

If the ping was not successful, troubleshoot the router configurations until the ping is successful.

Task 6: Configure OSPF Routing on Both Area 0 Routers

Step 1.   Configure OSPF routing on each router. Use OSPF process number 1 and ensure that all networks are in area 0. Refer to Lab 2-2, "Configuring OSPF with Loopback Addresses," for a review on configuring OSPF routing.

Did the IOS version automatically add lines under router OSPF 1? _____

Step 2.   Show the routing table for the Tokyo router.

```
Tokyo#show ip route
```

Do entries exist in the routing table? _____

Task 7: Test Network Connectivity

Ping the Tokyo host from the Madrid host. Was it successful? _____

If not, troubleshoot as necessary.

Task 8: Observe OSPF Traffic

Step 1.   At privileged EXEC mode, type the command **debug ip ospf events** and observe the output.

Is there OSPF traffic? _____

Step 2.   Turn off debugging by typing **no debug ip ospf events** or **undebug all**.

Task 9: Create a Default Route to the ISP

On the Madrid router only, type a static default route via the serial 1 interface.

```
Madrid(config)#ip route 0.0.0.0 0.0.0.0 200.200.200.1
```

Task 10: Verify the Default Static Route

Verify the default static route by looking at the Madrid routing table.

Is the default route in the routing table? _____

Task 11: Verify Connectivity from the Madrid Router

Step 1.   Verify connectivity from the Madrid router by pinging the ISP serial 1 interface from the Madrid router.

Can the interface be pinged? _____

Step 2.   Ping from a DOS window on the host that is attached to the Madrid router Fast Ethernet interface to the ISP router serial 1 interface.

Can the interface be pinged? _____

Step 3.   Ping again from the host to the loopback address on the ISP router, which represents the ISP connection to the Internet.

Can the loopback interface be pinged? _____

Step 4.   All these pings should be successful. If they are not, troubleshoot the configurations on the host and the Madrid and ISP routers.

Task 12: Verify Connectivity from the Tokyo Router

Verify connectivity from the Tokyo router by pinging the ISP router serial 1 interface from the Tokyo router.

Can the interface be pinged? _____

If yes, why? If not, why not?

_____

Task 13: Redistribute the Static Default Route

Propagate the gateway of last resort to the other routers in the OSPF domain. At the configure router prompt on the Madrid router, type **default-information originate**.

```
Madrid(config-router)#default-information originate
```

Does a default route now exist on the Tokyo router? _____

What is the address of the gateway of last resort? _____

There is an O*E2 entry in the routing table. What type of route is it?

_____

Can the ISP server address at 138.25.16.33 be pinged from both workstations? _____

If not, troubleshoot both hosts and all three routers.

After you complete the previous steps, log off (by typing **exit**) and turn the router off. Then, remove and store the cables and adapter.

Comprehensive Lab 2-7: OSPF Configuration

Figure 2-16   OSPF Configuration

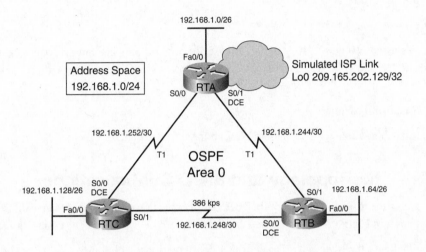

Table 2-14   Lab 2-7 Addressing Scheme

Device	Interface	IP Address	Subnet Mask
RTA	Fa0/0	192.168.1.1	255.255.255.192
	S0/1	192.168.1.245	255.255.255.252
	S0/0	192.168.1.254	255.255.255.252
	Lo0	209.165.202.129	255.255.255.255
RTB	S0/1	192.168.1.246	255.255.255.252
	Fa0/0	192.168.1.65	255.255.255.192
	S0/0	192.168.1.249	255.255.255.252
RTC	S0/1	192.168.1.250	255.255.255.252
	Fa0/0	192.168.1.129	255.255.255.192
	S0/0	192.168.1.253	255.255.255.252

Objectives

- Configure OSPF routing

- Modify OSPF cost

- Configure MD5 authentication

- Adjust OSPF timers

- Configure and propagate a default route

Equipment

The topology shown in Figure 2-16 is using 2600 series routers. This lab can be done with any combination of 1700, 2500, and 2600 series routers. Connectivity to an ISP is simulated with a loopback interface on RTA.

NetLab Compatibility Notes

This lab is fully compatible with a standard NetLab three router pod.

Task 1: Cable the Topology and Basic Configurations

Step 1.   Cable the topology as shown. If DCE/DTE connections and interfaces are different from those shown in Figure 2-16 and the table, relabel the figure to match your connections.

Step 2.   Configure the routers with basic router configurations, including

- Hostnames and host tables

- Enable secret password and MOTD banner

- Line configurations

- IOS-specific commands (e.g. **ip subnet-zero** with IOS versions prior to 12)

Step 3.   The following is a basic configuration for RTA:

```
Router(config)#hostname RTA
RTA(config)#ip subnet-zero
RTA(config)#no ip domain-lookup
RTA(config)#ip host RTC 192.168.1.253 192.168.1.254
RTA(config)#ip host RTB 192.168.1.246 192.168.1.249
RTA(config)#banner motd &
**********************************
   !!!AUTHORIZED ACCESS ONLY!!!
**********************************
&
RTA(config)#line con 0
RTA(config-line)#exec-timeout 30 0
RTA(config-line)#password cisco
RTA(config-line)#logging synchronous
RTA(config-line)#login
RTA(config-line)#line aux 0
RTA(config-line)#exec-timeout 30 0
RTA(config-line)#password cisco
RTA(config-line)#logging synchronous
RTA(config-line)#login
```

```
RTA(config-line)#line vty 0 4
RTA(config-line)#exec-timeout 30 0
RTA(config-line)#password cisco
RTA(config-line)#logging synchronous
RTA(config-line)#login
RTA(config-line)#end
RTA#copy run start
```

Task 2: Configure Interfaces and OSPF Routing

Step 1. Use Table 2-14 and the topology shown in Figure 2-16 to configure each router with the correct interface addresses. To simulate an ISP connection, use the following configuration on RTA:

```
RTA(config)#interface Loopback0
RTA(config-if)#description Simulated Link to ISP
RTA(config-if)#ip address 209.165.202.129 255.255.255.255
```

Step 2. Configure OSPF routing on RTA, RTB, and RTC. *Do not* configure the simulated ISP loopback interface as part of OSPF. The configuration for RTA is as follows:

```
RTA(config)#router ospf 1
RTA(config-router)#network 192.168.1.0 0.0.0.63 area 0
RTA(config-router)#network 192.168.1.244 0.0.0.3 area 0
RTA(config-router)#network 192.168.1.252 0.0.0.3 area 0
```

Task 3: Verify Connectivity

Step 1. You should now have full connectivity between RTA, RTB, and RTC. Issue the **show ip route** command to verify full convergence.

Routing table on RTA:

```
RTA#show ip route
Codes: C - connected, S - static, I - IGRP, R - RIP, M - mobile, B - BGP
       D - EIGRP, EX - EIGRP external, O - OSPF, IA - OSPF inter area
       N1 - OSPF NSSA external type 1, N2 - OSPF NSSA external type 2
       E1 - OSPF external type 1, E2 - OSPF external type 2, E - EGP
       i - IS-IS, L1 - IS-IS level-1, L2 - IS-IS level-2, ia - IS-IS inter
area
       * - candidate default, U - per-user static route, o - ODR
       P - periodic downloaded static route

Gateway of last resort is not set

     209.165.202.0/32 is subnetted, 1 subnets
C       209.165.202.129 is directly connected, Loopback0
     192.168.1.0/24 is variably subnetted, 6 subnets, 2 masks
O       192.168.1.64/26 [110/65] via 192.168.1.246, 00:00:48, Serial0/1
C       192.168.1.0/26 is directly connected, FastEthernet0/0
O       192.168.1.248/30 [110/128] via 192.168.1.246, 00:00:48, Serial0/1
                         [110/128] via 192.168.1.253, 00:00:48, Serial0/0
C       192.168.1.252/30 is directly connected, Serial0/0
C       192.168.1.244/30 is directly connected, Serial0/1
O       192.168.1.128/26 [110/65] via 192.168.1.253, 00:00:49, Serial0/0
```

Step 2.   Notice that RTA has four connected routes (including the simulated ISP link) and three OSPF routes. RTB and RTC should both have three connected routes and three OSPF routes.

Step 3.   Pings sourced from any router to a LAN interface on another router should succeed.

```
RTA#ping 192.168.1.65

Type escape sequence to abort.
Sending 5, 100-byte ICMP Echos to 192.168.1.65, timeout is 2 seconds:
!!!!!
Success rate is 100 percent (5/5), round-trip min/avg/max = 28/28/32 ms
RTA#ping 192.168.1.129

Type escape sequence to abort.
Sending 5, 100-byte ICMP Echos to 192.168.1.129, timeout is 2 seconds:
!!!!!
Success rate is 100 percent (5/5), round-trip min/avg/max = 28/29/32 ms
```

Task 4: Modify OSPF Cost

Step 1.   At this point, all routers are using the default bandwidth for serial interfaces: for 2500s and 2600s, 1544 kbps; for 1700s, 128 kbps. Use the **show interface serial** command to view the bandwidth used to calculate cost.

```
RTB#show interface s0/0
Serial0/0 is up, line protocol is up
  Hardware is PowerQUICC Serial
  Description: Link to RTC
  Internet address is 192.168.1.249/30
  MTU 1500 bytes, BW 1544 Kbit, DLY 20000 usec,
     reliability 255/255, txload 1/255, rxload 1/255
(output omitted)
```

Step 2.   When RTB pings the LAN interface on RTC, it sends it directly to RTC even though the path through RTA is faster.

```
RTB#traceroute 192.168.1.129

Type escape sequence to abort.
Tracing the route to 192.168.1.129

  1 RTC (192.168.1.250) 16 msec *  12 msec
RTB#
```

Step 3.   Configure both RTB and RTC with the correct bandwidth.

```
RTB(config)#interface s0/0
RTB(config-if)#bandwidth 386
!
RTC(config)#interface s0/1
RTC(config-if)#bandwidth 386
```

Step 4.   Verify that RTB sends pings destined for the LAN on RTC to RTA, which then routes the ping to RTC.

```
RTB#traceroute 192.168.1.129
```

```
Type escape sequence to abort.
Tracing the route to 192.168.1.129

  1 RTA (192.168.1.245) 16 msec 12 msec 16 msec
  2 RTC (192.168.1.253) 28 msec *   16 msec
RTB#
```

Task 5: Configure MD5 Authentication

Step 1.   To make sure routing updates come from trusted sources, configure each router to use MD5 authentication. The configuration for RTA follows:

```
RTA(config)#interface serial 0/0
RTA(config-if)#ip ospf message-digest-key 1 md5 7 allrouters
RTA(config)#interface serial 0/1
RTA(config-if)#ip ospf message-digest-key 1 md5 7 allrouters
RTA(config-if)#router ospf 1
RTA(config-router)#area 0 authentication message-digest
```

Step 2.   After configuring authentication on each router, neighbor adjacency will go to the DOWN state and then reinitialize. Make sure that all routing tables have reconverged by issuing the **show ip route** command. The table for RTA follows:

```
RTA#show ip route
Codes: C - connected, S - static, I - IGRP, R - RIP, M - mobile, B - BGP
       D - EIGRP, EX - EIGRP external, O - OSPF, IA - OSPF inter area
       N1 - OSPF NSSA external type 1, N2 - OSPF NSSA external type 2
       E1 - OSPF external type 1, E2 - OSPF external type 2, E - EGP
       i - IS-IS, L1 - IS-IS level-1, L2 - IS-IS level-2, ia - IS-IS inter
area
       * - candidate default, U - per-user static route, o - ODR
       P - periodic downloaded static route

Gateway of last resort is not set

     209.165.202.0/32 is subnetted, 1 subnets
C       209.165.202.129 is directly connected, Loopback0
     192.168.1.0/24 is variably subnetted, 6 subnets, 2 masks
O       192.168.1.64/26 [110/65] via 192.168.1.246, 00:06:25, Serial0/1
C       192.168.1.0/26 is directly connected, FastEthernet0/0
O       192.168.1.248/30 [110/323] via 192.168.1.246, 00:06:25, Serial0/1
                        [110/323] via 192.168.1.253, 00:06:25, Serial0/0
C       192.168.1.252/30 is directly connected, Serial0/0
C       192.168.1.244/30 is directly connected, Serial0/1
O       192.168.1.128/26 [110/65] via 192.168.1.253, 00:06:26, Serial0/0
```

Step 3.   You can verify authentication by using the **show ip ospf** command or the **show ip ospf interface** command.

```
RTA#show ip ospf
 Routing Process "ospf 1" with ID 209.165.202.129
 Supports only single TOS(TOS0) routes
 Supports opaque LSA
 SPF schedule delay 5 secs, Hold time between two SPFs 10 secs
 Minimum LSA interval 5 secs. Minimum LSA arrival 1 secs
 Number of external LSA 0. Checksum Sum 0x0
 Number of opaque AS LSA 0. Checksum Sum 0x0
 Number of DCbitless external and opaque AS LSA 0
 Number of DoNotAge external and opaque AS LSA 0
 Number of areas in this router is 1. 1 normal 0 stub 0 nssa
 External flood list length 0
    Area BACKBONE(0)
        Number of interfaces in this area is 3
        Area has message digest authentication
        SPF algorithm executed 2 times
        Area ranges are
        Number of LSA 3. Checksum Sum 0x1F45E
        Number of opaque link LSA 0. Checksum Sum 0x0
        Number of DCbitless LSA 0
        Number of indication LSA 0
        Number of DoNotAge LSA 0
        Flood list length 0


RTA#show ip ospf interface s0/0
Serial0/0 is up, line protocol is up
  Internet Address 192.168.1.254/30, Area 0
  Process ID 1, Router ID 209.165.202.129, Network Type POINT_TO_POINT, Cost:
64
  Transmit Delay is 1 sec, State POINT_TO_POINT,
  Timer intervals configured, Hello 10, Dead 40, Wait 40, Retransmit 5
    Hello due in 00:00:01
  Index 3/3, flood queue length 0
  Next 0x0(0)/0x0(0)
  Last flood scan length is 1, maximum is 1
  Last flood scan time is 0 msec, maximum is 0 msec
  Neighbor Count is 1, Adjacent neighbor count is 1
    Adjacent with neighbor 10.0.0.1
  Suppress hello for 0 neighbor(s)
  Message digest authentication enabled
    Youngest key id is 1
```

Task 6: Adjust OSPF Timers

Step 1.   Notice in the previous output for **show ip ospf interface** that the Hello and dead interval timers are shown as 10 and 40, respectively. Configure these intervals to be 40 and 160 on all three routers.

```
RTA(config)#interface s0/0
RTA(config-if)#ip ospf hello-interval 40
RTA(config-if)#ip ospf dead-interval 160
```

```
RTA(config)#interface s0/1
RTA(config-if)#ip ospf hello-interval 40
RTA(config-if)#ip ospf dead-interval 160
```

Step 2. Verify that all routers have full routing tables and have re-established neighbor adjacencies. If adjacency has not been re-established, you can use the **debug ip ospf events** command to find where there might be a timing mismatch.

```
RTA#show ip route
Codes: C - connected, S - static, I - IGRP, R - RIP, M - mobile, B - BGP
       D - EIGRP, EX - EIGRP external, O - OSPF, IA - OSPF inter area
       N1 - OSPF NSSA external type 1, N2 - OSPF NSSA external type 2
       E1 - OSPF external type 1, E2 - OSPF external type 2, E - EGP
       i - IS-IS, L1 - IS-IS level-1, L2 - IS-IS level-2, ia - IS-IS inter
area
       * - candidate default, U - per-user static route, o - ODR
       P - periodic downloaded static route


Gateway of last resort is not set

     209.165.202.0/32 is subnetted, 1 subnets
C       209.165.202.129 is directly connected, Loopback0
     192.168.1.0/24 is variably subnetted, 6 subnets, 2 masks
O       192.168.1.64/26 [110/65] via 192.168.1.246, 00:00:04, Serial0/1
C       192.168.1.0/26 is directly connected, FastEthernet0/0
O       192.168.1.248/30 [110/323] via 192.168.1.246, 00:00:04, Serial0/1
                        [110/323] via 192.168.1.253, 00:00:04, Serial0/0
C       192.168.1.252/30 is directly connected, Serial0/0
C       192.168.1.244/30 is directly connected, Serial0/1
O       192.168.1.128/26 [110/65] via 192.168.1.253, 00:00:05, Serial0/0
RTA#show ip ospf neighbor


Neighbor ID     Pri   State      Dead Time   Address        Interface
192.168.1.253    1    FULL/  -   00:02:19    192.168.1.253  Serial0/0
192.168.1.249    1    FULL/  -   00:02:16    192.168.1.246  Serial0/1
```

Task 7: Configure and Propagate a Default Route

Step 1. Because the ISP is only simulated, RTA does not have a real default route. However, you can simulate a default route by configuring it to forward to a null interface.

```
RTA(config)#ip route 0.0.0.0 0.0.0.0 null 0
```

Step 2. Now, you can configure RTA to propagate the default route to RTB and RTC.

```
RTA(config)#router ospf 1
RTA(config-router)#default-information originate
```

Step 3. RTB and RTC should now be able to successfully ping the 209.165.202.129 interface, which verifies that both routers have a working default route.

```
RTB#ping 209.165.202.129


Type escape sequence to abort.
Sending 5, 100-byte ICMP Echos to 209.165.202.129, timeout is 2 seconds:
!!!!!
```

```
Success rate is 100 percent (5/5), round-trip min/avg/max = 28/28/28 ms
RTC#ping 209.165.202.129

Type escape sequence to abort.
Sending 5, 100-byte ICMP Echos to 209.165.202.129, timeout is 2 seconds:
!!!!!
Success rate is 100 percent (5/5), round-trip min/avg/max = 28/33/48 ms
```

Challenge Lab 2-8: OSPF Design and Configuration

Figure 2-17   OSPF Design and Configuration

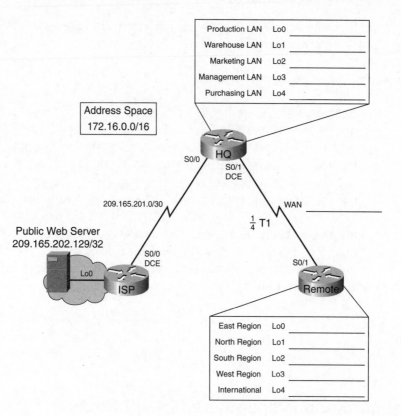

Table 2-15   Lab 2-8 Addressing Scheme

Device	Interface	IP Address	Subnet Mask
ISP	Lo0	209.165.202.129	255.255.255.255
	S0/0	209.165.201.1	255.255.255.252
HQ	S0/0	209.165.201.2	255.255.255.252
	S0/1		
	Lo0		
	Lo1		
	Lo2		
	Lo3		
	Lo4		
REMOTE	S0/1		
	Lo0		
	Lo1		
	Lo2		
	Lo3		
	Lo4		

Objectives

- Design a VLSM addressing scheme.

- Configure routers with basic configurations using your addressing scheme.

- Configure dynamic, static, and default routing.

- Verify connectivity and troubleshoot problems.

Equipment

The topology shown in Figure 2-17 uses 2600 series routers. This lab can be done with any combination of 1700, 2500, and 2600 series routers.

NetLab Compatibility Notes

This lab can be completed on a standard NetLab three router pod.

Task 1: Design the Addressing Scheme

You are given the address space, 172.16.0.0/16. The five loopback interfaces on HQ and five loopback interfaces on REMOTE are used to simulate different parts of a global network. Use the following specifications to design your addressing scheme.

Table 2-16   LAN Addressing Specifications

HQ	Hosts Needed
Production LAN	16,000
Warehousing LAN	8000
Marketing LAN	4000
Management LAN	2000
Purchasing LAN	1000

REMOTE	Hosts Needed
Eastern Region	4000
Northern Region	4000
Western Region	4000
Southern Region	4000
International	4000

Label the topology in Figure 2-17 with the networks and finish filling in the IP addresses in Table 2-16 with your chosen addressing scheme. Use the first IP address in each subnet for the interface address. For the WAN link between HQ and REMOTE, assign HQ the first address.

Task 2: Cable the Topology and Basic Configuration

Step 1.   Choose three routers and cable them according to the topology. You will not need any LAN interfaces or switches for this lab. (If using NetLab, choose a three router pod).

Step 2.   Configure the routers with basic configurations including interface addresses.

Task 3: Configure OSPF Routing and Default Routing

Step 1.   Configure both HQ and REMOTE to use OSPF as the routing protocol. Enter the simulated LAN subnets and the WAN link between HQ and REMOTE. *Do not* advertise the 209.165.201.0/30 network.

Step 2.   Configure ISP with a static route pointing the 172.16.0.0/16 Address Space. Configure HQ with a default route pointing to ISP. Configure HQ to advertise the default route to REMOTE.

Step 3.   Verify HQ and REMOTE routing tables.

- HQ should have seven directly connected routes, five OSPF routes, and one static route.
- REMOTE should have six directly connected routes, five OSPF routes, and one OSPF E2 route.
- Verify that REMOTE can ping the Simulated Web Server at 209.165.202.129.

Task 4: Other OSPF Configurations

Step 1.   Change the OSPF hello interval to 20 seconds.

Step 2.   The link between HQ and REMOTE is a 1/4 T1. Change the bandwidth on both HQ and REMOTE to match the actual link speed.

Step 3.   Configure OSPF authentication with MD5 between HQ and REMOTE. Use "allrouters" as the key.

Task 5: Verification and Documentation

Step 1.   **Capture the following verifications to a text file called verify.txt:**

- Ping output from REMOTE pinging the Simulated Web Server.

- Capture **show ip route** on all three routers: ISP, HQ, and REMOTE.

- Capture **show ip ospf**, **show ip ospf neighbor**, and **show ip ospf interface** on HQ and REMOTE.

Step 2.   Capture the running configurations on all three routers to separate text files. Use the hostname of the router to name each text file.

Step 3.   Clean up the verify.txt, HQ.txt, REMOTE.txt, and ISP.txt files. Add appropriate notes to assist in your studies.

CHAPTER 3

EIGRP and Troubleshooting Routing Protocols

The Study Guide portion of this chapter uses a combination of matching, fill in the blank, multiple choice, open-ended question, and unique custom exercises to test your knowledge on the theory of EIGRP concepts, EIGRP configuration, and basic routing protocol troubleshooting.

The Lab Exercises portion of this chapter includes all of the online curriculum labs as well as a comprehensive lab and a challenge lab to ensure that you have mastered the practical, hands-on skills needed about EIGRP and routing troubleshooting.

Study Guide

EIGRP Concepts

EIGRP is the enhanced version of the Cisco-proprietary Interior Gateway Routing Protocol (IGRP). The speed of convergence, ease of configuration, and blending of the best of both distance vector and link-state routing protocols make EIGRP the most powerful of IGPs. To get the absolute best of both worlds, use EIGRP if all of your equipment is from Cisco.

The exercises in this section walk you through the terminology and concepts of EIGRP. Pay particular attention to the similarities and differences between EIGRP and other routing protocols.

Vocabulary Exercise: Matching

Directions: Match the definition on the left with a term on the right. This exercise is not necessarily a one-to-one matching. Some definitions may be used more than once and some terms may have multiple definitions. However, all terms and definitions are used.

Definition

a. table that includes route entries for all destinations that the router has learned

b. a route selected as the primary route to reach a destination

c. table that ensures bidirectional communication between each of the directly connected neighbors

d. a backup route kept in the topology table in case the primary route goes down

e. used by EIGRP to discover, verify, and rediscover neighbor routers

f. a route that is in a reachable and operational status

g. guarantees loop-free operation at every instant throughout a route computation and allows all devices involved in a topology change to synchronize at the same time

h. table in which EIGRP places the routes it chooses from the topology table as the best (successor) routes to a destination

i. status of a route that has no feasible successors yet; router is waiting on replies from EIGRP routers

j. used by EIGRP to guarantee ordered delivery of EIGRP packets to all neighbors

k. used when a router discovers a new neighbor

l. used when a router needs specific information from one or all of its neighbors

Term

___ feasible successor

___ hello packets

___ Diffusing Update Algorithm

___ Reliable Transport Protocol

___ neighbor table

___ update packet

___ topology table

___ query packet

___ successor

___ routing table

___ active state

___ passive state

Vocabulary Exercise: Completion

Directions: Complete the paragraphs that follow by filling in appropriate words and phrases.

_____ and EIGRP are compatible with each other, which provides seamless interoperability between the two processes. EIGRP uses metric calculations similar to those used by _____, and EIGRP supports the same _____-cost path load balancing as _____ does.

Although the metric (_____ and _____ by default) is the same for both _____ and EIGRP, the weight assigned to the metric is _____ times greater for EIGRP. That is because EIGRP uses a metric that is __ bits long, and _____ uses a ___-bit metric. By multiplying or dividing by ____, EIGRP can easily exchange information with _____.

_____ has a maximum hop count of 255. _____ has a maximum hop count of 224. By default, the Cisco IOS limits the hop count for EIGRP limited to _____ as displayed by the **show ip protocols** command. This is more than adequate to support the largest, properly designed internetworks.

EIGRP's convergence technology employs the _____, which guarantees loop-free operation at every instant throughout a route. Routers that are *not* affected by topology changes are not involved in recomputations.

Redistribution, the sharing of routes, is automatic between _____ and EIGRP as long as both processes use the same _____ number.

Like OSPF, EIGRP maintains three tables for use with its computations. These tables include the _____ table (called the _____ database in OSPF), the _____ table (called the _____ database in OSPF), and the _____ table (called the _____ database in OSPF).

The following are some additional features of EIGRP:

- EIGRP converges rapidly on network topology changes. In some situations, convergence can be almost instantaneous. EIGRP stores backup routes, called _____ _____, so that it can quickly adapt to these alternate routes if the primary route, called the _____, becomes unavailable. If no backup route exists, then EIGRP sends a _____ packet to its neighbors to discover an alternate route.

- During normal operations when the network topology is fully converged, only _____ packets are sent to neighbors. These packets are also used to establish _____ _____.

- EIGRP supports automatic route _____ at _____ network boundaries. But it can be _____ configured to advertise on arbitrary network boundaries to reduce the size of routing tables.

- EIGRP uses its own Layer 4 protocol called the _____. Because EIGRP provides support for multiple routed protocols, including _____ and _____, it must be protocol independent. That means it cannot depend on _____ for reliability services.

EIGRP Packet Type Exercise

Like OSPF, EIGRP relies on different types of packets to maintain its tables and establish relationships with neighbor routers. Complete the missing elements that follow by filling in appropriate words or phrases. When given the choice, circle whether the packet is reliable or unreliable and whether it is unicast or multicast.

_____ packets:

- (Reliable/Unreliable) (unicast/multicast) sent to the address _____ to discover and maintain neighbors; contains the router's neighbor table

- Default _____ interval depends on the bandwidth:

  — ≤1.544 Mbps = __ sec. _____ interval (___ sec. holdtime)

  — > 1.544 Mbps = __ sec. _____ interval (__ sec. holdtime)

_____ **packets**. Sent (reliably/unreliably), there are two types:

- (Unicast/Multicast) to new neighbor discovered; contains routing table

- (Unicast/Multicast) to all neighbors when topology changes

_____ **packets**. Queries are (unicast/multicast) (reliably/unreliably) during route recomputation, asking neighbors for a new successor to a lost route.

_____ **packets**. Neighbors (unicast/multicast) a reply to a query of whether or not they have a route.

_____ **packets**. "Dataless" (unicast/multicast) packet that acknowledges the receipt of a packet that was sent reliably.

EIGRP Configuration

Now that you have a firm grasp of EIGRP concepts, it is time to learn how to configure EIGRP. The exercise in this section takes you step-by-step through an EIGRP configuration.

Learn the EIGRP Commands Exercise

Document the command syntax, including router prompt, to configure the EIGRP routing process.

True or False: All routers in an area must have the same *autonomous-system-number*.

Like the *process-id* in OSPF, the value for *autonomous-system-number* can be any number between __ and _____ as long as it does not have to be registered with IANA.

Refer to Figure 3-1. In the space provided, document the correct commands, including router prompt, to configure RTA to advertise all directly connected networks in EIGRP.

Figure 3-1   RTA EIGRP Configuration

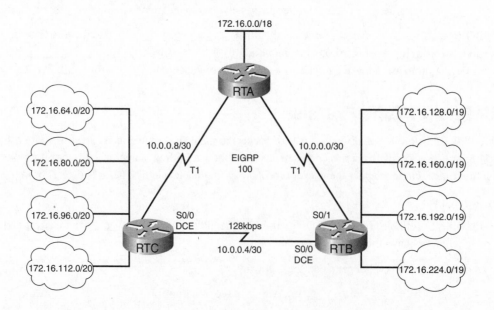

_____

_____

_____

In Figure 3-1, RTB and RTC are distribution routers for several networks. Each router has six networks attached: two WANs and four simulated LANs. If configuring OSPF, you would have to enter each network in the routing process. But for EIGRP, the configuration is greatly simplified. You need to enter only the classful networks. Therefore, the EIGRP configuration for RTB and RTC is identical to that of RTA. In the space provided, document the correct commands, including router prompt, to configure RTB and RTC to advertise all directly connected networks in EIGRP.

_____

_____

_____

_____

_____

_____

In Figure 3-1, notice that the WAN links are labeled with the contracted bandwidth. Because EIGRP calculates the metric using _____ and _____, you need to configure the links for the correct bandwidth. Assume that the default bandwidth for the three routers is 1544 kbps. Document the commands, including router prompt, to configure RTB and RTC with the correct bandwidth.

_____

_____

_____

_____

_____

The following output was sent to the console by the IOS when RTA and RTB established a new adjacency. Document the command, including router prompt, that you need to configure to have this message sent to the console on RTA.

```
RTA#
00:24:44: %DUAL-5-NBRCHANGE: IP-EIGRP 100: Neighbor 10.0.0.2 (Serial0/1) is up:
new adjacency
```

_____

Figure 3-1 has discontiguous subnets. Subnets of the 10.0.0.0 classful network separate subnets of the 172.16.0.0 classful network. As the configuration stands now, no router can send traffic to any of the LANs connected to another router. The routing table for RTA follows. Document the command, including router prompt, that must be configured on all three routers before all subnets will be reachable from anywhere in the network.

```
RTA#show ip route
Codes: C - connected, S - static, I - IGRP, R - RIP, M - mobile, B - BGP
       D - EIGRP, EX - EIGRP external, O - OSPF, IA - OSPF inter area
       N1 - OSPF NSSA external type 1, N2 - OSPF NSSA external type 2
       E1 - OSPF external type 1, E2 - OSPF external type 2, E - EGP
       i - IS-IS, L1 - IS-IS level-1, L2 - IS-IS level-2, ia - IS-IS inter area
       * - candidate default, U - per-user static route, o - ODR
       P - periodic downloaded static route
```

```
Gateway of last resort is not set


     172.16.0.0/16 is variably subnetted, 2 subnets, 2 masks
D       172.16.0.0/16 is a summary, 00:23:16, Null0
C       172.16.0.0/18 is directly connected, FastEthernet0/0
     10.0.0.0/8 is variably subnetted, 2 subnets, 2 masks
D       10.0.0.0/8 is a summary, 00:23:20, Null0
C       10.0.0.0/30 is directly connected, Serial0/1
```

Note: Now is a good time to complete Curriculum Lab 3-1: Configuring EIGRP Routing (3.2.1).

The output that follows shows the current routing table for RTA with automatic summarization disabled, and then shows the same routing table after manual summarization. Even in this simulated network, the table is rather large. In production networks, this table could be huge. Unlike single-area OSPF configurations, EIGRP provides a method to manually summarize subnets within the same address space into one route table entry. Document the commands necessary to configure RTB and RTC to manually summarize the simulated LANs into one advertisement.

RTA routing table before manual summarization:

```
RTA#show ip route
(output omitted)
Gateway of last resort is not set


     172.16.0.0/16 is variably subnetted, 9 subnets, 3 masks
D       172.16.160.0/19 [90/2297856] via 10.0.0.2, 00:00:16, Serial0/1
D       172.16.128.0/19 [90/2297856] via 10.0.0.2, 00:00:16, Serial0/1
D       172.16.224.0/19 [90/2297856] via 10.0.0.2, 00:00:16, Serial0/1
D       172.16.192.0/19 [90/2297856] via 10.0.0.2, 00:00:16, Serial0/1
C       172.16.0.0/18 is directly connected, FastEthernet0/0
D       172.16.112.0/20 [90/2297856] via 10.0.0.9, 00:00:29, Serial0/0
D       172.16.96.0/20 [90/2297856] via 10.0.0.9, 00:00:30, Serial0/0
D       172.16.80.0/20 [90/2297856] via 10.0.0.9, 00:00:30, Serial0/0
D       172.16.64.0/20 [90/2297856] via 10.0.0.9, 00:00:30, Serial0/0
     10.0.0.0/30 is subnetted, 3 subnets
C       10.0.0.8 is directly connected, Serial0/0
C       10.0.0.0 is directly connected, Serial0/1
D       10.0.0.4 [90/21024000] via 10.0.0.9, 00:00:30, Serial0/0
                 [90/21024000] via 10.0.0.2, 00:00:30, Serial0/1
```

RTA routing table after manual summarization:

```
RTA#show ip route
(output omitted)
Gateway of last resort is not set


     172.16.0.0/16 is variably subnetted, 3 subnets, 2 masks
D       172.16.128.0/17 [90/2297856] via 10.0.0.2, 00:00:36, Serial0/1
```

```
C          172.16.0.0/18 is directly connected, FastEthernet0/0
D          172.16.64.0/18 [90/2297856] via 10.0.0.9, 00:02:43, Serial0/0
      10.0.0.0/30 is subnetted, 3 subnets
C          10.0.0.8 is directly connected, Serial0/0
C          10.0.0.0 is directly connected, Serial0/1
D          10.0.0.4 [90/21024000] via 10.0.0.9, 00:00:36, Serial0/0
                   [90/21024000] via 10.0.0.2, 00:00:36, Serial0/1
```

_____

_____

_____

_____

_____

_____

_____

_____

_____

Troubleshooting Routing Protocols

Learning how to troubleshoot network problems and misconfigurations is paramount to your CCNA skill set. Not only will this skill save you countless hours on the job, your ability to problem solve will be thoroughly tested on the CCNA exam. The only way to develop troubleshooting or problem-solving skills is by practicing. The more "hands on" experience you gain from cabling and configuring networks, the more problems you will run across and solve.

By far, the most common errors occur at Layer 1. Always check your physical layer first when a problem occurs. Then, work your way up the layers. Too often, students issue the command **show run** to find a problem. Rarely is this the best or most efficient method of troubleshooting your network. In addition, on production networks the running configuration can span many pages. Learn the **show** and **debug** commands. Develop an understanding of what the output from these commands means. Not only will this skill better assist you in troubleshooting your network configurations, you will be better prepared for the troubleshooting scenarios you encounter on the CCNA exam.

In the following exercises, you will document a problem-solving flow chart and then work through **show** and **debug** commands for RIP, EIGRP, and OSPF. The Internet Research Exercise asks you to research the fields of an IP packet header.

Problem-Solving Cycle

In the space provided, draw a flow chart showing a generic problem-solving cycle that starts with "identify problem" and ends with "document problem and solution." Your flow chart should have no less than six steps, but it can have more.

Figure 3-2   Problem-Solving Cycle

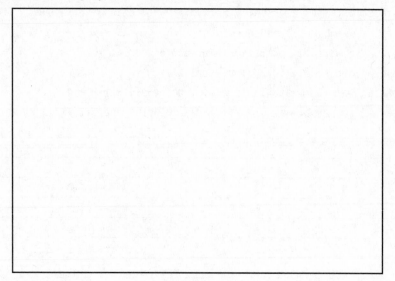

Troubleshooting RIP

The most common problem found in RIP that prevents RIP routes from being advertised is discontiguous subnets because RIP Version 1 does not support VLSM. First, make sure both Layer 1 and Layer 2 are functioning. Then, use the commands reviewed in this exercise to verify and troubleshoot the network.

What command generates the following output?

```
Router#_____

Codes: C - connected, S - static, I - IGRP, R - RIP, M - mobile, B - BGP
       D - EIGRP, EX - EIGRP external, O - OSPF, IA - OSPF inter area
       N1 - OSPF NSSA external type 1, N2 - OSPF NSSA external type 2
       E1 - OSPF external type 1, E2 - OSPF external type 2, E - EGP
       i - IS-IS, L1 - IS-IS level-1, L2 - IS-IS level-2, ia - IS-IS inter area
       * - candidate default, U - per-user static route, o - ODR
       P - periodic downloaded static route


Gateway of last resort is 192.168.1.253 to network 0.0.0.0

     192.168.1.0/24 is variably subnetted, 6 subnets, 2 masks
R       192.168.1.64/26 [120/1] via 192.168.1.246, 00:00:03, Serial0/1
C       192.168.1.0/26 is directly connected, FastEthernet0/0
R       192.168.1.248/30 [120/1] via 192.168.1.246, 00:00:03, Serial0/1
                         [120/1] via 192.168.1.253, 00:00:07, Serial0/0
C       192.168.1.252/30 is directly connected, Serial0/0
C       192.168.1.244/30 is directly connected, Serial0/1
R       192.168.1.128/26 [120/1] via 192.168.1.253, 00:00:08, Serial0/0
R*   0.0.0.0/0 [120/9] via 192.168.1.253, 00:00:02, Serial0/0
```

Using the preceding output, answer the following questions.

In the shaded entry for 192.168.1.128/26, what does the 120 mean in the [120/1] portion of the entry?

What does the 1 mean?

_____

Why are there two entries to the 192.168.1.248/30 network?

_____

How many subnets and masks are used in the 192.168.1.0/24 address space?

_____

What command generates the following output?

```
Router#_____
Routing Protocol is "rip"
  Sending updates every 30 seconds, next due in 15 seconds
  Invalid after 180 seconds, hold down 180, flushed after 240
  Outgoing update filter list for all interfaces is not set
  Incoming update filter list for all interfaces is not set
  Redistributing: rip
  Default version control: send version 2, receive version 2
    Interface            Send  Recv  Triggered RIP  Key-chain
    FastEthernet0/0       2     2
    Serial0/0             2     2
    Serial0/1             2     2
  Automatic network summarization is not in effect
  Maximum path: 6
  Routing for Networks:
    192.168.1.0
  Routing Information Sources:
    Gateway          Distance      Last Update
    192.168.1.253        120       00:00:17
    192.168.1.246        120       00:00:12
  Distance: (default is 120)
```

Using the preceding output, answer the following questions.

How many routers are advertising RIP routes to this router?

_____

How many equal-cost routes to the same destination can this router use (not the default)?

_____

What are the timers for RIP:

- Update: _____

- Holddown: _____

- Invalid: _____

- Flushed: _____

What command generates the following output?

```
Router#_____
00:29:04: RIP: received v2 update from 192.168.1.253 on Serial0/0
00:29:04:      192.168.1.64/26 via 0.0.0.0 in 2 hops
```

```
00:29:04:         192.168.1.128/26 via 0.0.0.0 in 1 hops
00:29:04:         192.168.1.248/30 via 0.0.0.0 in 1 hops
00:29:05: RIP: sending v2 update to 224.0.0.9 via FastEthernet0/0 (192.168.1.1)
00:29:05: RIP: build update entries
00:29:05:         192.168.1.64/26 via 0.0.0.0, metric 2, tag 0
00:29:05:         192.168.1.128/26 via 0.0.0.0, metric 2, tag 0
00:29:05:         192.168.1.244/30 via 0.0.0.0, metric 1, tag 0
00:29:05:         192.168.1.248/30 via 0.0.0.0, metric 2, tag 0
00:29:05:         192.168.1.252/30 via 0.0.0.0, metric 1, tag 0
00:29:05: RIP: sending v2 update to 224.0.0.9 via Serial0/0 (192.168.1.254)
00:29:05: RIP: build update entries
00:29:05:         192.168.1.0/26 via 0.0.0.0, metric 1, tag 0
00:29:05:         192.168.1.64/26 via 0.0.0.0, metric 2, tag 0
00:29:05:         192.168.1.244/30 via 0.0.0.0, metric 1, tag 0
```

Using the preceding output, answer the following questions.

How many RIP neighbors does this router have?

_____

Notice that this router sent two updates. How many routes did RIP advertise out FastEthernet0/0?

_____

How many routes did RIP advertise out Serial0/0?

_____

What routes that were advertised out Fa0/0 were not advertised out S0/0?

_____

Why do you think these routes were not advertised out the S0/0 interface?

_____

_____

_____

_____

Is it necessary to advertise out the Fast Ethernet interface? If not, what can you do to stop advertisements? If so, why?

_____

_____

_____

Troubleshooting EIGRP

Normal EIGRP operation is stable, efficient in bandwidth utilization, and relatively simple to monitor and troubleshoot. Make sure your Layer 1 and Layer 2 are functioning. Then use the following commands to verify and troubleshoot the network.

What command generates the following output?

```
Router#_____
Codes: C - connected, S - static, I - IGRP, R - RIP, M - mobile, B - BGP
        D - EIGRP, EX - EIGRP external, O - OSPF, IA - OSPF inter area
```

```
    N1 - OSPF NSSA external type 1, N2 - OSPF NSSA external type 2
    E1 - OSPF external type 1, E2 - OSPF external type 2, E - EGP
    i - IS-IS, L1 - IS-IS level-1, L2 - IS-IS level-2, ia - IS-IS inter area
    * - candidate default, U - per-user static route, o - ODR
    P - periodic downloaded static route

Gateway of last resort is not set

    172.16.0.0/16 is variably subnetted, 3 subnets, 2 masks
D       172.16.128.0/17 [90/2297856] via 10.0.0.2, 00:00:19, Serial0/1
C       172.16.0.0/18 is directly connected, FastEthernet0/0
D       172.16.64.0/18 [90/2297856] via 10.0.0.9, 00:00:19, Serial0/0
    10.0.0.0/30 is subnetted, 3 subnets
C       10.0.0.8 is directly connected, Serial0/0
C       10.0.0.0 is directly connected, Serial0/1
D       10.0.0.4 [90/21024000] via 10.0.0.2, 00:00:19, Serial0/1
                [90/21024000] via 10.0.0.9, 00:00:19, Serial0/0
```

Using the preceding output, answer the following questions.

In the shaded entry for 172.16.128.0/17, what does the 90 mean in the [90/2297856] portion of the entry?

_____

What does the 2297856 mean?

_____

Why are there two entries to the 10.0.0.4/30 network?

_____

How many subnets and masks are used in the 192.168.1.0/24 address space?

_____

What command generates the following output?

```
Router#_____
Routing Protocol is "eigrp 100"
  Outgoing update filter list for all interfaces is not set
  Incoming update filter list for all interfaces is not set
  Default networks flagged in outgoing updates
  Default networks accepted from incoming updates
  EIGRP metric weight K1=1, K2=0, K3=1, K4=0, K5=0
  EIGRP maximum hopcount 100
  EIGRP maximum metric variance 1
  Redistributing: eigrp 100
  Automatic network summarization is not in effect
  Maximum path: 5
  Routing for Networks:
    10.0.0.0
    172.16.0.0
```

```
Routing Information Sources:
   Gateway          Distance      Last Update
   10.0.0.9              90        00:00:53
   10.0.0.2              90        00:00:53
Distance: internal 90 external 170
```

Using the preceding output, answer the following questions.

How many routers are advertising EIGRP routes to this router?

_____

How many equal-cost routes to the same destination can this router use (not the default)?

_____

The K1 and K3 values in the metric weight have a value of 1 each. What are these values for?

_____

_____

The K2, K4, and K5 values are all 0. What do these values represent and why are they 0?

_____

_____

What command generates the following output?

Router#_____

```
H    Address                 Interface   Hold Uptime    SRTT   RTO  Q  Seq Type
                                         (sec)          (ms)      Cnt Num
1    10.0.0.9                Se0/0       11 00:23:21    24     200  0  4
0    10.0.0.2                Se0/1       10 00:23:35    32     200  0  8
```

What command generates the following output?

Router#_____

```
Codes: P - Passive, A - Active, U - Update, Q - Query, R - Reply,
       r - reply Status, s - sia Status

P 10.0.0.8/30, 1 successors, FD is 2169856
        via Connected, Serial0/0
P 10.0.0.0/30, 1 successors, FD is 2169856
        via Connected, Serial0/1
P 10.0.0.4/30, 2 successors, FD is 21024000
        via 10.0.0.2 (21024000/20512000), Serial0/1
        via 10.0.0.9 (21024000/20512000), Serial0/0
P 172.16.128.0/17, 1 successors, FD is 2297856
        via 10.0.0.2 (2297856/128256), Serial0/1
P 172.16.0.0/18, 1 successors, FD is 28160
        via Connected, FastEthernet0/0
P 172.16.64.0/18, 1 successors, FD is 2297856
        via 10.0.0.9 (2297856/128256), Serial0/0
```

What command generates the following output?

Router#_____

```
  Hellos sent/received: 1044/696
  Updates sent/received: 9/9
```

```
Queries sent/received: 0/0

Replies sent/received: 0/0

Acks sent/received: 7/7

Input queue high water mark 1, 0 drops

SIA-Queries sent/received: 0/0

SIA-Replies sent/received: 0/0
```

What command generates the following output?

```
Router#_____

IP-EIGRP: Processing incoming UPDATE packet

IP-EIGRP: Ext 192.168.3.0 255.255.255.0 M 386560 - 256000 130560 SM 360960 - 256000
104960

IP-EIGRP: Ext 192.168.0.0 255.255.255.0 M 386560 - 256000 130560 SM 360960 - 256000
104960

IP-EIGRP: Ext 192.168.3.0 255.255.255.0 M 386560 - 256000 130560 SM 360960 - 256000
104960

IP-EIGRP: 172.69.43.0 255.255.255.0, - do advertise out Ethernet0/1

IP-EIGRP: Ext 172.68.43.0 255.255.255.0 metric 371200 - 25600 115200

IP-EIGRP: 192.135.246.0 255.255.255.0, - do advertise out Ethernet0/1

IP-EIGRP: Ext 192.135.246.0 255.255.255.0 metric 46310656 - 45714176 596480

IP-EIGRP: 172.69.40.0 255.255.255.0, - do advertise out Ethernet0/1

IP-EIGRP: Ext 172.68.40.0 255.255.255.0 metric 2272256 - 1657856 614400

IP-EIGRP: 192.135.245.0 255.255.255.0, - do advertise out Ethernet0/1

IP-EIGRP: Ext 192.135.245.0 255.255.255.0 metric 40622080 - 40000000 622080

IP-EIGRP: 192.135.244.0 255.255.255.0, - do advertise out Ethernet0/1
```

Troubleshooting OSPF

The majority of problems encountered with OSPF relate to the formation of adjacencies and the synchronization of the link-state databases.

Make sure your Layer 1 and Layer 2 are functioning. Then use the following commands to verify and troubleshoot the network.

What command generates the following output?

```
Router#_____

Codes: C - connected, S - static, I - IGRP, R - RIP, M - mobile, B - BGP

       D - EIGRP, EX - EIGRP external, O - OSPF, IA - OSPF inter area

       N1 - OSPF NSSA external type 1, N2 - OSPF NSSA external type 2

       E1 - OSPF external type 1, E2 - OSPF external type 2, E - EGP

       i - IS-IS, L1 - IS-IS level-1, L2 - IS-IS level-2, ia - IS-IS inter area

       * - candidate default, U - per-user static route, o - ODR

       P - periodic downloaded static route


Gateway of last resort is 192.168.1.245 to network 0.0.0.0


     192.168.1.0/24 is variably subnetted, 6 subnets, 2 masks

C       192.168.1.64/26 is directly connected, FastEthernet0/0

O       192.168.1.0/26 [110/65] via 192.168.1.245, 00:00:06, Serial0/1

C       192.168.1.248/30 is directly connected, Serial0/0

O       192.168.1.252/30 [110/128] via 192.168.1.245, 00:00:06, Serial0/1

C       192.168.1.244/30 is directly connected, Serial0/1
```

```
O         192.168.1.128/26 [110/129] via 192.168.1.245, 00:00:06, Serial0/1
O*E2 0.0.0.0/0 [110/1] via 192.168.1.245, 00:00:07, Serial0/1
```

Using the preceding output, answer the following questions.

In the entry for 192.168.1.0/26, what does the 110 mean in the [110/65] portion of the entry?

_____

What does the 65 mean?

_____

How many subnets and masks are used in the 192.168.1.0/24 address space?

_____

What does O*E2 stand for and what does it mean?

_____

_____

_____

What command generates the following output?

```
Router#_____
Routing Protocol is "ospf 1"
  Outgoing update filter list for all interfaces is not set
  Incoming update filter list for all interfaces is not set
  Router ID 209.165.202.129
  It is an autonomous system boundary router
  Redistributing External Routes from,
  Number of areas in this router is 1. 1 normal 0 stub 0 nssa
  Maximum path: 4
  Routing for Networks:
     192.168.1.0 0.0.0.63 area 0
     192.168.1.244 0.0.0.3 area 0
     192.168.1.252 0.0.0.3 area 0
  Routing Information Sources:
     Gateway          Distance      Last Update
     209.165.202.129      110       00:08:10
     192.168.1.249        110       00:08:10
     192.168.1.253        110       00:08:10
  Distance: (default is 110)
```

Notice in the preceding output the line that states, "It is an autonomous system boundary router." What does this mean?

_____

_____

_____

_____

_____

What command generates the following output?

```
Router#_____
00:09:46: OSPF: Rcv hello from 192.168.1.249 area 0 from Serial0/1 192.168.1.246
```

```
00:09:46: OSPF: Mismatched hello parameters from 192.168.1.246
00:09:46: OSPF: Dead R 160 C 120, Hello R 40 C 40


00:10:26: OSPF: Rcv hello from 192.168.1.253 area 0 from Serial0/0 192.168.1.253
00:10:26: OSPF: End of hello processing
00:10:26: OSPF: Rcv hello from 192.168.1.249 area 0 from Serial0/1 192.168.1.246
00:10:26: OSPF: Mismatched hello parameters from 192.168.1.246
00:10:26: OSPF: Dead R 160 C 120, Hello R 40 C 40


00:11:06: OSPF: Rcv hello from 192.168.1.253 area 0 from Serial0/0 192.168.1.253
00:11:06: OSPF: End of hello processing
00:11:06: OSPF: Rcv hello from 192.168.1.249 area 0 from Serial0/1 192.168.1.246
00:11:06: OSPF: Mismatched hello parameters from 192.168.1.246
00:11:06: OSPF: Dead R 160 C 120, Hello R 40 C 40


00:11:46: OSPF: Rcv hello from 192.168.1.253 area 0 from Serial0/0 192.168.1.253
00:11:46: OSPF: End of hello processing
00:11:46: OSPF: Rcv hello from 192.168.1.249 area 0 from Serial0/1 192.168.1.246
00:11:46: OSPF: Mismatched hello parameters from 192.168.1.246
00:11:46: OSPF: Dead R 160 C 120, Hello R 40 C 40
00:11:46: OSPF: 192.168.1.249 address 192.168.1.246 on Serial0/1 is dead


00:11:46: %OSPF-5-ADJCHG: Process 1, Nbr 192.168.1.249 on Serial0/1 from FULL to
DOWN, Neighbor Down: Dead timer expired
```

From the preceding command output, what is the problem?

_____

_____

_____

_____

_____

_____

_____

What command would fix the "mismatch of hello parameters"?

_____

_____

_____

Suppose that after you fixed the mismatch problem, you wanted to watch the processing of packets as the two neighbors re-establish adjacency. What command generated the following output?

```
Router#_____
00:24:26: OSPF: rcv. v:2 t:1 l:44 rid:192.168.1.249
        aid:0.0.0.0 chk:0 aut:2 keyid:1 seq:0x2B91532F from Serial0/1
00:24:29: OSPF: rcv. v:2 t:2 l:32 rid:192.168.1.249
        aid:0.0.0.0 chk:0 aut:2 keyid:1 seq:0x2B915330 from Serial0/1
```

```
00:24:29: OSPF: rcv. v:2 t:2 l:112 rid:192.168.1.249
        aid:0.0.0.0 chk:0 aut:2 keyid:1 seq:0x2B915331 from Serial0/1
00:24:29: OSPF: rcv. v:2 t:2 l:32 rid:192.168.1.249
        aid:0.0.0.0 chk:0 aut:2 keyid:1 seq:0x2B915332 from Serial0/1
00:24:29: OSPF: rcv. v:2 t:2 l:32 rid:192.168.1.249
        aid:0.0.0.0 chk:0 aut:2 keyid:1 seq:0x2B915333 from Serial0/1
00:24:30: OSPF: rcv. v:2 t:4 l:112 rid:192.168.1.249
        aid:0.0.0.0 chk:0 aut:2 keyid:1 seq:0x2B915335 from Serial0/1
00:24:32: OSPF: rcv. v:2 t:5 l:44 rid:192.168.1.249
        aid:0.0.0.0 chk:0 aut:2 keyid:1 seq:0x2B915337 from Serial0/1
```

In the following table, fill in the description for each field shown in the preceding output.

Note: You may have to search Cisco.com to find the answers.

Field	Description
v:	
t:	
l:	
rid:	
aid:	
chk:	
aut:	
auk:	
keyid:	
seq:	

Internet Research Exercise

The CCNA objectives cover all of the layers of the OSI model to some extent. Some layers are less important than others to your studies. For example, the presentation and session layers can be thought of as belonging to the application layer, as shown when comparing the TCP/IP model and the OSI model side by side. The most important layer of the OSI model for CCNA candidates is the network layer. And the most important protocol of the network layer is the Internet Protocol (IP).

Your assignment is to research IP to discover detailed information about the structure of its packet header. You can use any trusted Internet resource, but the original source is the RFC. Make sure you list your sources in the place provided at the end of this exercise.

The IP Packet Header

In Figure 3-3, label all the fields of the IP packet header.

Figure 3-3   IP Packet Header

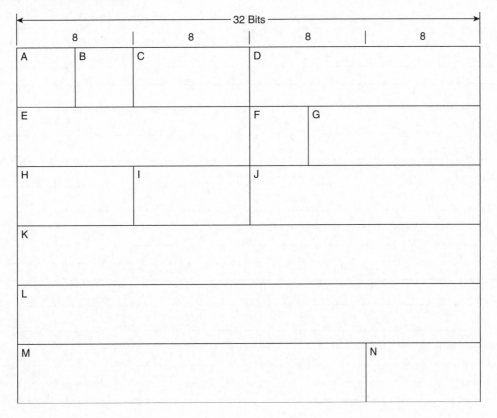

Field Descriptions

Describe in as much detail as possible the purpose of each field in the IP packet header.

Field A _____

_____

_____

Field B _____

_____

_____

_____

Field C _____

_____

_____

_____

_____

Field D _____

_____

_____

Field E _____

_____

_____

_____

_____

Field F _____

_____

_____

■ _____

■ _____

■ _____

Field G _____

_____

_____

_____

_____

_____

Field H _____

_____

_____

_____

_____

_____

Field I _____

_____

_____

Field J _____

_____

Field K _____

_____

Field L _____

_____

Field M _____

_____

Field N _____

_____

_____

Sources

Lab Exercises

Command Reference

In the table that follows, record the command, including the correct router prompt, that fits the description. Fill in any blanks with the appropriate missing information.

Command	Description
	Turns on the EIGRP process. **100** is the _____ (AS) number, which can be a number between __ and _____. All routers in the same AS must use the same AS number.
	Logs any changes to an EIGRP neighbor adjacency.
	Turns off the automatic summarization of networks at _____ boundaries.
	Changes the bandwidth of an interface to 128 kbps.
	Enables manual summarization on this specific interface for the 10.10.0.0/16 address space.
	Displays a neighbor table.
	Displays a detailed neighbor table.
	Displays EIGRP information for each interface.
	Displays the topology table. This command shows you where your feasible successors are.
	Displays the number and type of packets sent and received.
	Displays events/actions related to the DUAL FSM.
	Displays events/actions related to EIGRP packets.
	Displays events/actions related to EIGRP neighbors.

Curriculum Lab 3-1: Configuring EIGRP Routing (3.2.1)

Figure 3-4   Topology for Lab 3-1

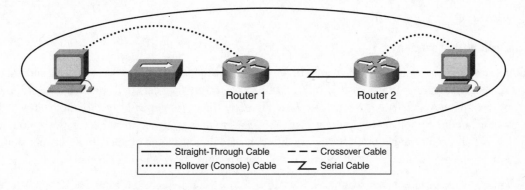

Router 1   Router 2

——— Straight-Through Cable	– – – Crossover Cable
······· Rollover (Console) Cable	⌐Z⌐ Serial Cable

Table 3-1   Lab Equipment Configuration: Part I

Router Designation	Router Name	Routing Protocol	Network Statements
Router 1	Paris	EIGRP	192.168.3.0
			192.168.2.0
Router 2	Warsaw	EIGRP	192.168.1.0
			192.168.2.0

The enable secret password for both routers is **class**.

The enable, VTY, and console password for both routers is **cisco**.

Table 3-2   Lab Equipment Configuration: Part II

Router Designation	IP Host Table Entry	Fast Ethernet 0 Address/ Subnet Mask	Interface Type Serial 0	Serial 0 Address/ Subnet Mask	Loopback 0 Subnet Mask Address/
Router 1	Warsaw	192.168.3.1/24	DCE	192.168.2.1/30	192.168.0.2/24
Router 2	Paris	192.168.1.1/24	DTE	192.168.2.2/30	No address

The interface type and address/subnet mask for the serial 1 interface on both routers is not applicable for this lab.

The "IP Host Table Entry" column contents indicate the names of the other routers in the IP host table.

Objectives

- Set up an IP addressing scheme for the network.

- Configure and verify EIGRP routing.

Background/Preparation

Cable a network that is similar to the one in Figure 3-4. You can use any router that meets the interface requirements in Figure 3-4 (that is, 800, 1600, 1700, 2500, and 2600 routers or a combination). Refer to the information in Appendix A, "Router Interface Summary Chart," to correctly specify the interface identifiers based on the equipment in your lab. The 1721 series routers produced the configuration output in this lab. Another router might produce slightly different output. You should execute the following steps on each router unless you are specifically instructed otherwise. Start a HyperTerminal session.

Implement the procedure that is documented in Appendix C, "Erasing and Reloading the Router," on all routers before you continue with this lab.

Task 1: Configure the Routers

On the routers, enter global configuration mode and configure the hostname as shown in the chart. Then, configure the console, virtual terminal, and enable passwords. Next, configure the interfaces according to Table 3-2. Finally, configure the IP hostnames. If you have problems configuring the router basics, refer to Lab 1-2, "Review of Basic Router Configuration with RIP."

Note: Do not configure the routing protocol until you are specifically told to.

Task 2: Save the Configuration Information from Privileged EXEC Command Mode

```
Paris#copy running-config startup-config
Destination filename [startup-config]? [Enter]
```

Task 3: Configure the Hosts

Step 1.   Configure the hosts with the proper IP address, subnet mask, and default gateway.

Step 2.   Each workstation should be able to ping the attached router. Troubleshoot as necessary. Hint: Remember to assign a specific IP address and default gateway to the workstation. If you are running Windows 98, check using **Start > Run > winipcfg**. If you are running Windows 2000 or later, check using **ipconfig** in a DOS window.

Step 3.   At this point, the workstations will not be able to communicate with each other. The following tasks demonstrate the process that is required to get communication working while using EIGRP as the routing protocol.

Task 4: View the Router's Configuration and Interface Information

Step 1.   At the privileged EXEC mode prompt, type the following:

```
Paris#show running-config
```

Step 2.   Using the **show ip interface brief** command, check the status of each interface.

What is the state of the interfaces on each router?

Paris:

- Fast Ethernet 0: _____
- Serial 0: _____

Warsaw:

- Fast Ethernet 0: _____
- Serial 0: _____

Step 3.   Ping from one of the connected serial interfaces to the other.

Was the ping successful? _____

Step 4.   If the ping was not successful, troubleshoot the router's configuration until the ping is successful.

Task 5: Configure EIGRP Routing on Router Paris

Step 1.   Enable the EIGRP routing process on router Paris and configure the networks it will advertise. Use EIGRP autonomous system number 101.

```
Paris(config)#router eigrp 101
Paris(config-router)#network 192.168.3.0
Paris(config-router)#network 192.168.2.0
Paris(config-router)#network 192.168.0.0
Paris(config-router)#end
```

Step 2.   Show the routing table for the Paris router.

```
Paris#show ip route
```

Do entries exist in the routing table? _____

Why?

_____

Task 6: Configure EIGRP Routing on Router Warsaw

Step 1.   Enable the EIGRP routing process on router Warsaw and configure the networks it will advertise. Use EIGRP autonomous system number 101.

```
Warsaw(config)#router eigrp 101
Warsaw(config-router)#network 192.168.2.0
Warsaw(config-router)#network 192.168.1.0
Warsaw(config-router)#end
```

Step 2.   Show the routing table for the Warsaw router.

```
Warsaw#show ip route
```

Task 7: Test Network Connectivity

Ping the Paris host from the Warsaw host. Was it successful? _____

If not, troubleshoot as necessary.

After you complete the previous steps, log off (by typing **exit**) and turn the router off. Then, remove and store the cables and adapter.

Curriculum Lab 3-2: Verifying Basic EIGRP Configuration (3.2.3)

Figure 3-5   Topology for Lab 3-2

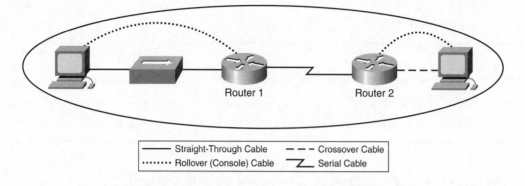

Router 1   Router 2

```
———— Straight-Through Cable      — — — Crossover Cable
········· Rollover (Console) Cable      ⅃ Serial Cable
```

Table 3-3   Lab Equipment Configuration: Part I

Router Designation	Router Name	Routing Protocol	Network Statements
Router 1	Paris	EIGRP	192.168.3.0
			192.168.2.0
Router 2	Warsaw	EIGRP	192.168.1.0
			192.168.2.0

The enable secret password for both routers is **class**.

The enable, VTY, and console password for both routers is **cisco**.

Table 3-4   Lab Equipment Configuration: Part II

Router Designation	IP Host Table Entry	Fast Ethernet 0 Address/ Subnet Mask	Interface Type Serial 0	Serial 0 Address/ Subnet Mask	Loopback 0 Address/ Subnet Mask
Router 1	Warsaw	192.168.3.1/24	DCE	192.168.2.1/30	192.168.0.2/24
Router 2	Paris	192.168.1.1/24	DTE	192.168.2.2/30	No address

The "IP Host Table Entry" column contents indicate the names of the other routers in the IP host table.

Objectives

- Set up an IP addressing scheme for the network.

- Configure and verify EIGRP routing.

Background/Preparation

Cable a network that is similar to the one in Figure 3-5. You can use any router that meets the interface requirements in Figure 3-5 (that is, 800, 1600, 1700, 2500, and 2600 routers or a combination). Refer to the information in Appendix A to correctly specify the interface identifiers based on the equipment in your lab. The 1721 series routers produced the configuration output in this lab. Another router might produce slightly different output. You should execute the following steps on each router unless you are specifically instructed otherwise. Start a HyperTerminal session.

Implement the procedure documented in Appendix C on all routers before you continue with this lab.

Task 1: Configure the Routers

On the routers, enter global configuration mode and configure the hostname as shown in Tables 3-3 and 3-4. Then, configure the console, virtual terminal, and enable passwords. Next, configure the interfaces according to Tables 3-3 and 3-4. Finally, configure the IP hostnames. If you have problems configuring the router basics, refer to Lab 1-2, "Review of Basic Router Configuration with RIP."

Note: Do not configure the routing protocol until you are specifically told to.

Task 2: Save the Configuration Information from Privileged EXEC Command Mode

```
PARIS#copy running-config startup-config
Destination filename [startup-config]? [Enter]
```

Task 3: Configure the Hosts

Step 1.   Configure the hosts with the proper IP address, subnet mask, and default gateway.Host connected to router Paris

Step 2.   Each workstation should be able to ping the attached router. Troubleshoot as necessary. Hint: Remember to assign a specific IP address and default gateway to the workstation. If you are running Windows 98, check using **Start > Run > winipcfg**. If you are running Windows 2000 or later, check using **ipconfig** in a DOS window.

Step 3.   At this point, the workstations will not be able to communicate with each other. The following tasks demonstrate the process that is required to get communication working while using EIGRP as the routing protocol.

Task 4: View the Router's Configuration and Interface Information

Step 1.   At the privileged EXEC mode prompt, type **show running-config**.

Step 2.   Using the **show ip interface brief** command, check the status of each interface.

Step 3.   What is the state of the interfaces on each router?

Paris:

- Fast Ethernet 0: _____

- Serial 0: _____

Warsaw:

- Fast Ethernet 0:_____

- Serial 0: _____

Step 4.   Ping from one of the connected serial interfaces to the other.

Step 5.   Was the ping successful? _____

Step 6.   If the ping was not successful, troubleshoot the router's configuration until the ping is successful.

Task 5: Configure EIGRP Routing on Router Paris

Step 1. Enable the EIGRP routing process on router Paris and configure the networks it will advertise. Use EIGRP autonomous system number 101.

```
Paris(config)#router eigrp 101
Paris(config-router)#network 192.168.3.0
Paris(config-router)#network 192.168.2.0
Paris(config-router)#network 192.168.0.0
Paris(config-router)#end
```

Step 2. Show the routing table for the Paris router.

```
Paris#show ip route
```

Do entries exist in the routing table? _____

Why?

_____

Task 6: Configure EIGRP Routing on Router Warsaw

Step 1. Enable the EIGRP routing process on router Warsaw and configure the networks it will advertise. Use EIGRP autonomous system number 101.

```
Warsaw(config)#router eigrp 101
Warsaw(config-router)#network 192.168.2.0
Warsaw(config-router)#network 192.168.1.0
Warsaw(config-router)#end
```

Step 2. Show the routing table for the Warsaw router.

```
Warsaw#show ip route
```

Do EIGRP entries exist in the routing table now? _____

What is the address type in the EIGRP 192.168.2.0 route? _____

What does the D mean in the first column of the routing table? _____

_____

Task 7: Show EIGRP Neighbors

From the Paris router, show any neighbors that are connected by using the **show ip eigrp neighbors** command at the privileged EXEC mode prompt.

Are neighbors shown? _____

Task 8: Test Network Connectivity

Ping the Paris host from the Warsaw host. Was it successful? <u>Yes</u>

If not, troubleshoot as necessary.

Task 9: View the Topology Table

Step 1.   To view the topology table, issue the **show ip eigrp topology all-links** command.

How many routes are in passive mode? _____

Step 2.   To view more specific information about a topology table entry, use an IP address with this command:

```
Paris#show ip eigrp topology 192.168.1.0
```

Based on the output of this command, does it tell what external protocol originated this route to 192.168.2.0? _____

Does it tell which router originated the route? _____

Step 3.   Use **show** commands to view key EIGRP statistics. On the Paris router, issue the **show ip eigrp traffic** command.

How many hello packets has the Paris router received? _____

How many has it sent? _____

After you complete the previous steps, log off (by typing **exit**) and turn the router off. Then, remove and store the cables and adapter.

Comprehensive Lab 3-3: Comprehensive EIGRP Configuration

Figure 3-6   EIGRP Configuration

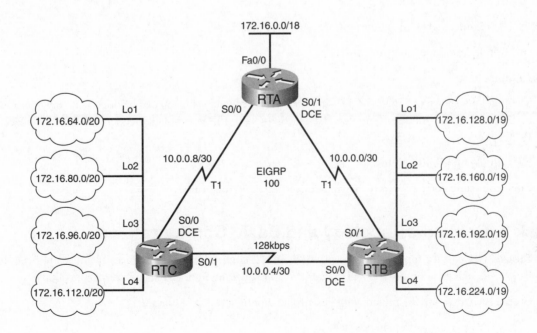

Table 3-5   Addressing Table for Lab 3-3

Device	Interface	IP Address	Subnet Mask
RTA	S0/1	10.0.0.1	255.255.255.252
	S0/0	10.0.0.10	255.255.255.252
	Fa0/0	172.16.0.1	255.255.192.0
RTB	S0/1	10.0.0.2	255.255.255.252
	S0/0	10.0.0.5	255.255.255.252
	Lo1	172.16.128.1	255.255.255.224
	Lo2	172.16.160.1	255.255.255.224
	Lo3	172.16.192.1	255.255.255.224
	Lo4	172.16.224.1	255.255.255.224
RTC	S0/1	10.0.0.6	255.255.255.252
	S0/0	10.0.0.9	255.255.255.252
	Lo1	172.16.64.1	255.255.255.240
	Lo2	172.16.80.1	255.255.255.240
	Lo3	172.16.96.1	255.255.255.240
	Lo4	172.16.112.1	255.255.255.240

Objectives

- Configure EIGRP routing.

- Configure bandwidth and turn off automatic summarization.

- Configure manual summarization.

Equipment

The topology shown in Figure 3-6 is using 2600 series routers. This lab can be done with any combination of 1700, 2500, and 2600 series routers. Connectivity to an ISP is simulated with a Loopback interface on RTA.

NetLab Compatibility Notes

This lab is fully compatible with a standard NetLab three router pod.

Task 1: Cable the Topology and Basic Configurations

Step 1.   Cable the topology as shown. If DCE/DTE connections and interfaces are different from those shown in Figure 3-6 and the table, then relabel the figure to match your connections.

Step 2.   Configure the routers with basic router configurations, including:

- Hostnames and host tables

- Enable secret password and MOTD banner

- Line configurations

- IOS-specific commands (e.g. **ip subnet-zero** with IOS versions prior to 12)

Step 3.   The following is a basic configuration for RTA:

```
Router(config)#hostname RTA
RTA(config)#ip subnet-zero
RTA(config)#no ip domain-lookup
RTA(config)#ip host RTC 10.0.0.9 10.0.0.6
RTA(config)#ip host RTB 10.0.0.2 10.0.0.5
RTA(config)#banner motd &
***********************************
  !!!AUTHORIZED ACCESS ONLY!!!
***********************************
&
RTA(config)#line con 0
RTA(config-line)#exec-timeout 30 0
RTA(config-line)#password cisco
RTA(config-line)#logging synchronous
RTA(config-line)#login
RTA(config-line)#ine aux 0
RTA(config-line)#exec-timeout 30 0
RTA(config-line)#password cisco
RTA(config-line)#logging synchronous
RTA(config-line)#login
RTA(config-line)#line vty 0 4
RTA(config-line)#exec-timeout 30 0
RTA(config-line)#password cisco
RTA(config-line)#logging synchronous
RTA(config-line)#login
RTA(config-line)#end
RTA#copy run start
```

Task 2: Configure Interfaces and EIGRP Routing

Step 1.   Use Table 3-5 and the topology shown in Figure 3-6 to configure each router with the correct interface addresses. The interface configuration for RTA is as follows:

```
RTA(config)#interface FastEthernet0/0
RTA(config-if)#description Link to RTA LAN
RTA(config-if)#ip address 172.16.0.1 255.255.192.0
RTA(config-if)#no shutdown
RTA(config-if)#interface Serial0/0
RTA(config-if)#description Link to RTC
RTA(config-if)#ip address 10.0.0.10 255.255.255.252
RTA(config-if)#clockrate 64000
RTA(config-if)#no shutdown
RTA(config-if)#interface Serial0/1
RTA(config-if)#description Link to RTB
RTA(config-if)#ip address 10.0.0.1 255.255.255.252
RTA(config-if)#clockrate 64000
RTA(config-if)#no shutdown
```

Step 2. Configure each router with EIGRP routing. The configuration for RTA follows. All routers have the same basic EIGRP configuration.

```
RTA(config)#router eigrp 100
RTA(config-router)#network 10.0.0.0
RTA(config-router)#network 172.16.0.0
```

Task 3: Configure Bandwidth and Automatic Summarization

Step 1. According to the topology shown in Figure 3-6, RTB and RTC are connected with a 128-kbps link. Enter the commands on both routers necessary to adjust the default bandwidth to match the actual speed.

Step 2. Display the routing table on RTA.

```
RTA#show ip route
(output omitted)
Gateway of last resort is not set

     172.16.0.0/16 is variably subnetted, 2 subnets, 2 masks
D       172.16.0.0/16 is a summary, 00:23:16, Null0
C       172.16.0.0/18 is directly connected, FastEthernet0/0
     10.0.0.0/8 is variably subnetted, 2 subnets, 2 masks
D       10.0.0.0/8 is a summary, 00:23:20, Null0
C       10.0.0.0/30 is directly connected, Serial0/1
```

Step 3. Notice that RTA does not have routes to the simulated LANs on RTB and RTC. Enter the command to disable automatic summarization on all three routers.

Task 4: Configure Manual Summarization

Step 1. Display the routing table on RTA.

```
RTA#show ip route
(output omitted)
Gateway of last resort is not set

     172.16.0.0/16 is variably subnetted, 9 subnets, 3 masks
D       172.16.160.0/19 [90/2297856] via 10.0.0.2, 00:00:16, Serial0/1
D       172.16.128.0/19 [90/2297856] via 10.0.0.2, 00:00:16, Serial0/1
D       172.16.224.0/19 [90/2297856] via 10.0.0.2, 00:00:16, Serial0/1
D       172.16.192.0/19 [90/2297856] via 10.0.0.2, 00:00:16, Serial0/1
C       172.16.0.0/18 is directly connected, FastEthernet0/0
D       172.16.112.0/20 [90/2297856] via 10.0.0.9, 00:00:29, Serial0/0
D       172.16.96.0/20 [90/2297856] via 10.0.0.9, 00:00:30, Serial0/0
D       172.16.80.0/20 [90/2297856] via 10.0.0.9, 00:00:30, Serial0/0
D       172.16.64.0/20 [90/2297856] via 10.0.0.9, 00:00:30, Serial0/0
     10.0.0.0/30 is subnetted, 3 subnets
C       10.0.0.8 is directly connected, Serial0/0
C       10.0.0.0 is directly connected, Serial0/1
D       10.0.0.4 [90/21024000] via 10.0.0.9, 00:00:30, Serial0/0
                 [90/21024000] via 10.0.0.2, 00:00:30, Serial0/1
```

Step 2. Notice that RTA has 12 routes. Some of these routes can be summarized to reduce the size of the routing table.

The simulated LANs on RTB share the same bit pattern for the first 17 bits of the network prefix 172.16.128.0.

The simulated LANS on RTC share the same bit pattern for the first 18 bits of the network prefix 172.16.64.0.

What command would you configure on both serial interfaces for RTB?

_____

What command would you configure on both serial interfaces for RTC?

_____

Step 3.   Display the routing table for RTA. You should have only six routes.

```
RTA#show ip route
(output omitted)
Gateway of last resort is not set

     172.16.0.0/16 is variably subnetted, 3 subnets, 2 masks
D       172.16.128.0/17 [90/2297856] via 10.0.0.2, 01:36:05, Serial0/1
C       172.16.0.0/18 is directly connected, FastEthernet0/0
D       172.16.64.0/18 [90/2297856] via 10.0.0.9, 01:38:11, Serial0/0
     10.0.0.0/30 is subnetted, 3 subnets
C       10.0.0.8 is directly connected, Serial0/0
C       10.0.0.0 is directly connected, Serial0/1
D       10.0.0.4 [90/21024000] via 10.0.0.9, 01:36:05, Serial0/0
                [90/21024000] via 10.0.0.2, 01:36:05, Serial0/1
```

Challenge Lab 3-4: EIGRP Design and Configuration

Figure 3-7   EIGRP Design and Configuration

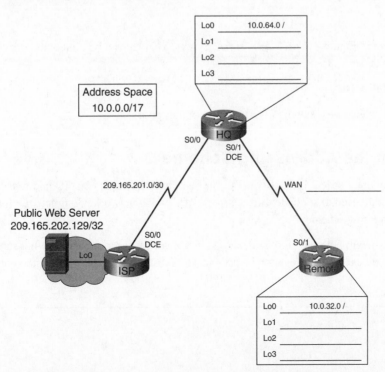

Table 3-6   Addressing Table for Lab 3-4

Device	Interface	IP Address	Subnet Mask
ISP	Lo0	209.165.202.129	255.255.255.255
	S0/0	209.165.201.1	255.255.255.252
HQ	S0/0	209.165.201.2	255.255.255.252
	S0/1		
	Lo0		
	Lo1		
	Lo2		
	Lo3		
REMOTE	S0/1		
	Lo0		
	Lo1		
	Lo2		
	Lo3		

Objectives

- Design a VLSM addressing scheme.

- Configure routers with basic configurations using your addressing scheme.

- Configure dynamic, static, and default routing.

- Configure manual summarization.

- Verify connectivity and troubleshoot problems.

Equipment

The topology shown in Figure 3-7 uses 2600 series routers. This lab can be done with any combination of 1700, 2500, and 2600 series routers.

NetLab Compatibility Notes

This lab can be completed on a standard NetLab three router pod.

Task 1: Design the Addressing Scheme

You are given the address space, 10.0.0.0/17. The four loopback interfaces on HQ and four loopback interfaces on REMOTE are used to simulate different parts of a global network. Complete the following steps to design your addressing scheme.

Step 1.   For HQ, begin with the 10.0.64.0 address as the subnet for loopback 0. What subnet mask would you use to provide enough space for 4000 users while maximizing the number of subnets?

Step 2. Starting with 10.0.64.0, contiguously assign the next three subnets, all supporting 4000 hosts. List all four subnets here:

_____

_____

_____

_____

Step 3. For REMOTE, begin with the 10.0.32.0 address as the subnet for loopback 0. What subnet mask would you use to provide enough space for 2000 users while maximizing the number of subnets?

_____

Step 4. Starting with 10.0.32.0, contiguously assign the next three subnets, all supporting 2000 hosts. List all four subnets here:

_____

_____

_____

_____

Step 5. Now pick a WAN subnet for the link shared by HQ and REMOTE. List the subnet you assigned here:

_____

Step 6. Label the topology in Figure 3-7 with the networks and finish filling in the IP address table with your chosen addressing scheme. Use the first available IP address in each subnet as the interface address. For the WAN subnet, assign HQ the first address.

Task 2: Cable the Topology and Basic Configuration

Step 1. Choose three routers and cable them according to the topology. You do not need any LAN interfaces or switches for this lab. (If using NetLab, choose a three router pod.)

Step 2. Configure the routers with basic configurations including interface addresses.

Task 3: Configure EIGRP Routing and Default Routing

Step 1. Configure both HQ and REMOTE to use EIGRP as the routing protocol. Enter the simulated LAN subnets and the WAN link between HQ and REMOTE. _Do not_ advertise the 209.165.201.0/30 network. Make sure you disable automatic summarization.

Step 2. Configure ISP with a static route pointing to the 10.0.0.0/17 Address Space.

Step 3. Configure HQ with a default route pointing to ISP.

Step 4. Configure HQ to advertise the default route to REMOTE with the **redistribute static** command within the EIGRP routing process.

```
HQ(config-router)#redistribute static
```

Step 5. Verify HQ and REMOTE routing tables:

- HQ should have six directly connected routes, four EIGRP routes, and one static route.

- REMOTE should have five directly connected routes, four EIGRP routes, and one EIGRP external route.

■ Verify that REMOTE can ping the Simulated Web Server at 209.165.202.129.

```
REMOTE#ping web

Type escape sequence to abort.
Sending 5, 100-byte ICMP Echos to 209.165.202.129, timeout is 2 seconds:
!!!!!
Success rate is 100 percent (5/5), round-trip min/avg/max = 56/56/56 ms
```

Task 4: Manual Summarization

Because the simulated LANs on both HQ and REMOTE were assigned contiguously, you can summarize the routing updates to reduce the size of the routing tables. What command will summarize the simulated LANs on HQ?

_____

_____

What command will summarize the simulated LANs on REMOTE?

_____

_____

Task 5: Verification and Documentation

Step 1.   Capture the following verifications to a text file called **verify.txt**:

■ Ping output from REMOTE pinging the Simulated Web Server.

■ Capture **show ip route** on all three routers: ISP, HQ, and REMOTE.

■ Capture **show ip eigrp neighbor** and **show ip eigrp topology** on HQ and REMOTE.

Step 2.   Capture the running configurations on all three routers to separate text files. Use the hostname of the router to name each text file.

Step 3.   Clean up the verify.txt, HQ.txt, REMOTE.txt, and ISP.txt files. Add appropriate notes to assist in your studies.

CHAPTER 4

Switching Concepts

The Study Guide portion of this chapter uses a combination of matching, fill in the blank, open-ended question, journal entry, and unique custom exercises to test your knowledge on the theory of switching and switch operation.

There are no Lab Exercises for this chapter.

Study Guide

Introduction to Ethernet/802.3 LANs

LAN design continues to evolve. Network designers until very recently used hubs and bridges to build networks. Now switches and routers are the key components in LAN design, and the capabilities and performance of these devices continue to improve.

As a CCNA candidate, you should have a firm grasp of the concepts involved in the evolution of Ethernet/802.3, the most commonly deployed LAN architecture. This section offers some exercises to help you master these concepts.

Vocabulary Exercise: Matching

Match the definition on the left with a term on the right. This exercise is not necessarily a one-to-one matching. Some definitions may be used more than once and some terms may have multiple definitions.

Definition

a. Ethernet's collision resolution methodology

b. the fading of a data signal as it travels through the media

c. reading the entire frame to check for errors before sending on to the destination

d. filters traffic at Layer 3; segments broadcast domains

e. Layer 2 device that provides network access to hosts

f. Layer 2 error-checking mechanism

g. capable of simultaneous transmission and reception

h. basic unit of time in which one bit can be sent

i. multiport repeater or LAN concentrator

j. sending a frame out all ports except for the port it was received on

k. frames are stored in queues that are linked to specific incoming ports`

l. temporary, dedicated path between two hosts created by the switch

m. sending out frames as soon as the destination MAC address is read

n. deposits all frames into a common memory buffer

o. address contained within the frame header for Ethernet encapsulations

p. sending a frame out a port based on the unicast MAC address

q. filters traffic based on Layer 2 addressing; no longer used in today's networks

r. forwarding frames after the first 64 bytes are read

s. delay inherent in sending data from the source to the destination

t. area of a LAN where frames from two different sources can run into each other

u. can either send or receive, but not both at the same time

v. filters traffic at Layer 2; capable of microsegmentation

Term

___ collision domains

___ hub

___ MAC

___ bridge

___ switch

___ virtual circuit

___ router

___ carrier sense multiple access collision detect (CSMA/CD)

___ half duplex

___ full duplex

___ network interface card (NIC)

___ latency

___ bit time (slot time)

___ attenuation

___ cyclic redundancy check (CRC)

___ store and forward

___ flooding

___ filtering

___ port-based memory buffering

___ shared memory buffering

___ frame check sequence (FCS)

___ cut-through

___ fragment-free

Vocabulary Exercise: Completion

Directions: Complete the paragraphs that follow by filling in appropriate words and phrases.

A hub is a Layer _ device and is sometimes referred to as a LAN or Ethernet _____ or a _____ repeater.

Ethernet is fundamentally a _____ technology through which all users on a given LAN segment compete for the same available _____. If two or more devices try to transmit at the same time, a _____ occurs.

Bridges and switches operate at the _____ layer of the Open System Interconnection (OSI) model. These Layer 2 devices make forwarding decisions based on _____ addresses contained within the headers of transmitted data frames.

Switches create a _____ circuit between two connected devices that want to communicate, which is a dedicated communication path established between the two devices.

The implementation of a switch on the network is called _____, which creates a collision-free environment for each device connected to the switch.

The disadvantage of Layer 2 devices is that they forward _____ frames to all connected devices on the network.

Routers operate at the _____ layer of the OSI model and will not forward _____ frames unless specifically programmed to do so. Therefore, routers reduce the size of both the _____ domains and the _____ domains in a network.

_____ is Ethernet's access control method. Originally Ethernet was a _____ technology, which allows hosts to either transmit or receive at one time, but not both.

_____ Ethernet significantly improves network performance without the expense of installing new media and offers ___ percent of the bandwidth in both directions because it is a _____-free environment. Frames sent by the two connected end nodes cannot collide, because the end nodes use two separate circuits in the Category 3, 5, 5e, or 6 cable.

Nodes that are attached to hubs that share their connection to a switch port must operate in _____ mode, because the end stations must be able to detect collisions.

_____, or delay, is the time a frame or a packet takes to travel from the source station to the final destination.

The networking device that adds the *most* latency is a _____.

A __-byte frame is the smallest frame that allows CSMA/CD to operate properly, and a ____-byte frame is the largest.

The distance that a LAN can cover is limited due to _____, which means that the signal weakens as it travels through the network.

CSMA/CD Process Flow Chart Exercise

Draw a flow chart of the CSMA/CD process. Your flow chart should have a minimum of six steps, but can have more.

Figure 4-1   CSMA/CD Process Flow Chart

Concept Questions

In your own words, describe the function of a router.

_____

_____

In your own words, explain how CSMA/CD works in half-duplex Ethernet LANs.

_____

_____

_____

_____

_____

_____

Journal Entry

In your own words, describe the various forms of latency. Draw a topology with several networking devices between two communicating computers as part of your explanation.

Figure 4-2   Your Topology Illustrating Latency

The forms of latency are as follows:

- _____
  _____
  _____

- _____
  _____
  _____

- _____
  _____
  _____

Introduction to LAN Switching

In the past, repeaters were used in most Ethernet networks. Because Ethernet is a broadcast topology, adding repeaters enlarged the domain in which collisions can occur causing a reduction in the bandwidth available for data transfer. Bridges were soon introduced to create multiple collision domains. Bridges evolved into switches capable of microsegmenting a LAN, effectively creating a collision-free environment.

Many modern switches are capable of performing varied and complex tasks in the network. For example, some switches are capable of performing both Layer 2 and Layer 3 functions. The exercises in this section focus on how a switch or router makes a decision to forward data on its way to the intended destination. This section provides an introduction to network segmentation and describes the basics of switch operation.

Vocabulary Exercise: Completion

Directions: Complete the paragraphs that follow by filling in appropriate words and phrases.

Networks can be divided into smaller units by a _____ or a _____. These smaller units are called _____. Each unit is its own _____ domain.

Bridges and switches are Layer _ devices that forward data frames based on the _____. Bridges read the _____ MAC address of the data packets to discover the devices that are on each segment. The _____ MAC address is used to populate the MAC address table.

Bridges and switches provide segmentation within a single network or subnetwork. _____ provide connectivity between networks and subnetworks. _____ do not forward broadcasts, whereas switches and bridges do forward broadcast frames.

When a switch or bridge is first initialized, the MAC address table is empty. With an empty MAC address table, the switch or bridge must _____ each frame to all connected ports other than the one on which the frame arrived. Sending a frame out all connected ports except the incoming port is called _____ the frame. Once a switch or a bridge has learned the topology, it can stop frames from propagating onto segments where the destination does not exist. This process is called _____.

Building the MAC Address Table Exercise

Assume that the bridge in Figure 4-3 was just installed and powered on. The MAC address table is empty. Answer the following questions and complete the table as the bridge would build it.

Figure 4-3   Building the MAC Address Table

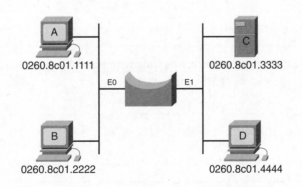

Port	MAC Address

1. Host A sends a unicast frame to Host B. What entry, if any, will the bridge enter in its MAC address table?

   _____

   What will the bridge do with the frame?

   _____

   _____

2. Host B responds to Host A with a unicast frame. What entry, if any, will the bridge enter in its MAC address table?

   _____

   What will the bridge do with the frame?

   _____

   _____

3. Host D attempts to log in to Server C. What entry, if any, will the bridge enter in its MAC address table?

   _____

   What will the bridge do with the frame?

   _____

   _____

4. Server C responds to the login attempt by Host D. What entry, if any, will the bridge enter in its MAC address table?

   _____

   _____

   What will the bridge do with the frame?

   _____

   _____

5. Server C sends out a broadcast frame announcing its services to all potential clients. What entry, if any, will the bridge enter in its MAC address table?

   _____

   What will the bridge do with the frame?

   _____

   _____

Concept Questions

Explain the difference between bridges and switches.

_____

_____

_____

Explain why routers cause more latency than do switches, bridges, or hubs.

_____

_____

_____

_____

_____

_____

Explain the difference between Layer 2 and Layer 3 switching.

_____

_____

_____

_____

_____

_____

_____

Journal Entry

Explain how a Layer 2 switch can operate in three different switching modes. Include in your explanation how much of the frame each method reads, what kind of error checking is performed by the method, and what the method's latency is. Include a diagram of a frame illustrating each method.

_____

_____

_____

_____

_____

_____

_____

_____

Figure 4-4   Solution Diagram

Switch Operation

The exercises in this section reinforce your knowledge of collision and broadcast domains. In addition, you revisit the concept of picking the correct cable when connecting devices.

Vocabulary Exercise: Completion

Directions: Complete the paragraphs that follow by filling in appropriate words and phrases.

Even though the LAN switch reduces the size of _____ domains, all hosts connected to the switch are still in the same _____ domain.

Communication in a network occurs in three ways. The most common way of communication is by _____ transmissions, in which one transmitter tries to reach one receiver.

Another way to communicate is known as a _____ transmission, in which one transmitter tries to reach only a subset, or a group, of the entire segment.

The final way to communicate is as a _____, in which one transmitter tries to reach all the receivers in the network.

When a device wants to send out a Layer 2 broadcast, the destination MAC address in the frame is set to all 1s. A broadcast MAC address is _____ in hexadecimal. By setting the destination to this value, all the devices will accept and process the broadcasted frame.

Routers are used to segment both _____ and _____ domains.

Collision and Broadcast Domains Exercises

Using Figure 4-5, circle all the collision domains with a solid line and all the broadcast domains with a dashed line.

Figure 4-5   Collision and Broadcast Domains: Topology 1

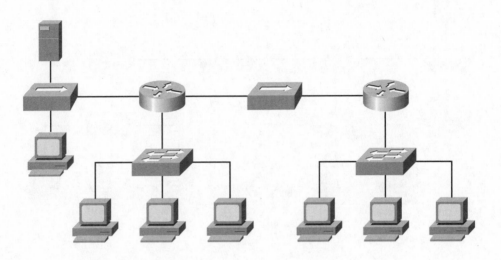

Using Figure 4-6, circle all the collision domains with a solid line and all the broadcast domains with a dashed line.

Figure 4-6   Collision and Broadcast Domains: Topology 2

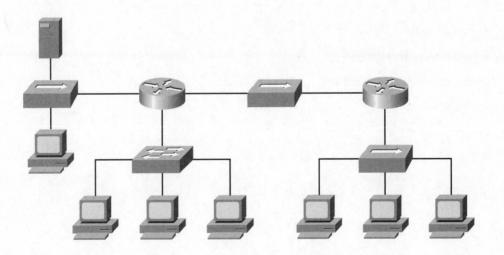

Using Figure 4-7, circle all the collision domains with a solid line and all the broadcast domains with a dashed line.

Figure 4-7   Collision and Broadcast Domains: Topology 3

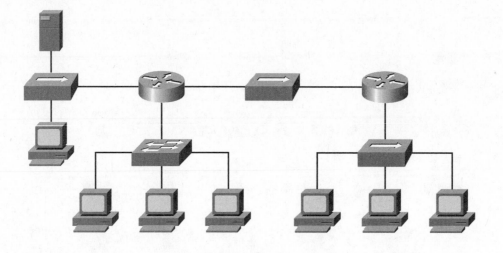

Choose the Correct Cable Exercise

In the blank provided, indicate with an **S** for straight-through and **C** for cross which type of cable would be used to connect the two devices.

_____ Hub to workstation or server

_____ Switch to switch

_____ Hub to hub

_____ Router to PC

_____ Switch to router

_____ Workstation to workstation

_____ Switch to workstation or server

_____ Switch to hub

_____ Router to router

Lab Exercises

There are no Lab Exercises for this chapter.

CHAPTER 5

LAN Design and Switches

The Study Guide portion of this chapter uses a combination of matching, fill in the blank, open-ended question, and identification exercises to test your knowledge on the theory of LAN design and the three-layer hierarchical model.

There are no Lab Exercises for this chapter.

Study Guide

LAN Design

A network design needs to be functional, scalable, adaptable, and manageable. Designing a network can be a challenge because it involves much more than just connecting users. A network requires many features in order to be reliable and available based on the needs of the organization. Understanding the basic design process and structure of networks will help you to ensure that you are meeting the needs of the network users.

Vocabulary Exercise: Matching

Match the definition on the left with a term on the right. This exercise is not necessarily a one-to-one matching. Some definitions may be used more than once and some terms may have multiple definitions.

Definition

a. area of a LAN where frames from two different sources can run into each other

b. switching between ports of different bandwidth

c. local and remote user access

d. cabling that runs between wiring closets

e. responsible for fast switching, redundancy, and remote access

f. cabling that runs from workstations to the wiring closet

g. primary wiring closet where POP is located

h. all ports on the switch have the same bandwidth

i. responsible for policy-based connectivity

j. secondary wiring closet

k. used to connect cable runs from user to the Layer 2 LAN switch ports

l. used to interconnect the various IDFs to the central MDF

Term

___ access layer

___ distribution layer

___ core layer

___ main distribution facility (MDF)

___ intermediate distribution facility (IDF)

___ collision domain

___ horizontal cross-connect (HCC)

___ vertical cross-connect (VCC)

___ asymmetric switching

___ symmetric switching

___ backbone or vertical cabling

Vocabulary Exercise: Completion

Complete the paragraphs that follow by filling in appropriate words and phrases.

The first step in designing a LAN is to _____ and _____ the goals of the design.

Most LANs are designed to meet four major requirements:

- _____, which enables users to meet their job requirements with speed and reliability

- _____, which means that the network should be designed with future growth in mind

- _____, which means that the network design will easily incorporate new technologies

- _____, which facilitates network monitoring

Servers can be categorized into two distinct classes:

- _____ servers support all the users on the network by offering services such as e-mail, DNS, and corporate intranet access.

- _____ servers support a specific set of users, offering services such as word processing and file sharing specific to that group's needs.

_____ servers should be placed in the MDF, and _____ servers should be placed in the IDF closest to the users who need it.

One of the most important components to consider when designing a network is the _____ because the _____ layer is the cause of most network problems.

_____ cable should be used in the backbone and risers in all cable designs. _____ _____ cable should be used in the horizontal runs. The cable upgrade should take priority over any other necessary changes.

The _____ standard specifies that every device connected to the network should be linked to a central location with horizontal cabling. In a simple star topology, this central location is the _____ (acronym) and includes one or more _____ used to connect the Layer 1 horizontal cabling coming into the wiring closet from work areas to the Layer 2 LAN switch inside the wiring closet.

In larger network environments, multiple wiring closets are often needed. These extra or secondary wiring closets are referred to as _____.

A _____ in each wiring closet is used to interconnect the various IDFs to the central MDF. The type of backbone or vertical cabling used is usually _____ because the cable lengths are typically longer than the 100-meter limit for Category 5e UTP cable.

Complete Figure 5-1 by filling in all the missing text labeling the components of this multibuilding campus LAN.

Figure 5-1   Extended Star Topology in a Multibuilding Campus

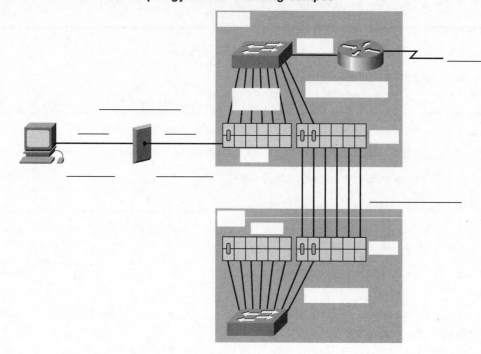

Devices at Layer 2 determine the size of the _____ domains, which can negatively affect the performance of a network. Switches are capable of _____, which effectively eliminates _____ because only one host is attached to a switch port.

A _____ is a Layer 3 device and is one of the most intelligent devices in the network topology. Layer 3 devices allow communication between segments based on Layer 3 _____.

A router does not forward _____, such as Address Resolution Protocol (ARP) requests. Therefore, routers segment _____ domains.

VLAN implementation combines Layer 2 switching and Layer 3 routing technologies to limit both _____ domains and _____ domains. To communicate between two VLANs, you must use a _____.

Concept Questions

List at least four issues that should be addressed in LAN design if you are going to maximize bandwidth and performance.

- _____
- _____
- _____
- _____
- _____
- _____

List and briefly explain the four steps of an effective LAN design methodology.

_____

_____

_____

_____

_____

_____

_____

_____

_____

_____

_____

_____

List three purposes of Layer 2 devices.

■ _____

■ _____

■ _____

Why do you want vertical cabling to have a greater data capacity than horizontal cabling?

_____

_____

What factors need to be considered when choosing whether to use a router or switch at a particular point in the network?

_____

_____

_____

LAN Switches

Cisco recommends designing your networks based on the three-layer hierarchical model. Each of the LAN design layers discussed in this chapter requires switches and routers that are best suited for the task at hand. The features, functions, and technical specifications for each switch or router vary based on the LAN design layer for which the device is intended. For the best network performance, it is important to understand the role of each layer and then choose the device that best suits the layer requirements.

Vocabulary Exercise: Completion

Directions: Complete the paragraphs that follow by filling in appropriate words and phrases.

The hierarchical design model includes the following three layers:

■ The _____ layer provides users in workgroups access to the network.

■ The _____ layer provides policy-based connectivity.

■ The _____ layer provides optimal transport between sites.

The _____ layer is the entry point for user workstations and servers to the network. In a campus LAN, the device used at this layer is typically a _____.

This layer's functions also include _____ filtering, which allows switches to direct frames to only the port the destination is attached to, and _____, which creates collision-free connections.

The purpose of the _____ layer is to provide a boundary definition in which packet manipulation can take place. Networks are segmented into _____ domains by this layer. Policies can be applied and access control lists can filter packets. This layer isolates network problems to the workgroups in which they occur and prevents these problems from affecting the _____ layer. Switches in this layer operate at Layer _____ and Layer _____.

The _____ layer is responsible for fast packet switching across the backbone, whether WANs or LANs, and providing redundant paths.

Three-Layer Hierarchical Model Exercise

For each of the following figures, indicate whether the scenario is an **access** layer function, **distribution** layer function, or **core** layer function.

Figure 5-2   Scenario 1

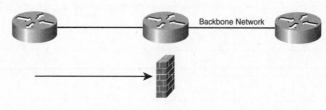

In Figure 5-2, an access control list (denoted by the firewall) is implemented to prevent unnecessary network traffic on the backbone network. The _____ layer is responsible for the implementation of access control lists.

Figure 5-3   Scenario 2

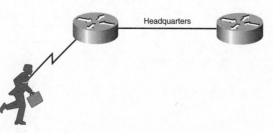

In Figure 5-3, a telecommuter is shown connecting to headquarters through a modem connection. The _____ layer is responsible for allowing telecommuters to connect to the network.

Figure 5-4   Scenario 3

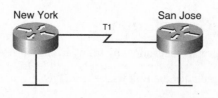

In Figure 5-4, the _____ layer is responsible for connecting New York and San Jose across a T1 link.

Figure 5-5   Scenario 4

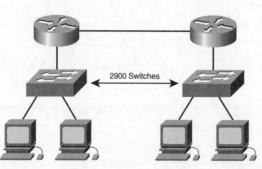

In Figure 5-5, the _____ layer is using 2900 series switches to connect end users to the network.

Figure 5-6 Scenario 5

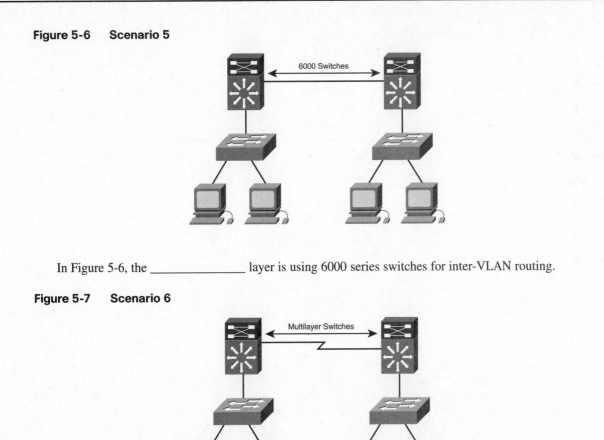

In Figure 5-6, the _____ layer is using 6000 series switches for inter-VLAN routing.

Figure 5-7 Scenario 6

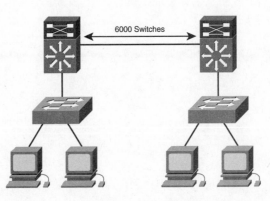

In Figure 5-7, the _____ layer is using multilayer switches for fast switching and no packet manipulation.

Figure 5-8 Scenario 7

In Figure 5-8, the _____ layer is using multilayer switches to summarize OSPF routes.

Concept Questions

List three functions of the access layer.

- _____

- _____

- _____

List five functions of the distribution layer

- _____
- _____
- _____
- _____
- _____

List three functions of the core layer

- _____
- _____
- _____

Lab Exercises

There are no Lab Exercises for this chapter.

CHAPTER 6

Catalyst Switch Configuration

The Study Guide portion of this chapter uses a combination of fill in the blank and unique custom exercises to test your knowledge of switch configuration.

The Lab Exercises portion of this chapter includes all of the online curriculum labs as well as a challenge lab to ensure that you have mastered the practical, hands-on skills needed about switch configuration.

Study Guide

Starting the Switch

The exercises in this section focus on knowledge and skills you need before you begin to configure switches. You should know how to connect to a switch to configure it. You should also be able to interpret the LEDs.

Vocabulary Exercise: Completion

Complete the paragraphs that follow by filling in appropriate words and phrases.

Before configuring a switch, make sure it is plugged in and that the system LED is _____. If the system LED is _____, the switch failed _____ and is not operational. To configure a switch, use a _____ cable to connect the _____ port on the back of the switch to a _____ port on the back of the computer. If using HyperTerminal as your terminal emulator, you need to configure the port settings in the Properties dialog box as follows:

Bit per second: _____

Data bits: _____

Parity: _____

Stop bits: _____

Flow control: _____

However, simply clicking the _____ button enters these settings automatically.

After the switch boots, you are asked the following question:

```
Would you like to enter the initial configuration dialog? [yes/no]:
```

Just as with a router, answering **yes** begins Setup mode, in which you are asked a series of basic configuration questions. If you accidentally answer yes or want to abort Setup mode, use the key combination _____. You can also enter setup mode from the privileged user prompt by entering the command _____.

Answering **no** gives you the Switch> prompt, from which you can use the _____ to configure the switch.

You will find that many of the basic configurations of a switch are identical to what you have already learned for a router. This is because both devices use the Cisco _____. For example, to enter privileged mode, type the _____ command. The prompt changes to _____. To enter global configuration mode, enter _____. The prompt changes to _____. At any point in your configuration, you can enter the _____ key to get help.

Switch LED Interpretation Exercise

The LEDs on a switch provide a wealth of information about the switch. Being able to interpret the meanings of different LED colors and statuses is important for troubleshooting problems and gives the network engineer a snapshot of current network performance. Refer to Figure 6-1 and answer the following questions about a switch's LED.

Figure 6-1   Four Main LEDs on the Catalyst 2950 Switch

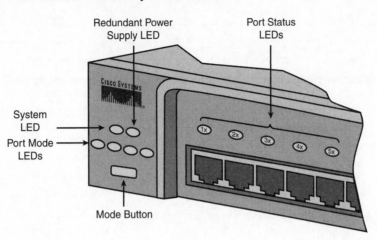

System LED

The system LED is off. What does this indicate?

_____

What does an amber system LED indicate?

_____

RPS LED

What does the acronym RPS stand for?

_____

The RPS LED is off. What does this indicate?

_____

What does a green RPS LED indicate?

_____

What does a flashing green RPS LED indicate?

_____

What does an amber RPS LED indicate?

_____

What does a flashing amber RPS LED indicate?

_____

Port Mode LEDs

The STAT mode is currently selected. What does each of the following indicate?

The port LED is off.

_____

The port LED is flashing green.

_____

The port LED is amber (three reasons).

_____

_____

_____

The UTIL mode is currently selected. Briefly explain this mode's purpose assuming the switch is a 2950-24.

_____

_____

_____

For the DUPLEX and SPEED modes, what does a green LED indicate?

_____

For the SPEED mode, what does a flashing green LED indicate?

_____

Configuring the Switch

The exercises in this section focus on switch configuration.

Learn Basic Switch Commands Exercise

For this exercise, refer to Figure 6-2 to answer the following configuration questions. The router is named DIST because it is a distribution layer router and the switch is named ALSW because it is an access layer switch.

Figure 6-2   Basic Switch Configuration Exercise

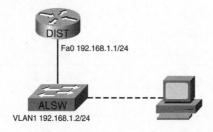

For a Catalyst 2950 switch, the following default configurations are in place:

IP address: _____

CDP: _____

100BASE-T port: _____

Spanning tree: _____

Console password: _____

The default hostname is _____. Record the switch prompt and command to change the hostname to ALSW.

_____

Record the switch prompt and command to configure **class** as the encrypted enable password.

_____

Record the switch prompt and command to enter console line configuration mode.

_____

Record the switch prompt and command to configure the password **cisco** on the console line.

_____

Record the switch prompt and command to require users to log in.

_____

The preceding commands should also be entered on the Telnet lines. A switch has _____ Telnet lines numbered _____ to _____. The command to enter Telnet line configuration mode is _____.

A switch should be assigned an IP address so that it can be accessed remotely using Telnet or other TCP/IP applications. Referring to Figure 6-2, record the switch prompt and commands to enter interface configuration mode and then to configure ALSW with an IP address. Then record the command to activate the interface.

_____

_____

_____

To receive and send IP packets, the management interface needs a default gateway. Record the switch prompt and command to configure ALSW with a default gateway.

ALSW(config)#**ip default-gateway 192.168.1.1**

The ports on a switch are defaulted to autonegotiate the speed and duplex. However, it is a good idea to set these to the correct setting for the attached host, because autonegotiation can produce unpredictable results. Record the switch prompt and commands to configure a port's interface to 100 Mbps and full duplex.

_____

Note: The commands must be entered in this order. If you try to enter the **duplex** command first, you will get the message: "Duplex can not be set until speed is set to non-auto value."

_____

_____

To enhance security, you can statically configure a port with the MAC address of the host or hosts attached to that port. Record the switch prompt and command to statically configure the MAC address 0005.9a3c.7800 on port 6.

_____

Instead of explicitly configuring the MAC address, you can configure a port to dynamically learn MAC addresses and have them "stick" to the current configuration. When in interface configuration mode for port 5, you need several commands to enable the following security requirements. Be sure the port is in access mode and do not forget to enable port security. Set the maximum addresses that the port can learn to **1** and set the port to shut down if another MAC address is detected.

_____

_____

_____

_____

_____

Briefly explain what each of the following port security violation keywords enables on the interface:

- **protect**— _____
  _____
  _____

- **restrict**— _____
  _____

- **shutdown**— _____
  _____
  _____
  _____

Lab Exercises

Command Reference

In the following table, record the command, including the correct switch prompt, that fits the description for a 2950 Catalyst switch. Fill in any blanks with the appropriate missing information.

Command	Description
	Displays the current VLAN configuration
	Removes the VLAN database from Flash memory
	Enables the virtual interface for _____, the default VLAN on the switch
	Configures a gateway to allow IP packets an exit
	Forces full-duplex operation on an interface
	Enables auto-duplex configuration
	Forces half-duplex operation on an interface
	Forces 10-Mbps operation on an interface
	Forces 100-Mbps operation on an interface
	Enables autospeed configuration
	Displays the current MAC address forwarding table
	Deletes all learned entries from the current MAC address forwarding table
address table for Fa0/1	Sets a static address of *aaaa.aaaa.aaaa* in the MAC
	Enables port security on the interface
	Sets the maximum number of MAC addresses that a port can learn to 1
	Configures the port to dynamically learn MAC addresses and "stick" them to the configuration
	Configures the port to be disabled if there is a security violation
	Configures the port to send a SNMP trap if a security violation is detected but does not shut down the port
	Configures the port to drop all frames from unknown source MAC addresses after the maximum configured MAC addresses have been learned

Curriculum Lab 6-1: Verifying Default Switch Configuration (6.2.1)

Figure 6-3   Topology for Lab 6-1

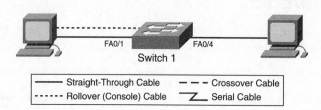

FA0/1
Switch 1
FA0/4

——— Straight-Through Cable   — — — Crossover Cable
· · · · · · Rollover (Console) Cable   ⌐Z⌐ Serial Cable

Objective

Investigate the default configuration of a 2900 series switch.

Background/Preparation

Cable a network that is similar to the one in Figure 6-3. The 2950 series switch produced the configuration output in this lab. Another switch might produce different output. You should execute the following steps on each switch unless you are specifically instructed otherwise. Instructions are also provide for the 1900 series switch, which initially displays a User Interface Menu. Select the **Command Line** option from the menu to perform the steps for this lab.

Start a HyperTerminal session.

Implement the procedure documented in Appendix B, "Erasing and Reloading the Switch," on all switches before you continue with this lab.

General Configuration Tips

- Use the question mark (?) and arrow keys to help to enter commands.

- Each command mode restricts the set of available commands. If you have difficulty entering a command, check the prompt and then enter **?** for a list of available commands. You might be using the wrong command mode or the wrong syntax.

- To disable a feature, enter the keyword **no** before the command, such as **no ip address**.

- Save the configuration changes to NVRAM so that you do not lose the changes if there is a system reload or power outage.

Table 6-1 shows the switch command modes that you should be familiar with for all labs in this chapter.

Table 6-1   Switch Command Modes

Command Mode	Access Method	Switch Prompt Displayed	Exit Method
User EXEC	Log in.	Switch>	Use the logout command.
Privileged EXEC	From user EXEC mode, enter the **enable** command.	Switch#	To exit to user EXEC mode, use the **disable**, **exit**, or **logout** command.
Global configuration	From privileged EXEC mode, enter the **configure terminal** command.	Switch (config)#	To exit to privileged EXEC mode, use the **exit** or **end** command, or press **Ctrl-Z**.
Interface configuration	From global configuration mode, enter the **interface** *type number* command, such as **interface serial 0**.	Switch (config-if)#	To exit to global configuration mode, use the **exit** command.

Task 1: Enter Privileged Mode

Step 1. Privileged mode gives access to all the switch commands. Because many of the privileged mode commands configure operating parameters, privileged mode access should be password-protected to prevent unauthorized use. The privileged mode command set includes those commands that are contained in user EXEC mode, as well as the **configure** command through which access to the remaining command modes is gained.

```
Switch>enable
Switch#
```

Step 2. Notice that the prompt changed to reflect privileged EXEC mode.

Task 2: Examine the Current Switch Configuration

Step 1. Examine the current running configuration file:

```
Switch#show running-config
```

How many Ethernet and Fast Ethernet interfaces does the switch have?

_____

What is the range of values shown for the VTY lines? _____

Step 2. Examine the current contents of NVRAM.

```
Switch#show startup-config
%% Non-volatile configuration memory is not present
```

Why does the switch give this response?

_____

Step 3. Show the current IP address of the switch.

```
Switch#show interface VLAN 1
```

Is an IP address set on the switch? _____

What is the MAC address of this virtual switch interface?

_____

Is this interface up? _____

Step 4. You can show the IP properties of the interface by entering the following command:

```
Switch#show ip interface VLAN 1
```

Step 5. The following command provides the switch IP address information for the 1900:

```
#show ip
```

Task 3: Get Cisco IOS Software Information

Examine the version information that the switch reports.

```
Switch#show version
```

What is the IOS version that the switch is running?

_____

What is the system image filename?

_____

What is the base MAC address of this switch?

_____

Is the switch running Enterprise Edition software?

_____

Is the switch running Enhanced Image software, indicated by the letters EA in the IOS filename (2950 series)? _____

Task 4: Examine the Fast Ethernet Interfaces

Examine the default properties of the Fast Ethernet interfaces. As an example, examine the properties of the fourth interface:

Switch#**show interface fastethernet 0/4**

1900:

`#show interface fastethernet 0/26`

_____

Note: This is a trunk port.

or

`#show interface ethernet 0/4`

_____

Note: This is an access port.

2950:

`#show interface fastethernet 0/4`

_____

Note: This can be a trunk or access port.

or

`#show interface gigabitethernet 0/1`

_____

Note: This can be a trunk or access port.

Is the interface up or down? _____

What event would make an interface go up?

_____

What is the MAC address of the interface?

_____

What is the speed and duplex setting of the interface?

_____

Task 5: Examine VLAN Information

Examine the default VLAN settings of the switch.

```
Switch#show vlan
```

What is the name of VLAN 1? _____

Which ports are in this VLAN? _____

Is VLAN 1 active? _____

What type of VLAN is the default VLAN? _____

Task 6: Examine Flash Memory (1900: Skip to Step 8)

Examine the contents of the Flash directory.

```
Switch#dir flash:
```

or

```
Switch#show flash
```

Name the files and directories found.

_____

_____

_____

_____

_____

Task 7: Examine the Startup Configuration File

Step 1.   To see the contents of the startup configuration file, enter the **show running-config** command in privileged EXEC mode.

```
Switch#show startup-config
```

Step 2.   The switch responds with the following:

```
Non-volatile configuration memory is not present
```

Why does this message appear?

_____

Step 3.   Copy the current configuration to NVRAM. This step ensures that any changes made will be available to the switch if there is a reload or if the power goes off.

```
Switch#copy running-config startup-config
Destination filename [startup-config]?
Building configuration...
[OK]
Switch#
```

Step 4.   Show the contents of NVRAM.

Switch#**show startup-config**

What is displayed now?

_____

_____

Task 8: Exit the Switch

Step 1.   Exit to the switch welcome screen.

Switch#**exit**

Step 2.   Remove and store the cables and adapter.

Curriculum Lab 6-2: Basic Switch Configuration (6.2.2)

Figure 6-4   Topology for Lab 6-2

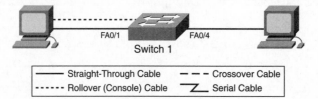

FA0/1   FA0/4

Switch 1

——— Straight-Through Cable   — — — Crossover Cable
------- Rollover (Console) Cable   ⁔ Serial Cable

Table 6-2   Lab Equipment Configuration

Switch Designation	Switch Name	Enable Secret Password	Enable/VTY/Console Password
Switch 1	ALSwitch	**class**	**cisco**

Objectives

- Configure a switch with a name and an IP address.

- Configure passwords to ensure that access to the CLI is secured.

- Configure switch port speed and duplex properties for an interface.

- Save the active configuration.

- View the switch browser interface.

Background/Preparation

Cable a network that is similar to the one in Figure 6-4. The 2950 series switch produced the configuration output used in this lab. Another switch might produce different output. You should execute the following steps on each switch unless you are specifically instructed otherwise. Instructions are also provided for the 1900 series switch, which initially displays a User Interface Menu. Select the **Command Line** option from the menu to perform the steps for this lab.

Start a HyperTerminal session.

Implement the procedure documented in Appendix B before you continue with this lab.

Task 1: Enter Privileged Mode

Step 1.   Privileged mode gives access to all the switch commands. Because many of the privileged mode commands configure operating parameters, privileged mode access should be password-protected to prevent unauthorized use. The privileged mode command set includes those commands that are contained in user EXEC mode, as well as the **configure** command through which access to the remaining command modes is gained.

```
Switch>enable
Switch#
```

1900:

```
>enable
#
```

Step 2.   Notice that the prompt changed to reflect privileged EXEC mode.

Task 2: Examine the Current Switch Configuration

Step 1.   Examine the current running configuration file.

```
Switch#show running-config
```

How many Ethernet or Fast Ethernet interfaces does the switch have? _____

What is the range of values shown for the VTY lines? _____

Step 2.   Examine the current contents of NVRAM.

```
Switch#show startup-config
startup-config is not present
```

Why does the switch give this response?

_____

Task 3: Assign a Name to the Switch

Step 1.   Enter enable and then configuration mode. Configuration mode allows the management of the switch. Enter the name by which this switch will be referred, ALSwitch.

```
Switch#configure terminal
Enter configuration commands, one per line. End with Ctrl+Z.
Switch(config)#hostname ALSwitch
ALSwitch(config)#exit
```

Step 2.   Notice that the prompt changed to reflect its new name. Type **exit** or press **Ctrl-Z** to go back into privileged mode.

Task 4: Examine the Current Running Configuration

Examine the current configuration to verify that there is no configuration except for the hostname.

```
ALSwitch#show running-config
```

Are passwords set on lines? _____

What does the configuration show as the hostname of this switch? _____

Task 5: Set the Access Passwords (1900: Skip to Task 6)

Enter config-line mode for the console. Set the password on this line to **cisco** for login. Configure the VTY lines 5 to 15 with the password **cisco**.

```
ALSwitch#configure terminal
Enter configuration commands, one per line. End with Ctrl-Z.
ALSwitch(config)#line con 0
ALSwitch(config-line)#password cisco
ALSwitch(config-line)#login

ALSwitch(config-line)#line vty 0 15
ALSwitch(config-line)#password cisco
ALSwitch(config-line)#login

ALSwitch(config-line)#exit
```

Task 6: Set the Command Mode Passwords

Set the enable password to **cisco** and the enable secret password to **class**.

```
ALSwitch(config)#enable password cisco

ALSwitch(config)#enable secret class
```

1900:

```
ALSwitch(config)#enable password level 15 cisco

ALSwitch(config)#enable secret class
```

Which password takes precedence: the enable password or the enable secret password? _____

Task 7: Configure Layer 3 Access to the Switch

Step 1.   Set the IP address of the switch to 192.168.1.2 with a subnet mask of 255.255.255.0. Note that this is done on the internal virtual interface VLAN 1.

```
ALSwitch(config)#interface VLAN 1
ALSwitch(config-if)#ip address 192.168.1.2 255.255.255.0
ALSwitch(config-if)#exit
```

1900:

```
ALSwitch(config)#ip address 192.168.1.2 255.255.255.0
ALSwitch(config)#exit
```

Step 2.   Set the default gateway for the switch and the default management VLAN as 192.168.1.1.

```
ALSwitch(config)#ip default-gateway 192.168.1.1
ALSwitch(config)#exit
```

1900:

```
ALSwitch(config)#ip default-gateway 192.168.1.1
ALSwitch(config)#exit
```

Task 8: Verify the Management LAN Settings (1900: Skip to Step 9)

Step 1.   Verify the interface settings on VLAN 1.

```
ALSwitch#show interface VLAN 1
```

What is the bandwidth on this interface?

_____

What are the VLAN states? VLAN1 is _____, and line protocol is _____.

Step 2.   Enable the virtual interface using the **no shutdown** command.

```
ALSwitch(config)#interface VLAN 1
ALSwitch(config-if)#no shutdown
ALSwitch(config-if)#exit
```

What is the queuing strategy? _____

Task 9: Configure Port Speed and Duplex Properties for a Fast Ethernet Interface

Note: 1900 switch access ports can operate only at 10 Mbps, but duplex can be set to full. If the switch has 10/100-Mbps trunk ports, the speed and duplex can be set for these.

Step 1.   Prepare to configure the fastethernet 0/4 interface.

```
ALSwitch#configure terminal
```

Step 2.   Enter configuration commands, one per line. End with **Ctrl-Z**.

```
ALSwitch(config)#interface fastethernet 0/4
```

Step 3.   Set the port speed of interface fastethernet 0/4 to 100 Mbps and to operate in full-duplex mode.

```
ALSwitch(config-if)#speed 100
ALSwitch(config-if)#duplex full
```

Step 4.   If you know that the devices that are connected to a port must operate at a certain speed and in duplex mode, you should set the interface to that speed and mode.

Task 10: Verify the Settings on a Fast Ethernet Interface

```
ALSwitch#show interface fastethernet 0/4
```

Task 11: Save the Configuration

Step 1.   The basic configuration of the switch has just been completed. Back up the running configuration file to NVRAM. This ensures that the changes made will not be lost if the system is rebooted or loses power.

```
ALSwitch#copy running-config startup-config
Destination filename [startup-config]?[Enter]
Building configuration...
[OK]
ALSwitch#
```

Step 2. The configuration is automatically saved to NVRAM within approximately 1 minute of enter- ing a command. To save the configuration to a TFTP server, enter the following:

```
ALSwitch#copy nvram tftp://tftp server ip address/destination_filename
```

Task 12: Examine the Startup Configuration File (1900: Skip to Task 13)

To see the configuration that is stored in NVRAM, enter **show startup-config** from privileged EXEC (enable) mode.

```
ALSwitch#show startup-config
```

What is displayed?

_____

Are all the changes that were entered recorded in the file? _____

Task 13: Remove the Enable and Enable Secret Passwords

```
ALSwitch#configure terminal
Enter configuration commands, one per line.  End with Ctrl+Z.
ALSwitch(config)#no enable password
ALSwitch(config)#no enable secret
```

1900:

```
ALSwitch(config)#no enable password level 15
ALSwitch(config)#no enable secret
```

Task 14: Access the Switch Web Interface

Step 1. Access to the web interface of the switch may be on by default. If it is not on, issue the following command:

```
ALSwitch(config)#ip http server
```

Step 2. Start your web browser.

Step 3. Type the switch IP address into the Location field (Netscape) or Address field (Internet Explorer) and press **Enter**.

Step 4. Because you have not secured access to the switch web interface, you will get a web page from the switch. You will not be asked to supply a username or password.

Task 15: Exit the Switch

Step 1. Exit to the switch welcome screen.

```
Switch#exit
```

Step 2. Remove and store the cables and adapter.

Curriculum Lab 6-3: Managing the MAC Address Table (6.2.3)

Figure 6-5   Topology for Lab 6-3

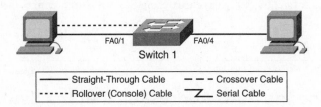

Table 6-3   Lab Equipment Configuration

Switch Designation	Switch Name	VLAN 1 IP Address	Default Gateway IP Address	Subnet Mask
Switch 1	ALSwitch	192.168.1.2	192.168.1.1	255.255.255.0

The enable secret password is **class**.

The enable, VTY, and console password is **cisco**.

Objective

Create a basic switch configuration and manage the switch MAC table.

Background/Preparation

Cable a network that is similar to the one in Figure 6-5. The 2950 switch produced the configuration output in this lab. Another switch might produce different output. Instructions are also provided for the 1900 series switch, which initially displays a User Interface Menu. Select the **Command Line** option from the menu to perform the steps for this lab.

Start a HyperTerminal session.

Implement the procedure documented in Appendix B on all switches before you continue with this lab.

Task 1: Configure the Switch

Configure the hostname and passwords, as well as the management VLAN 1 settings for the switch, as indicated in Table 6-3. If you have problems while performing this configuration, refer to Curriculum Lab 6-2, "Basic Switch Configuration (6.2.2)."

Task 2: Configure the Hosts that Are Attached to the Switch

Configure the hosts to use the same IP subnet for addresses, masks, and the default gateway as the switch.

Task 3: Verify Connectivity

To verify that the hosts and switch are correctly configured, ping the switch IP address from the hosts.

Were the pings successful? _____

If the answer is no, troubleshoot the hosts and switch configurations.

Task 4: Record the Host MAC Addresses

Determine and record the Layer 2 addresses of the PC network interface cards.

If you are running Windows 98, check using **Start > Run > winipcfg**. Click **More info**.

If you are running Windows 2000 or higher, check using **Start > Run > cmd > ipconfig /all**.

PC1: _____

PC4: _____

Task 5: Determine the MAC Addresses that the Switch Has Learned

Determine the MAC addresses that the switch has learned by using the **show mac-address-table** command at the privileged EXEC mode prompt.

ALSwitch#**show mac-address-table**

How many dynamic addresses exist? _____

How many MAC addresses exist? _____

How many addresses have been user defined? _____

Do the MAC addresses match the host MAC addresses? _____

Task 6: Determine the show mac-address-table Options

Step 1.   Determine the options that the **show mac-address-table** command has by using the **?** option.

ALSwitch#**show mac-address-table ?**

How many options are available for the **show mac-address-table** command? _____

Step 2.   Show the MAC address table for the switch.

How many total MAC addresses exist? _____

Step 3.   Show only the MAC address table addresses that were learned dynamically.

How many exist? _____

Task 7: Clear the MAC Address Table

Remove the existing MAC addresses by using the **clear mac-address-table** command from the privileged EXEC mode prompt.

ALSwitch#**clear mac-address-table dynamic**

Task 8: Verify the Results

Verify that the **mac-address-table** was cleared.

ALSwitch#**show mac-address-table**

How many MAC addresses exist now? _____

How many dynamic addresses exist? _____

Task 9: Determine the clear mac-address-table Options

Determine the options that are available with the command **clear mac-address-table ?** at the privileged EXEC mode prompt.

```
ALSwitch#clear mac-address-table ?
```

How many options exist? _____

In what circumstances would these options be used?

_____

Task 10: Examine the MAC Table Again

Step 1.   Look at the MAC address table again by using the **show mac-address-table** command at the privileged EXEC mode prompt.

```
ALSwitch#show mac-address-table
```

How many dynamic addresses exist? _____

Why did this change from the last display?

_____

_____

Step 2.   If the table has not changed yet, ping the switch IP address from the hosts two times each and repeat step 10.

Task 11: Exit the Switch

Step 1.   Exit to the switch welcome screen.

```
Switch#exit
```

Step 2.   Remove and store the cables and adapter.

Curriculum Lab 6-4: Configuring Static MAC Addresses (6.2.4)

Figure 6-6   Topology for Lab 6-4

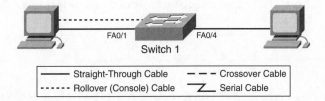

Table 6-4   Lab Equipment Configuration

Switch Designation	Switch Name	VLAN 1 IP Address	Default Gateway IP Address	Subnet Mask
Switch 1	ALSwitch	192.168.1.2	192.168.1.1	255.255.255.0

The enable secret password is **class**.

The enable, VTY, and console password is **cisco**.

Objectives

- Create a static address entry in the switch MAC table.

- Remove the created static MAC address entry.

Background/Preparation

Cable a network that is similar to the one in Figure 6-6. The 2950 switch produced the configuration output in this lab. Another switch might produce different output. Instructions are also provided for the 1900 series switch, which initially displays a User Interface Menu. Select the **Command Line** option from the menu to perform the steps for this lab.

Start a HyperTerminal session.

Implement the procedure documented in Appendix B on all switches before you continue with this lab.

Task 1: Configure the Switch

Configure the hostname and passwords, as well as the management VLAN 1 settings for the switch, as indicated in Table 6-4. If you have problems while performing this configuration, refer to Curriculum Lab 6-2, "Basic Switch Configuration (6.2.2)."

Task 2: Configure the Hosts Attached to the Switch

Configure the hosts to use the same IP subnet for addresses, masks, and the default gateway as the switch.

Task 3: Verify Connectivity

To verify that the hosts and switch are correctly configured, ping the switch IP address from the hosts.

Were the pings successful? _____

If the answer is no, troubleshoot the hosts and switch configurations.

Task 4: Record the Host MAC Addresses

Determine and record the Layer 2 addresses of the PC network interface cards.

If you are running Windows 98, check using **Start > Run > winipcfg**. Click **More info**.

If you are running Windows 2000, check using **Start > Run > cmd > ipconfig /all**.

PC1: _____

PC4: _____

Task 5: Determine the MAC Addresses that the Switch Has Learned

Determine the MAC addresses that the switch has learned by using the **show mac-address-table** command at the privileged EXEC mode prompt.

```
ALSwitch#show mac-address-table
```

How many dynamic addresses exist? _____

How many MAC addresses exist? _____

Do the MAC addresses match the host MAC addresses? _____

Task 6: Determine the mac-address-table Options

Determine the options that the **mac-address-table** command has by using the **?** option.

ALSwitch(config)#**mac-address-table ?**

How many options are available for the **mac-address-table** command? _____

There is an option to set a static MAC address in the table. Under what circumstances would you use this option?

_____

Task 7: Set Up a Static MAC Address

Set up a static MAC address on Fast Ethernet interface 0/4. Use the address that was recorded for PC4 in Task 4. The MAC address 00e0.2917.1884 is used in the example statement only.

ALSwitch(config)#**mac-address-table static 00e0.2917.1884 interface fastethernet 0/4 vlan 1**

1900:

ALSwitch(config)#**mac-address-table permanent 00e0.2917.1884 ethernet 0/4**

Task 8: Verify the Results

Verify the MAC address table entries.

ALSwitch#**show mac-address-table**

How many MAC addresses exist now? _____

How many static addresses exist? _____

Under what circumstances can other static or dynamic learning of addresses occur on switch port 4?

_____

Task 9: Remove the Static MAC Entry

You might need to reverse the **static mac-address-table** entry. To do this, enter configuration mode and reverse the command by putting **no** in front of the entire old command string. The MAC address 00e0.2917.1884 is used in the example statement only. Use the MAC address that was recorded for the host on port 0/4.

ALSwitch(config)#**no mac-address-table static 00e0.2917.1884 interface**
    fastethernet 0/4 vlan 1

1900:

ALSwitch(config)#**no mac-address-table permanent 00e0.2917.1884**
    ethernet 0/4

Task 10: Verify the Results

Verify that the static MAC address was cleared.

```
ALSwitch#show mac-address-table static
```

How many static MAC addresses exist now? _____

Task 11: Exit the Switch

Step 1.   Exit to the switch welcome screen.

```
Switch#exit
```

Step 2.   Remove and store the cables and adapter.

Curriculum Lab 6-5: Configuring Port Security (6.2.5)

Figure 6-7   Topology for Lab 6-5

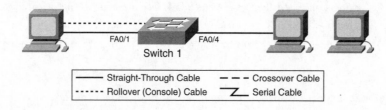

Table 6-5   Lab Equipment Configuration

Switch Designation	Switch Name	VLAN 1 IP Address	Default Gateway IP Address	Subnet Mask
Switch 1	ALSwitch	192.168.1.2	192.168.1.1	255.255.255.0

The enable secret password is **class**.

The enable, VTY, and console password is **cisco**.

Objectives

- Create and verify a basic switch configuration.

- Configure port security on individual Fast Ethernet ports.

Background/Preparation

Cable a network that is similar to the one in Figure 6-7. The 2950 switch produced the configuration output in this lab. Another switch might produce different output. Instructions are also provided for the 1900 series switch, which initially displays a User Interface Menu. Select the **Command Line** option from the menu to perform the steps for this lab.

Start a HyperTerminal session.

Implement the procedure documented in Appendix B on all switches before you continue with this lab.

Task 1: Configure the Switch

Configure the hostname and passwords, as well as the management VLAN 1 settings for the switch, as indicated in Table 6-5. If you have problems while performing this configuration, refer to Curriculum Lab 6-2, "Basic Switch Configuration (6.2.2)."

Task 2: Configure the Hosts Attached to the Switch

Step 1.   Configure the hosts to use the same IP subnet for addresses, masks, and the default gateway as the switch.

Step 2.   You need a third host for this lab. You must configure this host with the address 192.168.1.7. The subnet mask is 255.255.255.0 and the default gateway is 192.168.1.1. Do *not* connect this PC to the switch yet.

Task 3: Verify Connectivity

To verify that the hosts and switch are configured correctly, ping the switch IP address from the hosts.

Were the pings successful? _____

If the answer is no, troubleshoot the hosts and switch configurations.

Task 4: Record the Hosts' MAC Addresses

Determine and record the Layer 2 addresses of the PC network interface cards.

If you are running Windows 98, check using **Start > Run > winipcfg**. Click **More info**.

If you are running Windows 2000, check using **Start > Run > cmd > ipconfig /all**.

PC1: _____

PC4: _____

Task 5: Determine the MAC Addresses that the Switch Has Learned

Determine the MAC addresses that the switch has learned by using the **show mac-address-table** command at the privileged EXEC mode prompt.

```
ALSwitch#show mac-address-table
```

How many dynamic addresses exist? _____

How many MAC addresses exist? _____

Do the MAC addresses match the host MAC addresses? _____

Task 6: Determine the mac-address-table Options

Determine the options that the **mac-address-table** command has by using the **?** option.

```
ALSwitch(config)#mac-address-table ?
```

Task 7: Set Up a Static MAC Address

Set up a static MAC address on Fast Ethernet interface 0/4. Use the address that was recorded for PC4 in Task 4. The MAC address 00e0.2917.1884 is used in the example statement only.

```
ALSwitch(config)#mac-address-table static 00e0.2917.1884 interface
fastethernet 0/4 vlan 1
```

1900:

```
ALSwitch(config)#mac-address-table permanent 00e0.2917.1884 ethernet
0/4
```

Task 8: Verify the Results

Verify the MAC address table entries.

```
ALSwitch#show mac-address-table
```

How many static addresses exist? _____

Task 9: List Port Security Options

Step 1. Determine options for setting port security on interface Fast Ethernet 0/4. Enter **switchport port security ?** from the interface configuration prompt for Fast Ethernet port 0/4.

```
ALSwitch(config)#interface fastethernet 0/4
```

```
ALSwitch(config-if)#switchport port-security  ?
  aging        Port-security aging commands
  mac-address  Secure mac address
  maximum      Max secure addresses
  violation    Security violation mode
  <cr>
```

1900:

```
ALSwitch(config)#interface ethernet 0/4
ALSwitch(config-if)#port secure ?
  max-mac-count  Maximum number of addresses allowed on the port
  <cr>
```

Step 2. Allow the switch port fastethernet 0/4 to accept only one device by using the following commands:

```
ALSwitch(config-if)#switchport mode access
ALSwitch(config-if)#switchport port-security
ALSwitch(config-if)#switchport port-security mac-address sticky
```

1900:

```
ALSwitch(config-if)#port secure
```

Task 10: Verify the Results

Step 1. Verify the MAC address table entries.

```
ALSwitch#show mac-address-table
```

How are the address types listed for the two MAC addresses?

_____

_____

Step 2. Show port security settings.

```
ALSwitch#show port-security
```

1900:

```
ALSwitch#show mac-address-table security
```

Task 11: Show the Running Configuration File

Do some statements directly reflect the security implementation in the listing of the running configuration?

_____

What do those statements mean?

Task 12: Limit the Number of Hosts Per Port

Step 1.   On interface fastethernet 0/4, set the port security maximum MAC count to 1.

```
ALSwitch(config)#interface fastethernet 0/4
ALSwitch(config-if)#switchport port-security maximum 1
```

1900:

```
ALSwitch(config)#interface Ethernet 0/4
ALSwitch(config-if)#port secure max-mac-count 1
```

Step 2.   Disconnect the PC that is attached to fastethernet 0/4 and connect to that port the PC that has been given the IP address 192.168.1.7. This PC has not been attached to the switch. To generate some traffic, you might need to ping the switch address 192.168.1.2.

Record your observations.

Task 13: Configure the Port to Shut Down if a Security Violation Occurs

Step 1.   If a security violation occurs, you should shut down the interface. Make the port security action **shutdown**.

2950

```
ALSwitch(config-if)#switchport port-security violation shutdown
```

1900:

```
ALSwitch(config-if)#port security action shutdown
```

In addition to shutdown, what other violation options are available with port security?

_____

Step 2.   If necessary, ping the switch address 192.168.1.2 from the PC 192.168.1.7 that is now connected to interface fastethernet 0/4. This ensures that there is traffic from the PC to the switch.

Record your observations.

_____

Task 14: Show Port 0/4 Configuration Information

To see the configuration information for Fast Ethernet port 0/4, enter **show interface fastethernet 0/4** at the privileged EXEC mode prompt.

```
ALSwitch#show interface fastethernet 0/4
```

1900:

```
ALSwitch#show interface ethernet 0/4
```

What is the state of this interface?

Fast Ethernet 0/4 is _____, and line protocol is _____.

Task 15: Reactivate the Port

Step 1.   If a security violation occurs and the port is shut down, use the **no shutdown** command to reactivate it.

Step 2.   Try this a few times, switching between the original port 0/4 host and the new one. Plug in the original host, enter the **no shutdown** command on the interface, and ping by using the DOS window. You have to repeat the ping multiple times or use the **ping 192.168.1.2 -n 200** command. This sets the number of ping packets to 200 instead of 4. Then, switch hosts and try again.

Task 16: Exit the Switch

Step 1.   Exit to the switch welcome screen.

```
Switch#exit
```

Step 2. Remove and store the cables and adapter.

Curriculum Lab 6-6: Add, Move, and Change MAC Addresses (6.2.6)

Figure 6-8   Topology for Lab 6-6

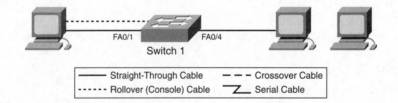

Table 6-6   Lab Equipment Configuration

Switch Designation	Switch Name	VLAN 1 IP Address	Default Gateway IP Address	Subnet Mask
Switch 1	ALSwitch	192.168.1.2	192.168.1.1	255.255.255.0

The enable secret password is **class**.

The enable, VTY, and console password is **cisco**.

Objectives

- Create and verify a basic switch configuration.

- Move a PC from one switch port to another and add a new PC to the switch.

Background/Preparation

Cable a network that is similar to the one in Figure 6-8. The 2950 switch produced the configuration output in this lab. Another switch might produce different output. Instructions are also provided for the 1900 series switch, which initially displays a User Interface Menu. Select the **Command Line** option from the menu to perform the steps for this lab.

Start a HyperTerminal session.

Implement the procedure documented in Appendix B before you continue with this lab.

Task 1: Configure the Switch

Configure the hostname and passwords, as well as the management VLAN 1 settings for the switch, as indicated in Table 6-6. If you have problems while performing this configuration, refer to Curriculum Lab 6-2, "Basic Switch Configuration (6.2.2)."

Task 2: Configure the Hosts Attached to the Switch

Step 1.   Configure the hosts to use the same IP subnet for addresses, masks, and the default gateway as the switch.

Step 2.   You need a third host for this lab. You must configure it with the address 192.168.1.7. The subnet mask is 255.255.255.0 and the default gateway is 192.168.1.1. Do *not* connect this PC to the switch yet.

Task 3: Verify Connectivity

To verify that the hosts and switch are correctly configured, ping the switch IP address from the hosts.

Were the pings successful? _____

If the answer is no, troubleshoot the hosts and switch configurations.

Task 4: Record the Hosts' MAC Addresses

Determine and record the Layer 2 addresses of the PC network interface cards.

If you are running Windows 98, check using **Start > Run > winipcfg**. Click **More info**.

If you are running Windows 2000, check using **Start > Run > cmd > ipconfig /all**.

PC1: _____

PC4: _____

Task 5: Determine the MAC Addresses that the Switch Has Learned

Determine the MAC addresses that the switch has learned by using the **show mac-address-table** command at the privileged EXEC mode prompt.

```
ALSwitch#show mac-address-table
```

How many dynamic addresses exist? _____

How many MAC addresses exist? _____

Do the MAC addresses match the host MAC addresses? _____

Task 6: Determine the mac-address-table Options

Determine the options that the **mac-address-table** command has by using the **?** option.

```
ALSwitch(config)#mac-address-table ?
```

Task 7: Set Up a Static MAC Address

Set up a static MAC address on Fast Ethernet interface 0/4. Use the address that was recorded for PC4 in Step 4. The MAC address 00e0.2917.1884 is used in the example statement only.

```
ALSwitch(config)#mac-address-table static 00e0.2917.1884 interface
  fastethernet 0/4 vlan 1
```

1900:

```
ALSwitch(config)#mac-address-table permanent 00e0.2917.1884 ethernet
  0/4
```

Task 8: Verify the Results

Verify the MAC address table entries.

```
ALSwitch#show mac-address-table
```

How many static addresses exist? _____

Task 9: List Port Security Options

Step 1. Determine options for setting port security on interface Fast Ethernet 0/4. Enter **switchport port security ?** from the interface configuration prompt for Fast Ethernet port 0/4.

```
ALSwitch(config)#interface fastethernet 0/4
ALSwitch(config-if)#port security ?
  aging          Port-security aging commands
  mac-address    Secure mac address
  maximum        Max secure addrs
  violation      Security Violation Mode
  <cr>
```

1900:

```
ALSwitch(config)#interface ethernet 0/4
ALSwitch(config-if)#port secure ?
  max-mac-count  Maximum number of addresses allowed on the port
  <cr>
```

Step 2. Allow the switch port Fast Ethernet 0/4 to accept only one device by using the following commands:

```
ALSwitch(config-if)#switchport mode access
ALSwitch(config-if)#switchport port-security
ALSwitch(config-if)#switchport port-security mac-address sticky
```

1900:

```
ALSwitch(config-if)#port secure
```

Task 10: Verify the Results

Verify the MAC address table entries.

```
ALSwitch#show mac-address-table
```

How are the address types listed for the two MAC addresses?

Task 11: Show the Running Configuration File

In the listing of the running configuration, do some statements directly reflect the security implementation? _____

What do those statements mean?

Task 12: Limit the Number of Hosts Per Port

Step 1.   On interface Fast Ethernet 0/4, set the port security maximum MAC count to 1.

```
ALSwitch(config)#interface fastethernet 0/4
ALSwitch(config-if)#switchport port-security maximum 1
```

1900:

```
ALSwitch(config)#interface ethernet 0/4
ALSwitch(config-if)#port secure max-mac-count 1
```

Step 2.   Disconnect the PC that is attached to Fast Ethernet 0/4 and connect to that port the PC that has been given the IP address 192.168.1.7. This PC has not been attached to the switch. To generate some traffic, ping the switch address 192.168.1.2 with the **-n 50** option. For example, use **ping 192.168.1.2 -n 50**, where 50 is the number of pings sent.

Task 13: Move Host

Step 1.   Reconnect the PC that had previously been connected to Fast Ethernet 0/4 to Fast Ethernet 0/8. The PC has been moved to a new location. This could be to another VLAN, but in this instance, all switch ports are in VLAN 1 and network 192.168.1.0.

Step 2.   From this PC on Fast Ethernet 0/8, ping **192.168.1.2 -n 50.**

Was this successful? _____

Why or why not?

_____

Step 3.   Show the MAC address table.

```
ALSwitch#show mac-address-table
```

Step 4.   Record the VLAN 1 MAC addresses that are displayed.

Task 14: Clear the MAC Address Table

Step 1.   Clear the MAC address table. Doing so unlocks the MAC addresses from security and allows a new address to be registered.

```
ALSwitch#clear mac-address-table dynamic
```

Step 2.   From the PC on the Fast Ethernet 0/8, ping **192.168.1.2 -n 50**.

Was this successful? _____

Step 3.   If not, troubleshoot as necessary.

Task 15: Change the Security Settings

Step 1.   Show the MAC address table.

```
ALSwitch#show mac-address-table
```

Step 2.   Observe that Fast Ethernet 0/4 is secure but that the security should be applied to the machine on port 0/8 because that is the machine that was moved form port 0/4. Remove port security from interface Fast Ethernet 0/4.

```
ALSwitch(config)#interface fastethernet 0/4
ALSwitch(config-if)#no switchport port-security
ALSwitch(config-if)#no switchport port-security mac-address sticky
ALSwitch(config-if)#no switchport port-security mac-address sticky
0008.744d.8ee2
ALSwitch(config-if)#shutdown
ALSwitch(config-if)#no shutdown
```

1900:

```
ALSwitch(config)#interface ethernet 0/4
ALSwitch(config-if)#no port secure
```

Step 3.   Apply port security with a **max-mac-count** of 1 to interface Fast Ethernet 0/8.

```
ALSwitch(config)#interface fastethernet 0/8
ALSwitch(config-if)#switchport mode access
ALSwitch(config-if)#switchport port-security
ALSwitch(config-if)#switchport port-security mac-address sticky
ALSwitch(config-if)#switchport port-security maximum 1
```

1900:

```
ALSwitch(config)#interface ethernet 0/8
ALSwitch(config-if)#port secure max-mac-count 1
```

Step 4.   Clear the MAC address table.

Note: You also could have cleared individual entries.

ALSwitch#**clear mac-address-table dynamic**

Task 16: Verify the Results

Verify that the MAC address table has been cleared.

ALSwitch#**show mac-address-table**

Can all PCs still successfully ping each other? _____

If not, troubleshoot the switch and PCs.

Task 17: Exit the Switch

Step 1.   Exit to the switch welcome screen.

```
Switch#exit
```

Step 2.   Remove and store the cables and adapter.

Curriculum Lab 6-7: Managing Switch Operating System Files (6.2.7a)

Figure 6-9   Topology for Lab 6-7

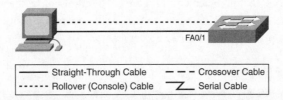

	Straight-Through Cable	– – –	Crossover Cable
------	Rollover (Console) Cable	Z	Serial Cable

Table 6-7   Lab Equipment Configuration

Switch Designation	Switch Name	VLAN 1 IP Address	Default Gateway IP Address
Switch 1	ALSwitch	192.168.1.2	192.168.1.1

The enable secret password is **class**.

The enable, VTY, and console password is **cisco**.

The subnet mask is 255.255.255.0.

Objectives

- Create and verify a basic switch configuration.

- Back up the switch IOS to a TFTP server and then restore it.

Background/Preparation

Cable a network that is similar to the one in Figure 6-9. The 2950 switch produced the configuration output in this lab. Another switch might produce different output. Instructions are also provided for the 1900 series switch, which initially displays a User Interface Menu. Select the **Command Line** option from the menu to perform the steps for this lab.

Start a HyperTerminal session.

Implement the procedure documented in Appendix B before you continue with this lab.

Task 1: Configure the Switch

Configure the hostname and passwords, as well as the management VLAN 1 settings for the switch, as indicated in Table 6-7. If you have problems while performing this configuration, refer to Curriculum Lab 6-2, "Basic Switch Configuration (6.2.2)."

Task 2: Configure the Host that Is Attached to the Switch

Configure the host to use the same subnet for addresses, masks, and the default gateway as the switch. This host will act as the TFTP server in this lab. Be sure to take note of the IP address that is assigned.

Task 3: Verify Connectivity

To verify that the host and switch are configured correctly, ping the switch IP address from the host.

Was the ping successful? _____

If the answer is no, troubleshoot the host and switch configurations.

Task 4: Start and Configure the Cisco TFTP Server

Step 1.   The TFTP server that is indicated in Figure 6-10 might not be the same one that is used in this classroom. Please check with the instructor for the operating instructions for the TFTP server that is used in place of the Cisco TFTP server.

Figure 6-10   TFTP Server Startup

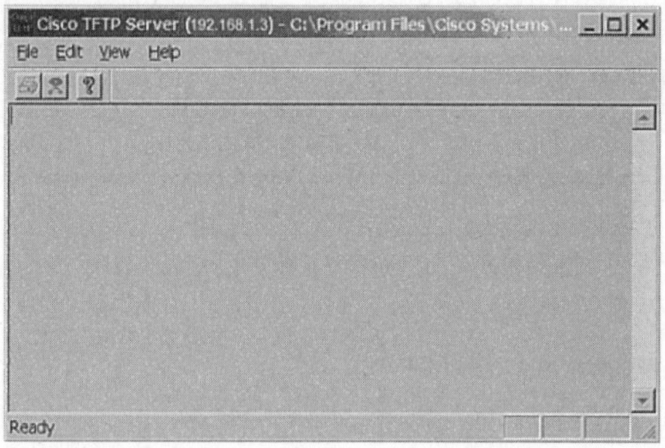

Step 2.   After the TFTP server is running and shows the proper address configured on the workstation, proceed to the actual copying of the Cisco IOS Software image file to the switch.

Task 5: Copy the IOS Image to the TFTP Server (1900: Skip to Step 9)

Step 1.   Before you try to copy the files, verify that the TFTP server is running.

What is the IP address of the TFTP server? _____

Step 2.   From the console session, enter **show flash**.

What is the name and length of the IOS image that is stored in Flash memory?

_____

What attributes can you identify from codes in the IOS filename?

_____

Step 3.   From the console session in privileged EXEC mode, enter the **copy flash tftp** command. At the prompt, enter the IP address of the TFTP server.

Task 6: Verify the Transfer to the TFTP Server

Step 1.   Verify the transfer by choosing **View > Log File** to check the TFTP server log file. The output should look something like the following:

```
Mon Sep 19 14:10:08 2005: Receiving 'c2950-i6q4l2-mz.121-9.EA1.bin' in binary
mode
Mon Sep 19 14:11:14 2005: Successful.
```

Step 2.   Verify the Flash image size in the TFTP server directory. To locate it, choose **View > Options**. This shows the TFTP server root directory. It should be similar to the following, unless the default directories were changed:

C:\Program Files\Cisco Systems\Cisco TFTP Server

Step 3.   Locate this directory by using File Manager and look at the detail listing of the file. The file length in the **show flash** command should be the same file size as the file stored on the TFTP server. If the file sizes are not identical, check with your instructor.

Task 7: Copy the IOS Image from the TFTP Server

Step 1.   Now that the IOS image is backed up, the image must be tested and the IOS image must be restored to the switch. Verify again that the TFTP server is running, is sharing a network with the switch, and can be reached by pinging the TFTP server IP address.

Record the IP address of the TFTP server. _____

Step 2.   Start the actual copying, from the privileged EXEC prompt. Do *not* interrupt the process!

The switch might prompt you to overwrite Flash. Will the image fit in available Flash? _____

What is the size of the file that is being loaded? _____

What happened on the switch console screen as the file was being downloaded?

_____

Was the verification successful? _____

Was the whole operation successful? _____

Task 8: Test the Restored IOS Image

Step 1.   To verify that the switch IOS image is correct, cycle the switch power and observe the startup process to confirm that there were no Flash errors. If there were no errors, then the switch's IOS image should have started correctly. Also, to further verify the IOS image in Flash, issue the **show version** command, which shows output similar to the following:

```
System image file is "flash:/c2950-i6q4I2-mz.121-9.EA1.bin"
```

Step 2.   Exit to the switch welcome screen.

```
Switch#exit
```

Step 3.   Remove and store the cables and adapter.

Task 9: Procedure for 1900 Switch Firmware Upgrade Using TFTP

Step 1. Select option **F** to go to the Firmware Configuration menu from the Main Menu. An example of the Firmware Configuration menu follows:

```
          Catalyst 1900 - Firmware Configuration


        — — — — — — — — — · System Information  — — — — — — — — — — —
        FLASH:  1024K bytes
        V8.01.00   : Enterprise Edition
        Upgrade status:
        No upgrade currently in progress.


        — — — — — — — — — · Settings  — — — — — — — — — — — — — —
        [S] TFTP Server name or IP address          192.168.1.3
        [F] Filename for firmware upgrades          cat1900.bin
        [A] Accept upgrade transfer from other hosts    Enabled


        — — — — — — — — — · Actions  — — — — — — — — — — — — — — — ·
        [U] System XMODEM upgrade            [D] Download test subsystem
(XMODEM)
        [T] System TFTP upgrade             [X] Exit to Main Menu
```

Step 2. Ensure that the switch firmware upgrade file is available on the TFTP server in the default directory. The file can be copied from another networking device or computer or it can be downloaded to the server from an appropriate website.

Step 3. Select option **S** from the Firmware Configuration menu and enter the IP address of the server where the switch upgrade file is located.

Step 4. Select option **F** from the Firmware Configuration menu and enter the name of the firmware-upgrade file.

Step 5. Select **T** from the Firmware Configuration menu to initiate the upgrade.

Step 6. Verify that the upgrade is in progress by checking the Upgrade Status field of the Firmware Configuration menu. If the upgrade is in progress, the field reads "in-progress."

Step 7. When the transfer is complete, the switch resets automatically and executes the newly downloaded firmware.

Caution: During the transfer of the upgrade file, the switch might not respond to commands for as long as 1 minute. This is normal and correct. If you interrupt the transfer by turning the switch off and on, the firmware could be corrupted.

Curriculum Lab 6-8: Managing Switch Startup Configuration Files (6.2.7b)

Figure 6-11   Topology for Lab 6-8

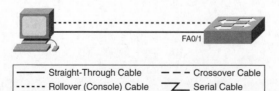

Straight-Through Cable	– – – Crossover Cable
····· Rollover (Console) Cable	Serial Cable

Table 6-8   Lab Equipment Configuration

Switch Designation	Switch Name	VLAN 1 IP Address	Default Gateway IP Address
Switch 1	ALSwitch	192.168.1.2	192.168.1.1

The enable secret password is **class**.

The enable, VTY, and console password is **cisco**.

The subnet mask is 255.255.255.0.

Objectives

- Create and verify a basic switch configuration.

- Back up the switch startup configuration file to a TFTP server and then restore it.

Background/Preparation

Cable a network that is similar to the one in Figure 6-11. The 2950 switch produced the configuration output in this lab. Another switch might produce different output. Instructions are also provided for the 1900 series switch, which initially displays a User Interface Menu. Select the **Command Line** option from the menu to perform the steps for this lab.

Start a HyperTerminal session.

Implement the procedure documented in Appendix B before you continue with this lab.

Task 1: Configure the Switch

Configure the hostname and passwords, as well as the management VLAN 1 settings for the switch, as indicated in Table 6-8. If you have problems while performing this configuration, refer to Curriculum Lab 6-2, "Basic Switch Configuration (6.2.2)."

Task 2: Configure the Host that Is Attached to the Switch

Configure the host to use the same subnet for addresses, masks, and the default gateway as the switch. This host will act as the TFTP server in this lab. Be sure to take note of the IP address that is assigned.

Task 3: Verify Connectivity

To verify that the host and switch are correctly configured, ping the switch IP address from the host.

Was the ping successful? _____

If the answer is no, troubleshoot the host and switch configurations.

Task 4: Start and Configure the Cisco TFTP Server

Step 1.   The TFTP server that is indicated in Figure 6-12 might not be the same one that is used in this classroom. Please check with the instructor for the operating instructions for the TFTP server that is used in place of the Cisco TFTP server.

Figure 6-12   TFTP Server Startup

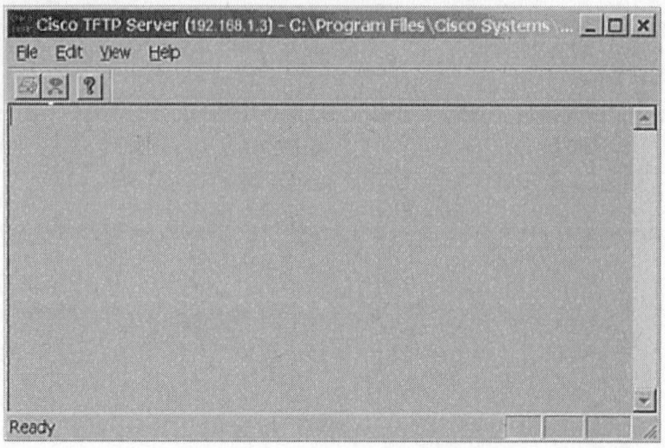

Step 2.   After the TFTP server is running and shows the proper address configured on the workstation, proceed to the copying of the configuration file to the switch.

Task 5: Copy the Startup Configuration File to the TFTP Server

Step 1.   Before you try to copy the files, verify that the TFTP server is running.

What is the IP address of the TFTP server?

_____

Step 2.   From the console session, enter **show flash**.

For a 2900 switch, use the command **dir flash:**.

Note: This function is not supported on the 1900 switch.

What is the name and length of the startup configuration image that is stored in Flash?

Step 3.   From the console session in privileged EXEC mode, enter **copy running-config startup-config** to make sure that the running configuration file is saved to the startup configuration file. Then, enter the **copy startup-config tftp** command. At the prompt, enter the IP address of the TFTP server.

```
ALSwitch#copy running-config startup-config
Destination filename [startup-config]?[Enter]
Building configuration...
[OK]

ALSwitch#copy startup-config tftp
Address or name of remote host []? 192.168.1.10
Destination filename [alswitch-confg]?[Enter]
!!
1278 bytes copied in 1.60 secs (744 bytes/sec)
ALSwitch#
```

Step 4.   For the 1900 switch, use the following to copy the switch configuration file to a TFTP server:

```
ALSwitch#copy  nvram  tftp://192.168.1.3/alswitch-config
```

```
Configuration upload is successfully completed
```

Task 6: Verify the Transfer to the TFTP Server

Step 1.   Verify the transfer by choosing **View > Log File** to check the TFTP server log file. The output should look something like the following:

```
Mon Sep 19 14:10:08 2005: Receiving 'alswitch.confg' file from 192.168.1.2 in
binary mode
Mon Sep 19 14:11:14 2005: Successful.
```

Step 2.   Verify the Flash image size in the TFTP server directory. To locate it, choose **View > Options**. This shows the TFTP server root directory. It should be similar to the following, unless the default directories were changed:

C:\Program Files\Cisco Systems\Cisco TFTP Server

Step 3.   Locate this directory by using File Manager and look at the detail listing of the file. The file length in the **show flash** command should be the same file size as the file that is stored on the TFTP server. If the file sizes are not identical, check with your instructor.

Task 7: Restore the Startup Configuration File from the TFTP Server

Step 1.   Erase the switch startup configuration file.

Step 2.   Reconfigure the file with just the VLAN 1 IP address of 192.168.1.2 255.255.255.0.

Step 3.   Enter the command **copy tftp startup-config** at the privileged EXEC mode prompt. Do *not* interrupt the process!

```
Switch#copy tftp startup-config
Address or name of remote host []? 192.168.1.10
Source filename []? alswitch-confg
Destination filename [startup-config]?
Accessing tftp://192.168.1.10/alswitch-confg...
Loading alswitch-confg from 192.168.1.10 (via VLAN1): !
[OK - 744 bytes]
[OK]
1278 bytes copied in 0.100 secs
Switch#
```

Was the operation successful? _____

Step 4.   For the 1900 switch, use the following to copy the switch configuration file to a TFTP server:

```
ALSwitch#copy tftp://192.168.1.10/alswitch-config nvram
TFTP successfully downloaded configuration file
```

Task 8: Test the Restored Startup Configuration Image (Not Supported on the 1900)

Step 1.   To verify that the switch image is correct, cycle the switch power and observe the switch prompt. If it has returned to the name that was assigned to it in the original configuration, the restoration is complete. Enter the command **show startup-config** to see the restored configuration.

Step 2.   Exit to the switch welcome screen.

```
Switch#exit
```

Step 3.   Remove and store the cables and adapter.

Curriculum Lab 6-9: Password Recovery Procedure on a Catalyst 2900 Series Switch (6.2.8)

Figure 6-13   Topology for Lab 6-9

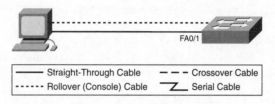

FA0/1

Straight-Through Cable	– – – Crossover Cable
------ Rollover (Console) Cable	Serial Cable

Table 6-9   Lab Equipment Configuration

Switch Designation	Switch Name	VLAN 1 IP Address	Default Gateway IP Address
Switch 1	ALSwitch	192.168.1.2	192.168.1.1

The enable secret password is **class**.

The enable, VTY, and console password is **cisco**.

The subnet mask is 255.255.255.0.

Objectives

- Create a basic switch configuration and verify it.

- Change passwords so that the password recovery procedure must be performed.

Background/Preparation

Cable a network that is similar to the one in Figure 6-13. The 2950 switch produced the configuration output in this lab. Another switch might produce different output. Instructions are also provided for the 1900 series switch, which initially displays a User Interface Menu. Select the **Command Line** option from the menu to perform the steps for this lab.

Start a HyperTerminal session.

Implement the procedure documented in Appendix B before you continue with this lab.

Task 1: Configure the Switch

Configure the hostname and passwords, as well as the management VLAN 1 settings for the switch, as indicated in Table 6-9. If you have problems while performing this configuration, refer to Curriculum Lab 6-2, "Basic Switch Configuration (6.2.2)."

Task 2: Configure the Host that Is Attached to the Switch

Configure the host to use the same subnet for addresses, masks, and the default gateway as the switch.

Task 3: Verify Connectivity

To verify that the host and switch are correctly configured, ping the switch IP address from the host.

Was the ping successful? _____

If the answer is no, troubleshoot the host and switch configurations.

Task 4: Reset the Console Password

Step 1.   Have a classmate change the console and VTY passwords on the switch, save the changes to the **startup-config** file, and reload the switch.

Step 2.   Without knowing the passwords, try to gain access to the switch.

Task 5: Recover Access to the Switch

Step 1.   Make sure that a PC is connected to the console port and that a HyperTerminal window is open.

Step 2.   Power off the switch and turn it back on by holding down the **Mode** button on the front of the switch at the same time that the switch is powered on. Release the **Mode** button a few seconds after the STAT LED is no longer lit.

Step 3.   The following should be displayed:

```
C2950 Boot Loader (C2950-HBOOT-M) Version 12.1(11r)EA1, RELEASE SOFTWARE (fc1)
Compiled Mon 22-Jul-02 18:57 by antonino
WS-C2950-24 starting...
Base ethernet MAC Address: 00:0a:b7:72:2b:40
Xmodem file system is available.
```

The system has been interrupted prior to initializing the Flash file system. The following commands initialize the Flash file system and finish loading the operating system software:

```
flash_init
load_helper
boot
```

Step 4.   To initialize the file system and finish loading the operating system:

Type **flash_init**.

Type **load_helper**.

Type **dir flash:** (do not forget to type the : (colon) after the word *flash*).

Step 5.   Type **rename flash:config.text flash:config.old** to rename the configuration file.

This file contains the password definition.

Task 6: Restart the System

Step 1.   Type **boot** to boot the system.

Step 2.   Enter **N** at the prompt to start the Setup program.

```
Continue with the configuration dialog? [yes/no] : N
```

Step 3.   Type **rename flash:config.old flash:config.text** to rename the configuration file with its original name at the privileged EXEC mode prompt.

Step 4.　Copy the configuration file into memory.

```
Switch#copy flash:config.text system:running-config
Source filename [config.text]?[Enter]
Destination filename [running-config][Enter]
```

Step 5.　The configuration file is now reloaded, so change the old unknown passwords and save the new configuration.

```
ALSwitch#configure terminal
ALSwitch(config)#no enable secret
ALSwitch(config)#enable password Cisco
ALSwitch(config)#line console 0
ALSwitch(config-line)#password cisco
ALSwitch(config-line)#exit
ALSwitch(config)#line vty 0 15
ALSwitch(config-line)#password cisco
ALSwitch(config-line)#exit
ALSwitch(config)#exit
ALSwitch#copy running-config startup-config
Destination filename [startup-config]?[Enter]
Building configuration...
[OK]
ALSwitch#
```

Step 6.　Power cycle the switch and verify that the passwords are now functional.

If they are not, repeat the procedure.

After you complete the previous steps, log off (by typing **exit**) and turn all the devices off. Then, remove and store the cables and adapter.

Task 7: Procedure for the 1900 and 2800 Switches

Check the boot firmware version number from the Systems Engineering menu. To access the Systems Engineering menu, follow this procedure:

Step 1.　Disconnect the power cord from the rear panel.

Step 2.　Press and hold the **Mode** button on the front panel.

Step 3.　Power-cycle the switch.

Step 4.　Release the **Mode** button one or two seconds after the LED above port 1x goes off or when the diagnostic console is displayed.

```
Cisco Systems Diagnostic Console
Copyright Cisco Systems, Inc. 1999
All rights reserved.


Ethernet Address: 00-E0-1E-7E-B4-40

_ _ _ _ _ _ _ _ _ _ _ _ _ _ _ _ _ _ _ _ _ _ _ _ _ _ .
```

Press **Enter** to continue.

Step 5.　Press **Enter** to display the Diagnostic Console [nd] Systems Engineering menu:

```
Diagnostic Console - Systems Engineering
Operation firmware version: 8.00.00 Status: valid
```

```
Boot firmware version: 3.02
[C] Continue with standard system start up
[U] Upgrade operation firmware (XMODEM)
[S] System Debug Interface
Enter Selection:
```

The bold letters show the Boot firmware version.

Clearing the Password (Firmware Version 1.10 and Later)

Step 1. Power-cycle the switch.

After POST completes, the following prompt displays:

```
Do you wish to clear the passwords? [Y]es or [N]o:
```

Note: You have 10 seconds to respond. If you do not respond within that time, the Management Console Logon screen appears. You cannot change this waiting period.

Step 2. Enter **Y** to delete the existing password from NVRAM.

Note: If you type **N**, the existing password remains valid.

Step 3. Assign a password from the switch management interfaces (management console or CLI).

Viewing the Password (Firmware Versions Between 1.10 and 3.02)

For firmware versions between 1.10 and 3.02, you can view the password you are trying to recover (instead of clearing it as described in the previous section).

Step 1. Access the diagnostic console:

Press and hold the **Mode** button.

Power-cycle the switch.

Release the **Mode** button one or two seconds after the LED above port 1x goes off or the diagnostics console appears.

You will see the following logon screen:

```
— — — — — — — — — — — — — — — — — — — — — — — — — .
Cisco Systems Diagnostic Console
Copyright Cisco Systems, Inc. 1999
All rights reserved.


Ethernet Address: 00-E0-1E-7E-B4-40
— — — — — — — — — — — — — — — — — — — — — — — — — .
```

Press **Enter** to continue.

Step 2. Press **Enter** and select the **[S]** option on the Diagnostic Console – Systems Engineering menu, and then select the **[V]** option on the Diagnostic Console – System Debug Interface menu to display the management console password.

Step 3. If you want to change the password, select the **[M]** option on the Console Settings menu.

Password Recovery for Firmware Version 1.09 and Earlier

Note: If the shipping date is before June 1997, gather the information listed in this section and contact the Cisco Technical Assistance Center (TAC) for password recovery.

Note: This section is also applicable for those Catalyst 2800 switches that do not have the Mode button in their front panel.

To recover your password, follow these steps:

Step 1. Contact the Cisco TAC for the factory-installed password.

Step 2. Provide the serial number or MAC address of the switch.

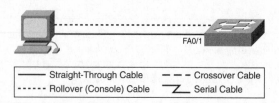

——— Straight-Through Cable	– – – Crossover Cable
------ Rollover (Console) Cable	╱ Serial Cable

The serial number is usually located on the back of the unit. To obtain the MAC address, remove the cover and read the Ethernet address of the PROM.

Curriculum Lab 6-10: Firmware Upgrade of a Catalyst 2950 Series Switch (6.2.9)

Figure 6-14   Topology for Lab 6-10

Table 6-10   Lab Equipment Configuration

Switch Designation	Switch Name	VLAN 1 IP Address	Default Gateway IP Address
Switch 1	ALSwitch	192.168.1.2	192.168.1.1

The enable secret password is **class**.

The enable, VTY, and console password is **cisco**.

The subnet mask is 255.255.255.0.

Objectives

- Create a basic switch configuration and verify it.

- Upgrade the IOS and HTML files from a file that the instructor supplies.

Background/Preparation

Cable a network that is similar to the one in Figure 6-14. The 2950 switch produced the configuration output in this lab. Another switch might produce different output.

Start a HyperTerminal session.

Implement the procedure documented in Appendix B before you continue with this lab.

Important Note: This lab requires that a combined IOS image and HTML file c2950-c3h2s-mz.120-5.3.WC.1.tar be in the default file directory of the TFTP server. The instructor should download this file from the Cisco Connection online software center. This file is the latest update for the Catalyst 2950. It has the same filename stem as the current image, but for the purpose of the lab, assume that this is an update. The IOS update release contains new HTML files to support changes to the web interface.

This lab requires that there be a saved copy of the current configuration file as backup.

Task 1: Configure the Switch

Configure the hostname and passwords, as well as the management VLAN 1 settings for the switch, as indicated in Table 6-10. If you have problems while performing this configuration, refer to Curriculum Lab 6-2, "Basic Switch Configuration (6.2.2)."

Task 2: Configure the Host Attached to the Switch

Configure the host to use the same IP subnet for addresses, masks, and the default gateway as the switch.

Task 3: Verify Connectivity

To verify that the host and switch are correctly configured, ping the switch IP address from the host.

Was the ping successful? _____

If the answer is no, troubleshoot the host and switch configurations.

Task 4: Display the Name of the Running Image File

Step 1. Display the name of the running image file by using the **show boot** command from the privileged EXEC mode prompt.

```
ALSwitch#show boot
BOOT path-list:
Config file:            flash:config.text
Enable Break:           no
Manual Boot:            no
HELPER path-list:
NVRAM/Config file
buffer size:            32768
ALSwitch#
```

Step 2. If, as shown in the previous step, no software image is defined in the boot path, enter **dir flash:** or **show flash** to display the contents.

```
ALSwitch#dir flash:
Directory of flash:/

2 -rwx 1674921 Mar 01 1993 01:28:10 c2950-c3h2s-mz.120-5.3.WC.1.bin
3 -rwx 269 Jan 01 1970 00:00:57 env_vars
4 drwx 10240 Mar 01 1993 00:21:13 html
```

```
165-rwx 965 Mar 01 1993 00:22:23 config.text

7741440 bytes total (4778496 bytes free)
```

Task 5: Prepare for the New Image

Step 1.   If the switch has enough free memory, as shown in the previous step, rename the existing IOS image file to the same name with the .old extension. If there is not enough memory, make sure that a copy of the IOS image exists on the TFTP server.

```
ALSwitch#rename flash: c2950-c3h2s-mz.120-5.3.WC.1.bin flash:
  c2950-c3h2s-mz.120-5.3.WC.1.old
```

Step 2.   Verify that the renaming was successful.

```
ALSwitch#dir flash:
Directory of flash:/

  2 -rwx 1674921 Mar 01 1993 01:28:10 c2950-c3h2s-mz.120-5.3.WC.1.old
  3 -rwx 269 Jan 01 1970 00:00:57 env_vars
  4 drwx 10240 Mar 01 1993 00:21:13 html
167 -rwx 965 Mar 01 1993 00:22:23 config.text

7741440 bytes total (4778496 bytes free)
ALSwitch#
```

Step 3.   As a precaution, disable access to the switch HTML pages.

```
ALSwitch(config)#no ip http server
```

Task 6: Extract the New IOS Image and HTML Files into Flash Memory

Step 1.   Use the **tar** command as shown:

```
ALSwitch#tar /x tftp://192.168.1.3//c2950-c3h2s-mz.120-
  5.4.WC.1.tar flash:
```

Note: Depending on the TFTP server that is being used, you might need only one slash (/) after the IP address of the server.

Step 2.   Re-enable access to the switch HTML pages.

```
ALSwitch(config)#ip http server
```

Step 3.   Remove existing HTML files.

```
ALSwitch#delete flash:html/*
```

Task 7: Associate the New Boot File

Enter the **boot** command with the name of the *new image* filename at the configuration mode prompt.

```
ALSwitch(config)#boot system flash:c2950-c3h2s-mz.120-5.4.WC.1.bin
```

Step 1.   Restart the switch by using the **reload** command to see if the new IOS loaded. Use the **show version** command to see the IOS filename.

What is the name of the IOS file that the switch booted from?

_____

Is this the proper filename? _____

Step 2.   If the IOS filename is now correct remove the backup file from flash memory using the command **delete flash: c2950-c3h2s-mz.120-5.3.WC.1.old** from the Privileged EXEC mode prompt to remove the backup file.

Step 3.   Exit to the switch welcome screen.

```
Switch#exit
```

Step 4.   Remove and store the cables and adapter.

Challenge Lab 6-11: Basic Switch Configuration with Port Security

Figure 6-15   Basic Switch Configuration with Port Security

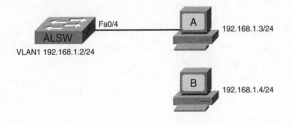

Objectives

- Prepare the switch for a new configuration.

- Apply basic configurations.

- Enable and test port security.

Equipment

The topology shown in Figure 6-15 is using a 2950 Catalyst series switch. You also need two different PCs to test the port security.

Note: Command output for this lab is based on a 2950 series switch running Cisco IOS version 12.1(13)EA1. The commands you need to use and the output may differ. If necessary, consult with your instructor for the correct commands. Alternatively, you can research the commands for your particular switch platform and IOS at Cisco.com. This would be an excellent way to enhance your Cisco device configuration skills and to simulate a "real-world" situation, namely, researching the command set for a particular device that is a part of your production network.

NetLab Compatibility Notes

Much of this lab can be completed on a NetLab basic switch pod. However, to test port security, your NetLab setup must support PCs.

Task 1: Cable the Topology and Clear the Configuration

Step 1.   Choose a 2950 switch and attach a workstation to FastEthernet 0/4.

Step 2.   Make sure the switch has an empty startup configuration and that the VLAN database has been deleted. Then, reload the switch. What commands must be used to carry out this instruction? How do you verify that the VLAN database has been deleted?

```
Switch#erase startup-config
Switch#delete flash:vlan.dat
Switch#reload
```

Task 2: Configure the Switch

Step 1.   Configure the switch with the following basic requirements:

- Hostname
- Enable password
- Banner MOTD
- Line configurations
- Other instructor-required global configurations

Step 2.   Check your configurations. What command did you use?

```
show running-config
```

Step 3.   Although there is not a router shown in Figure 6-15, one would eventually be attached. Configure the management interface, activate it, and configure 192.168.1.1 as the default gateway. What commands did you use?

Step 4.   Configure the two hosts. What configurations did you use?

Host A:

- IP address: _____
- Subnet Mask: _____
- Default Gateway: _____

Host B:

- IP address: _____
- Subnet Mask: _____
- Default Gateway: _____

Step 5.   Verify that host A can ping ALSW. If it cannot, troubleshoot.

Task 3: Configure and Test Port Security

Step 1.   For FastEthernet 0/4, implement the following port security requirements:

- Use port security to dynamically learn only one MAC address.
- Set the port to be disabled if there is a violation.

What commands did you use?

_____

_____

_____

_____

_____

Step 2. Verify that the MAC address for host A is now part of the configuration for ALSW. What command did you use?

Is the MAC address for host A "stuck" to the configuration for ALSW? If not, troubleshoot.

Step 3. What commands can you use to verify port security?

_____

_____

_____

Step 4. Test port security by removing host A and attaching host B to the FastEthernet 0/4 port. The port LED should turn from green to OFF. If it does not, send a frame to ALSW by pinging its VLAN interface from host B. Watch for console messages from the switch. You should see the following:

```
   00:06:03: %PM-4-ERR_DISABLE: psecure-violation error detected on Fa0/4, put-
ting Fa0/4 in err-disable state
00:06:03: %PORT_SECURITY-2-PSECURE_VIOLATION: Security violation occurred,
caused by MAC address 00b0.d092.80c3 on port FastEthernet0/4.
00:06:04: %LINEPROTO-5-UPDOWN: Line protocol on Interface FastEthernet0/4,
changed state to down
00:06:05: %LINK-3-UPDOWN: Interface FastEthernet0/4, changed state to down
```

Step 5. Assume that host B is the new workstation for FastEthernet 0/4. How would you clear the disabled status of the port so that the MAC address for host B will be accepted?

Step 6. Verify that the MAC address for host B is now part of the configuration for ALSW. What command did you use?

CHAPTER 7

Spanning Tree Protocol

The Study Guide portion of this chapter uses a combination of matching, fill in the blank, open-ended question, journal entry, and unique custom exercises to test your knowledge on the theory of redundant topologies and Spanning Tree Protocol (STP).

The Lab Exercises portion of this chapter includes all of the online curriculum labs to ensure that you have mastered the practical, hands-on skills needed about redundant topologies and STP.

Study Guide

Redundant Topologies

Redundancy in a network is required to protect against loss of connectivity due to the failure of an individual component. However, this provision can result in physical topologies with loops. Physical layer loops can cause serious problems in switched networks. This section includes exercises to reinforce your understanding of redundant networks and the unique problem of broadcast storms.

Vocabulary Exercise: Completion

Complete the paragraphs that follow by filling in appropriate words and phrases.

Redundancy allows networks to be fault _____, which protects against network downtime. Focusing specifically on networking, list a few things that can cause network downtime:

_____

_____

_____

Network engineers are often required to balance the cost of redundancy with the need for network _____ _____. Networks that demand close to 100 percent uptime often strive for "_____" uptime, a network that is available _____ percent of the time. A goal of redundant topologies is to eliminate network outages caused by a single point of _____.

However, redundancy in switched topologies introduces a new problem called _____, which is when frames loop endlessly through the network, eventually consuming all the available bandwidth.

Concept Questions

List and describe three of the problems that can occur with redundant links and devices in switched or bridged networks.

- _____

- _____

- _____

_____

What mechanism does the IP have to stop packets from endlessly looping throughout an internetwork?

_____

_____

_____

Journal Entry

Draw and label a topology with two switches. In your own words, explain how a broadcast storm would occur in this redundantly switched network without some sort of mechanism to stop loops.

_____

_____

_____

_____

Figure 7-1   Redundant Topology

Spanning Tree Protocol

STP is used in redundantly switched networks to create a loop-free logical topology from a physical topology that has loops. The STP is a powerful tool that gives network administrators the security of a redundant topology without the risk of problems caused by switching loops. In this section, you work through exercises that will strengthen your understanding of what STP is and how it operates.

Vocabulary Exercise: Matching

Match the definition on the left with a term on the right. This exercise is not necessarily a one-to-one matching. Some definitions may be used more than once and some terms may have multiple definitions.

Definition

a. calculated based on the speed of the link

b. port is only receiving BPDUs

c. status messages sent between switches every 2 seconds

d. 20 seconds or a cycle of 10 BPDUs

e. the time it takes for a port to transition from the listening state to the learning state or from the learning state to the forwarding state

f. actively building a MAC address table but not forwarding user traffic

g. used in redundantly switched networks to create a loop-free logical topology

h. can send and receive traffic

i. port is sending and receiving BPDUs, but not user traffic

j. without loop avoidance, frames are flooded endlessly

k. includes the priority and MAC address of the bridge

l. lowest-cost path from the non-root bridge to the root bridge

m. an improved version of IEEE 802.1d

n. reduces the time of reconvergence when a topology change occurs in a redundantly switched network

o. called "blocking" in IEEE 802.1d

p. ports connected to a single end station

q. only one in a given network; all ports are designated ports

r. operating in full-duplex mode

s. a port that is currently in the discarding state, but will transition to forwarding if the designated root port on that segment fails

t. automatically transitions from the blocking state to the forwarding state

Term

___ broadcast storms

___ Spanning Tree Protocol (STP)

___ bridge ID (BID)

___ path cost

___ root bridge

___ designated ports

___ root port

___ bridge protocol data unit (BPDU)

___ IEEE 802.1d

___ blocking

___ listening

___ learning

___ forward delay

___ max-age

___ PortFast

___ Rapid Spanning Tree Protocol (RSTP)

___ alternate port

___ discarding state

___ IEEE 802.1w

___ edge ports

___ point-to-point links

Vocabulary Exercise: Completion

Complete the paragraphs that follow by filling in appropriate words and phrases.

The _____, originally developed by Digital Equipment Corporation, is used to maintain a loop-free topology. STP is also known as IEEE _____. STP builds a loop-free topology using two key concepts: the _____ (BID) and _____, which is based on the speed of the link. STP accumulates cost based on the bandwidth of all the links in the path.

Originally, the cost of a link was calculated on a linear scale based on a maximum bandwidth of _____ Mbps. Because LANs now incorporate 10GigE links, the costs have been revised. Complete the following table showing the difference in IEEE costs for STP links.

Link Speed	Cost (Revised IEEE Spec)	Cost (Previous IEEE Spec)
10 Gbps		
1 Gbps		
100 Mbps		
10 Mbps		

Root ports and designated ports are used for _____ data traffic. Nondesignated ports _____ data traffic. These ports are called _____ or _____ ports. When using STP, the root bridge is the bridge with the _____ bridge ID (BID).

The BID is made up of two parts: the _____ field, which is ___ bytes, and _____ field, which is ___ bytes. The BID is included in messages that are sent every ___ seconds. These messages are called

_____.

Record the command, including the switch prompt, to change a switch's priority from the default, which is _____, to 4096. Assume that you are using IOS version 12.1 or later.

If you do not configure priority, which switch in a given topology will be elected the root bridge?

With STP, ports transition through four states: _____, _____, _____, and _____. A fifth state, _____, is configured when the administrator manually shuts down the port. A port in the _____ state listens only to BPDUs. If the port does not receive BPDUs for ____ seconds, which is the _____ timer, then it transitions to the _____ state. During the _____ state, the port is sending and receiving BPDUs to determine the active topology. After ____ seconds, which is called the _____ _____, the port transitions to the _____ state. During the _____ state, the port is actively building a MAC address table in preparation for the _____ state. After another _____ of ____ seconds, the port transitions to the _____ state, in which it is either a root port or a designated port and is sending and receiving user traffic. The total convergence time to move from a _____ state to a _____ state is ____ seconds.

If a switch port is connected only to end-user stations, with no chance of ever connecting to another switch, then it can be configured with the _____ feature by using the **spanning-tree** _____ interface command.

The Rapid Spanning Tree Protocol (RSTP), or IEEE _____, was developed to reduce the time it takes to reconverge the active topology when a change occurs. RSTP uses three port states: _____, _____, and _____. In addition, ports can have five different roles.

Note: Port roles are not the same as port states.

Complete the following table.

RSTP Role	Definition
	A single port on each switch in which the switch hears the best BPDU out of all the received BPDUs
	Of all switch ports on all switches attached to the same segment/collision domain, the port that advertises the "best" root BPDU
	A port on a switch that receives a suboptimal root BPDU
	A nondesignated port on a switch that is attached to the same segment/collision domain as another port on the same switch
	A port that is administratively disabled

RSTP calls Ethernet connections between switches _____ and calls Ethernet connections to end-user devices _____. If the link is full duplex, RSTP designates it as a _____ link. If the link is half duplex, RSTP designates it as a _____ link. An example of a shared link is a port attached to a hub.

Determine the Root Bridge and Port Roles Exercise

The root bridge is chosen based on the _____ BID. After the root bridge is selected, a non-root bridge looks at the following components in sequence to determine which ports will process user data and which ports will discard user data:

1. On each non-root bridge, the port with the lowest path cost to root is the root port.

2. If two or more bridges are members of the same segment and have the same cost to reach the root bridge, the bridge with the lowest BID is the designated port for that segment.

3. If a bridge has two or more equal cost paths to root, the port with the lowest ID is designated port. The other port(s) is blocking.

In the topologies shown in Figures 7-2, 7-3, and 7-4, circle the root bridge. On non-root bridges, label root ports with an **R**, designated ports with a **D**, and ports that are in the blocking state with a **B**. Use the revised IEEE costs to make your determinations. In the space provided after each topology, draw the logical loop-free spanning-tree topology with the root bridge at the top.

Figure 7-2   Determine the Root Bridge and Port Roles: Topology 1

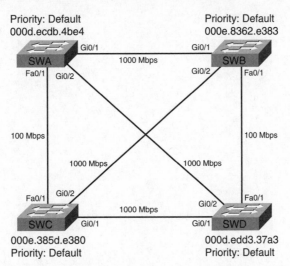

Priority: Default
000d.ecdb.4be4

Priority: Default
000e.8362.e383

SWA   SWB

Gi0/1   Gi0/1

1000 Mbps

Fa0/1   Gi0/2   Gi0/2   Fa0/1

100 Mbps   100 Mbps

1000 Mbps   1000 Mbps

Fa0/1   Gi0/2   Gi0/2   Fa0/1

SWC   1000 Mbps   SWD

Gi0/1   Gi0/1

000e.385d.e380   000d.edd3.37a3
Priority: Default   Priority: Default

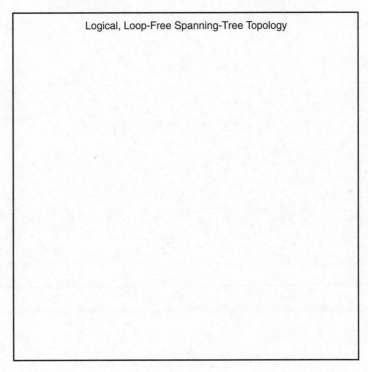

Logical, Loop-Free Spanning-Tree Topology

Figure 7-3   Determine the Root Bridge and Port Roles: Topology 2

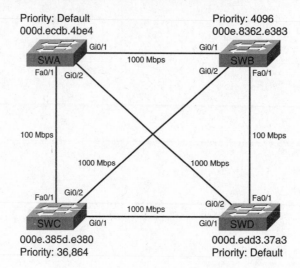

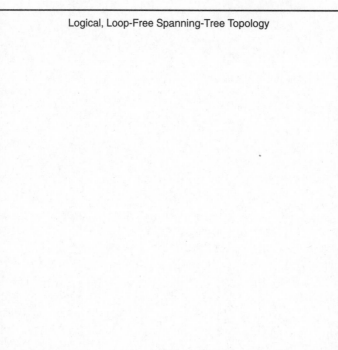

Figure 7-4   Determine the Root Bridge and Port Roles: Topology 3

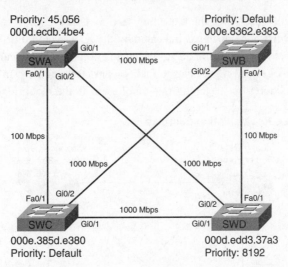

Priority: 45,056
000d.ecdb.4be4

Priority: Default
000e.8362.e383

Gi0/1 — 1000 Mbps — Gi0/1

SWA   SWB

Fa0/1   Gi0/2   Gi0/2   Fa0/1

100 Mbps   100 Mbps

1000 Mbps   1000 Mbps

Fa0/1   Gi0/2   Gi0/2   Fa0/1

SWC   Gi0/1 — 1000 Mbps — Gi0/1   SWD

000e.385d.e380
Priority: Default

000d.edd3.37a3
Priority: 8192

Logical, Loop-Free Spanning-Tree Topology

Spanning-Tree Recalculation Exercise

Figure 7-5 is the same as Figure 7-3 in the preceding section. However, now the Gigabit Ethernet link between SWC and SWB has gone down. as indicated by the X. As you did before, circle the root bridge. On non-root bridges, label root ports with an **R**, designated ports with a **D**, and ports that are in the blocking state with a **B**. Use the revised IEEE costs to make your determinations. In the space provided after the topology, draw the logical loop-free spanning-tree topology with the root bridge at the top.

Figure 7-5   Spanning-Tree Recalculation Exercise

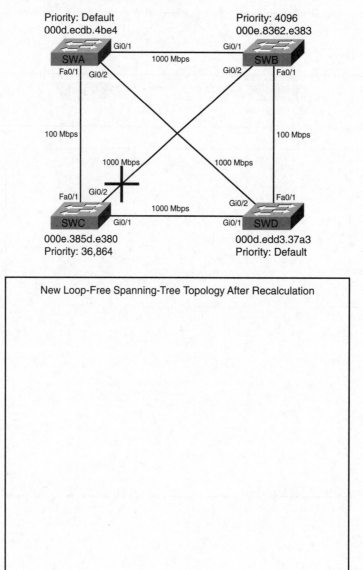

Concept Questions

What are the basic steps STP performs to converge a loop-free network?

_____

_____

_____

_____

_____

_____

How is the root bridge selected?

_____

_____

_____

What happens if two devices have the same priority number?

_____

What are BPDUs?

_____

What happens if BPDUs are not received for a set amount of time?

_____

_____

Lab Exercises

Command Reference

In the table that follows, record the command, including the correct switch prompt, that fits the description for a 2950 Catalyst switch. Fill in any blanks with the appropriate missing information.

Command	Description
	Cisco IOS Software Release 12.0 Displays the spanning-tree table of the switch.
	Cisco IOS Software Release 12.1 Displays the spanning-tree table of the switch.
	Cisco IOS Software Release 12.0 Sets the priority for root bridge elections. Number can be from 1 to 65535. The default is _____.
	Cisco IOS Software Release 12.1 Sets the priority for root bridge elections. Number can be from 0 to 65535 and must be configured in increments of _____. The default is _____.
	Sets an access port that will never be attached to another switch to move immediately into the forwarding state.

Curriculum Lab 7-1: Selecting the Root Bridge (7.2.4)

Figure 7-6   Topology for Lab 7-1

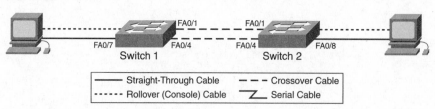

———	Straight-Through Cable	– – –	Crossover Cable
------	Rollover (Console) Cable	⟋Z⟋	Serial Cable

Table 7-1   Lab Equipment Configuration

Switch Designation		Switch Name	VLAN 1 IP Address	Default Gateway IP Address
Switch 1	Switch_A	192.168.1.2	192.168.1.1	
Switch 2	Switch_B	192.168.1.3	192.168.1.1	

The enable secret password for both switches is **class**.

The enable, VTY, and console password for both switches is **cisco**.

The subnet mask for both switches is 255.255.255.0.

Objectives

- Create a basic switch configuration and verify it.

- Determine which switch is selected as a root switch with factory default settings.

- Force the other switch to be selected as a root switch.

Background/Preparation

Cable a network that is similar to the one in Figure 7-6. The 2950 series switch produced the configuration output in this lab. Another switch might produce different output. You should execute the following steps on each switch unless you are specifically instructed otherwise:

- Start a HyperTerminal session.

- Implement the procedure that is documented in Appendix B, "Erasing and Reloading the Switch," on all switches before you continue with this lab.

Task 1: Configure the Switches

Configure the hostnames and passwords, as well as the management VLAN 1 settings for each switch, as indicated in Table 7-1. If you have problems while performing this configuration, refer to Lab 6-2, "Basic Switch Configuration."

Task 2: Configure the Hosts that Are Attached to the Switches

Configure the hosts as part of the same subnet as the switches. The hosts also share the same subnet mask and the same default gateway.

Task 3: Verify Connectivity

Step 1.   To verify that the hosts and switches are correctly configured, ping the switches from the hosts.

Step 2.   Were the pings successful?

Step 3.   If the answer is no, troubleshoot the host and switch configurations.

Note: If your pings were not successful, remember the troubleshooting methodology you learned in your CCNA 2 studies. Start with the physical layer first. Are all the link lights lit that need to be lit? What other Layer 1 issues might be the problem? If Layer 1 is not the problem, proceed to Layer 2. What Layer 2 issues are likely to be causing a problem? Layer 3? For a review of the method of testing by the layers, refer to the online curriculum CCNA 2 Routers and Routing Basics: Module 9, Objective 9.2, "Network Testing."

Task 4: Look at the show interface vlan Options

Step 1.   Type **show interface vlan1 ?**.

Step 2.   List some of the options that are available.

Task 5: Look at the VLAN Interface Information

Step 1.   On Switch_A, type the command **show interface vlan 1** at the privileged EXEC mode prompt.

Step 2.   What is the MAC address of the switch?

_____

Step 3.   On Switch_B, type the command **show interface vlan 1** at the privileged EXEC mode prompt.

Step 4.   What is the MAC address of the switch?

_____

Step 5.   Which switch should be the root of the spanning tree for VLAN 1?

_____

Step 6.   What would you do if you wanted to change which switch is root for VLAN 1?

_____

True or False: After changing which switch is root, you must reload the switches for the change to take effect.

_____

Task 6: Look at the Switches' Spanning-Tree Tables

Step 1.   On Switch_A, type **show spanning-tree brief** at the privileged EXEC mode prompt if you are running Cisco IOS Software Release 12.0. If you are running Cisco IOS Software Release 12.1, type **show spanning-tree**.

Step 2.   On Switch_B, type **show spanning-tree brief** at the privileged EXEC mode prompt.

Step 3.   Examine your output and answer the following questions.

Which switch is the root switch?

_____

What is the priority of the root switch?

_____

What is the bridge ID of the root switch?

_____

Which ports are forwarding on the root switch?

_____

Which ports are blocking on the root switch?

_____

What is the priority of the non-root switch?

_____

What is the bridge ID of the non-root switch?

_____

Which ports are forwarding on the non-root switch?

_____

Which ports are blocking on the non-root switch?

___

What is the status of the link light on the blocking port?

___

Task 7: Reassign the Root Bridge

Step 1.   The switch that has been selected as the root bridge, by using default values, is not the best choice. You must force the other switch to become the root switch.

For the purposes of this step, assume that the root switch by default is Switch_A. Also assume that Switch_B is preferred as the root switch. If your implementation has Switch_B as the default root, then you will want to configure Switch_A to be the root. Go to the console and enter configuration mode for the switch you want to change to root.

Step 2.   Determine the parameters that you can configure for the STP.

Step 3.   List the options.

___

Step 4.   Set the priority of the switch that is not root to 4096.

If you are using Cisco IOS Software Release 12.0:

```
Switch_B(config)#spanning-tree priority 1
Switch_B(config)#exit
```

If you are using Cisco IOS Software Release 12.1:

```
Switch_B(config)#spanning-tree vlan 1 priority 4096
Switch_B(config)#exit
```

Task 8: Look at the Switch Spanning-Tree Table

Step 1.   On Switch_A, type **show spanning-tree brief** at the privileged EXEC mode prompt if you are running Cisco IOS Software Release 12.0. If you are running Cisco IOS Software Release 12.1, type **show spanning-tree**.

Step 2.   On Switch_B, type **show spanning-tree brief** at the privileged EXEC mode prompt.

Step 3.   Examine your output and answer the following questions.

Which switch is the root switch?

___

What is the priority of the root switch?

___

Which ports are forwarding on the root switch?

___

Which ports are blocking on the root switch?

___

What is the priority of the non-root switch?

___

Which ports are forwarding on the non-root switch?

Which ports are blocking on the non-root switch?

What is the status of the link light on the blocking port?

Task 9: Verify the Running Configuration File on the Root Switch

Step 1. On the switch that was changed to be the root bridge, type **show running-config** at the privileged EXEC mode prompt.

Step 2. Does an entry exist in the running configuration file that specifies the spanning-tree priority for this switch?

Step 3. What does that entry say?

Note: The output is different depending on whether the Cisco IOS software is Release 12.0 or Release 12.1.

After you complete the previous steps, log off (by typing **exit**) and turn all the devices off. Then remove and store the cables and adapter.

Curriculum Lab 7-2: Spanning-Tree Recalculation (7.2.6)

Figure 7-7   Topology for Lab 7-2

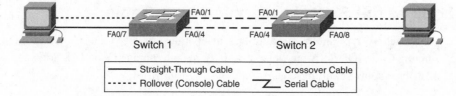

Table 7-2   Lab Equipment Configuration

Switch Designation	Switch Name	VLAN 1 IP Address	Default Gateway IP Address
Switch 1	Switch_A	192.168.1.2	192.168.1.1
Switch 2	Switch_B	192.168.1.3	192.168.1.1

The enable secret password for both switches is **class**.

The enable, VTY, and console password for both switches is **cisco**.

The subnet mask for both switches is 255.255.255.0.

Objectives

- Create a basic switch configuration and verify it.

- Observe the behavior of the spanning-tree algorithm in the presence of switched network topology changes.

Background/Preparation

Cable a network that is similar to the one in Figure 7-7. The 2950 series switch produced the configuration output in this lab. Another switch might produce different output. You should execute the following steps on each switch unless you are specifically instructed otherwise:

- Start a HyperTerminal session.

- Implement the procedure documented in Appendix B on all switches before you continue with this lab.

Task 1: Configure the Switches

Configure the hostnames and passwords, as well as the management VLAN 1 settings for each switch, as indicated in Table 7-2. If you have problems while performing this configuration, refer to Lab 6-2, "Basic Switch Configuration."

Task 2: Configure the Hosts that Are Attached to the Switches

Configure the hosts as part of the same subnet as the switches. The hosts also share the same subnet mask and the same default gateway.

Task 3: Verify Connectivity

Step 1.   To verify that the hosts and switches are configured correctly, ping the switches from the hosts.

Step 2.   Were the pings successful?

Step 3.   If the answer is no, troubleshoot the host and switch configurations.

Task 4: Look at the VLAN Interface Information

Step 1.   On both switches, type the command **show interface vlan 1** at the privileged EXEC prompt.

Step 2.   What is the MAC address of Switch_A?

Step 3.   What is the MAC address of Switch_B?

Step 4.   Which switch should be the root of the spanning tree for VLAN 1?

Task 5: Look at the Switches' Spanning-Tree Tables

Step 1.   On Switch_A, type **show spanning-tree brief** at the privileged EXEC mode prompt if you are running Cisco IOS Software Release 12.0. If you are running Cisco IOS Software Release 12.1, type **show spanning-tree**. Different releases of IOS have different options for this command.

Step 2.   On Switch_B, type **show spanning-tree brief** at the privileged EXEC mode prompt.

Step 3. Examine the command output and answer the following questions.

Which switch is the root switch?

_____

Record the states of the first 12 interfaces and ports of each switch in the following table.

Switch_A	Port No.	Switch_B
	1	
	2	
	3	
	4	
	5	
	6	
	7	
	8	
	9	
	10	
	11	
	12	

Task 6: Remove a Cable on the Switch

Step 1. Remove the cable from the forwarding port on the non-root switch. If Switch_A is your root switch, then remove the cable from the forwarding port on Switch_B. If Switch_B is your root switch, then remove the cable from the forwarding port on Switch_A.

Step 2. Wait for at least 2 minutes.

Step 3. What has happened to the switch port LEDs?

_____

Task 7: Look at the Spanning-Tree Table for the Switches

Step 1. On Switch_A, type **show spanning-tree brief** at the privileged EXEC mode prompt if you are running Cisco IOS Software Release 12.0. If you are running Cisco IOS Software Release 12.1, type **show spanning-tree**. Different releases of IOS have different options for this command.

Step 2. On Switch_B, type **show spanning-tree brief** at the privileged EXEC mode prompt.

Step 3. What changes have taken place in the command output?

On Switch_A?

_____

_____

On Switch_B?

_____

_____

Task 8: Replace the Cable in the Switch

Step 1. Replace the cable in the port that it was removed from. For the previous example, this is interface FastEthernet 0/1 on Switch_A.

Step 2. Wait for at least 2 minutes.

Step 3. What has happened to the switch port LEDs?

_____

Task 9: Redisplay the Spanning-Tree Table for the Switches

Step 1. On Switch_A, type **show spanning-tree brief** at the privileged EXEC mode prompt if you are running Cisco IOS Software Release 12.0. If you are running Cisco IOS Software Release 12.1, type **show spanning-tree**. Different releases of IOS have different options for this command.

Step 2. On Switch_B, type **show spanning-tree brief** at the privileged EXEC mode prompt.

Step 3. What changes have taken place in the command output?

On Switch_A?

_____

On Switch_B?

_____

After you complete the previous steps, log off (by typing **exit**) and turn all the devices off. Then remove and store the cables and adapter.

CHAPTER 8

Virtual LANs

The Study Guide portion of this chapter uses a combination of fill in the blank and unique custom exercises to test your knowledge on the theory of VLANs, VLAN configuration, and VLAN troubleshooting.

The Lab Exercises portion of this chapter includes all of the online curriculum labs as well as a challenge lab to ensure that you have mastered the practical, hands-on skills needed about VLANs.

Study Guide

VLAN Concepts

As a network engineer, it is important that you understand the logical function of a VLAN and how VLANs can improve network performance. The completion exercise in this brief section provides a quick review of VLAN concepts.

Vocabulary Exercise: Completion

Directions: Complete the paragraphs that follow by filling in appropriate words and phrases.

Up to this point in your studies, you have learned that a LAN includes all devices in the same _____ domain and that a switch is used to microsegment the _____ domain. In this chapter, you learned that switches can be configured with _____ LANs, or VLANs, to segment the _____ domain at Layer __ Without VLANs, a switch treats all interfaces on the switch as being in the same _____ domain.

A VLAN is a _____ domain created by one or more switches. Configuration is as simple as putting some interfaces in one VLAN and other interfaces in another VLAN.

List a few reasons or benefits for using VLANs:

- _____

- _____

- _____

- _____

Layer 2 switches cannot forward traffic between VLANs. In fact, the switch maintains a separate _____ table for each VLAN so that broadcasts are contained within each VLAN. To communicate between users on different VLANs, the traffic must pass through a _____ or _____ switch. This can be done by using a different Ethernet interface for each VLAN. Note that each VLAN would be on a different _____ It is more common to use one Fast Ethernet interface to trunk multiple VLANs and configure logical subinterfaces.

Two basic VLAN configuration methods are available to the network engineer: _____ configuration, which is port based, and _____ configuration, which uses a VLAN Management Policy Server (VMPS). _____ VLAN configuration is by far the most widely implemented of these two methods. Dynamic VLAN configuration is not currently a CCNA objective.

VLAN Configuration

Currently, the Cisco IOS is in a transition phase from configuring VLANs in VLAN database configuration mode to configuring VLANs in global configuration mode. Because both ways are currently supported, you need to be familiar with each. The configuration exercise in this section will walk you through both methods for creating, modifying, applying, and deleting VLANs.

Learn VLAN Configuration Commands Exercise

True or False: You can assign a VLAN to an interface without creating the VLAN first. If true, what confirmation message does the switch display? If false, what error message does the switch display?

_____

_____

_____

_____

VLANs can be created using VLAN database mode or global configuration mode. VLAN global configuration mode is preferred because the user interface is familiar. In addition, you must use the **exit** command in VLAN database mode to have changes applied to the VLAN database. Finally, VLAN database configuration mode has been deprecated and will be removed in some future releases.

For the following exercise, refer to Figure 8-1.

Figure 8-1   VLAN Configuration Commands

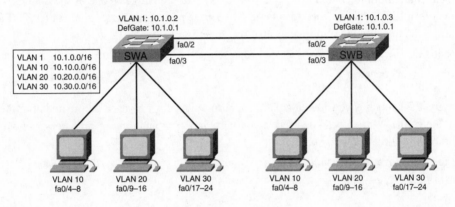

Record the commands, including the switch prompt, to configure SWA with the VLANs, shown in Figure 8-1. The commands would be the same on SWB.

VLAN database configuration mode

_____

_____

_____

_____

_____

_____

_____

_____

_____

_____

_____

_____

VLAN global configuration mode

_____

_____

_____

_____

_____

_____

_____

_____

From global configuration mode if you type **interface ?** and see **range** as one of the options, you are in luck. Your Cisco IOS Software Release supports the **range** parameter. This argument to the **interface** command allows you to configure multiple ports at one time. For example:

```
Switch(config)#interface range fa0/1 - 8
Switch(config-if-range)#
```

Interestingly, the hyphen is considered a parameter. You must enter a space before and after the hyphen. Note that the **range** argument can be used to configure any combination of ports. For example, the following would be a legitimate command:

```
Switch(config)#interface range fa 0/4 - 5, fa 0/3 , fa 0/10 - 12 , gi 0/1
Switch(config-if-range)#
```

Record the commands, including the switch prompt, to assign interfaces with the VLANs shown in Figure 8-1. You only need to show the commands for SWA. The commands are the same for SWB.

_____

_____

_____

_____

_____

_____

_____

_____

_____

_____

You need to move ports Fa0/17 through Fa0/20 to the Marketing VLAN. Record the command or commands, including switch prompt, to make the move.

_____

_____

_____

The Purchasing department has been eliminated. All Purchasing department functions are now handled by Accounting. You no longer need the Purchasing VLAN. Record the command or commands, including switch prompt, to delete the Purchasing VLAN.

VLAN database configuration mode

_____

_____

_____

_____

_____

_____

_____

VLAN global configuration mode

_____

_____

_____

What happens to the ports that were members of a deleted VLAN?

_____

What must be done to fix this problem?

_____

_____

Record the commands, including switch prompt, to reassign ports Fa0/21 through Fa0/24 to VLAN 1.

_____

_____

_____

_____

Troubleshooting VLANs

Now that you are comfortable configuring VLANS, it is time to review the commands that will help you to verify and troubleshoot your VLAN implementation. This section covers the **show** commands most commonly used with VLANs.

Identify the Troubleshooting Command Exercise

In this exercise, you are asked to identify what command was used to display the output. You may need to use a switch to help research your answers. The following output is from a Cisco 2950 running Cisco IOS Software Version 12.1(13)EA1.

```
Switch _____

VLAN0001
  Spanning tree enabled protocol ieee
  Root ID    Priority    4097
             Address     000e.385d.e380
             This bridge is the root
             Hello Time   2 sec  Max Age 20 sec  Forward Delay 15 sec
```

```
   Bridge ID  Priority    4097   (priority 4096 sys-id-ext 1)
              Address     000e.385d.e380
              Hello Time   2 sec  Max Age 20 sec  Forward Delay 15 sec
              Aging Time 300


Interface         Role Sts Cost      Prio.Nbr Type
---------------- ---- --- ------- -------- --------------------------------

Fa0/1             Desg FWD 19        128.1    P2p
Fa0/2             Desg FWD 19        128.2    P2p
Fa0/3             Desg FWD 19        128.3    P2p


Switch _____


VLAN Name                        Status     Ports
---- ---------------------------- --------- --------------------------------

10   Accounting                   active    Fa0/1, Fa0/2, Fa0/3, Fa0/4
                                            Fa0/5, Fa0/6, Fa0/7, Fa0/8


VLAN Type  SAID      MTU   Parent RingNo BridgeNo Stp  BrdgMode Trans1 Trans2
---- ----- --------- ----- ------ ------ -------- ---- -------- ------ ------

10   enet  100010    1500  -      -      -        -    -        0      0


Remote SPAN VLAN
----------------
Disabled


Primary Secondary Type          Ports
------- --------- ------------- -------------------------------------------


Switch# _____
Name: Fa0/2
Switchport: Enabled
Administrative Mode: trunk
Operational Mode: trunk
Administrative Trunking Encapsulation: dot1q
Operational Trunking Encapsulation: dot1q
Negotiation of Trunking: On
Access Mode VLAN: 1 (default)
Trunking Native Mode VLAN: 1 (default)
Voice VLAN: none
Administrative private-vlan host-association: none
Administrative private-vlan mapping: none
Operational private-vlan: none
Trunking VLANs Enabled: ALL
Pruning VLANs Enabled: 2-1001
```

```
Capture Mode Disabled
Capture VLANs Allowed: ALL


Protected: false


Voice VLAN: none (Inactive)
Appliance trust: none


Switch _____


VLAN Name                            Status    Ports
__ _____ ____. _____

1    default                         active    Gi0/1, Gi0/2
10   Accounting                      active    Fa0/4, Fa0/5, Fa0/6, Fa0/7
                                               Fa0/8
20   Marketing                       active    Fa0/9, Fa0/10, Fa0/11, Fa0/12
                                               Fa0/13, Fa0/14, Fa0/15, Fa0/16
30   Purchasing                      active    Fa0/17, Fa0/18, Fa0/19, Fa0/20
                                               Fa0/21, Fa0/22, Fa0/23, Fa0/24
1002 fddi-default                    active
1003 token-ring-default              active
1004 fddinet-default                 active
1005 trnet-default                   active


Switch _____
Port        Mode        Encapsulation  Status     Native vlan
Fa0/1       on          802.1q         trunking   1
Fa0/2       on          802.1q         trunking   1
Fa0/3       on          802.1q         trunking   1


Port        Vlans allowed on trunk
Fa0/1       1-4094
Fa0/2       1-4094
Fa0/3       1-4094


Port        Vlans allowed and active in management domain
Fa0/1       1,10,20,30
Fa0/2       1,10,20,30
Fa0/3       1,10,20,30


Port        Vlans in spanning tree forwarding state and not pruned
Fa0/1       1,10,20,30
Fa0/2       1,10,20,30
Fa0/3       1,10,30
```

Lab Exercises

Command Reference

In the table that follows, record the command, including the correct switch prompt, that fits the description for a 2950 Catalyst switch.

Command	Description
	Enters VLAN database configuration mode
	Creates VLAN 2 and names it Engineering
	Creates VLAN 2 and names it Marketing
	Applies changes and exits VLAN database mode
	Creates VLAN 10 using global configuration mode
	Assigns the name Accounting to VLAN 10
	Enters interface configuration mode for interfaces Fa0/2 through Fa0/8
	Sets these ports to access mode
	Assigns these ports to VLAN 2
	Deletes VLAN 3 in VLAN database configuration mode
	Deletes VLAN 3 in global configuration mode
	Removes an interface from VLAN 10
	Removes the entire VLAN database from Flash memory
	Displays the complete VLAN database
	Displays a summary of the VLAN database

Curriculum Lab 8-1: Configuring Static VLANs (8.2.3)

Figure 8-2   Topology for Lab 8-1

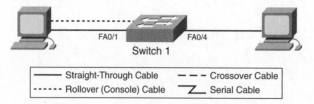

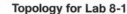

Table 8-1   Lab Equipment Configuration

Switch Designation	Switch Name	VLAN 1 IP Address	Default Gateway IP Address	Subnet Mask
Switch 1	Switch_A	192.168.1.2	192.168.1.1	255.255.255.0

The enable secret password is **class**.

The enable, VTY, and console password is **cisco**.

Objectives

- Create a basic switch configuration and verify it.

- Determine the switch firmware version.

- Create two VLANs, name them, and assign member ports to them.

Background/Preparation

When you are managing a switch, the management domain is always VLAN 1. The network administrator's workstation must have access to a port in the VLAN 1 management domain. All ports are assigned to VLAN 1 by default. This lab will help demonstrate how you can use VLANs to separate traffic and reduce broadcast domains.

Cable a network that is similar to the one in Figure 8-2. The 2950 series switch produced the configuration output in this lab. Another switch might produce different output. You should execute the following steps on each switch unless you are specifically instructed otherwise. Instructions are also provided for the 1900 series switch, which initially displays a User Interface Menu. Select the **Command Line** option from the menu to perform the steps for this lab.

Start a HyperTerminal session.

Implement the procedure documented in Appendix B, "Erasing and Reloading the Switch," on all switches before you continue with this lab.

Task 1: Configure the Switch

Configure the hostnames and passwords, as well as the management VLAN 1 settings for the switch, as indicated in Table 8-1. If you have problems while performing this configuration, refer to Lab 6-2, "Basic Switch Configuration."

Task 2: Configure the Hosts Attached to the Switch

Configure the host to use the same subnet for addresses, masks, and the default gateway as the switch.

Task 3: Verify Connectivity

To verify that the hosts and switch are correctly configured, ping the switch from the hosts.

Were the pings successful? _____

If the answer is no, troubleshoot the hosts and switch configurations.

Task 4: Show the Cisco IOS Version

It is important that you know the version of the operating system. Differences between versions might change how you enter commands. Enter the **show version** command at the user EXEC or privileged EXEC mode prompt.

```
Switch_A#show version
```

What version of the switch IOS is displayed? _____

Does this switch have Standard Edition or Enterprise Edition software? _____

Task 5: Display the VLAN Interface Information

On Switch_A, enter the command **show vlan** at the privileged EXEC mode prompt.

```
Switch_A#show vlan
```

Which ports belong to the default VLAN? _____

How many VLANs are set up by default on the switch? _____

What does the VLAN 1003 represent?

_____

How many ports are in the 1003 VLAN? 0

Task 6: Create and Name Two VLANs

Enter the following commands to create two named VLANs:

```
Switch_A#vlan database
Switch_A(vlan)#vlan 2 name VLAN2
Switch_A(vlan)#vlan 3 name VLAN3
Switch_A(config)#exit
```

1900:

```
Switch_A#config t
Switch_A(config)#vlan 2 name VLAN2
Switch_A(config)#vlan 3 name VLAN3
```

Task 7: Display the VLAN Interface Information

On Switch_A, enter the command **show vlan** at the privileged EXEC mode prompt.

```
Switch_A#show vlan
```

Are new VLANs in the listing? If so, which ones? _____

Do these VLANs have ports assigned to them yet? _____

Task 8: Assign a Port to VLAN 2

You must assign ports to VLANs from the interface mode. Enter the following commands to add port 2 to VLAN 2:

```
Switch_A#configure terminal
Switch_A(config)#interface fastethernet 0/2
Switch_A(config-if)#switchport mode access
Switch_A(config-if)#switchport access vlan 2
Switch_A(config-if)#end
```

1900:

```
Switch_A#config t
Switch_A(config)#interface Ethernet 0/2
Switch_A(config-if)#vlan static 2
Switch_A(config)#end
```

Task 9: Display the VLAN Interface Information

On Switch_A, enter the command **show vlan** at the privileged EXEC mode prompt.

```
Switch_A#show vlan
```

Is port 2 assigned to VLAN 2? _____

Is the port still listed in the default VLAN? _____

Task 10: Assign a Port to VLAN 3

You must assign ports to VLANs from the interface mode. Enter the following commands to add port 3 to VLAN 3:

```
Switch_A#configure terminal
Switch_A(config)#interface fastethernet 0/3
Switch_A(config-if)#switchport mode access
Switch_A(config-if)#switchport access vlan 3
Switch_A(config-if)#end
```

1900:

```
Switch_A#config t
Switch_A(config)#interface Ethernet 0/3
Switch_A(config)#vlan static 3
Switch_A(config)#end
```

Task 11: Display the VLAN Interface Information

On Switch_A, enter the command **show vlan** at the privileged EXEC mode prompt.

```
Switch_A#show vlan
```

Is port 3 assigned to VLAN 3? _____

Is the port still listed in the default VLAN? _____

Task 12: Look Only at VLAN 2 Information

Instead of displaying all the VLANs, enter the **show vlan id 2** command at the privileged EXEC mode prompt.

```
Switch_A#show vlan id 2
```

1900:

```
Switch_A#show vlan 2
```

Does this command supply more information than the **show vlan** command? _____

Task 13: Look Only at VLAN 2 Information with a Different Command (1900: Skip this Task)

Instead of displaying all the VLANs, enter the **show vlan name VLAN2** command at the privileged EXEC mode prompt.

```
Switch_A#show vlan name VLAN2
```

Does this command supply more information than the other **show** commands? _____

After you complete the previous step, log off (by typing **exit**) and turn all the devices off. Then, remove and store the cables and adapter.

Curriculum Lab 8-2: Verifying VLAN Configurations (8.2.4)

Figure 8-3   Topology for Lab 8-2

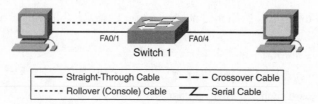

Switch 1

FA0/1   FA0/4

| Straight-Through Cable | — — Crossover Cable |
| ----- Rollover (Console) Cable | Serial Cable |

Table 8-2   Lab Equipment Configuration

Switch Designation	Switch Name	VLAN 1 IP Address	Default Gateway IP Address	Subnet Mask
Switch 1	Switch_A	192.168.1.2	192.168.1.2	255.255.255.0

The enable secret password is **class**.

The enable, VTY, and console password is **cisco**.

Objectives

- Create a basic switch configuration and verify it.

- Create two VLANs.

- Name the VLANs and assign multiple member ports to them.

- Test functionality by moving a workstation from one VLAN to another.

Background/Preparation

When you are managing a switch, the management domain is always VLAN 1. The network administrator's workstation must have access to a port in the VLAN 1 management domain. All ports are assigned to VLAN 1 by default. This lab will also help demonstrate how VLANs can be used to separate traffic and reduce broadcast domains.

Cable a network that is similar to the one in Figure 8-3. The 2950 series switch produced the configuration output in this lab. Another switch might produce different output. You should execute the following steps on each switch unless you are specifically instructed otherwise. Instructions are also provided for the 1900 series switch, which initially displays a User Interface Menu. Select the **Command Line** option from the menu to perform the steps for this lab.

Start a HyperTerminal session.

Implement the procedure documented in Appendix B on all switches before you continue with this lab.

Task 1: Configure the Switch

Configure the hostnames and passwords, as well as the management VLAN 1 settings for the switch, as indicated in Table 8-2. If you have problems while performing this configuration, refer to Lab 6-2, "Basic Switch Configuration."

Task 2: Configure the Hosts Attached to the Switch

Configure the host to use the same subnet for addresses, masks, and the default gateway as the switch.

Task 3: Verify Connectivity

To verify that the hosts and switch are correctly configured, ping the switch from the hosts.

Were the pings successful? _____

If the answer is no, troubleshoot the hosts and switch configurations.

Task 4: Display the VLAN Interface Information

On Switch_A, enter the command **show vlan** at the privileged EXEC mode prompt.

```
Switch_A#show vlan
```

Which ports belong to the default VLAN? _____

Task 5: Create and Name Two VLANs

Enter the following commands to create two named VLANs:

```
Switch_A#vlan database
Switch_A(vlan)#vlan 2 name VLAN2
Switch_A(vlan)#vlan 3 name VLAN3
Switch_A(config)#exit
```

1900:

```
Switch_A#config t
Switch_A(config)#vlan 2 name VLAN2
Switch_A(config)#vlan 3 name VLAN3
Switch_A(config)#exit
```

Task 6: Assign Ports to VLAN 2

You must assign ports to VLANs from the interface mode. Enter the following commands to add ports 4, 5, and 6 to VLAN 2:

```
Switch_A#configure terminal
Switch_A(config)#interface fastethernet 0/4
Switch_A(config-if)#switchport mode access
Switch_A(config-if)#switchport access vlan 2
Switch_A(config)#interface fastethernet 0/5
Switch_A(config-if)#switchport mode access
Switch_A(config-if)#switchport access vlan 2
Switch_A(config)#interface fastethernet 0/6
Switch_A(config-if)#switchport mode access
Switch_A(config-if)#switchport access vlan 2
Switch_A(config-if)#end
```

1900:

```
Switch_A#config t
Switch_A(config)#interface ethernet 0/4
Switch_A(config-if)#vlan static 2
Switch_A(config-if)#interface ethernet 0/5
Switch_A(config-if)#vlan static 2
Switch_A(config-if)#interface ethernet 0/6
Switch_A(config-if)#vlan static 2
Switch_A(config-if)#end
```

Task 7: Display the VLAN Interface Information

On Switch_A, enter the command **show vlan** at the privileged EXEC mode prompt.

```
Switch_A#show vlan
```

Are ports 4 through 6 assigned to VLAN 2? _____

Task 8: Assign Ports to VLAN 3

Enter the following commands to assign ports 7, 8, and 9 to VLAN 3:

```
Switch_A#configure terminal
Switch_A(config)#interface fastethernet 0/7
Switch_A(config-if)#switchport mode access
Switch_A(config-if)#switchport access vlan 3
Switch_A(config)#interface fastethernet 0/8
Switch_A(config-if)#switchport mode access
Switch_A(config-if)#switchport access vlan 3
Switch_A(config)#interface fastethernet 0/9
Switch_A(config-if)#switchport mode access
Switch_A(config-if)#switchport access vlan 3
Switch_A(config-if)#end
```

Task 9: Display the VLAN Interface Information

On Switch_A, enter the command **show vlan** at the privileged EXEC mode prompt.

Switch_A#**show vlan**

Are ports 7 through 9 assigned to VLAN 3? _____

Task 10: Test the VLANs

Step 1.   Ping from the host in port 0/4 to the host in port 0/1.

Was the ping successful? _____

Why?_____

Step 2.   Ping from the host in port 0/1 to the host in port 0/4.

Was the ping successful? _____

Why?

_____

Step 3.   Ping from the host in port 0/4 to the switch IP 192.168.1.2.

Was the ping successful?

_____

Why?

_____

Step 4.   Ping from the host in port 0/1 to the switch IP 192.168.1.2.

Was the ping successful? _____

Why?

_____

Task 11: Move a Host

Move the host in port 0/4 to port 0/3, wait until the port LED turns green, and then go to the next task.

Task 12: Test the VLANs

Step 1.   Ping from the host in port 0/3 to the host in port 0/1.

Was the ping successful? _____

Why?

_____

Step 2.   Ping from the host in port 0/1 to the host in port 0/3.

Was the ping successful? _____

Step 3.   Ping from the host in port 0/3 to the switch IP 192.168.1.2.

Was the ping successful? _____

Task 13: Move Hosts

Move the host in port 0/3 to port 0/4 and the host in port 0/1 to port 0/5, wait until the port LED turns green, and then go to the next task.

Task 14: Test the VLANs

Step 1.   Ping from the host in port 0/4 to the host in port 0/5.

Was the ping successful? _____

Why?

_____

Step 2.   Ping from the host in port 0/5 to the host in port 0/4.

Was the ping successful? _____

Step 3.   Ping from the host in port 0/4 to the switch IP 192.168.1.2.

Was the ping successful? _____

Step 4.   Ping from the host in port 0/5 to the switch IP 192.168.1.2.

Was the ping successful? _____

Why?

_____

Task 15: Move the Hosts

Move the host in port 0/4 to port 0/8, wait until the port LED turns green, and then go to the next task.

Task 16: Test the VLANs

Step 1.   Ping from the host in port 0/5 to the host in port 0/8.

Was the ping successful? _____

Why?

_____

Step 2.   Ping from the host in port 0/8 to the host in port 0/5.

Was the ping successful? _____

Step 3.   Ping from the host in port 0/5 to the switch IP 192.168.1.2.

Was the ping successful? _____

Step 4.   Ping from the host in port 0/8 to the switch IP 192.168.1.2.

Was the ping successful? _____

After you complete the previous steps, log off (by typing **exit**) and turn all the devices off. Then, remove and store the cables and adapter.

Curriculum Lab 8-3: Deleting VLAN Configurations (8.2.6)

Figure 8-4   Topology for Lab 8-3

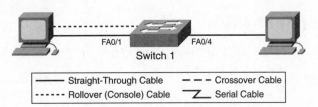

Straight-Through Cable	— — Crossover Cable
------ Rollover (Console) Cable	Z Serial Cable

Table 8-3   Lab Equipment Configuration

Switch Designation	Switch Name	VLAN 1 IP Address	Default Gateway IP Address	Subnet Mask
Switch 1	Switch_A	192.168.1.2	192.168.1.1	255.255.255.0

The enable secret password is **class**.

The enable, VTY, and console password is **cisco**.

Objectives

- Create a basic switch configuration and verify it.

- Create two VLANs.

- Name the VLANs and assign multiple member ports to them.

- Delete VLANs.

- Understand why it is not possible to delete VLAN 1.

Background/Preparation

When you are managing a switch, the management domain is always VLAN 1. The network administrator's workstation must have access to a port in the VLAN 1 management domain. All ports are assigned to VLAN 1 by default. This lab will help demonstrate how you can use VLANs to separate traffic and reduce broadcast domains.

Cable a network that is similar to the one in Figure 8-4. The 2950 series switch produced the configuration output in this lab. Another switch might produce different output. You should execute the following steps on each switch unless you are specifically instructed otherwise.

Instructions are also provided for the 1900 series switch, which initially displays a User Interface Menu. Select the **Command Line** option from the menu to perform the steps for this lab.

Start a HyperTerminal session.

Implement the procedure documented in Appendix B on all switches before you continue with this lab.

Task 1: Configure the Switch

Configure the hostnames and passwords, as well as the management VLAN 1 settings for the switch, as indicated in Table 8-3. If you have problems while performing this configuration, refer to Lab 6-2, "Basic Switch Configuration."

Task 2: Configure the Hosts Attached to the Switch

Configure the host to use the same subnet for addresses, masks, and the default gateway as the switch.

Task 3: Verify Connectivity

To verify that the hosts and switch are correctly configured, ping the switch from the hosts.

Were the pings successful? _____

If the answer is no, troubleshoot the hosts and switch configurations.

Task 4: Display the VLAN Interface Information

On Switch_A, enter the command **show vlan** at the privileged EXEC mode prompt.

```
Switch_A#show vlan
```

Which ports belong to the default VLAN? _____

Task 5: Create and Name Two VLANs

Enter the following commands to create two named VLANs:

```
Switch_A#vlan database
Switch_A(vlan)#vlan 2 name VLAN2
Switch_A(vlan)#vlan 3 name VLAN3
Switch_A(config)#exit
```

1900:

```
Switch_A#configure terminal
Switch_A(config)#vlan 2 name VLAN2
Switch_A(config)#vlan 3 name VLAN3
```

Task 6: Assign Ports to VLAN 2

Assigning ports to VLANs must be done from the interface mode. Enter the following commands to add ports 4, 5, and 6 to VLAN 2:

```
Switch_A#configure terminal
Switch_A(config)#interface fastethernet 0/4
Switch_A(config-if)#switchport mode access
Switch_A(config-if)#switchport access vlan 2
Switch_A(config)#interface fastethernet 0/5
Switch_A(config-if)#switchport mode access
Switch_A(config-if)#switchport access vlan 2
Switch_A(config)#interface fastethernet 0/6
Switch_A(config-if)#switchport mode access
Switch_A(config-if)#switchport access vlan 2
Switch_A(config-if)#end
```

1900:

```
Switch_A#configure terminal
Switch_A(config)#interface Ethernet 0/4
Switch_A(config-if)#vlan static 2
Switch_A(config-if)#interface Ethernet 0/5
Switch_A(config-if)#vlan static 2
Switch_A(config-if)#interface Ethernet 0/6
Switch_A(config-if)#vlan static 2
Switch_A(config)#end
```

Task 7: Display the VLAN Interface Information

On Switch_A, enter the command **show vlan** at the privileged EXEC mode prompt.

```
Switch_A#show vlan
```

Are ports 4 through 6 assigned to VLAN 2? _____

Task 8: Assign Ports to VLAN 3

Enter the following commands to assign ports to VLAN 3:

```
Switch_A#configure terminal
Switch_A(config)#interface fastethernet 0/7
Switch_A(config-if)#switchport mode access
Switch_A(config-if)#switchport access vlan 3
Switch_A(config)#interface fastethernet 0/8
Switch_A(config-if)#switchport mode access
Switch_A(config-if)#switchport access vlan 3
Switch_A(config)#interface fastethernet 0/9
Switch_A(config-if)#switchport mode access
Switch_A(config-if)#switchport access vlan 3
Switch_A(config-if)#end
```

Task 9: Display the VLAN Interface Information

On Switch_A, enter the command **show vlan** at the privileged EXEC mode prompt.

```
Switch_A#show vlan
```

Are ports 7 through 9 assigned to VLAN 3? _____

Task 10: Test the VLANs

Step 1. Ping from the host in port 0/4 to the host in port 0/1.

Was the ping successful? _____

Why?

_____

Step 2. Ping from the host in port 0/1 to the host in port 0/4.

Was the ping successful? _____

Why?

_____

Step 3. Ping from the host in port 0/4 to the switch IP 192.168.1.2.

Was the ping successful? _____

Why?

_____

Step 4. Ping from the host in port 0/1 to the switch IP 192.168.1.2.

Was the ping successful? _____

Why?

_____

Task 11: Delete a Host from a VLAN

To remove a host from a VLAN, use the **no** form of the **switchport** commands in port interface configuration mode.

```
Switch_A#configure terminal
Switch_A(config)#interface fastethernet 0/4
Switch_A(config-if)#no switchport mode access
Switch_A(config-if)#no switchport access vlan 2
```

1900:

```
Switch_A#config t
Switch_A(config)#interface Ethernet 0/4
Switch_A(config-if)#no vlan static 2
Switch_A(config-if)#end
```

Task 12: Display the VLAN Interface Information

On Switch_A, enter the command **show vlan** at the privileged EXEC mode prompt.

```
Switch_A#show vlan
```

Is port 0/4 removed from VLAN 2? _____

Task 13: Delete a VLAN

To remove an entire VLAN, enter the VLAN database mode and use the negative form of the command.

```
Switch_A#vlan database
Switch_A(vlan)#no vlan 3
Deleting VLAN 3...
Switch_A(vlan)#exit
```

1900:

```
Switch_A#config t
Switch_A(config)#no vlan 3
Switch_A(config)#exit
```

Task 14: Display the VLAN Interface Information

On Switch_A, enter the command **show vlan** at the privileged EXEC mode prompt.

`Switch_A#`**`show vlan`**

Is VLAN 3 removed? _____

What happened to the ports that were released from the VLANs?

_____

Task 15: Delete VLAN 1

Try to delete VLAN 1, which is the default VLAN, the same way that you deleted VLAN 3.

`Switch_A#`**`vlan database`**
`Switch_A(vlan)#`**`no vlan 1`**
`A default VLAN may not be deleted.`
`Switch_A(vlan)#`**`exit`**

1900:

`Switch_A#`**`config t`**
`Switch_A(config)#`**`no vlan 1`**
`Switch_A(config)#`**`no vlan 1`**

`                          ^`

`% Invalid input detected at '^' marker.`
`Switch_A(config)#`**`exit`**

Can the default VLAN be deleted? _____

After you complete the previous step, log off (by typing **exit**) and turn all the devices off. Then, remove and store the cables and adapter.

Challenge Lab 8-4: Static VLANs, STP, and Port Security

Figure 8-5   Static VLANs, STP, and Port Security

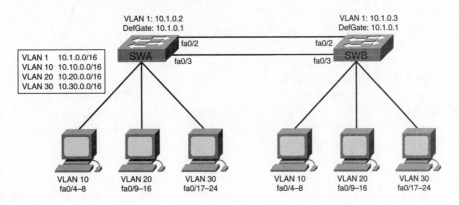

Objectives

- Create and assign VLANs.
- Configure root bridges for STP.
- Configure port security.

Equipment

The topology shown in Figure 8-5 is using 2950 switches.

NetLab Compatibility Notes

This lab is fully compatible with a standard NetLab Basic Switch Pod although you will not be able to fully test your VLANs or port security.

Task 1: Cable the Topology and Basic Configuration

Step 1. Choose two 2950 switches and cable them according to the topology. (If using NetLab, choose a Basic Switch Pod. Portions of this lab will not be verifiable.)

Step 2. Configure the switches according to your instructor's required basic configurations, including hostnames, passwords, host tables, banner, and lines. Configure each of the switches with the correct VLAN 1 IP addresses and the correct default gateway.

Step 3. Verify connectivity between SWA and SWB. Pings should be successful. If not, troubleshoot. Note: Switches should *not* be able to ping the router yet.

Task 2: Configure VLANs

Step 1. Configure the following VLANs on both SWA and SWB:

- VLAN 10 is the Accounting VLAN
- VLAN 20 is the Marketing VLAN
- VLAN 30 is the Purchasing VLAN

Step 2. Configure the appropriate ports on SWA and SWB for trunking with the **switchport mode trunk** command. Verify trunking is properly configured with the **show interface trunk** command on both SWA and SWB.

```
SWA#show interface trunk

Port        Mode         Encapsulation  Status        Native vlan
Fa0/2       on           802.1q         trunking      1
Fa0/3       on           802.1q         trunking      1

Port        Vlans allowed on trunk
Fa0/2       1-4094
Fa0/3       1-4094

Port        Vlans allowed and active in management domain
Fa0/2       1,10,20,30
Fa0/3       1,10,20,30

Port        Vlans in spanning tree forwarding state and not pruned
Fa0/2       1,10,20,30
Fa0/3       1,10,20,30
```

Step 3. The Fa0/1 port is unused on both SWA and SWB. For enhanced security, administratively shut down this port. Otherwise, the port will activate whenever it detects a device on the other end.

Step 4. Configure access mode on the rest of the ports using the **switchport mode access** command. Assign the access ports to their correct VLAN as specified in the topology.

Step 5. Verify the VLAN configuration on both switches with the **show vlan brief** command. Your output should look similar to the following output:

```
SWA#show vlan brief

VLAN Name                             Status    Ports
__ _____ _____ _____
1    default                          active    Fa0/1
10   Accounting                       active    Fa0/4, Fa0/5, Fa0/6, Fa0/7
                                                Fa0/8
20   Marketing                        active    Fa0/9, Fa0/10, Fa0/11,
                                                Fa0/12
                                                Fa0/13, Fa0/14, Fa0/15,
                                                Fa0/16
30   Purchasing                       active    Fa0/17, Fa0/18, Fa0/19,
                                                Fa0/20
                                                Fa0/21, Fa0/22, Fa0/23,
                                                Fa0/24
1002 fddi-default                     active
1003 token-ring-default               active
1004 fddinet-default                  active
1005 trnet-default                    active
```

Task 3: Configure the Root Bridge for STP

Step 1. For VLANs 1, 10, and 30, SWA should always be the root bridge. Configure SWA with a spanning-tree priority of 4096 for these three VLANs.

For VLAN 20, SWA is to never be the root bridge. Configure SWA with a spanning-tree priority of 61,440.

What is the default priority?

_____

Why would you want to configure some VLANs with a different STP root bridge?

_____

_____

Step 2. Verify SWA is the root with the **show spanning-tree summary** command. SWA should be listed as the root bridge, as shown in the following output below:

```
SWA#show spanning-tree summary
Switch is in pvst mode
Root bridge for: VLAN0001, VLAN0010, VLAN0030
EtherChannel misconfiguration guard is enabled
Extended system ID    is enabled
Portfast              is disabled by default
PortFast BPDU Guard   is disabled by default
Portfast BPDU Filter  is disabled by default
Loopguard             is disabled by default
UplinkFast            is disabled
BackboneFast          is disabled
Pathcost method used is short
```

Name	Blocking	Listening	Learning	Forwarding	STP Active
VLAN0001	0	0	0	3	3
VLAN0010	0	0	0	3	3
VLAN0020	1	0	0	2	3
VLAN0030	0	0	0	3	3
4 vlans	1	0	0	11	12

```
SWB#show spanning-tree summary
Switch is in pvst mode
Root bridge for: VLAN0020
EtherChannel misconfiguration guard is enabled
Extended system ID   is enabled
Portfast             is disabled by default
PortFast BPDU Guard  is disabled by default
Portfast BPDU Filter is disabled by default
Loopguard            is disabled by default
UplinkFast           is disabled
BackboneFast         is disabled
Pathcost method used is short
```

Name	Blocking	Listening	Learning	Forwarding	STP Active
VLAN0001	1	0	0	1	2
VLAN0010	1	0	0	1	2
VLAN0020	0	0	1	1	2
VLAN0030	1	0	0	1	2
4 vlans	3	0	1	4	8

Task 4: Configure Port Security

Step 1.   Configure the access ports (Fa0/4 through 24) for access mode and turn on port security.

Step 2.   Enter the command to make the first MAC address learned "stick" to the port. No other MAC addresses should be allowed (maximum of one MAC per port).

Step 3.   Enter the command that will automatically shut down the port if a security violation occurs.

Step 4.   Verify port security with the show port-security command. Your output should look similar to the following output:

```
SWA#show port-security
Secure Port      MaxSecureAddr   CurrentAddr   SecurityViolation   Security
Action
                 (Count)         (Count)       (Count)

_____

        Fa0/4    1               0             0                   Shutdown
        Fa0/5    1               0             0                   Shutdown
        Fa0/6    1               0             0                   Shutdown
        Fa0/7    1               0             0                   Shutdown
        Fa0/8    1               0             0                   Shutdown
        Fa0/9    1               0             0                   Shutdown
        Fa0/10   1               0             0                   Shutdown
        Fa0/11   1               0             0                   Shutdown
        Fa0/12   1               0             0                   Shutdown
        Fa0/13   1               0             0                   Shutdown
        Fa0/14   1               0             0                   Shutdown
        Fa0/15   1               0             0                   Shutdown
        Fa0/16   1               0             0                   Shutdown
        Fa0/17   1               0             0                   Shutdown
        Fa0/18   1               0             0                   Shutdown
        Fa0/19   1               0             0                   Shutdown
        Fa0/20   1               0             0                   Shutdown
        Fa0/21   1               0             0                   Shutdown
        Fa0/22   1               0             0                   Shutdown
        Fa0/23   1               0             0                   Shutdown
        Fa0/24   1               0             0                   Shutdown

_____

Total Addresses in System : 0
Max Addresses limit in System : 1024
```

Task 5: Verify VLANs and Port Security

Step 1.   Test the VLAN configuration by verifying that a host attached to VLAN 10 cannot ping the hosts of VLAN 20 or VLAN 30.

Step 2.   Test the port security configuration by disconnecting a host from a port and connecting a different host to the same port. The port should automatically shut down. How do you, as the administrator, re-enable the port?

_____

_____

_____

CHAPTER 9

VLAN Trunking Protocol

The Study Guide portion of this chapter uses a combination of fill in the blank, open-ended question, and unique custom exercises to test your knowledge on the theory of VLAN Trunking Protocol.

The Lab Exercises portion of this chapter includes all of the online curriculum labs as well as a comprehensive lab and a challenge lab to ensure that you have mastered the practical, hands-on skills needed about VTP.

Study Guide

Trunking

For the purposes of this chapter, a trunk is a physical and logical connection between two switches across which network traffic travels. In a switched network, a trunk is a point-to-point link that supports several VLANs. The purpose of a trunk is to conserve ports when a link between two devices that implement VLANs is created.

In this section, you work through exercises that review trunking, the concept of frame tagging, and basic trunk configuration.

Vocabulary Exercise: Completion

Directions: Complete the paragraphs that follow by filling in appropriate words and phrases.

Two switches directly connected can send and receive traffic for multiple VLANs across a _____ link. The term _____ originated in the telephone industry to describe a link used to carry multiple conversations. In switching technologies, you need to identify which VLAN a frame belongs to. To make this identification possible, switches can use one of two major methods of _____: _____, a Cisco proprietary protocol that used to be the most common, and IEEE _____, which is now the standard for frame tagging. Newer Cisco IOS Software Releases do not even support _____ anymore. It is important to understand that a trunk link does not belong to a specific VLAN. A trunk link is a conduit for VLANs between_____ and _____.

With ___, an Ethernet frame is encapsulated with an additional header that contains a VLAN ID. With _____, a tag containing the VLAN ID is embedded into the Ethernet frame.

A port can be configured as a **trunk** port, an **access** port, or a **dynamic** port. Trunk links should be manually configured, although the Cisco IOS will, by default, detect a trunk link because all ports are set to **dynamic desirable**. Record the command, including correct prompt, to configure a port for trunking.

_____

For the 1900 series switches and the 2950 series switches, you do not have to configure the encapsulation type on a trunk link. However, if you are using a 2900 series switch, which supports both ISL and IEEE 802.1q, then you have to configure the encapsulation type. Record the command, including correct prompt, to configure a port to use ISL encapsulation.

_____

Note: If you are not sure about this command, check Curriculum Lab 9-1, "Trunking with ISL (9.1.5a)."

Now record the command, including correct prompt, to configure a port to use IEEE 802.1q encapsulation.

_____

If your switch is a _____ series, you do *not* configure the encapsulation type. The command is not even available. However, when configuring a router with a VLAN trunk to a switch, you must specify the encapsulation type because the router IOS does not auto-detect it. These commands are reviewed later in the chapter, in the section, "Inter-VLAN Routing Overview."

To quickly verify trunking, you can use the _____ command to display output similar to the following:

```
Port        Mode          Encapsulation  Status       Native vlan
Fa0/1       on            802.1q         trunking     1
Fa0/2       on            802.1q         trunking     1
Fa0/3       on            802.1q         trunking     1


Port        Vlans allowed on trunk
Fa0/1       1-4094
Fa0/2       1-4094
Fa0/3       1-4094


Port        Vlans allowed and active in management domain
Fa0/1       1,10,20,30
Fa0/2       1,10,20,30
Fa0/3       1,10,20,30


Port        Vlans in spanning tree forwarding state and not pruned
Fa0/1       1,10,20,30
Fa0/2       1,10,20,30
Fa0/3       1,10,30
```

You can also view more specific information about a port by using the _____ command to display output similar to the following:

```
Name: Fa0/1
Switchport: Enabled
Administrative Mode: trunk
Operational Mode: trunk
Administrative Trunking Encapsulation: dot1q
Operational Trunking Encapsulation: dot1q
Negotiation of Trunking: On
Access Mode VLAN: 1 (default)
Trunking Native Mode VLAN: 1 (default)
Administrative private-vlan host-association: none
Administrative private-vlan mapping: none
Operational private-vlan: none
Trunking VLANs Enabled: ALL
Pruning VLANs Enabled: 2-1001


Protected: false


Voice VLAN: none (Inactive)
Appliance trust: none
```

Basic Trunk Configuration Exercise

Use Figure 9-1 to answer the following configuration scenario questions.

Figure 9-1   Basic Trunk Configuration

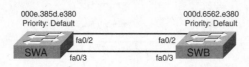

SWA and SWB are both 1900 switches. Record the command or commands, including prompt, needed to set the Fa0/2 and Fa0/3 interfaces to trunking. If necessary, specify ISL as the encapsulation. You may need to research the answer for this question. Try your favorite search engine or Cisco.com.

_____

_____

_____

_____

_____

SWA and SWB are both 2900 switches. Record the command or commands, including prompt, needed to set the Fa0/2 and Fa0/3 interfaces to trunking. If necessary, specify ISL as the encapsulation.

_____

_____

_____

_____

_____

SWA and SWB are both 2950 switches. Record the command or commands, including prompt, needed to set the Fa0/2 and Fa0/3 interfaces to trunking. If necessary, specify IEEE 802.1q as the encapsulation.

_____

_____

_____

_____

_____

Which switch is the STP root bridge and why?

_____

VTP

VTP was created by Cisco to solve operational problems in a switched network with VLANs. It is a Cisco proprietary protocol. With VTP, VLAN configuration is consistently maintained across a common administrative domain. Additionally, VTP reduces management and monitoring complexities of networks with VLANs.

In this section, you will work through exercises that cover the basic concepts and configurations of VTP. You will also find several concept questions to answer. A lesson from Cisco.com will round out your study of VTP.

Vocabulary Exercise: Completion

Directions: Complete the paragraphs that follow by filling in appropriate words and phrases.

The role of _____, or VTP, is to maintain VLAN configuration consistency across a common network administration domain. Although switch ports are normally assigned to only a single VLAN, trunk ports by default carry frames from _____.

Switches can operate in one of three VTP modes. The default mode is VTP _____. A switch operating in VTP _____ mode propagates configuration changes as VTP messages across _____ links to all connected switches in the network. Switches that are in VTP _____ mode and share the same _____ name and _____ as the server use VTP messages to adjust the local VLAN database. Switches that are in VTP _____ mode do *not* use VTP messages. However, a switch in this mode forwards the VTP messages out all _____ links except for the link the messages were originally received on. In addition, a switch in _____ mode can create, modify, and delete its own local _____. Provide the missing information in Table 9-1.

Table 9-1   VTP Mode Comparisons

Feature	_____ Mode	_____ Mode	_____ Mode
Source VTP messages			
Listen to VTP messages	Yes		
Create VLANs	Yes	No	Yes[1]
Remember VLANs			

1. Locally significant only.

Before the VTP _____ will propagate VTP messages, it must be configured with a VTP _____ name. The default name is _____. Because all switches are in VTP _____ mode by default, there must be a method to determine which VLAN database will have priority. This is done through the concept of a _____ number, which is __ when the switch first boots. Each time a VLAN is added, deleted, or modified by the VTP _____, the _____ number is _____ and a VTP _____ is sent out all _____ ports. If more than one VTP _____ exists in the same VTP _____, then messages from the server with the highest _____ number take precedence over all other messages. As a precaution against misconfigurations, it is always a good idea to configure both VTP _____ and VTP _____ with a VTP _____.

VTP Basic Configuration Exercise

Use Figure 9-2 to answer the following configuration scenario questions.

Figure 9-2   VTP Basic Configuration

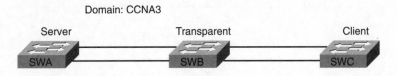

You want to configure local VLANs on SWB that will not be propagated to SWA or SWC. In addition, you do not want SWB to apply any VLANs created by SWA or SWC. Therefore, you need to configure SWB to be in VTP transparent mode. Record the commands, including prompt, to configure SWB in this mode.

_____
_____
_____
_____
_____

All your domain-wide VLANs are going to be created on SWA and propagated throughout the domain. Therefore, you need to configure SWA to be in VTP server mode. Record the commands, including prompt, to configure SWA in this mode.

_____
_____
_____
_____
_____

You do not want SWC to inadvertently be able to create VLANs. Therefore, you need to configure SWC to be in VTP client mode. Record the commands, including prompt, to configure SWC in this mode.

_____
_____
_____
_____
_____

Are there any problems with your configuration? Will SWC update its VLANs when SWA makes VLAN changes? Explain any problems and how to fix them.

_____
_____
_____
_____
_____
_____
_____
_____
_____
_____
_____
_____
_____

Concept Questions

Explain why VTP was developed by Cisco to solve operational problems in a switched network with VLANs.

_____
_____
_____
_____

List the two main types of VTP advertisements.

_____

_____

List and describe the three types of VTP messages.

_____

_____

_____

_____

_____

_____

_____

List at least three actions that can trigger a server to send subset advertisements.

- _____

- _____

- _____

- _____

- _____

Internet Research: VTP

At Cisco.com, you will find a very thorough review of VTP including information not covered in this chapter. Use the following link to access this VTP lesson online:

http://www.cisco.com/warp/public/473/vtp_flash/

When you are done, answer the questions that follow.

Introduction to VTP

VTP is a Layer 2 messaging protocol used to maintain _____ configuration consistency by managing the _____, _____, and _____ of _____ on a network-wide basis.

In a network with six switches and VLANs that are shared across switches, what would you have to do if you did not use VTP?

Manually configure and maintain the VLANs on every switch.

A VTP frame consists of a VTP _____ and a VTP _____ type. The VTP information is inserted in the _____ portion of an Ethernet frame.

What kind of address do VTP messages use?

_____

How often are summary advertisements sent and what is their purpose?

_____

_____

_____

What does an advertisement request cause to happen?

_____

VTP Domain and VTP Modes

When a switch has been cleared and rebooted, it has the following VTP configuration:

- VTP Domain Name = _____
- VTP Mode = _____
- Configuration Revision = _____
- VLANs = _____

The VTP _____ can add, delete, or rename VLANs. It also advertises the _____ name, _____ configuration, and _____ number to all other switches in the VTP domain. It also maintains a list of all VLANs in _____ so that it can retrieve this information if the switch is reset.

A VTP _____ cannot add, delete, or rename VLANs. It does not store VLANs in _____.

Switches in VTP _____ mode must have their VLANs configured manually. They do not participate in VTP or advertise their VLAN configuration. When is it useful to configure a switch in this mode?

_____

_____

Before VLANs will be advertised by the VTP server, you must configure a domain name.

Assume that VLANs 10, 20, and 30 have been added to a VTP server with appropriate names. What is the configuration revision number? _____

Now assume that the name for VLAN 10 is changed, VLAN 30 is deleted, and VLAN 40 is added. What is the configuration revision number? _____

List the three types of _____ links that VTP messages will be sent across.

_____

What MAC address are VTP messages sent to?

_____

Assume that you configure six VLANs on a VTP transparent switch. What would be the configuration revision number? __

_____

It what situations will a VTP transparent switch forward VTP messages to other switches.

_____

Common VTP Issues

Assuming that a new switch was configured with the correct domain name, what would happen if you were to add a VTP client or server switch with a higher configuration revision number to the network?

_____

_____

_____

_____

_____

_____

List three possible ways to reset the configuration revision number on a switch. (Only two methods are discussed in the presentation. Can you think of another way?)

_____

_____

_____

Internet Research: VTP Pruning

There will be a lot of traffic on a large switched network with VLANs that span multiple switches. VTP pruning is a method of reducing traffic. Research VTP pruning and briefly describe what it is, how it operates, and what configuration commands, if any, you would use. Make sure to list your sources.

_____

_____

_____

_____

_____

_____

_____

_____

_____

_____

Inter-VLAN Routing Overview

Inter-VLAN communication cannot occur without a Layer 3 device, such as a router. You will use ISL or IEEE 802.1q to enable trunking on a router subinterface. In this section, you will briefly review the concept of inter-VLAN routing. Then, you will work through a inter-VLAN routing configuration exercise.

Vocabulary Exercise: Completion

Directions: Complete the paragraphs that follow by filling in appropriate words and phrases.

Inter-VLAN communication crosses _____ domains. When a host in one _____ domain wishes to communicate with a host in another _____ domain, you must use a _____. When connecting a router to a switched network with multiple VLANs, one interface is needed per _____ because each is on its own logical network or _____. You can reduce the number of physical interfaces needed to route VLANs by using a _____ link between the switch and router. You achieve logical division of a physical interface by implementing _____. One _____ would be configured per _____. Each _____ would also be configured with an IP address from a separate logical _____.

Basic Inter-VLAN Configuration Exercise

Use Figure 9-3 to answer the following configuration scenario questions.

Figure 9-3   Basic Inter-VLAN Configuration

VLAN 1	192.168.1.0/24
VLAN 100	192.168.100.0/24
VLAN 200	192.168.200.0/24
VLAN 300	192.168.300.0/24

What does a router like RTA require in order to route between VLANs?

_____

Record the commands, including prompt, to configure RTA to route for all the VLANs shown in Figure 9-3. Use IEEE 802.1q encapsulation. Describe all interfaces and make sure you append the word **native** to the end of the encapsulation configuration for VLAN 1. Use the first available IP address in each network.

_____
_____
_____
_____
_____
_____
_____
_____
_____
_____
_____
_____
_____
_____
_____
_____
_____
_____
_____
_____
_____
_____
_____
_____

Lab Exercises

Command Reference

In the table that follows, record the command, including the correct switch prompt, that fits the description for a 1900 Catalyst switch.

1900 Switch Command	Description
Switch(config)#`interface fa 0/26`	
Switch(config-if)#	Turns port to trunking mode
	Displays trunking information about port 0/26, which is trunk A
	Changes the switch to client mode
	Changes the switch to server mode
	Changes the switch to transparent mode
	Sets the name of the VTP management domain to CCNA3
	Set the VTP password to cisco
	Displays all VTP information

In the table that follows, record the command, including the correct switch prompt, that fits the description for a 2900 Catalyst switch. When appropriate, use VLAN database configuration mode.

2900 Switch Command	Description
	Turns port to trunking mode
	Sets encapsulation type to ISL
	Sets encapsulation type to Dot1Q— the default encapsulation type
	Enters VLAN database mode
	Changes the switch to client mode
	Changes the switch to server mode
	Changes the switch to transparent mode
	Sets the name of the VTP management domain to CCNA3
	Set the VTP password to cisco
	Sets VTP mode to version 2
	Enables VTP pruning
	Applies the VLAN database changes and exits the mode

In the table that follows, record the command, including the correct switch prompt, that fits the description for a 2950 Catalyst switch. When appropriate, use global configuration mode. Do *not* use VLAN database configuration mode.

2950 Switch Command	Description
Switch(config)#**interface fa 0/1**	
	Turns port to trunking mode
	Shows the status of interface Fa0/1, including trunking information (works with both 2900 and 2950 switches)
	Changes the switch to client mode
	Changes the switch to server mode
	Changes the switch to transparent mode
	Sets the name of the VTP management domain to CCNA3
	Set the VTP password to cisco
	Sets VTP mode to version 2
	Enables VTP pruning
	Displays VTP domain status (works with both 2900 and 2950 switches)
	Displays VTP statistics (works with both 2900 and 2950 switches)

In the table that follows, record the command, including the correct router prompt, that fits the description for a 2600 series router.

2600 Command	Description
	Enters interface mode for interface Fa0/0
	Turns on the interface
	Creates subinterface 0/0.1
	Assigns the native VLAN to this logical subinterface using Dot1Q encapsulation
	Assigns the IP address 192.168.1.1/24 to this logical interface
	Creates subinterface 0/0.10
	Assigns VLAN 10 to this logical interface using Dot1Q encapsulation
	Assigns the IP address 192.168.10.1/24 to this logical interface

Curriculum Lab 9-1: Trunking with ISL (9.1.5a)

Figure 9-4   Topology for Lab 9-1

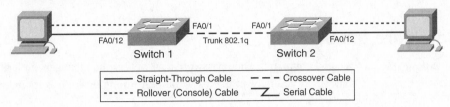

Switch 1 FA0/12 ——— FA0/1 Trunk 802.1q FA0/1 Switch 2 FA0/12

Switch 1   Switch 2

Straight-Through Cable   — — — Crossover Cable
Rollover (Console) Cable   Serial Cable

Table 9-2   Lab Equipment Configuration

Switch Designation	Switch Name	VLAN 1 IP Address	VLAN Names and Numbers	Switch Port Assignments
Switch 1	Switch_A	192.168.1.2	VLAN 1 Native VLAN 10 Accounting VLAN 20 Marketing VLAN 30 Engineering	Fa0/2–0/3 Fa0/4–0/6 Fa0/7–0/9 Fa0/10–0/12
Switch 2	Switch_B	192.168.1.3	VLAN 1 Native VLAN 10 Accounting VLAN 20 Marketing VLAN 30 Engineering	Fa0/2–0/3 Fa0/4–0/6 Fa0/7–0/9 Fa0/10–0/12

The enable secret password for both routers is **class**.

The enable, VTY, and console password for both routers is **cisco**.

The subnet mask for both routers is 255.255.255.0.

Objectives

- Create a basic switch configuration and verify it.

- Create multiple VLANs, name them, and assign multiple member ports to them.

- Create an ISL trunk line between the two switches to allow communication between paired VLANs.

- Test the VLANs' functionality by moving a workstation from one VLAN to another.

Background/Preparation

Important Note: The use of Catalyst 2950 switches is not appropriate for this lab, because those switches support only 802.1q trunking.

Trunking changes the formatting of the packets. The ports need to be in agreement as to which format is being used to transmit data on the trunk, or no data will be passed. If different trunking encapsulation occurs on the two ends of the link, they will not able to communicate. A similar situation will occur if one of your ports is configured in trunking mode (unconditionally) and the other one is in access mode (unconditionally).

When you are managing a switch, the management domain is always VLAN 1. The network administrator's workstation must have access to a port in the VLAN 1 management domain. All ports are assigned to VLAN 1 by default. This lab will help demonstrate how you can use VLANs to separate traffic and reduce broadcast domains.

Cable a network that is similar to the one in Figure 9-4. The configuration output used in this lab is produced from a 2900 switch. Another switch might produce different output. You should execute the following steps on each switch unless you are specifically instructed otherwise.

Start a HyperTerminal session.

Implement the procedure documented in Appendix B, "Erasing and Reloading the Switch," before you continue with this lab.

Task 1: Configure the Switch

Configure the hostname, access, and command mode passwords, as well as the management LAN settings. These values are shown in Table 9-2. If you have problems while performing this configuration, refer to Lab 6-2, "Basic Switch Configuration."

Task 2: Configure the Hosts Attached to the Switch

Configure the host to use the same subnet for addresses, masks, and the default gateway as the switch.

Task 3: Verify Connectivity

To verify that the hosts and switch are correctly configured, ping the switch from the hosts.

Were the pings successful? _____

If the answer is no, troubleshoot the hosts and switch configurations.

Task 4: Display the VLAN Interface Information

On Switch_A, enter the command **show vlan** at the privileged EXEC mode prompt.

```
Switch_A#show vlan
```

Task 5: Create and Name Three VLANs

Use the following commands to create three named VLANs:

2900 Switch
```
Switch_A#vlan database
Switch_A(vlan)#vlan 10 name Accounting
Switch_A(vlan)#vlan 20 name Marketing
Switch_A(vlan)#vlan 30 name Engineering
Switch_A(vlan)#exit
```

2950 Switch
```
Switch_A#configure terminal
Switch_A(config)#vlan 10
Switch_A(config-vlan)#name Accounting
Switch_A(config-vlan)#vlan 20
Switch_A(config-vlan)#name Marketing
Switch_A(config-vlan)#vlan 30
Switch_A(config-vlan)#name Engineering
```

Note: VLAN database mode is being deprecated in future releases of Cisco IOS. For now, both VLAN database mode and global configuration mode are supported for creating VLANs.

Task 6: Assign Ports to VLAN 10

You must assign ports to VLANs from the interface mode. Enter the following commands to add ports 0/4 to 0/6 to VLAN 10:

```
Switch_A#configure terminal
Switch_A(config)#interface fastethernet 0/4
Switch_A(config-if)#switchport mode access
Switch_A(config-if)#switchport access vlan 10
Switch_A(config-if)#interface fastethernet 0/5
Switch_A(config-if)#switchport mode access
Switch_A(config-if)#switchport access vlan 10
Switch_A(config-if)#interface fastethernet 0/6
Switch_A(config-if)#switchport mode access
Switch_A(config-if)#switchport access vlan 10
Switch_A(config-if)#end
```

Note: Use the **range** parameter to quickly configure several interfaces with the same command. For example:

```
Switch_A#configure terminal
Switch_A(config)#interface range fastethernet 0/4 - 6
Switch_A(config-if-range)#switchport mode access
Switch_A(config-if-range)#switchport access vlan 10
Switch_A(config-if-range)#end
```

Task 7: Assign Ports to VLAN 20

Enter the following commands to add ports 0/7 to 0/9 to VLAN 20:

```
Switch_A#configure terminal
Switch_A(config)#interface fastethernet 0/7
Switch_A(config-if)#switchport mode access
Switch_A(config-if)#switchport access vlan 20
Switch_A(config-if)#interface fastethernet 0/8
Switch_A(config-if)#switchport mode access
Switch_A(config-if)#switchport access vlan 20
Switch_A(config-if)#interface fastethernet 0/9
Switch_A(config-if)#switchport mode access
Switch_A(config-if)#switchport access vlan 20
Switch_A(config-if)#end
```

Task 8: Assign Ports to VLAN 30

Enter the following commands to add ports 0/10 to 0/12 to VLAN 30:

```
Switch_A#configure terminal
Switch_A(config)#interface fastethernet 0/10
Switch_A(config-if)#switchport mode access
Switch_A(config-if)#switchport access vlan 30
Switch_A(config-if)#interface fastethernet 0/11
Switch_A(config-if)#switchport mode access
```

```
Switch_A(config-if)#switchport access vlan 30
Switch_A(config-if)#interface fastethernet 0/12
Switch_A(config-if)#switchport mode access
Switch_A(config-if)#switchport access vlan 30
Switch_A(config-if)#end
```

Task 9: Create VLANs on Switch_B

Repeat Tasks 5 through 8 on Switch_B to create its VLANs.

Task 10: Display the VLAN Interface Information

On Switch_A, enter the command **show vlan** at the privileged EXEC mode prompt.

```
Switch_A#show vlan
```

Are ports 0/10 to 0/12 assigned to VLAN 30? _____

Task 11: Test the VLANs

Step 1.   Ping from the host in Switch_A port 0/12 to the host in Switch_B port 0/12.

Was the ping successful? _____

Why?

_____

Step 2.   Ping from the host in Switch_A port 0/12 to the switch IP 192.168.1.2.

Was the ping successful? _____

Why?

_____

Task 12: Create the ISL Trunk

On both Switch_A and Switch_B, enter the following command at the Fast Ethernet 0/1 interface command prompt:

```
Switch_A(config)#interface fastethernet 0/1
Switch_A(config-if)#switchport trunk encapsulation isl
Switch_A(config-if)#switchport mode trunk
Switch_A(config-if)#end

Switch_B(config)#interface fastethernet 0/1
Switch_B(config-if)#switchport mode trunk
Switch_B(config-if)#switchport trunk encapsulation isl
Switch_B(config-if)#end
```

Task 13: Verify the ISL Trunk

To verify that port Fast Ethernet 0/1 has been established as a trunk port, enter **show interface fastethernet 0/1 switchport** at the privileged EXEC mode prompt.

What type of trunking encapsulation is shown in the output? _____

According to the output with **show interface fastethernet 0/1 switchport** on Switch_B, is there a difference between the Administrative Trunking Encapsulation and the Operational Trunking Encapsulation?

_____

On the fragment "Trunking VLANs Enable" from the last output, what does the word ALL mean?

_____

What would happen if the two ports of the trunk were using different encapsulation?

_____

Explain.

_____

Task 14: Test the VLANs and the Trunk

Step 1.   To test the VLANs and the trunk, ping from the host in Switch_A port 0/12 to the host in Switch_B port 0/12.

Was the ping successful? _____

Why?

_____

Step 2.   Ping from the host in Switch_A port 0/12 to the switch IP 192.168.1.2.

Was the ping successful? _____

Why?

_____

Task 15: Move the Hosts

Move the host in Switch_A from port 0/12 to port 0/8, wait until the port LED turns green, and then go to the next task.

Task 16: Test the VLANs and the Trunk

Step 1.   To test the VLANs and the trunk, ping from the host in Switch_A port 0/8 to the host in Switch_B port 0/12.

Was the ping successful? _____

Why?

_____

Step 2.   Ping from the host in Switch_A port 0/8 to the switch IP 192.168.1.2.

Was the ping successful? _____

Why?

_____

Task 17: Move the Hosts

Move the host in Switch_B from port 0/12 to port 0/7, wait until the port LED turns green, and then go to the next task.

Task 18: Test the VLANs and the Trunk

Step 1.   To test the VLANs and the trunk, ping from the host in Switch_A port 0/8 to the host in Switch_B port 0/7.

Was the ping successful? _____

Why?

_____

Step 2.   Ping from the host in Switch_A port 0/8 to the switch IP 192.168.1.2.

Was the ping successful? _____

Why?

_____

Task 19: Move the Hosts

Move the host in Switch_A from port 0/8 to port 0/2, wait until the port LED turns green, and then go to the next task.

Task 20: Test the VLANs and the Trunk

Step 1.   To test the VLANs and the trunk, ping from the host in Switch_A port 0/2 to the host in Switch_B port 0/7.

Was the ping successful? _____

Step 2.   Ping from the host in Switch_A port 0/2 to the switch IP 192.168.1.2.

Was the ping successful? _____

Why?

_____

Task 21: Move the Hosts

Move the host in Switch_B from port 0/7 to port 0/3, wait until the port LED turns green, and then go to the next task.

Task 22: Test the VLANs and the Trunk

Step 1.   To test the VLANs and the trunk, ping from the host in Switch_A port 0/2 to the host in Switch_B port 0/3.

Was the ping successful? _____

Why?

_____

Step 2.   Ping from the host in Switch_B port 0/3 to the switch IP 192.168.1.2.

Was the ping successful? _____

Why?

_____

Step 3. Ping from the host in Switch_B port 0/3 to the switch IP 192.168.1.3.

Was the ping successful? _____

Why?

_____

What conclusions can you draw from the testing that you just performed in regard to VLAN membership and VLANs across a trunk?

_____

_____

_____

Step 4. After you complete the previous steps, log off (by typing **exit**) and turn all the devices off. Then, remove and store the cables and adapter.

Curriculum Lab 9-2: Trunking with 802.1q (9.1.5b)

Figure 9-5   Topology for Lab 9-2

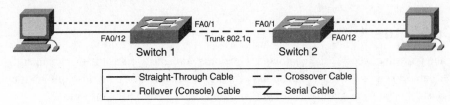

		FA0/1	FA0/1		
FA0/12		Trunk 802.1q		FA0/12	
	Switch 1		Switch 2		

——— Straight-Through Cable	– – – Crossover Cable	
······ Rollover (Console) Cable	⌿ Serial Cable	

Table 9-3   Lab Equipment Configuration

Switch Designation	Switch Name	VLAN 1 IP Address	VLAN Names and Numbers	Switch Port Assignments
Switch 1	Switch_A	192.168.1.2	VLAN 1 Native	Fa0/2–0/3
			VLAN 10 Accounting	Fa0/4–0/6
			VLAN 20 Marketing	Fa0/7–0/9
			VLAN 30 Engineering	Fa0/10–0/12
Switch 2	Switch_B	192.168.1.3	VLAN 1 Native	Fa0/2–0/3
			VLAN 10 Accounting	Fa0/4–0/6
			VLAN 20 Marketing	Fa0/7–0/9
			VLAN 30 Engineering	Fa0/10–0/12

The enable secret password for both routers is **class**.

The enable, VTY, and console password for both routers is **cisco**.

The subnet mask for both routers is 255.255.255.0.

Objectives

- Create a basic switch configuration and verify it.

- Create multiple VLANs, name them, and assign multiple member ports to them.

- Create an 802.1q trunk line between the two switches to allow communication between paired VLANs.

- Test the VLANs' functionality by moving a workstation from one VLAN to another.

Background/Preparation

Trunking changes the formatting of the packets. The ports need to be in agreement as to which format is being used to transmit data on the trunk, or no data will be passed. If the two ends of the link have a different trunking encapsulation, they will not be able to communicate. A similar situation will occur if one of your ports is configured in trunking mode (unconditionally) and the other one is in access mode (unconditionally).

When you are managing a switch, the management domain is always VLAN 1. The network administrator's workstation must have access to a port in the VLAN 1 management domain. All ports are assigned to VLAN 1 by default. This lab will help demonstrate how you can use VLANs to separate traffic and reduce broadcast domains.

Cable a network that is similar to the one in Figure 9-5. The configuration output that is used in this lab is produced from a 2950 series switch. Another switch might produce different output. You should execute the following steps on each switch unless you are specifically instructed otherwise.

Start a HyperTerminal session.

Implement the procedure documented in Appendix B before you continue with this lab.

Task 1: Configure the Switch

Configure the hostname, access, and command mode passwords, as well as the management LAN settings. These values are shown in Table 9-3. If you have problems while performing this configuration, refer to Lab 6-2, "Basic Switch Configuration." Do *not* configure VLANs and trunking yet.

Task 2: Configure the Hosts Attached to the Switch

Configure the host to use the same subnet for addresses, masks, and the default gateway as the switch.

Task 3: Verify Connectivity

To verify that the hosts and switch are configured correctly, ping the switch from the hosts.

Were the pings successful? _____

If the answer is no, troubleshoot the hosts and switch configurations.

Task 4: Display the VLAN Interface Information

On Switch_A, enter the command **show vlan** at the privileged EXEC mode prompt.

```
Switch_A#show vlan
```

Task 5: Create and Name Three VLANs

Enter the following commands to create three named VLANs:

2900 Switch

```
Switch_A#vlan database

Switch_A(vlan)#vlan 10 name Accounting

Switch_A(vlan)#vlan 20 name Marketing

Switch_A(vlan)#vlan 30 name Engineering

Switch_A(vlan)#exit
```

2950 Switch

```
Switch_A#configure terminal

Switch_A(config)#vlan 10

Switch_A(config-vlan)#name Accounting

Switch_A(config-vlan)#vlan 20

Switch_A(config-vlan)#name Marketing

Switch_A(config-vlan)#vlan 30

Switch_A(config-vlan)#name Engineering
```

Note: VLAN database mode is being deprecated in future releases of Cisco IOS. For now, both VLAN database mode and global configuration mode are supported for creating VLANs.

Task 6: Assign Ports to VLAN 10

You must assign ports to VLANs from the interface mode. Enter the following commands to add ports 0/4 to 0/6 to VLAN 10:

```
Switch_A#configure terminal

Switch_A(config)#interface fastethernet 0/4

Switch_A(config-if)#switchport mode access

Switch_A(config-if)#switchport access vlan 10

Switch_A(config-if)#interface fastethernet 0/5

Switch_A(config-if)#switchport mode access

Switch_A(config-if)#switchport access vlan 10

Switch_A(config-if)#interface fastethernet 0/6

Switch_A(config-if)#switchport mode access

Switch_A(config-if)#switchport access vlan 10

Switch_A(config-if)#end
```

Note: Use the **range** parameter to quickly configure several interfaces with the same command. For example:

```
Switch_A#configure terminal

Switch_A(config)#interface range fastethernet 0/4 - 6

Switch_A(config-if-range)#switchport mode access

Switch_A(config-if-range)#switchport access vlan 10

Switch_A(config-if-range)#end
```

Task 7: Assign Ports to VLAN 20

Enter the following commands to add ports 0/7 to 0/9 to VLAN 20:

```
Switch_A#configure terminal

Switch_A(config)#interface fastethernet 0/7

Switch_A(config-if)#switchport mode access
```

```
Switch_A(config-if)#switchport access vlan 20
Switch_A(config-if)#interface fastethernet 0/8
Switch_A(config-if)#switchport mode access
Switch_A(config-if)#switchport access vlan 20
Switch_A(config-if)#interface fastethernet 0/9
Switch_A(config-if)#switchport mode access
Switch_A(config-if)#switchport access vlan 20
Switch_A(config-if)#end
```

Task 8: Assign Ports to VLAN 30

Enter the following commands to add ports 0/10 to 0/12 to VLAN 30:

```
Switch_A#configure terminal
Switch_A(config)#interface fastethernet 0/10
Switch_A(config-if)#switchport mode access
Switch_A(config-if)#switchport access vlan 30
Switch_A(config-if)#interface fastethernet 0/11
Switch_A(config-if)#switchport mode access
Switch_A(config-if)#switchport access vlan 30
Switch_A(config-if)#interface fastethernet 0/12
Switch_A(config-if)#switchport mode access
Switch_A(config-if)#switchport access vlan 30
Switch_A(config-if)#end
```

Task 9: Create VLANs on Switch_B

Repeat Tasks 5 through 8 on Switch_B to create its VLANs.

Task 10: Display the VLAN Interface Information

On both switches, enter the command **show vlan** at the privileged EXEC mode prompt.

```
Switch_A#show vlan
```

Are ports 0/10 to 0/12 assigned to VLAN 30? _____

Task 11: Test the VLANs

Step 1.   Ping from the host in Switch_A port 0/12 to the host in Switch_B port 0/12.

Was the ping successful? _____

Why?

_____

Step 2.   Ping from the host in Switch_A port 0/12 to the switch IP 192.168.1.2.

Was the ping successful? _____

Why?

_____

Task 12: Create the Trunk

On both switches, Switch_A and Switch_B, enter the following command at the Fast Ethernet 0/1 interface command prompt. Note that it is not necessary to specify the encapsulation on a 2950, because it only supports 802.1q.

```
Switch_A(config)#interface fastethernet 0/1
Switch_A(config-if)#switchport mode trunk
Switch_A(config-if)#end
Switch_B(config)#interface fastethernet 0/1
Switch_B(config-if)#switchport mode trunk
Switch_B(config-if)#end
```

2900:

```
Switch_A(config)#interface fastethernet0/1
Switch_A(config-if)#switchport mode trunk
Switch_A(config-if)#switchport trunk encapsulation dot1q
Switch_A(config-if)#end

Switch_B(config)#interface fastethernet0/1
Switch_B(config-if)#switchport mode trunk
Switch_B(config-if)#switchport trunk encapsulation dot1q
Switch_B(config-if)#end
```

Task 13: Verify the Trunk

To verify that port Fast Ethernet 0/1 has been established as a trunk port, enter **show interface fastethernet 0/1 switchport** at the privileged EXEC mode prompt.

What type of trunking encapsulation is shown on the output results? _____

According to the output with **show interface fastethernet 0/1 switchport** on Switch_B, is there a difference between the Administrative Trunking Encapsulation and the Operational Trunking Encapsulation?

_____

On the fragment "Trunking VLANs Enable" from the last output, what does the word ALL mean?

_____

What would happen if the two ports of the trunk were using different encapsulation?

_____

Explain.

_____

Task 14: Test the VLANs and the Trunk

Step 1.   To test the VLANs and the trunk, ping from the host in Switch_A port 0/12 to the host in Switch_B port 0/12.

Was the ping successful? _____

Why?

_____

Step 2.   Ping from the host in Switch_A port 0/12 to the switch IP 192.168.1.2.

Was the ping successful? _____

Why?

_____

Task 15: Move the Hosts

Move the host in Switch_A from port 0/12 to port 0/8, wait until the port LED turns green, and then go to the next task.

Task 16: Test the VLANs and the Trunk

Step 1.   To test the VLANs and the trunk, ping from the host in Switch_A port 0/8 to the host in Switch_B port 0/12.

Was the ping successful?_____

Why?

_____

Step 2.   Ping from the host in Switch_A port 0/8 to the switch IP 192.168.1.2.

Was the ping successful? _____

Why?

_____

Task 17: Move the Hosts

Move the host in Switch_B from port 0/12 to port 0/7, wait until the port LED turns green, and then go to the next task.

Task 18: Test the VLANs and the Trunk

Step 1.   To test the VLANs and the trunk, ping from the host in Switch_A port 0/8 to the host in Switch_B port 0/7.

Was the ping successful? _____

Why?

_____

Step 2.   Ping from the host in Switch_A port 0/8 to the switch IP 192.168.1.2.

Was the ping successful? _____

Why?

_____

Task 19: Move the Hosts

Move the host in Switch_A from port 0/8 to port 0/2, wait until the port LED turns green, and then go to the next task.

Task 20: Test the VLANs and the Trunk

Step 1.   To test the VLANs and the trunk, ping from the host in Switch_A port 0/2 to the host in Switch_B port 0/7.

Was the ping successful? _____

Step 2.   Ping from the host in Switch_A port 0/2 to the switch IP 192.168.1.2.

Was the ping successful? _____

Why?

_____

Task 21: Move the Hosts

Move the host in Switch_B from port 0/7 to port 0/3, wait until the port LED turns green, and then go to the next task.

Task 22: Test the VLANs and the Trunk

Step 1.   To test the VLANs and the trunk, ping from the host in Switch_A port 0/2 to the host in Switch_B port 0/3.

Was the ping successful? _____

Why?

_____

Step 2.   Ping from the host in Switch_B port 0/3 to the switch IP 192.168.1.2.

Was the ping successful? _____

Why?

_____

Step 3.   Ping from the host in Switch_B port 0/3 to the switch IP 192.168.1.3.

Was the ping successful? _____

Why?

_____

What conclusions can you draw from the testing that you just performed in regard to VLAN membership and VLANs across a trunk?

_____

_____

After you complete the previous steps, log off (by typing **exit**) and turn all the devices off. Then, remove and store the cables and adapter.

Curriculum Lab 9-3: VTP Client and Server Configurations (9.2.5)

Figure 9-6   Topology for Lab 9-3

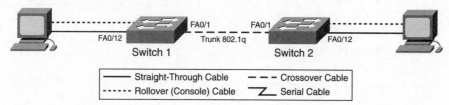

	Straight-Through Cable	– – – Crossover Cable
	Rollover (Console) Cable	Serial Cable

Table 9-4   Lab Equipment Configuration

Switch Designation	Switch Name	VLAN 1 IP Address	VLAN Names and Numbers	Switch Port Assignments
Switch 1	Switch_A	192.168.1.2	VLAN 1 Native	Fa0/2–0/3
			VLAN 10 Accounting	Fa0/4–0/6
			VLAN 20 Marketing	Fa0/7–0/9
			VLAN 30 Engineering	Fa0/10–0/12
Switch 2	Switch_B	192.168.1.3	VLAN 1 Native	Fa0/2–0/3
			VLAN 10 Accounting	Fa0/4–0/6
			VLAN 20 Marketing	Fa0/7–0/9
			VLAN 30 Engineering	Fa0/10–0/12

The enable secret password for both routers is **class**.

The enable, VTY, and console password for both routers is **cisco**.

The subnet mask for both routers is 255.255.255.0.

Objectives

- Create a basic switch configuration and verify it.

- Create multiple VLANs, name them, and assign multiple member ports to them.

- Configure the VTP protocol to establish server and client switches.

- Create an 802.1q trunk line between the two switches to allow communication between paired VLANs.

- Test the VLANs' functionality by moving a workstation from one VLAN to another.

Background/Preparation

When you are managing a switch, the management domain is always VLAN 1. The network administrator's workstation must have access to a port in the VLAN 1 management domain. All ports are assigned to VLAN 1 by default.

Cable a network that is similar to the one in Figure 9-6. The configuration output used in this lab is produced from a 2950 series switch. Another switch might produce different output. You should execute the following steps on each switch unless you are specifically instructed otherwise.

Start a HyperTerminal session.

Implement the procedure documented in Appendix B before you continue with this lab.

Task 1: Configure the Switches

Configure the hostname, access, and command mode passwords, as well as the management LAN settings. These values are shown in Table 9-4. If you have problems while performing this configuration, refer to Lab 6-2, "Basic Switch Configuration."

Task 2: Configure the Hosts Attached to the Switch

Configure the host to use the same subnet for addresses, masks, and the default gateway as the switch.

Task 3: Verify Connectivity

To verify that the hosts and switch are configured correctly, ping the switch from the hosts.

Were the pings successful? _____

If the answer is no, troubleshoot the hosts and switch configurations.

Task 4: Display the VLAN Interface Information

On Switch_A, enter the command **show vlan** at the privileged EXEC mode prompt.

```
Switch_A#show vlan
```

Task 5: Configure VTP

You need to configure VLAN Trunking Protocol (VTP) on both switches. VTP is the protocol that communicates information about which VLANs exist from one switch to another. If VTP did not provide this information, you would have to create VLANs on all switches individually.

By default, the Catalyst switch series are configured as VTP servers. If the server services are turned off, use the following command to turn it back on.

2900 Switch
```
Switch_A#vlan database

Switch_A(vlan)#vtp server

Switch_A(vlan)#exit
```

2950 Switch
```
Switch_A#configure terminal

Switch_A(config)#vtp mode server

Switch_A(config)#end
```

Note: VLAN database mode is being deprecated in future releases of Cisco IOS. For now, both VLAN database mode and global configuration mode are supported for creating VLANs.

Task 6: Create and Name Three VLANs

Enter the following commands to create three named VLANs:

2900 Switch
```
Switch_A#vlan database

Switch_A(vlan)#vlan 10 name Accounting

Switch_A(vlan)#vlan 20 name Marketing

Switch_A(vlan)#vlan 30 name Engineering

Switch_A(vlan)#exit
```

2950 Switch

```
Switch_A#configure terminal
Switch_A(config)#vlan 10
Switch_A(config-vlan)#name Accounting
Switch_A(config-vlan)#vlan 20
Switch_A(config-vlan)#name Marketing
Switch_A(config-vlan)#vlan 30
Switch_A(config-vlan)#name Engineering
```

Task 7: Assign Ports to VLAN 10

You must assign ports to VLANs from the interface mode. Enter the following commands to add ports 0/4 to 0/6 to VLAN 10:

```
Switch_A#configure terminal
Switch_A(config)#interface fastethernet 0/4
Switch_A(config-if)#switchport mode access
Switch_A(config-if)#switchport access vlan 10
Switch_A(config-if)#interface fastethernet 0/5
Switch_A(config-if)#switchport mode access
Switch_A(config-if)#switchport access vlan 10
Switch_A(config-if)#interface fastethernet 0/6
Switch_A(config-if)#switchport mode access
Switch_A(config-if)#switchport access vlan 10
Switch_A(config-if)#end
```

Note: Use the **range** parameter to quickly configure several interfaces with the same command. For example:

```
Switch_A#configure terminal
Switch_A(config)#interface range fastethernet 0/4 - 6
Switch_A(config-if-range)#switchport mode access
Switch_A(config-if-range)#switchport access vlan 10
Switch_A(config-if-range)#end
```

Task 8: Assign Ports to VLAN 20

Enter the following commands to add ports 0/7 to 0/9 to VLAN 20:

```
Switch_A#configure terminal
Switch_A(config)#interface fastethernet 0/7
Switch_A(config-if)#switchport mode access
Switch_A(config-if)#switchport access vlan 20
Switch_A(config-if)#interface fastethernet 0/8
Switch_A(config-if)#switchport mode access
Switch_A(config-if)#switchport access vlan 20
Switch_A(config-if)#interface fastethernet 0/9
Switch_A(config-if)#switchport mode access
Switch_A(config-if)#switchport access vlan 20
Switch_A(config-if)#end
```

Task 9: Assign Ports to VLAN 30

Enter the following commands to add ports 0/10 to 0/12 to VLAN 30:

```
Switch_A#configure terminal
Switch_A(config)#interface fastethernet 0/10
Switch_A(config-if)#switchport mode access
Switch_A(config-if)#switchport access vlan 30
Switch_A(config-if)#interface fastethernet 0/11
Switch_A(config-if)#switchport mode access
Switch_A(config-if)#switchport access vlan 30
Switch_A(config-if)#interface fastethernet 0/12
Switch_A(config-if)#switchport mode access
Switch_A(config-if)#switchport access vlan 30
Switch_A(config-if)#end
```

Task 10: Display the VLAN Interface Information

On Switch_A, enter the command **show vlan** at the privileged EXEC mode prompt.

```
Switch_A#show vlan
```

Are ports 0/10 to 0/12 assigned to VLAN 30? _____

Task 11: Configure the VTP Client

Configure Switch_B to be a VTP client.

```
Switch_B#vlan database
Switch_B(vlan)#vtp client
Switch_B(vlan)#vtp domain group1
Switch_B(vlan)#exit
```

Task 12: Create the Trunk

On both Switch_A and Switch_B, enter the following command at the Fast Ethernet 0/1 interface command prompt. Note that it is not necessary to specify the encapsulation on a 2950, because it only supports 802.1q.

```
Switch_A(config)#interface fastethernet 0/1
Switch_A(config-if)#switchport mode trunk
Switch_A(config-if)#end
```

```
Switch_B(config)#interface fastethernet 0/1
Switch_B(config-if)#switchport mode trunk
Switch_B(config-if)#end
```

2900:

```
Switch_A(config)#interface fastethernet0/1
Switch_A(config-if)#switchport mode trunk
Switch_A(config-if)#switchport trunk encapsulation dot1q
Switch_A(config-if)#end
```

```
Switch_B(config)#interface fastethernet0/1
Switch_B(config-if)#switchport mode trunk
Switch_B(config-if)#switchport trunk encapsulation dot1q
Switch_B(config-if)#end
```

Task 13: Verify the Trunk

To verify that port Fast Ethernet 0/1 has been established as a trunk port, enter **show interface fastethernet 0/1 switchport** at the privileged EXEC mode prompt.

What type of trunking encapsulation is shown in the output? _____

Task 14: Display the VLAN Interface Information

On Switch_B, enter the command **show vlan** at the privileged EXEC mode prompt.
```
Switch_B#show vlan
```

Do VLANs 10, 20, and 30 show without your having to type them in? _____

Why did this happen?

_____

Task 15: Assign Ports to VLAN 10

Although the VLAN definitions have migrated to Switch_B by using VTP, you still must assign ports to these VLANs on Switch_B. You must assign ports to VLANs from the interface mode. Enter the following commands to add ports 0/4 to 0/6 to VLAN 10:
```
Switch_B#configure terminal
Switch_B(config)#interface fastethernet 0/4
Switch_B(config-if)#switchport mode access
Switch_B(config-if)#switchport access vlan 10
Switch_B(config-if)#interface fastethernet 0/5
Switch_B(config-if)#switchport mode access
Switch_B(config-if)#switchport access vlan 10
Switch_B(config-if)#interface fastethernet 0/6
Switch_B(config-if)#switchport mode access
Switch_B(config-if)#switchport access vlan 10
Switch_B(config-if)#end
```

Task 16: Assign Ports to VLAN 20

Enter the following commands to add ports 0/7 to 0/9 to VLAN 20:
```
Switch_B#configure terminal
Switch_B(config)#interface fastethernet 0/7
Switch_B(config-if)#switchport mode access
Switch_B(config-if)#switchport access vlan 20
Switch_B(config-if)#interface fastethernet 0/8
Switch_B(config-if)#switchport mode access
```

```
Switch_B(config-if)#switchport access vlan 20
Switch_B(config-if)#interface fastethernet 0/9
Switch_B(config-if)#switchport mode access
Switch_B(config-if)#switchport access vlan 20
Switch_B(config-if)#end
```

Task 17: Assign Ports to VLAN 30

Enter the following commands to add ports 0/10 to 0/12 to VLAN 30:

```
Switch_B#configure terminal
Switch_B(config)#interface fastethernet 0/10
Switch_B(config-if)#switchport mode access
Switch_B(config-if)#switchport access vlan 30
Switch_B(config-if)#interface fastethernet 0/11
Switch_B(config-if)#switchport mode access
Switch_B(config-if)#switchport access vlan 30
Switch_B(config-if)#interface fastethernet 0/12
Switch_B(config-if)#switchport mode access
Switch_B(config-if)#switchport access vlan 30
Switch_B(config-if)#end
```

Task 18: Display the VLAN Interface Information

On Switch_B, enter the command **show vlan** at the privileged EXEC mode prompt.

```
Switch_B#show vlan
```

Are ports 0/10 to 0/12 assigned to VLAN 30? _____

Task 19: Test the VLANs and the Trunk

Step 1.   To test the VLANs and the trunk, ping from the host in Switch_A port 0/12 to the host in Switch_B port 0/12.

Was the ping successful? _____

Why?

_____

Step 2.   Ping from the host in Switch_A port 0/12 to the switch IP 192.168.1.2.

Was the ping successful? _____

Why?

_____

Task 20: Move the Hosts

Move the host in Switch_A from port 0/12 to port 0/8, wait until the port LED turns green, and then go to the next task.

Task 21: Test the VLANs and the Trunk

Step 1.   To test the VLANs and the trunk, ping from the host in Switch_A port 0/8 to the host in Switch_B port 0/12.

Was the ping successful? _____

Why?

_____

Step 2.   Ping from the host in Switch_A port 0/8 to the switch IP 192.168.1.2.

Was the ping successful? _____

Why?

_____

After you complete the previous steps, log off (by typing **exit**) and turn all the devices off. Then, remove and store the cables and adapter.

Curriculum Lab 9-4: Configuring Inter-VLAN Routing (9.3.6)

Figure 9-7   Topology for Lab 9-4

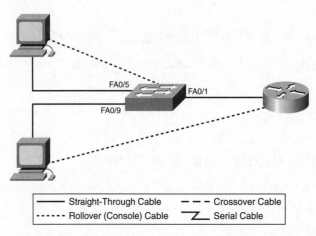

	Straight-Through Cable	— — Crossover Cable
	Rollover (Console) Cable	Serial Cable

Table 9-5   Lab Equipment Configuration

Switch Designation	Switch Name	VLAN 1 IP Address	VLAN Names and Numbers	Switch Port Assignments
Switch 1	Switch_A	192.168.1.2	VLAN 1 Native	
VLAN 10 Sales				
VLAN 20 SupportFa0/1–0/4				
Fa0/5–0/8				
Fa0/9–0/12				

The enable secret password is **class**.

The enable, VTY, and console password is **cisco**.

The subnet mask is 255.255.255.0.

Objectives

- Create a basic switch configuration and verify it.

- Create multiple VLANs, name them, and assign multiple member ports to them.

- Create a basic configuration on a router.

- Create an 802.1q trunk line between the switch and router to allow communication between VLANs.

- Test the routing functionality.

Background/Preparation

Cable a network that is similar to the one in Figure 9-7. The configuration output that is used in this lab is produced from a 2950 series switch. Another switch might produce different output. You should execute erase and reload procedures on each switch unless you are specifically instructed otherwise. Instructions are also provided for the 1900 series switch, which initially displays a User Interface Menu. Select the **Command Line** option from the menu to perform the steps for this lab.

Note: The router used must have a Fast Ethernet interface in order to support trunking and inter-VLAN routing. The 2500 series router cannot be used for this lab.

Start a HyperTerminal session.

Implement the procedure documented in Appendix B before you continue with this lab.

Task 1: Configure the Switch

Configure the hostname, access, and command mode passwords, as well as the management LAN settings. These values are shown in Table 9-5. If you have problems while performing this configuration, refer to Lab 6-2, "Basic Switch Configuration."

Task 2: Configure the Hosts Attached to the Switch

Configure the hosts by using the following information.

The host in port 0/5:

IP address: 192.168.5.2

Subnet mask: 255.255.255.0

Default gateway: 192.168.5.1

The host in port 0/9:

IP address: 192.168.7.2

Subnet mask: 255.255.255.0

Default gateway: 192.168.7.1

Task 3: Verify Connectivity

Step 1. Verify that the switch ports and host NIC link lights are lit.

Step 2. Ping the switch IP address from the hosts.

Were the pings successful? _____

Why or why not?

_____

Task 4: Create and Name Two VLANs

Enter the following commands to create two named VLANs:

```
Switch_A#vlan database
Switch_A(vlan)#vlan 10 name Sales
Switch_A(vlan)#vlan 20 name Support
Switch_A(vlan)#exit
```

1900:

```
Switch_A#config t
Switch_A(config)#vlan 10 name Sales
Switch_A(config)#vlan 20 name Support
Switch_A(config)#exit
```

Task 5: Assign Ports to VLAN 10

You must assign ports to VLANs from the interface mode. Enter the following commands to add ports 0/5 to 0/8 to VLAN 10:

```
Switch_A#configure terminal
Switch_A(config)#interface fastethernet0/5
Switch_A(config-if)#switchport mode access
Switch_A(config-if)#switchport access vlan 10
Switch_A(config-if)#interface fastethernet0/6
Switch_A(config-if)#switchport mode access
Switch_A(config-if)#switchport access vlan 10
Switch_A(config-if)#interface fastethernet0/7
Switch_A(config-if)#switchport mode access
Switch_A(config-if)#switchport access vlan 10
Switch_A(config-if)#interface fastethernet0/8
Switch_A(config-if)#switchport mode access
Switch_A(config-if)#switchport access vlan 10
Switch_A(config-if)#end
```

1900:

```
Switch_A#config t
Switch_A(config)#interface ethernet 0/5
Switch_A(config-if)#vlan static 10
Switch_A(config-if)#interface ethernet 0/6
```

```
Switch_A(config-if)#vlan static 10
Switch_A(config-if)#interface ethernet 0/7
Switch_A(config-if)#vlan static 10
Switch_A(config-if)#interface ethernet 0/8
Switch_A(config-if)#vlan static 10
Switch_A(config-if)#end
```

Task 6: Assign Ports to VLAN 20

Enter the following commands to add ports 0/9 to 0/12 to VLAN 20:

```
Switch_A#configure terminal
Switch_A(config)#interface fastethernet0/9
Switch_A(config-if)#switchport mode access
Switch_A(config-if)#switchport access vlan 20
Switch_A(config-if)#interface fastethernet0/10
Switch_A(config-if)#switchport mode access
Switch_A(config-if)#switchport access vlan 20
Switch_A(config-if)#interface fastethernet0/11
Switch_A(config-if)#switchport mode access
Switch_A(config-if)#switchport access vlan 20
Switch_A(config-if)#interface fastethernet0/12
Switch_A(config-if)#switchport mode access
Switch_A(config-if)#switchport access vlan 20
Switch_A(config-if)#end
```

1900:

```
Switch_A#config t
Switch_A(config)#interface ethernet 0/9
Switch_A(config-if)#vlan static 20
Switch_A(config-if)#interface ethernet 0/10
Switch_A(config-if)#vlan static 20
Switch_A(config-if)#interface ethernet 0/11
Switch_A(config-if)#vlan static 20
Switch_A(config-if)#interface ethernet 0/12
Switch_A(config-if)#vlan static 20
Switch_A(config-if)#end
```

Task 7: Display the VLAN Interface Information

On Switch_A, enter the command **show VLAN** at the privileged EXEC mode prompt.

```
Switch_A#show vlan
```

Are ports assigned correctly? _____

Task 8: Create the Trunk

On Switch_A, enter the following command at the Fast Ethernet 0/1 interface command prompt. Note that Fast Ethernet 0/1 and the other access ports on a 1900 switch only support 10-Mbps Ethernet and cannot be used as trunk ports. The trunk ports (if present) on a 24-port 1900 are typically Fast Ethernet 0/26 and 0/27.

```
Switch_A(config)#interface fastethernet0/1
Switch_A(config-if)#switchport mode trunk
Switch_A(config-if)#end
```

2900:

```
Switch_A(config)#interface fastethernet0/1
Switch_A(config-if)#switchport mode trunk
Switch_A(config-if)#switchport trunk encapsulation dot1q
Switch_A(config-if)#end
```

1900:

```
Switch_A#config t
Switch_A(config)#interface fastethernet0/26
Switch_A(config-if)#trunk on
```

Task 9: Configure the Router

Step 1.   Configure the router with the following data. Note that, to support trunking and inter-VLAN routing, the router must have a Fast Ethernet interface.

   Hostname: Router_A

   Console, VTY, and enable passwords: **cisco**

   Enable secret password: **class**

Step 2.   Configure the Fast Ethernet interface by using the following commands:

Note: If working with a 1900 switch, replace the **dot1.q** encapsulation with **isl** in the following router configuration commands.

```
Router_A(config)#interface fastethernet 0/0
Router_A(config-if)#no shutdown
Router_A(config-if)#interface fastethernet 0/0.1
Router_A(config-subif)#encapsulation dot1q 1
Router_A(config-subif)#ip address 192.168.1.1 255.255.255.0
Router_A(config-if)#interface fastethernet 0/0.2
Router_A(config-subif)#encapsulation dot1q 10
Router_A(config-subif)#ip address 192.168.5.1 255.255.255.0
Router_A(config-if)#interface fastethernet 0/0.3
Router_A(config-subif)#encapsulation dot1q 20
Router_A(config-subif)#end
```

Task 10: Save the Router Configuration

Enter the **copy run start** command to save the current running configuration to NVRAM.

Task 11: Display the Router Routing Table

Enter **show ip route** at the privileged EXEC mode prompt.

Do entries exist in the routing table? _____

What interface are the entries pointing to? _____

Why is there not a need to run a routing protocol?

_____

Task 12: Test the VLANs and the Trunk

Step 1. To test the VLANs and the trunk, ping from the host in Switch_A port 0/9 to the host in port 0/5.

Was the ping successful? _____

Why?

_____

Step 2. Ping from the host in Switch_A port 0/5 to the switch IP 192.168.1.2.

Was the ping successful? _____

Task 13: Move the Hosts

Move the hosts to other VLANs and try pinging the management VLAN 1. Note the results.

_____

After you complete the previous step, log off (by typing **exit**) and turn all the devices off. Then, remove and store the cables and adapter.

Comprehensive Lab 9-5: Inter-VLAN and VTP Configuration

Note: This lab continues where Challenge Lab 8-4, "Static VLANs, STP, and Port Security" ended. You need to complete that lab before proceeding with this lab. Another option is to continue on to Challenge Lab 9-6, "Advanced Switching," which is not dependent on any previous labs.

Figure 9-8   Inter-VLAN and VTP Configuration

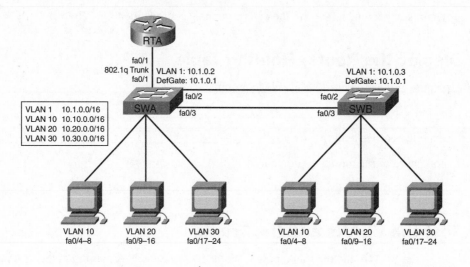

Table 9-6   Addressing Scheme

Device Mask	Interface	IP Address	Subnet
SWA	VLAN 1	10.1.0.2	255.255.0.0
SWB	VLAN 1	10.1.0.3	255.255.0.0
RTA	Fa0/1.1	10.1.0.1	255.255.0.0
	Fa0/1.10	10.10.0.1	255.255.0.0
	Fa0/1.20	10.20.0.1	255.255.0.0
	Fa0/1.30	10.30.0.1	255.255.0.0

Objectives

- Delete the VLAN database.

- Configure VTP parameters.

- Configure inter-VLAN routing.

- Modify VLANs.

- Verify and document configurations.

The topology shown in Figure 9-8 is using 2950 switches and a 2621 router. You can also use a 1700 series router that supports VLAN trunking.

NetLab Compatibility Notes

This lab is fully compatible with a standard NetLab Basic Switch Pod.

Task 1: Cable the Topology and Basic Configuration

Step 1. SWA and SWB should be loaded with your saved configurations for Challenge Lab 8-4, "Static VLANs, STP, and Port Security." If you did not complete that lab, you need to do so now.

Step 2. Configure RTA with basic router configurations, including:

- Hostname
- Line configurations
- Global passwords
- Host tables
- Banner
- Other instructor-required global configurations

Task 2: Configure VTP Parameters

Step 1. SWA will be the VTP server. Configure SWA with the domain name **CCNA3** and password **cisco**. Verify your configuration with the **show vtp status** command.

```
SWA#show vtp status
VTP Version                      : 2
Configuration Revision           : 3
Maximum VLANs supported locally  : 250
Number of existing VLANs         : 8
VTP Operating Mode               : Server
VTP Domain Name                  : CCNA3
VTP Pruning Mode                 : Disabled
VTP V2 Mode                      : Disabled
VTP Traps Generation             : Disabled
MD5 digest                       : 0x3B 0x01 0x37 0x7F 0x25 0x20 0xD0 0x0F
Configuration last modified by 0.0.0.0 at 3-1-93 00:30:56
Local updater ID is 10.1.0.2 on interface Vl1 (lowest numbered VLAN interface
found)
```

Step 2. Notice in the preceding output that the configuration revision number is 3. Why?

_____

_____

Step 3. On SWB, you need to remove the current VLAN configurations and reload the switch. What command will delete the VLAN database file?

_____

_____

_____

_____

Step 4. After you delete the VLAN database and reload the switch, your **show vlan brief** command should display the following:

```
SWB#show vlan brief
```

```
VLAN Name                        Status    Ports
---- -------------------------   -------   --------------------------
1    default                     active    Fa0/1
1002 fddi-default                active
1003 token-ring-default          active
1004 fddinet-default             active
1005 trnet-default               active
SWB#show vlan brief

VLAN Name                        Status    Ports
---- -------------------------   -------   --------------------------
1    default                     active    Fa0/1
1002 fddi-default                active
1003 token-ring-default          active
1004 fddinet-default             active
1005 trnet-default               active
```

Step 5.   Your VTP status should display the following output. Take note of the configuration revision number, the operating mode, and the domain name.

```
SWB#show vtp status
VTP Version                     : 2
Configuration Revision          : 0
Maximum VLANs supported locally : 64
Number of existing VLANs        : 5
VTP Operating Mode              : Server
VTP Domain Name                 :
VTP Pruning Mode                : Disabled
VTP V2 Mode                     : Disabled
VTP Traps Generation            : Disabled
MD5 digest                      : 0x57 0xCD 0x40 0x65 0x63 0x59 0x47 0xBD
Configuration last modified by 0.0.0.0 at 0-0-00 00:00:00
Local updater ID is 10.1.0.3 on interface Vl1 (lowest numbered VLAN interface found)
```

Step 6.   Enter the commands to configure SWB as a VTP client on the CCNA3 VTP domain with the password **cisco**. Record the commands you used.

\
\
\
\
\
\

Step 7.   It may take a while for SWB to receive a VTP message from the server, because, unless there is a change or unless a request is made, the server sends out VTP advertisements only every 5 minutes. You can speed up the process by shutting down the trunks attached to SWA and then reactivating them. This will force an exchange of VTP messages. Verify SWB now has the VLAN information from SWA.

```
SWB#show vtp status
VTP Version                     : 2
Configuration Revision          : 3
```

```
Maximum VLANs supported locally    : 64
Number of existing VLANs           : 8
VTP Operating Mode                 : Client
VTP Domain Name                    : CCNA3
VTP Pruning Mode                   : Disabled
VTP V2 Mode                        : Disabled
VTP Traps Generation               : Disabled
MD5 digest                         : 0x3B 0x01 0x37 0x7F 0x25 0x20 0xD0 0x0F
Configuration last modified by 0.0.0.0 at 3-1-93 00:30:56
SWB#show vlan brief

VLAN Name                             Status    Ports
__ _____      _____.  _____

1    default                          active    Fa0/1
10   Accounting                       active    Fa0/4, Fa0/5, Fa0/6, Fa0/7
                                                Fa0/8
20   Marketing                        active    Fa0/9, Fa0/10, Fa0/11,
                                                Fa0/12

                                                Fa0/13, Fa0/14, Fa0/15,
                                                Fa0/16
30   Purchasing                       active    Fa0/17, Fa0/18, Fa0/19,
                                                Fa0/20
                                                Fa0/21, Fa0/22, Fa0/23,
Fa0/24
1002 fddi-default                     active
1003 token-ring-default               active
1004 fddinet-default                  active
1005 trnet-default                    active
```

Task 3: Configure Inter-VLAN Routing

Step 1. The Fast Ethernet interface on RTA that is attached to SWA will trunk VLANs. Make sure you configure the Fa0/1 port on SWA to trunking mode and activate it.

Step 2. Configure RTA to trunk for all three VLANs by using the subinterface designations and IP addresses shown in Table 9-6. Make sure the physical interface is activated. Also, for VLAN 1, make sure you add the **native** argument to the end of the **encapsulation** command.

Output from the **show ip interface brief** command should look like the following:

```
RTA#show ip interface brief
Interface          IP-Address    OK?   Method   Status             Protocol
FastEthernet0/0    unassigned    YES   unset    administratively   down down

Serial0/0          unassigned    YES   unset    administratively   down down

FastEthernet0/1    unassigned    YES   unset    up                 up

FastEthernet0/1.1  10.1.0.1      YES   manual   up                 up

FastEthernet0/1.10 10.10.0.1     YES   manual   up                 up

FastEthernet0/1.20 10.20.0.1     YES   manual   up                 up

FastEthernet0/1.30 10.30.0.1     YES   manual   up                 up
```

Step 3. Attach two workstations to the network. One should be attached to a port on SWA. Attach the other to SWB on a port that belongs to a different VLAN from the workstation attached to SWA. Document your choices in the space provided. Remember that the default gateway will be the IP address of the router's subinterface that belongs to the same VLAN.

Workstation attached to SWA:

Port _____

VLAN _____

IP address _____

Subnet mask _____

Workstation attached to SWB:

Port _____

VLAN _____

IP address _____

Subnet mask _____

Step 4. Verify that the two workstations can ping each other. If they cannot, troubleshoot.

Task 4: Adding, Moving, and Deleting VLANs

Step 1. A few employees from the Warehousing department are relocating to the office serviced by the SWB switch. Create a new VLAN 40 named Warehousing. Record the commands, including switch prompt, to create this new VLAN.

_____

_____

Step 2. Verify that SWB has incremented its VTP configuration revision number and has the new VLAN listed.

```
SWB#show vtp status
VTP Version                     : 2
Configuration Revision          : 4
Maximum VLANs supported locally : 64
Number of existing VLANs        : 9
VTP Operating Mode              : Client
VTP Domain Name                 : CCNA3
VTP Pruning Mode                : Disabled
VTP V2 Mode                     : Disabled
VTP Traps Generation            : Disabled
MD5 digest                      : 0xBC 0xD2 0x4A 0x5B 0xF3 0x03 0x26 0x75
Configuration last modified by 10.1.0.2 at 3-1-93 01:17:40
SWB#show vlan brief
```

VLAN	Name	Status	Ports
1	default	active	Fa0/1
10	Accounting	active	Fa0/4, Fa0/5, Fa0/6, Fa0/7 Fa0/8
20	Marketing	active	Fa0/9, Fa0/10, Fa0/11, Fa0/12 Fa0/13, Fa0/14, Fa0/15, Fa0/16

```
30    Purchasing                active      Fa0/17, Fa0/18, Fa0/19, Fa0/20
                                            Fa0/21, Fa0/22, Fa0/23, Fa0/24

40    Warehousing               active
1002  fddi-default              active
1003  token-ring-default        active
1004  fddinet-default           active
1005  trnet-default             active
```

Step 3.   Because the Purchasing department has only four employees in the office serviced by SWB, reassign the last four ports on SWB to the new Warehousing VLAN. Record the commands you used and verify your configuration with the **show vlan brief** command.

_____

_____

```
SWB#show vlan brief

VLAN Name                      Status      Ports
__ _____          _____       _____

1    default                   active      Fa0/1
10   Accounting                active      Fa0/4, Fa0/5, Fa0/6, Fa0/7
                                           Fa0/8
20   Marketing                 active      Fa0/9, Fa0/10, Fa0/11, Fa0/12
                                           Fa0/13, Fa0/14, Fa0/15, Fa0/16
30   Purchasing                active      Fa0/17, Fa0/18, Fa0/19, Fa0/20
40   Warehousing               active      Fa0/21, Fa0/22, Fa0/23, Fa0/24
1002 fddi-default              active
1003 token-ring-default        active
1004 fddinet-default           active
1005 trnet-default             active
```

Step 4.   The Purchasing department has been consolidated with the Accounting department. The Purchasing employees on SWB have transferred to the office serviced by SWA. Record the command to delete VLAN 30. Verify with the **show vtp status** and **show vlan brief** commands on SWB.

_____

_____

```
SWB#show vtp status
VTP Version                         : 2
Configuration Revision              : 5
Maximum VLANs supported locally     : 64
Number of existing VLANs            : 8
VTP Operating Mode                  : Client
VTP Domain Name                     : CCNA3
VTP Pruning Mode                    : Disabled
VTP V2 Mode                         : Disabled
VTP Traps Generation                : Disabled
MD5 digest                          : 0x80 0xED 0x23 0x29 0x92 0x92 0xBE 0x09
Configuration last modified by 10.1.0.2 at 3-1-93 02:07:29
SWB#show vlan brief
```

```
VLAN Name                           Status   Ports
-- ------------------------------   -----.   ----------------------------
1    default                        active   Fa0/1
10   Accounting                     active   Fa0/4, Fa0/5, Fa0/6, Fa0/7
                                             Fa0/8
20   Marketing                      active   Fa0/9, Fa0/10, Fa0/11, Fa0/12
                                             Fa0/13, Fa0/14, Fa0/15, Fa0/16
40   Warehousing                    active   Fa0/21, Fa0/22, Fa0/23, Fa0/24
1002 fddi-default                   active
1003 token-ring-default            active
1004 fddinet-default               active
1005 trnet-default                 active
```

Step 5.   Notice from the **show vlan brief** output for SWB that ports Fa0/17 through Fa0/20 are not assigned to any VLAN. Correct this by assigning them to the Warehousing VLAN. Record the commands you used and then verify with the **show vlan brief** command.

_____

_____

```
SWB#show vlan brief

VLAN Name                           Status   Ports
-- ------------------------------   -----.   ----------------------------
1    default                        active   Fa0/1
10   Accounting                     active   Fa0/4, Fa0/5, Fa0/6, Fa0/7
                                             Fa0/8
20   Marketing                      active   Fa0/9, Fa0/10, Fa0/11, Fa0/12
                                             Fa0/13, Fa0/14, Fa0/15, Fa0/16
40   Warehousing                    active   Fa0/17, Fa0/18, Fa0/19, Fa0/20
                                             Fa0/21, Fa0/22, Fa0/23, Fa0/24
1002 fddi-default                   active
1003 token-ring-default            active
1004 fddinet-default               active
1005 trnet-default                 active
```

Step 6.   On SWA, assign the ports that belonged to the Purchasing VLAN to the Accounting VLAN. Record the commands you used and then verify with the **show vlan brief** command.

_____

_____

```
SWA#show vlan brief

VLAN Name                           Status   Ports
-- ------------------------------   -----.   ----------------------------
1    default                        active   Fa0/1, Gi0/1, Gi0/2
10   Accounting                     active   Fa0/4, Fa0/5, Fa0/6, Fa0/7
                                             Fa0/8, Fa0/17, Fa0/18, Fa0/19
                                             Fa0/20, Fa0/21, Fa0/22, Fa0/23
                                             Fa0/24
20   Marketing                      active   Fa0/9, Fa0/10, Fa0/11, Fa0/12
                                             Fa0/13, Fa0/14, Fa0/15, Fa0/16
40   Warehousing                    active
1002 fddi-default                   active
1003 token-ring-default            active
```

```
1004 fddinet-default                    active
1005 trnet-default                      active
```

Step 7.   If you attach a workstation to the Warehousing VLAN, it will not be able to ping any workstations outside its own VLAN. Try it. Why were the pings unsuccessful?

Step 8.   Record and implement the configuration changes necessary to ensure that Warehousing workstations have inter-VLAN communication ability. Verify that a Warehousing workstation can ping another workstation attached to a different VLAN.

Task 5: Documentation

Document your configurations by capturing the following output:

- **show run**
- **show vlan brief**
- **show vtp status**
- On RTA, capture **show run** and **show ip interface brief**

Challenge Lab 9-6: Advanced Switching

Figure 9-9   **Advanced Switching Challenge Lab**

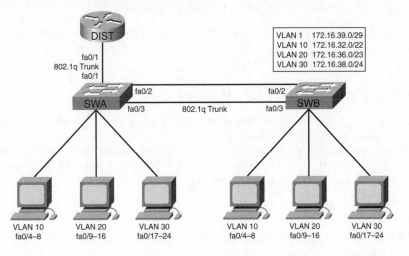

Table 9-7   **Addressing Scheme**

Device	Interface	IP Address	Subnet Mask
SWA	VLAN 1	172.16.39.2	255.255.255.248
SWB	VLAN 1	172.16.39.3	255.255.255.248
DIST	Fa0/1.1	172.16.39.1	255.255.255.248
	Fa0/1.10	172.16.32.1	255.255.252.0
	Fa0/1.20	172.16.36.1	255.255.254.0
	Fa0/1.30	172.16.38.1	255.255.255.0

Objectives

■ Configure STP.

■ Configure port security.

■ Configure the VTP server and client.

■ Configure and assign VLANs.

■ Configure inter-VLAN routing.

■ Verify and document configurations.

Equipment

The topology shown in Figure 9-9 is using 2950 switches and a 2621 router. You can also use a 1700 series router that supports VLAN trunking.

NetLab Compatibility Notes

This lab is fully compatible with a standard NetLab Basic Switch Pod although you will not be able to fully test your VLANs or port security.

Task 1: Cable the Topology and Basic Configuration

Step 1.   Choose two 2950 switches and one router with a Fast Ethernet interface (1700 or 2600) and cable them according to the topology. (If using NetLab, choose a switch router pod.)

Step 2.   Configure the switches and router according to your instructor's required basic configuration hostnames, host tables, lines, and banner. Configure each of the switches with the correct VLAN 1 IP addresses and the correct default gateway.

Step 3.   Verify connectivity between SWA and SWB. Pings should be successful. If they are not, troubleshoot.

Task 2: Configure the Root Bridge for STP

Step 1.   SWA should always be the root bridge. Configure SWA with a spanning-tree priority of 4096 for all four VLANs (1, 10, 20, and 30).

Step 2.   Verify that SWA is the root with the **show spanning-tree summary** command. SWA should be listed as the root bridge, as shown in the following output.

```
SWA#show spanning-tree summary
Switch is in pvst mode
Root bridge for: VLAN0001, VLAN0010, VLAN0020, VLAN0030
EtherChannel misconfiguration guard is enabled
Extended system ID    is enabled
Portfast              is disabled by default
PortFast BPDU Guard   is disabled by default
Portfast BPDU Filter  is disabled by default
Loopguard             is disabled by default
UplinkFast            is disabled
BackboneFast          is disabled
Pathcost method used  is short
```

```
Name                        Blocking Listening Learning Forwarding STP Active
---------------------- ---- ----- ---- ----- -----
VLAN0001                       0         0        0          3          3
VLAN0010                       0         0        0          3          3
VLAN0020                       0         0        0          3          3
VLAN0030                       0         0        0          3          3
---------------------- ---- ----- ---- ----- -----
4 vlans                        0         0        0         12         12
```

```
SWB#show spanning-tree summary
Switch is in pvst mode
Root bridge for: none
EtherChannel misconfiguration guard is enabled
Extended system ID      is enabled
Portfast                is disabled by default
PortFast BPDU Guard      is disabled by default
Portfast BPDU Filter     is disabled by default
Loopguard               is disabled by default
UplinkFast              is disabled
BackboneFast            is disabled
Pathcost method used     is short
```

```
Name                        Blocking Listening Learning Forwarding STP Active
---------------------- ---- ----- ---- ----- -----
VLAN0001                       1         0        0          1          2
VLAN0010                       1         0        0          1          2
VLAN0020                       1         0        0          1          2
VLAN0030                       1         0        0          1          2
---------------------- ---- ----- ---- ----- -----
4 vlans                        4         0        0          4          8
```

Task 3: Configure Port Security

Step 1. As a security precaution, disable the Fast Ethernet 0/1 interface on SWB, because this interface will not be used for access mode or trunk mode.

Perform the following steps on both SWA and SWB.

Step 2. Configure the access ports (Fa0/4 to 24) for access mode and turn on port security.

Step 3. Enter the command to make the first MAC address learned "stick" to the port. No other MAC addresses should be allowed (maximum of one MAC per port).

Step 4. Enter the command that will automatically shut down the port if a security violation occurs.

Step 5. Verify port security with the **show port-security** command. Your output should look similar to the following:

```
SWA#show port-security
Secure Port    MaxSecureAddr  CurrentAddr  SecurityViolation  Security
Action
               (Count)        (Count)      (Count)
------------------------------------------------------------------
       Fa0/4        1              0            0                 Shutdown
       Fa0/5        1              0            0                 Shutdown
       Fa0/6        1              0            0                 Shutdown
```

```
        Fa0/7           1               0               0               Shutdown
        Fa0/8           1               0               0               Shutdown
        Fa0/9           1               0               0               Shutdown
        Fa0/10          1               0               0               Shutdown
        Fa0/11          1               0               0               Shutdown
        Fa0/12          1               0               0               Shutdown
        Fa0/13          1               0               0               Shutdown
        Fa0/14          1               0               0               Shutdown
        Fa0/15          1               0               0               Shutdown
        Fa0/16          1               0               0               Shutdown
        Fa0/17          1               0               0               Shutdown
        Fa0/18          1               0               0               Shutdown
        Fa0/19          1               0               0               Shutdown
        Fa0/20          1               0               0               Shutdown
        Fa0/21          1               0               0               Shutdown
        Fa0/22          1               0               0               Shutdown
        Fa0/23          1               0               0               Shutdown
        Fa0/24          1               0               0               Shutdown
-------------------------------------------------------------------------

Total Addresses in System : 0
Max Addresses limit in System : 1024
```

SWB#**show port-security**

```
Secure Port    MaxSecureAddr   CurrentAddr  SecurityViolation  Security
Action
               (Count)         (Count)      (Count)
-------------------------------------------------------------------------
        Fa0/4           1               0               0               Shutdown
        Fa0/5           1               0               0               Shutdown
        Fa0/6           1               0               0               Shutdown
        Fa0/7           1               0               0               Shutdown
        Fa0/8           1               0               0               Shutdown
        Fa0/9           1               0               0               Shutdown
        Fa0/10          1               0               0               Shutdown
        Fa0/11          1               0               0               Shutdown
        Fa0/12          1               0               0               Shutdown
        Fa0/13          1               0               0               Shutdown
        Fa0/14          1               0               0               Shutdown
        Fa0/15          1               0               0               Shutdown
        Fa0/16          1               0               0               Shutdown
        Fa0/17          1               0               0               Shutdown
        Fa0/18          1               0               0               Shutdown
        Fa0/19          1               0               0               Shutdown
        Fa0/20          1               0               0               Shutdown
        Fa0/21          1               0               0               Shutdown
        Fa0/22          1               0               0               Shutdown
        Fa0/23          1               0               0               Shutdown
        Fa0/24          1               0               0               Shutdown
-------------------------------------------------------------------------

Total Addresses in System : 0
Max Addresses limit in System : 1024
```

Task 4: Configure VTP and VLANs

Step 1. Configure SWA as the VTP server with the domain name **CCNA3** and password **cisco**. Configure SWB as a VTP client in the same domain using the same password.

Step 2. Configure VLANs with names on the VTP server.

- VLAN 10 is the Accounting VLAN.

- VLAN 20 is the Marketing VLAN.

- VLAN 30 is the Purchasing VLAN.

Step 3. Configure the appropriate ports on SWA and SWB for trunking. Verify trunking is properly configured with the **show interface trunk** command on both SWA and SWB.

```
SWA#show interface trunk

Port        Mode        Encapsulation  Status      Native vlan
Fa0/1       on          802.1q         trunking    1
Fa0/2       on          802.1q         trunking    1
Fa0/3       on          802.1q         trunking    1

Port        Vlans allowed on trunk
Fa0/1       1-4094
Fa0/2       1-4094
Fa0/3       1-4094

Port        Vlans allowed and active in management domain
Fa0/1       1,10,20,30
Fa0/2       1,10,20,30
Fa0/3       1,10,20,30

Port        Vlans in spanning tree forwarding state and not pruned
Fa0/1       1,10,20,30
Fa0/2       1,10,20,30
Fa0/3       1,10,20,30

SWB#show interface trunk

Port        Mode        Encapsulation  Status      Native vlan
Fa0/2       on          802.1q         trunking    1
Fa0/3       on          802.1q         trunking    1

Port        Vlans allowed on trunk
Fa0/2       1-4094
Fa0/3       1-4094

Port        Vlans allowed and active in management domain
Fa0/2       1,10,20,30
Fa0/3       1,10,20,30

Port        Vlans in spanning tree forwarding state and not pruned
Fa0/2       1,10,20,30
Fa0/3       none
```

Step 4.　Assign access ports to their correct VLAN as specified in the topology.

Step 5.　Verify both the VTP status and VLAN configuration on both switches with the **show vtp status** and **show vlan brief** commands. Your output should look similar to the following:

```
SWA#show vtp status
VTP Version                     : 2
Configuration Revision          : 1
Maximum VLANs supported locally : 64
Number of existing VLANs        : 8
VTP Operating Mode              : Server
VTP Domain Name                 : CCNA3
VTP Pruning Mode                : Disabled
VTP V2 Mode                     : Disabled
VTP Traps Generation            : Disabled
MD5 digest                      : 0xE0 0x67 0x70 0x4A 0x3C 0xAB 0x44 0x67
Configuration last modified by 172.16.39.2 at 3-10-93 01:23:32
Local updater ID is 172.16.39.2 on interface Vl1 (lowest numbered VLAN inter-
face found)


SWA#show vlan brief


VLAN Name                         Status    Ports
---- ------------------------     -----.    --------------------------
1    default                      active
10   Accounting                   active    Fa0/4, Fa0/5, Fa0/6, Fa0/7
                                            Fa0/8
20   Marketing                    active    Fa0/9, Fa0/10, Fa0/11, Fa0/12
                                            Fa0/13, Fa0/14, Fa0/15, Fa0/16
30   Purchasing                   active    Fa0/17, Fa0/18, Fa0/19, Fa0/20
                                            Fa0/21, Fa0/22, Fa0/23, Fa0/24

1002 fddi-default                 active
1003 token-ring-default           active
1004 fddinet-default              active
1005 trnet-default                active


SWB#show vtp status
VTP Version                     : 2
Configuration Revision          : 1
Maximum VLANs supported locally : 64
Number of existing VLANs        : 8
VTP Operating Mode              : Client
VTP Domain Name                 : CCNA3
VTP Pruning Mode                : Disabled
VTP V2 Mode                     : Disabled
VTP Traps Generation            : Disabled
MD5 digest                      : 0xE0 0x67 0x70 0x4A 0x3C 0xAB 0x44 0x67
Configuration last modified by 172.16.39.2 at 3-10-93 01:23:32
```

```
SWB#show vlan brief

VLAN Name                             Status    Ports
--   --------------------------------  ------    --------------------------------
1    default                          active    Fa0/1
10   Accounting                       active    Fa0/4, Fa0/5, Fa0/6, Fa0/7
                                                Fa0/8
20   Marketing                        active    Fa0/9, Fa0/10, Fa0/11, Fa0/12
                                                Fa0/13, Fa0/14, Fa0/15, Fa0/16
30   Purchasing                       active    Fa0/17, Fa0/18, Fa0/19, Fa0/20
                                                Fa0/21, Fa0/22, Fa0/23, Fa0/24
1002 fddi-default                     active
1003 token-ring-default               active
1004 fddinet-default                  active
1005 trnet-default                    active
```

Task 5: Set Up DHCP on the DIST Router

Although DHCP (Dynamic Host Configuration Protocol) is a CCNA 4 objective, it will help in this lab to use dynamic assignment of IP addresses. Later in the lab, when you connect a workstation to one of the switches, a DHCP broadcast will be sent to DIST. DIST will send a DHCP offer to your workstation with an appropriate IP address for the VLAN the workstation is attached to. Make sure your workstations are set to "Obtain IP address automatically." Add the following commands while in global configuration mode on DIST:

```
ip dhcp excluded-address 172.16.32.1 172.16.32.10
ip dhcp excluded-address 172.16.36.1 172.16.36.10
ip dhcp excluded-address 172.16.38.1 172.16.38.10
!
ip dhcp pool VLAN10
   network 172.16.32.0 255.255.252.0
   default-router 172.16.32.1
!
ip dhcp pool VLAN20
   network 172.16.36.0 255.255.254.0
   default-router 172.16.36.1
!
ip dhcp pool VLAN30
   network 172.16.38.0 255.255.255.0
   default-router 172.16.38.1
```

Task 6: Configure Inter-VLAN Routing

Configure DIST to route all VLANs by completing the following:

Step 1.   Activate the physical interface.

Step 2.   Create subinterfaces for each of the four VLANs. Number each subinterface with the VLAN number. For example, the VLAN 1 subinterface should be numbered fa0.1 or fa0/0.1, depending on the router.

Step 3.   Configure each subinterface for 802.1q trunking and assign each subinterface the first IP address in the appropriate subnet for that VLAN (refer to the topology).

Step 4. Configure each subinterface with an appropriate description.

Step 5. Verify that the **show ip interface brief** command output is similar to the following output:

```
DIST#show ip interface brief
Interface           IP-Address    OK?  Method  Status                  Protocol
FastEthernet0/0     unassigned    YES  unset   administratively down   down
Serial0/0           unassigned    YES  unset   administratively down   down
FastEthernet0/1     unassigned    YES  unset   up                      up
FastEthernet0/1.1   172.16.39.1   YES  manual  up                      up
FastEthernet0/1.10  172.16.32.1   YES  manual  up                      up
FastEthernet0/1.20  172.16.36.1   YES  manual  up                      up
FastEthernet0/1.30  172.16.38.1   YES  manual  up                      up
```

Step 6. Verify connectivity between all three devices. Each device should be able to ping the other two devices.

```
DIST#ping SWA


Type escape sequence to abort.
Sending 5, 100-byte ICMP Echos to 172.16.39.2, timeout is 2 seconds:
!!!!!
Success rate is 100 percent (5/5), round-trip min/avg/max = 1/4/8 ms


DIST#ping SWB


Type escape sequence to abort.
Sending 5, 100-byte ICMP Echos to 172.16.39.3, timeout is 2 seconds:
!!!!!
Success rate is 100 percent (5/5), round-trip min/avg/max = 4/4/4 ms


SWB#ping SWA


Type escape sequence to abort.
Sending 5, 100-byte ICMP Echos to 172.16.39.2, timeout is 2 seconds:
!!!!!
Success rate is 100 percent (5/5), round-trip min/avg/max = 4/4/4 ms
```

Task 7: Verify Inter-VLAN Routing

Step 1. Attach two workstations to different VLANs.

Step 2. Verify that each workstation received an IP address from the DHCP server on DIST.

Step 3. Verify that the two workstations can ping each other. Traceroute should show that the ping packets are going through the router. The following is some sample output of this verification. Yours should look similar.

```
_____
Configuration for a Workstation attached to VLAN 10
_____


C:\>ipconfig


Windows IP Configuration
```

```
Ethernet adapter Local Area Connection:

        Connection-specific DNS Suffix   . :
        IP Address. . . . . . . . . . . : 172.16.32.11
        Subnet Mask . . . . . . . . . . : 255.255.252.0
        Default Gateway . . . . . . . . : 172.16.32.1


 _ _ _ _ _ _ _ _ _ _ _ _ _ _ _ _ _ _ _ _ _ _ _ _ _ _ _ _ .
Configuration for a Workstation attached to VLAN 20
 _ _ _ _ _ _ _ _ _ _ _ _ _ _ _ _ _ _ _ _ _ _ _ _ _ _ _ _ .


C:\>ipconfig

Windows IP Configuration


Ethernet adapter Local Area Connection:

        Connection-specific DNS Suffix   . :
        IP Address. . . . . . . . . . . : 172.16.36.11
        Subnet Mask . . . . . . . . . . : 255.255.255.0
        Default Gateway . . . . . . . . : 172.16.36.1


 _ _ _ _ _ _ _ _ _ _ _ _ _ _ _ _ _ _ _ _ _ _ _ .
VLAN 10 Workstation pings VLAN 20 workstation
 _ _ _ _ _ _ _ _ _ _ _ _ _ _ _ _ _ _ _ _ _ _ _ .


C:\>ping 172.16.36.11

Pinging 172.16.36.11 with 32 bytes of data:

Reply from 172.16.36.11: bytes=32 time=2ms TTL=127
Reply from 172.16.36.11: bytes=32 time=1ms TTL=127
Reply from 172.16.36.11: bytes=32 time=1ms TTL=127
Reply from 172.16.36.11: bytes=32 time<1ms TTL=127

Ping statistics for 172.16.36.11:
    Packets: Sent = 4, Received = 4, Lost = 0 (0% loss),
Approximate round trip times in milli-seconds:
    Minimum = 0ms, Maximum = 2ms, Average = 1ms


 _ _ _ _ _ _ _ _ _ _ _ _ _ _ _ _ _ _ _ _ _ _ _ _ _ _ _ _
VLAN 10 Workstation traces path to VLAN 20 workstation
 _ _ _ _ _ _ _ _ _ _ _ _ _ _ _ _ _ _ _ _ _ _ _ _ _ _ _ _


C:\>tracert 172.16.36.11

Tracing route to 172.16.36.12 over a maximum of 30 hops

  1     1 ms      1 ms     <1 ms  172.16.32.1
  2    <1 ms     <1 ms     <1 ms  172.16.36.11

Trace complete.
```

Step 4. Verify that the two workstation MAC addresses are "stuck" to the configuration. You can verify this with either the **show run** or **show mac-address-table** command. The sticky command used earlier causes the output to show that these two MAC addresses are now statically configured, as shown in the following output.

```
SWA#show mac-address-table
          Mac Address Table
-----------------------------------------

Vlan    Mac Address       Type        Ports
--      -----------       ----        ---
All     000d.2903.ef40    STATIC      CPU
All     0100.0ccc.cccc    STATIC      CPU
All     0100.0ccc.cccd    STATIC      CPU
All     0100.0cdd.dddd    STATIC      CPU
 1      000c.857f.9ea0    DYNAMIC     Fa0/1
 1      000d.28f2.6942    DYNAMIC     Fa0/2
 1      000d.28f2.6943    DYNAMIC     Fa0/3
10      000c.857f.9ea0    DYNAMIC     Fa0/1
10      000d.56a1.a975    STATIC      Fa0/4
20      000c.857f.9ea0    DYNAMIC     Fa0/1
20      000d.56a1.c8f7    STATIC      Fa0/9
Total Mac Addresses for this criterion: 11


SWA#show run

<output omitted>
!
interface FastEthernet0/4
 switchport port-security mac-address sticky 000d.56a1.a975
!
interface FastEthernet0/9
 switchport port-security mac-address sticky 000d.56a1.c8f7
```

Step 5. Enter the **show port-security** command. The output should now show that the two ports are counted.

```
SWA#show port-security
```

Secure Port	MaxSecureAddr (Count)	CurrentAddr (Count)	SecurityViolation (Count)	Security Action
Fa0/4	1	1	0	Shutdown
Fa0/5	1	0	0	Shutdown
Fa0/6	1	0	0	Shutdown
Fa0/7	1	0	0	Shutdown
Fa0/8	1	0	0	Shutdown
Fa0/9	1	1	0	Shutdown
Fa0/10	1	0	0	Shutdown
Fa0/11	1	0	0	Shutdown
Fa0/12	1	0	0	Shutdown
Fa0/13	1	0	0	Shutdown
Fa0/14	1	0	0	Shutdown

```
Fa0/15          1              0              0          Shutdown
Fa0/16          1              0              0          Shutdown
Fa0/17          1              0              0          Shutdown
Fa0/18          1              0              0          Shutdown
Fa0/19          1              0              0          Shutdown
Fa0/20          1              0              0          Shutdown
Fa0/21          1              0              0          Shutdown
Fa0/22          1              0              0          Shutdown
Fa0/23          1              0              0          Shutdown
Fa0/24          1              0              0          Shutdown
------------------------------------------------------------------

Total Addresses in System : 2
Max Addresses limit in System : 1024
```

Step 6.   Verify that a port currently used by one of your workstations will shut down when another workstation is attached to the same port. When you attach the workstation, you will see the link beat light go green for a brief moment. Then it will go dark as the port is automatically shut down. On the switch console, you may get syslog messages similar to the following output.

```
2d23h: %LINK-3-UPDOWN: Interface FastEthernet0/4, changed state to down

2d23h: %PORT_SECURITY-2-PSECURE_VIOLATION: Security violation occurred,
caused by MAC address 000d.56a1.acfc on port Fa0/4.

2d23h: %PM-4-ERR_DISABLE: psecure-violation error detected on Fa0/4,
putting Fa0/4 in err-disable state
```

Step 7.   Verify that the port is shut down with the **show interface** and **show port-security** commands.

```
SWA#show interface fastethernet 0/4
FastEthernet0/4 is down, line protocol is down (err-disabled)

SWA#show port-security
Secure Port   MaxSecureAddr  CurrentAddr  SecurityViolation  Security
Action
              (Count)        (Count)      (Count)

-----------------------------------------------------------------------
    Fa0/4         1              1              1          Shutdown
    Fa0/5         1              0              0          Shutdown
    Fa0/6         1              0              0          Shutdown
    Fa0/7         1              0              0          Shutdown
    Fa0/8         1              0              0          Shutdown
    Fa0/9         1              1              0          Shutdown
    Fa0/10        1              0              0          Shutdown
    Fa0/11        1              0              0          Shutdown
    Fa0/12        1              0              0          Shutdown
    Fa0/13        1              0              0          Shutdown
    Fa0/14        1              0              0          Shutdown
    Fa0/15        1              0              0          Shutdown
    Fa0/16        1              0              0          Shutdown
    Fa0/17        1              0              0          Shutdown
    Fa0/18        1              0              0          Shutdown
    Fa0/19        1              0              0          Shutdown
```

Fa0/20	1	0	0	Shutdown
Fa0/21	1	0	0	Shutdown
Fa0/22	1	0	0	Shutdown
Fa0/23	1	0	0	Shutdown
Fa0/24	1	0	0	Shutdown

```
Total Addresses in System : 2
Max Addresses limit in System : 1024
```

Step 8.   Complete the procedures necessary to remove this port from the err-disabled state and allow the new workstation's MAC address to "stick" to the configuration.

Task 8: Documentation

Document your configurations by capturing the following output:

- **show run**
- **show vlan brief**
- **show spanning-tree summary**
- **show vtp status**
- **show port-security**
- **show mac-address-table**
- **On DIST, capture show run**

Router Interface Summary Chart

For most of the CCNA 3 labs, you need to examine the following chart to correctly reference the router interface identifiers to use in commands based on the equipment in your lab.

Router Model	Ethernet Interface 1	Ethernet Interface 2	Serial Interface 1	Serial Interface 2
800 (806)	Ethernet 0 (E0)	Ethernet 1 (E1)		
1600	Ethernet 0 (E0)	Ethernet 1 (E1)	Serial 0 (S0)	Serial 1 (S1)
1700	FastEthernet 0 (FA0)	FastEthernet 1 (FA1)	Serial 0 (S0)	Serial 1 (S1)
2500	Ethernet 0 (E0)	Ethernet 1 (E1)	Serial 0 (S0)	Serial 1 (S1)
2600	FastEthernet 0/0 (FA0/0)	FastEthernet 0/1 (FA0/1)	Serial 0/0 (S0/0)	Serial 0/1 (S0/1)

To find out exactly how the router is configured, look at the interfaces to identify what type and how many the router has. There is no way to effectively list all of the combinations of configurations for each router class. The chart provides the identifiers for the possible combinations of interfaces in the device. This interface chart does not include any other type of interface even though a specific router might contain one. An example of this is an ISDN BRI interface. The string in parentheses is the legal abbreviation that you can use in Cisco IOS Software commands to represent the interface.

Erasing and Reloading the Switch

For the majority of the labs in CCNA 3 focusing on switch configuration, it is necessary to start with a basic unconfigured switch; otherwise, the configuration parameters you enter might combine with previous ones and produce unpredictable results. The instructions here enable you to prepare the switch prior to performing the lab so that previous configuration options do not interfere with your configurations.

The following is the procedure for clearing out previous configurations and starting with an unconfigured switch. Instructions are provided for the 2900, 2950, and 1900 series switches.

2900 and 2950 Series Switches

Step 1. Disconnect the switch to be erased from all other switches. Verify that there is no uplink or backbone cabling to any other switch, otherwise VLAN configuration information can be transferred automatically.

Step 2. Enter into privileged EXEC mode by typing **enable**. If prompted for a password, enter **class** (if that does not work, ask the instructor).

```
Switch> enable
```

Step 3. Remove the VLAN database information file:

```
Switch# delete flash:vlan.dat
Delete filename [vlan.dat]?[Enter]
Delete flash:vlan.dat? [confirm][Enter]
```

If there was no VLAN file, the following message appears:

```
%Error deleting flash:vlan.dat (No such file or directory)
```

Step 4. Remove the switch startup configuration file from NVRAM:

```
Switch#erase startup-config
```

The responding line prompt will be

```
Erasing the nvram filesystem will remove all files! Continue? [confirm]
```

Press **Enter** to confirm.

The response should be

```
Erase of nvram: complete
```

Step 5. Check that VLAN information was deleted.

Verify that the VLAN configuration was deleted in Step 3 using the **show vlan** command. If previous VLAN configuration information (other than the default management VLAN 1) is still present, it will be necessary to power cycle the switch (hardware restart) instead of issuing the **reload** command. To power cycle the switch, remove the power cord from the back of the switch or unplug it. Then plug it back in.

If the VLAN information was successfully deleted in Step 3, go to Step 6 and restart the switch using the **reload** command.

Step 6. Restart the software (using the **reload** command):

Note: This step is not necessary if the switch was restarted using the power cycle method.

1. In privileged EXEC mode, enter the command **reload**:

   ```
   Switch(config)# reload
   ```

   The responding line prompt will be

   ```
   System configuration has been modified. Save? [yes/no]:
   ```

2. Type **n** and then press **Enter**.

   The responding line prompt will be

   ```
   Proceed with reload? [confirm][Enter]
   ```

   The first line of the response will be

   ```
   Reload requested by console.
   ```

   After the switch has reloaded, the line prompt will be

   ```
   Would you like to enter the initial configuration dialog? [yes/no]:
   ```

3. Type **n** and then press **Enter**.

   The responding line prompt will be

   ```
   Press RETURN to get started![Enter]
   ```

1900 Series Switches

Step 1. Remove VLAN Trunking Protocol (VTP) information:

```
#delete vtp
This command resets the switch with VTP parameters set to factory defaults.
All other parameters will be unchanged.

Reset system with VTP parameters set to factory defaults, [Y]es or [N]o?
```

Enter **y** and press **Enter**.

Step 2. Remove the switch startup configuration from NVRAM:

```
#delete nvram
This command resets the switch with factory defaults.  All system
parameters will revert to their default factory settings.  All static
and dynamic addresses will be removed.

Reset system with factory defaults, [Y]es or [N]o?
```

Enter **y** and press **Enter**.

Erasing and Reloading the Router

For some of the CCNA 3 labs, it is necessary to start with a basic unconfigured router; otherwise, the configuration parameters you enter might combine with previous ones and produce unpredictable results. The instructions here allow you to prepare the router prior to performing the lab so that previous configuration options do not interfere with your configurations.

The following is the procedure for clearing out previous configurations and starting with an unconfigured router.

Step 1. Enter into privileged EXEC mode by typing **enable**.

```
Router>enable
```

If prompted for a password, enter **class**. (If that does not work, ask your instructor.)

Step 2. In privileged EXEC mode, enter the command **erase startup-config**.

```
Router#erase startup-config
```

The response from the router will be

```
Erasing the nvram filesystem will remove all files! Continue? [confirm]
```

Step 3. Press **Enter** to confirm.

The response will be

```
Erase of nvram: complete
```

Step 4. Now in privileged EXEC mode, enter the command **reload**.

```
Router#reload
response:
System configuration has been modified. Save? [yes/no]:
```

Step 5. Type **n** and then press **Enter**.

The router will respond with the following:

```
Proceed with reload? [confirm]
```

Step 6. Press **Enter** to confirm.

The first line of the response will be

```
Reload requested by console.
```

After the router reloads, the prompt will be

```
Would you like to enter the initial configuration dialog? [yes/no]:
```

Step 7. Type **n** and then press **Enter**.

The responding prompt will be

```
Press RETURN to get started!
```

Step 8. Press **Enter**.

Now, the router is ready for you to perform the assigned lab.

CCNA 3 Skills-Based Assessment Practice

Ultimately, your success on the CCNA exams, and in your networking career, will depend heavily upon your ability to plan, design, implement, operate, and troubleshoot internetworks. In *Switching Basics and Intermediate Routing CCNA 3*, you have learned many new skills. Now it is time to apply what you have learned to comprehensive skills-based assessments. Because your CCNA 3 coursework is divided into routing and switching, this appendix includes a skills-based assessment for routing and a skills-based assessment for switching. Then, you will combine skills from both routing and switching in the CCNA 3 comprehensive skills-based assessment.

CCNA 3 Skills-Based Assessment: Routing

Figure D-1   CCNA 3 Skills-Based Assessment: Routing

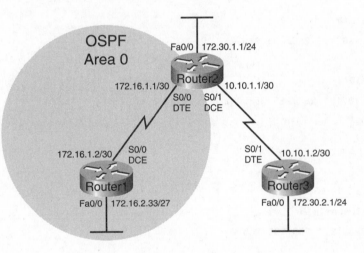

Objectives

- Configure OSPF with authentication

- Configure EIGRP

- Configure a default route and propagate it using OSPF

- Verify network connectivity and gather documentation

Equipment

The topology shown in Figure D-1 is using 2600 series routers. However, you can use any router series that supports OSPF, including the 1700 and 2500 series.

NetLab Compatibility Notes

This lab is fully compatible with a standard NetLab Basic Router Pod.

Preconfigurations

Use the following scripts to preconfigure the routers:

Router1

```
hostname Router1
interface FastEthernet0/0
 ip address 172.16.2.33 255.255.255.224
no shutdown
 interface Serial0/0
 ip address 172.16.1.2 255.255.255.252
 clockrate 56000
 no shutdown
```

Router2

```
hostname Router2
interface FastEthernet0/0
 ip address 172.30.1.1 255.255.255.0
no shutdown
interface Serial0/0
 ip address 172.16.1.1 255.255.255.252
 no shutdown
interface serial0/1
 ip address 10.10.1.1 255.255.255.252
 clockrate 56000
 no shutdown
```

Router3

```
hostname Router3
interface FastEthernet0/0
 ip address 172.30.2.1 255.255.255.0
no shutdown
interface serial0/1
 ip address 10.10.1.2 255.255.255.252
 no shutdown
```

Task 1: Configure OSPF with Authentication

Step 1.   Use a loopback interface to configure Router1 with an OSPF router ID of 192.168.1.1.

Step 2.   Use a loopback interface to configure Router2 with an OSPF router ID of 192.168.2.1.

Step 3.   Configure OSPF routing between Router1 and Router2 with a process ID of 50.

Step 4.   Configure OSPF so that only the following 172.16.0.0 subnets will be routed:

- **172.16.2.32/27**
- **172.16.1.0/30**

Step 5.   Configure the OSPF hello interval to 5 seconds and the OSPF dead interval to 20 seconds.

Step 6.   Configure the OSPF communication between the routers to use authentication with MD5 encryption.

Task 2: Configure EIGRP

Step 1. Configure EIGRP between Router2 and Router3 with an AS of 100.

Step 2. Configure EIGRP should only to route only for the following networks:

- **10.10.1.0/30**
- **172.30.1.0/24**
- **172.30.2.0/24**

Task 3: Configure Default Routing and Propagate It Using OSPF

Step 1. On Router2, configure a default static route to Router3.

Step 2. Propagate that default route to all routers in the OSPF routing domain.

Task 4: Verify Connectivity and Gather Documentation

Step 1. From Router2, verify connectivity by pinging all interfaces on all routers.

Step 2. From Router1, ping all OSPF-enabled interfaces.

Step 3. From Router3, ping all EIGRP-enabled interfaces.

Note: Router1 and Router3 will not be able to ping all interfaces, because there is no redistribution between OSPF and EIGRP in this scenario.

Step 4. For each of the routers, capture the following output:

- **show run**
- **show ip route**
- **ping** output showing successful pings according to Steps 1 to 3

Router1

```
Router1#show run
Building configuration...

hostname Router1
!
enable secret class
!
no ip domain lookup
ip host R2 172.16.1.1
!
interface Loopback0
 ip address 192.168.1.1 255.255.255.0
!
interface FastEthernet0/0
 ip address 172.16.2.33 255.255.255.224
 no shutdown
!
```

```
interface Serial0/0
 description Link to R2
 ip address 172.16.1.2 255.255.255.252
 ip ospf message-digest-key 1 md5 allrouters
 ip ospf hello-interval 5
 ip ospf dead-interval 20
 clock rate 56000
 no shutdown
!
router ospf 50
 log-adjacency-changes
 area 0 authentication message-digest
 network 172.16.1.0 0.0.0.3 area 0
 network 172.16.2.32 0.0.0.31 area 0
!
banner motd $
***********************************

  !!!AUTHORIZE ACCESS ONLY!!!
***********************************
$
!
line con 0
 exec-timeout 0 0
 password cisco
 logging synchronous
 login
line aux 0
 exec-timeout 0 0
 password cisco
 logging synchronous
 login
line vty 0 4
 exec-timeout 0 0
 password cisco
 logging synchronous
 login
end


Router1#show ip route
Codes: C - connected, S - static, R - RIP, M - mobile, B - BGP
       D - EIGRP, EX - EIGRP external, O - OSPF, IA - OSPF inter area
       N1 - OSPF NSSA external type 1, N2 - OSPF NSSA external type 2
       E1 - OSPF external type 1, E2 - OSPF external type 2
       i - IS-IS, su - IS-IS summary, L1 - IS-IS level-1, L2 - IS-IS level-2
       ia - IS-IS inter area, * - candidate default, U - per-user static route
       o - ODR, P - periodic downloaded static route
```

```
Gateway of last resort is 172.16.1.1 to network 0.0.0.0


     172.16.0.0/16 is variably subnetted, 2 subnets, 2 masks
C       172.16.2.32/27 is directly connected, FastEthernet0/0
C       172.16.1.0/30 is directly connected, Serial0/0
C     192.168.1.0/24 is directly connected, Loopback0
O*E2 0.0.0.0/0 [110/1] via 172.16.1.1, 00:06:43, Serial0/0


Router1#ping 172.16.1.1


Type escape sequence to abort.
Sending 5, 100-byte ICMP Echos to 172.16.1.1, timeout is 2 seconds:
!!!!!
Success rate is 100 percent (5/5), round-trip min/avg/max = 32/32/36 ms
Router1#ping 172.30.1.1


Type escape sequence to abort.
Sending 5, 100-byte ICMP Echos to 172.30.1.1, timeout is 2 seconds:
!!!!!
Success rate is 100 percent (5/5), round-trip min/avg/max = 32/33/36 ms


Router1#show version
Cisco Internetwork Operating System Software
IOS (tm) C2600 Software (C2600-J1S3-M), Version 12.3(17a), RELEASE SOFTWARE (fc2)
Technical Support: http://www.cisco.com/techsupport
Copyright (c) 1986-2005 by cisco Systems, Inc.
Compiled Mon 12-Dec-05 14:12 by evmiller
Image text-base: 0x80008098, data-base: 0x81A33618


ROM: System Bootstrap, Version 12.2(7r) [cmong 7r], RELEASE SOFTWARE (fc1)
ROM: C2600 Software (C2600-J1S3-M), Version 12.3(17a), RELEASE SOFTWARE (fc2)


Router1 uptime is 44 minutes
System returned to ROM by power-on
System image file is "flash:c2600-j1s3-mz.123-17a.bin"


cisco 2611XM (MPC860P) processor (revision 0x100) with 89088K/9216K bytes of mem
ory.
Processor board ID JAE07460SS1 (4270759778)
M860 processor: part number 5, mask 2
Bridging software.
X.25 software, Version 3.0.0.
TN3270 Emulation software.
2 FastEthernet/IEEE 802.3 interface(s)
2 Serial network interface(s)
32K bytes of non-volatile configuration memory.
```

32768K bytes of processor board System flash (Read/Write)

Configuration register is 0x2102

Router2

Router2#**show run**
Building configuration...

hostname Router2
!
enable secret class
!
no ip domain lookup
ip host R1 172.16.1.2
ip host R3 10.10.1.2
!
interface Loopback0
 ip address 192.168.2.1 255.255.255.0
!
interface FastEthernet0/0
 ip address 172.30.1.1 255.255.255.0
 no shutdown
!
interface Serial0/0
 description Link to R1
 ip address 172.16.1.1 255.255.255.252
 ip ospf message-digest-key 1 md5 allrouters
 ip ospf hello-interval 5
 ip ospf dead-interval 20
 no shutdown
!
interface Serial0/1
 description Link to R3
 ip address 10.10.1.1 255.255.255.252
 clock rate 56000
 no clockrate
!
router eigrp 100
 network 10.0.0.0
 network 172.30.0.0
 no auto-summary
!
router ospf 50
 area 0 authentication message-digest
 network 172.16.1.0 0.0.0.3 area 0
 default-information originate

```
!
ip route 0.0.0.0 0.0.0.0 Serial0/1
!
banner motd $
**********************************
  !!!AUTHORIZE ACCESS ONLY!!!
**********************************
$
!
line con 0
 exec-timeout 0 0
 password cisco
 logging synchronous
 login
line aux 0
 exec-timeout 0 0
 password cisco
 logging synchronous
 login
line vty 0 4
 exec-timeout 0 0
 password cisco
 logging synchronous
 login
end


Router2#show ip route
Codes: C - connected, S - static, R - RIP, M - mobile, B - BGP
       D - EIGRP, EX - EIGRP external, O - OSPF, IA - OSPF inter area
       N1 - OSPF NSSA external type 1, N2 - OSPF NSSA external type 2
       E1 - OSPF external type 1, E2 - OSPF external type 2
       i - IS-IS, su - IS-IS summary, L1 - IS-IS level-1, L2 - IS-IS level-2
       ia - IS-IS inter area, * - candidate default, U - per-user static route
       o - ODR, P - periodic downloaded static route


Gateway of last resort is 0.0.0.0 to network 0.0.0.0


     172.16.0.0/16 is variably subnetted, 2 subnets, 2 masks
O       172.16.2.32/27 [110/65] via 172.16.1.2, 00:08:04, Serial0/0
C       172.16.1.0/30 is directly connected, Serial0/0
     172.30.0.0/16 is variably subnetted, 2 subnets, 2 masks
D       172.30.0.0/16 [90/2172416] via 10.10.1.2, 00:08:31, Serial0/1
C       172.30.1.0/24 is directly connected, FastEthernet0/0
     10.0.0.0/30 is subnetted, 1 subnets
C       10.10.1.0 is directly connected, Serial0/1
C     192.168.2.0/24 is directly connected, Loopback0
```

```
S*   0.0.0.0/0 is directly connected, Serial0/1


Router2#ping 172.16.2.33


Type escape sequence to abort.
Sending 5, 100-byte ICMP Echos to 172.16.2.33, timeout is 2 seconds:
!!!!!
Success rate is 100 percent (5/5), round-trip min/avg/max = 40/44/60 ms
Router2#ping 172.30.2.1


Type escape sequence to abort.
Sending 5, 100-byte ICMP Echos to 172.30.2.1, timeout is 2 seconds:
!!!!!
Success rate is 100 percent (5/5), round-trip min/avg/max = 32/33/36 ms


Router2#show version
Cisco Internetwork Operating System Software
IOS (tm) C2600 Software (C2600-J1S3-M), Version 12.3(17a), RELEASE SOFTWARE (fc2)
Technical Support: http://www.cisco.com/techsupport
Copyright (c) 1986-2005 by cisco Systems, Inc.
Compiled Mon 12-Dec-05 14:12 by evmiller
Image text-base: 0x80008098, data-base: 0x81A33618


ROM: System Bootstrap, Version 12.2(7r) [cmong 7r], RELEASE SOFTWARE (fc1)
ROM: C2600 Software (C2600-J1S3-M), Version 12.3(17a), RELEASE SOFTWARE (fc2)


Router2 uptime is 43 minutes
System returned to ROM by power-on
System image file is "flash:c2600-j1s3-mz.123-17a.bin"


cisco 2621XM (MPC860P) processor (revision 0x100) with 118784K/12288K bytes of m
emory.
Processor board ID JAE07420G4S (1562611187)
M860 processor: part number 5, mask 2
Bridging software.
X.25 software, Version 3.0.0.
TN3270 Emulation software.
2 FastEthernet/IEEE 802.3 interface(s)
2 Serial network interface(s)
32K bytes of non-volatile configuration memory.
49152K bytes of processor board System flash (Read/Write)


Configuration register is 0x2102
```

Router3

```
Router3#show run
Building configuration...

!
hostname Router3
!
enable secret class
!
no ip domain lookup
ip host R2 10.10.1.1
!
interface FastEthernet0/0
 ip address 172.30.2.1 255.255.255.0
 no shutdown
!
interface Serial0/1
 description Link to R2
 ip address 10.10.1.2 255.255.255.252
 no shutdown
!
router eigrp 100
 network 10.0.0.0
 network 172.30.0.0
 auto-summary
!
banner motd $
**********************************
   !!!AUTHORIZE ACCESS ONLY!!!
**********************************
$
!
line con 0
 exec-timeout 0 0
 password cisco
 logging synchronous
 login
line aux 0
 exec-timeout 0 0
 password cisco
 logging synchronous
 login
```

```
line vty 0 4
 exec-timeout 0 0
 password cisco
 logging synchronous
 login
end


Router3#show ip route
Codes: C - connected, S - static, R - RIP, M - mobile, B - BGP
       D - EIGRP, EX - EIGRP external, O - OSPF, IA - OSPF inter area
       N1 - OSPF NSSA external type 1, N2 - OSPF NSSA external type 2
       E1 - OSPF external type 1, E2 - OSPF external type 2
       i - IS-IS, su - IS-IS summary, L1 - IS-IS level-1, L2 - IS-IS level-2
       ia - IS-IS inter area, * - candidate default, U - per-user static route
       o - ODR, P - periodic downloaded static route


Gateway of last resort is not set


     172.30.0.0/16 is variably subnetted, 3 subnets, 2 masks
C       172.30.2.0/24 is directly connected, FastEthernet0/0
D       172.30.0.0/16 is a summary, 00:12:12, Null0
D       172.30.1.0/24 [90/2172416] via 10.10.1.1, 00:12:11, Serial0/1
     10.0.0.0/8 is variably subnetted, 2 subnets, 2 masks
C       10.10.1.0/30 is directly connected, Serial0/1
D       10.0.0.0/8 is a summary, 00:12:12, Null0


Router3#ping 172.30.1.1


Type escape sequence to abort.
Sending 5, 100-byte ICMP Echos to 172.30.1.1, timeout is 2 seconds:
!!!!!
Success rate is 100 percent (5/5), round-trip min/avg/max = 40/44/64 ms


Router3#show version
Cisco Internetwork Operating System Software
IOS (tm) C2600 Software (C2600-J1S3-M), Version 12.3(17a), RELEASE SOFTWARE (fc2)
Technical Support: http://www.cisco.com/techsupport
Copyright (c) 1986-2005 by cisco Systems, Inc.
Compiled Mon 12-Dec-05 14:12 by evmiller
Image text-base: 0x80008098, data-base: 0x81A33618


ROM: System Bootstrap, Version 11.3(2)XA4, RELEASE SOFTWARE (fc1)
ROM: C2600 Software (C2600-J1S3-M), Version 12.3(17a), RELEASE SOFTWARE (fc2)


Router3 uptime is 44 minutes
System returned to ROM by power-on
```

System image file is "flash:c2600-j1s3-mz.123-17a.bin"

cisco 2621 (MPC860) processor (revision 0x102) with 56320K/9216K bytes of memory

.

Processor board ID JAD04300B3P (4106725847)

M860 processor: part number 0, mask 49

Bridging software.

X.25 software, Version 3.0.0.

TN3270 Emulation software.

2 FastEthernet/IEEE 802.3 interface(s)

2 Serial network interface(s)

32K bytes of non-volatile configuration memory.

16384K bytes of processor board System flash (Read/Write)

Configuration register is 0x2102

CCNA 3 Skills-Based Assessment: Switching

Figure D-2   CCNA 3 Skills-Based Assessment: Switching

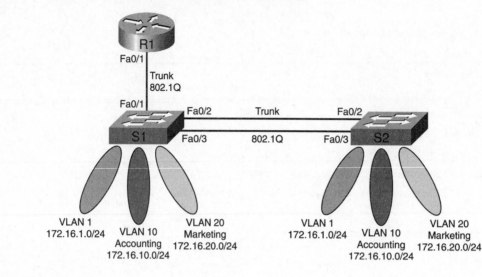

Objectives

- Router VLAN configuration
- Basic switch configuration
- Configure trunk links and port security
- Configure STP, VTP, and VLANs
- Configure VLAN interfaces on switches
- Configure VLAN trunking and spanning tree
- Verify connectivity and gather documentation

Equipment

The topology shown in Figure D-2 has been designed for the 2950 series switch. Other hardware may have different interface types and numbers. 1900 series switches do not support 802.1Q encapsulation and thus require ISL encapsulation.

NetLab Compatibility Notes

This lab is fully compatible with a standard NetLab Basic Switch Pod.

Task 1: Router VLAN Configuration

Step 1.   Configure the router hostname and any other basic configurations required by your instructor.

Step 2.   Configure the Ethernet interface to trunk for each VLAN on S1—VLAN 1, VLAN 10, and VLAN 20 using 802.1Q encapsulation:

Note: 1900 series switches do not support 802.1Q encapsulation. Use ISL encapsulation for 1900 series switches.

- **VLAN 1 = 172.16.1.0/24**
- **VLAN 10 = 172.16.10.0/24**
- **VLAN 20 = 172.16.20.0/24**

Task 2: Basic Switch Configuration

Step 1.   Configure the hostname on switch S1 to **S1**.

Step 2.   Configure S1 with a VLAN 1 IP address of 172.16.1.3/24.

Step 3.   Configure the hostname on S2 to **S2**.

Step 4.   Configure S2 with a VLAN 1 IP address of 172.16.1.4/24.

Step 5.   Configure both switches with a default gateway address of 172.16.1.1.

Task 3: Configure Trunk Links and Port Security

Step 1.   On S1, configure interfaces Fa0/1–3 in trunking mode.

Step 2.   On S2, configure interface Fa0/2–3 in trunking mode. Shut down interface Fa0/1, because it will not be used.

Note: If you are using a 2900 series switch, you have to specify the encapsulation type used on the switch's trunk links.

Step 3.   On both switches, configure the following on interfaces Fa0/4–24 (or 12 if using a 12-port switch):

- **Set the ports to access mode.**
- **Enable port security.**
- **Enable the first MAC address to stick to the configuration.**
- **Enable port shutdown if there is a security violation.**

Task 4: Configure STP, VTP, and VLANs

Step 1.   Configure S1 to be the root bridge for VLAN 1 and VLAN 10.

Step 2.   Configure S2 to be the root bridge for VLAN 20.

Step 3.   Configure both S1 and S2 as part of VTP domain Group1.

Step 4.   Configure S1 as the VTP server and S2 as the VTP client.

Step 5.   Configure **cisco** as the VTP password.

Step 6.   Create VLAN 10 with the name **Accounting**.

Step 7.   Create VLAN 20 with the name **Marketing**.

Task 5: Configure VLAN Interfaces on Switches

Step 1.   Configure the following on switch S1:

- **Assign interfaces Fa0/4–6 to VLAN 10.**
- **Assign interfaces Fa0/7–9 to VLAN 20.**
- **Verify that all other interfaces are in VLAN 1.**

Step 2.   Configure the following on switch S2:

- **Assign interfaces Fa0/4–6 to VLAN 10.**
- **Assign interfaces Fa0/7–9 to VLAN 20.**
- **Verify that all other interfaces are in VLAN 1.**

Task 6: Configure VLAN Trunking and Spanning Tree

Step 1.   Configure trunking between S1 and S2 with 802.1Q encapsulation using ports Fa0/2 and Fa0/3 on both switches.

Note: Use ISL encapsulation for 1900 series switches.

Step 2.   Configure S1 for trunking between S1 and R1 with 802.1Q encapsulation using port Fa0/1.

Step 3.   Configure S1 to be the root bridge for VLAN 1

Task 7: Verify Connectivity and Gather Documentation

Step 1.   It is not possible to verify inter-VLAN routing, because there are no hosts attached. However, the router and the two switches should be able to ping each other on their VLAN 1 interfaces.

Step 2.   For the router, capture the following output:

- **show run**
- **show ip interface brief**

Step 3.   For the switches, capture the following output:

- **show run**
- **show vlan brief**
- **show vtp status**
- **show spanning-tree summary**

R1

```
R1#show run
Building configuration...

hostname R1
!
enable secret class
!
no ip domain lookup
ip host S2 172.16.1.4
ip host S1 172.16.1.3
!
interface FastEthernet0/1
 no shutdown
!
interface FastEthernet0/1.1
 description Managment VLAN 1
 encapsulation dot1Q 1 native
 ip address 172.16.1.1 255.255.255.0
!
interface FastEthernet0/1.10
 description Accounting VLAN 10
 encapsulation dot1Q 10
 ip address 172.16.10.1 255.255.255.0
```

```
!
interface FastEthernet0/1.20
 description Marketing VLAN 20
 encapsulation dot1Q 20
 ip address 172.16.20.1 255.255.255.0
!
banner motd $
**********************************
   !!!AUTHORIZE ACCESS ONLY!!!
**********************************
$
!
line con 0
 exec-timeout 0 0
 password cisco
 logging synchronous
 login
line aux 0
 exec-timeout 0 0
 password cisco
 logging synchronous
 login
line vty 0 4
 exec-timeout 0 0
 password cisco
 logging synchronous
 login
end
```

```
R1#show ip interface brief
Interface                IP-Address      OK? Method Status                 Prot
ocol
FastEthernet0/0          unassigned      YES unset  administratively down down

Serial0/0                unassigned      YES unset  administratively down down

FastEthernet0/1          unassigned      YES unset  up                       up

FastEthernet0/1.1        172.16.1.1      YES manual up                       up

FastEthernet0/1.10       172.16.10.1     YES manual up                       up

FastEthernet0/1.20       172.16.20.1     YES manual up                       up
```

```
R1#show version
Cisco Internetwork Operating System Software
IOS (tm) C2600 Software (C2600-IPBASE-M), Version 12.3(1a), RELEASE SOFTWARE (fc1)
```

```
Copyright (c) 1986-2003 by cisco Systems, Inc.
Compiled Fri 06-Jun-03 22:08 by dchih
Image text-base: 0x80008098, data-base: 0x80F9CF68


ROM: System Bootstrap, Version 12.2(7r) [cmong 7r], RELEASE SOFTWARE (fc1)


R1 uptime is 1 hour, 47 minutes
System returned to ROM by power-on
System image file is "flash:c2600-ipbase-mz.123-1a.bin"


cisco 2621XM (MPC860P) processor (revision 0x100) with 125952K/5120K bytes of me
mory.
Processor board ID JAE07420G7D (326445113)
M860 processor: part number 5, mask 2
Bridging software.
X.25 software, Version 3.0.0.
2 FastEthernet/IEEE 802.3 interface(s)
1 Serial network interface(s)
32K bytes of non-volatile configuration memory.
49152K bytes of processor board System flash (Read/Write)


Configuration register is 0x2142 (will be 0x2102 at next reload)
```

S1

```
S1#show run
Building configuration...

hostname S1
!
enable secret class
!
no ip domain-lookup
ip host R1 172.16.1.1
ip host S2 172.16.1.4
!
!
spanning-tree vlan 1 priority 24576
spanning-tree vlan 10 priority 24576
!
!----------------------------------------
!VTP and VLAN Configurations
!----------------------------------------
vtp mode server
vtp domain Group1
vtp password cisco
```

```
vlan 10
name Accounting
vlan 20
name Marketing
!----------------------------------------
!
interface FastEthernet0/1
 switchport mode trunk
!
interface FastEthernet0/2
 switchport mode trunk
!
interface FastEthernet0/3
 switchport mode trunk
!
interface range FastEthernet0/4 - 6
 switchport access vlan 10
 switchport mode access
 switchport port-security
 switchport port-security mac-address sticky
 switchport port-security maximum 1
 switchport port-security violation shutdown
!
interface range FastEthernet0/7 - 9
 switchport access vlan 20
 switchport mode access
 switchport port-security
 switchport port-security mac-address sticky
 switchport port-security maximum 1
 switchport port-security violation shutdown
!
interface range FastEthernet0/10 - 24
 switchport mode access
 switchport port-security
 switchport port-security mac-address sticky
 switchport port-security maximum 1
 switchport port-security violation shutdown
!
interface Vlan1
 ip address 172.16.1.3 255.255.255.0
 no shutdown
!
ip default-gateway 172.16.1.1=
!
banner motd $
```

```
************************************
   !!!AUTHORIZE ACCESS ONLY!!!
************************************
$
!
line con 0
 exec-timeout 0 0
 password cisco
 logging synchronous
 login
line vty 0 4
 exec-timeout 0 0
 password cisco
 logging synchronous
 login
line vty 5 15
 exec-timeout 0 0
 password cisco
 logging synchronous
 login
!
end


S1#show vlan brief

VLAN Name                             Status    Ports
---- -------------------------------- --------- -------------------------------
1    default                          active    Fa0/10, Fa0/11, Fa0/12, Fa0/13
                                                Fa0/14, Fa0/15, Fa0/16, Fa0/17
                                                Fa0/18, Fa0/19, Fa0/20, Fa0/21
                                                Fa0/22, Fa0/23, Fa0/24, Gi0/1
                                                Gi0/2

10   Accounting                       active    Fa0/4, Fa0/5, Fa0/6
20   Marketing                        active    Fa0/7, Fa0/8, Fa0/9
1002 fddi-default                     active
1003 token-ring-default               active
1004 fddinet-default                  active
1005 trnet-default                    active


S1#show vtp status
VTP Version                     : 2
Configuration Revision          : 2
Maximum VLANs supported locally : 250
Number of existing VLANs        : 7
VTP Operating Mode              : Server
VTP Domain Name                 : Group1
```

```
VTP Pruning Mode           : Disabled
VTP V2 Mode                : Disabled
VTP Traps Generation       : Disabled
MD5 digest                 : 0xB9 0x8C 0x14 0x31 0x5F 0x85 0x67 0xFC
Configuration last modified by 172.16.1.3 at 3-1-93 00:02:29
Local updater ID is 172.16.1.3 on interface Vl1 (lowest numbered VLAN interface found)
```

```
S1#show spanning-tree summary
Switch is in pvst mode
Root bridge for: VLAN0001, VLAN0010
EtherChannel misconfiguration guard is enabled
Extended system ID    is enabled
Portfast              is disabled by default
PortFast BPDU Guard   is disabled by default
Portfast BPDU Filter  is disabled by default
Loopguard             is disabled by default
UplinkFast            is disabled
BackboneFast          is disabled
Pathcost method used is short


Name                 Blocking Listening Learning Forwarding STP Active
-------------------- -------- --------- -------- ---------- ----------
VLAN0001                 0         0        0         3          3
VLAN0010                 0         0        0         3          3
VLAN0020                 1         0        0         2          3
-------------------- -------- --------- -------- ---------- ----------
3 vlans                  1         0        0         8          9
```

```
S1#show version
Cisco Internetwork Operating System Software
IOS (tm) C2950 Software (C2950-I6Q4L2-M), Version 12.1(13)EA1, RELEASE SOFTWARE (fc1)
Copyright (c) 1986-2003 by cisco Systems, Inc.
Compiled Tue 04-Mar-03 02:14 by yenanh
Image text-base: 0x80010000, data-base: 0x805A8000


ROM: Bootstrap program is CALHOUN boot loader


S1 uptime is 34 minutes
System returned to ROM by power-on
System image file is "flash:c2950-i6q4l2-mz.121-13.EA1.bin"


cisco WS-C2950T-24 (RC32300) processor (revision K0) with 20839K bytes of memory
.
Processor board ID FOC0743Y1E3
Last reset from system-reset
Running Enhanced Image
```

```
24 FastEthernet/IEEE 802.3 interface(s)
2 Gigabit Ethernet/IEEE 802.3 interface(s)

32K bytes of flash-simulated non-volatile configuration memory.
Base ethernet MAC Address: 00:0E:38:5D:E3:80
Motherboard assembly number: 73-6114-09
Power supply part number: 34-0965-01
Motherboard serial number: FOC07430LSF
Power supply serial number: DAB0742EDCL
Model revision number: K0
Motherboard revision number: A0
Model number: WS-C2950T-24
System serial number: FOC0743Y1E3
Configuration register is 0xF
```

S2

```
S2#show run
Building configuration...

hostname S2
!
enable secret class
!
no ip domain-lookup
ip host S1 172.16.1.3
ip host R1 172.16.1.1
!
!
spanning-tree vlan 20 priority 24576
!
!----------------------------------------
!VTP and VLAN Configurations
!----------------------------------------
vtp mode client
vtp domain Group1
vtp password cisco
!----------------------------------------
!
interface FastEthernet0/1
 shutdown
!
interface FastEthernet0/2
 switchport mode trunk
!
interface FastEthernet0/3
 switchport mode trunk
```

```
!
interface range FastEthernet0/4 - 6
 switchport access vlan 10
 switchport mode access
 switchport port-security
 switchport port-security mac-address sticky
 switchport port-security maximum 1
 switchport port-security violation shutdown
!
interface range FastEthernet0/7 - 9
 switchport access vlan 20
 switchport mode access
 switchport port-security
 switchport port-security mac-address sticky
 switchport port-security maximum 1
 switchport port-security violation shutdown
!
interface range FastEthernet0/10 - 24
 switchport mode access
 switchport port-security
 switchport port-security mac-address sticky
 switchport port-security maximum 1
 switchport port-security violation shutdown
!
interface Vlan1
 ip address 172.16.1.4 255.255.255.0
 no shutdown
!
ip default-gateway 172.16.1.1
ip http server
!
banner motd $
**********************************
   !!!AUTHORIZE ACCESS ONLY!!!
**********************************
$
!
line con 0
 exec-timeout 0 0
 password cisco
 logging synchronous
 login
line vty 0 4
 exec-timeout 0 0
 password cisco
 logging synchronous
```

```
 login
line vty 5 15
 exec-timeout 0 0
 password cisco
 logging synchronous
 login
end
```

S2#**show vlan brief**

```
VLAN Name                             Status    Ports
---- -------------------------------- --------- -------------------------------
1    default                          active    Fa0/1, Fa0/10, Fa0/11, Fa0/12
                                                Fa0/13, Fa0/14, Fa0/15, Fa0/16
                                                Fa0/17, Fa0/18, Fa0/19, Fa0/20
                                                Fa0/21, Fa0/22, Fa0/23, Fa0/24
10   Accounting                       active    Fa0/4, Fa0/5, Fa0/6
20   Marketing                        active    Fa0/7, Fa0/8, Fa0/9
1002 fddi-default                     active
1003 token-ring-default               active
1004 fddinet-default                  active
1005 trnet-default                    active
```

S2#**show vtp status**

```
VTP Version                     : 2
Configuration Revision          : 2
Maximum VLANs supported locally : 64
Number of existing VLANs        : 7
VTP Operating Mode              : Client
VTP Domain Name                 : Group1
VTP Pruning Mode                : Disabled
VTP V2 Mode                     : Disabled
VTP Traps Generation            : Disabled
MD5 digest                      : 0xB9 0x8C 0x14 0x31 0x5F 0x85 0x67 0xFC
Configuration last modified by 172.16.1.3 at 3-1-93 00:02:29
```

S2#**show spanning-tree summary**

```
Switch is in pvst mode
Root bridge for: VLAN0020
EtherChannel misconfiguration guard is enabled
Extended system ID    is enabled
Portfast              is disabled by default
PortFast BPDU Guard   is disabled by default
Portfast BPDU Filter is disabled by default
Loopguard             is disabled by default
UplinkFast            is disabled
```

BackboneFast   is disabled
Pathcost method used is short

Name	Blocking	Listening	Learning	Forwarding	STP Active
VLAN0001	1	0	0	1	2
VLAN0010	1	0	0	1	2
VLAN0020	0	0	0	2	2
3 vlans	2	0	0	4	6

S2#**show version**
Cisco Internetwork Operating System Software
IOS (tm) C2950 Software (C2950-I6Q4L2-M), Version 12.1(13)EA1, RELEASE SOFTWARE (fc1)
Copyright (c) 1986-2003 by cisco Systems, Inc.
Compiled Tue 04-Mar-03 02:14 by yenanh
Image text-base: 0x80010000, data-base: 0x805A8000

ROM: Bootstrap program is CALHOUN boot loader

S2 uptime is 35 minutes
System returned to ROM by power-on
System image file is "flash:/c2950-i6q4l2-mz.121-13.EA1.bin"

cisco WS-C2950-24 (RC32300) processor (revision J0) with 20839K bytes of memory.
Processor board ID FHK0728W0XH
Last reset from system-reset
Running Standard Image
24 FastEthernet/IEEE 802.3 interface(s)

32K bytes of flash-simulated non-volatile configuration memory.
Base ethernet MAC Address: 00:0D:65:62:E3:80
Motherboard assembly number: 73-5781-11
Power supply part number: 34-0965-01
Motherboard serial number: FOC07280RA4
Power supply serial number: DAB07278PCM
Model revision number: J0
Motherboard revision number: A0
Model number: WS-C2950-24
System serial number: FHK0728W0XH
Configuration register is 0xF

S2#

CCNA 3 Comprehensive Skills-Based Assessment

Table D-1   VLSM Addressing Scheme

Device Name	Interface	Address	Subnet Mask
ISP			
CORE			
DIST-A			
DIST-B			
DIST-C			
ALSw-A			
ALSw-B			

Objectives

Demonstrate a comprehensive implementation of CCNA 3 skills by completing the following:

- Design a VLSM addressing scheme to meet requirements
- Configure OSPF, static, and default routing
- Configure STP and port security
- Configure VTP and VLANs
- Verify your configuration and gather documentation

Scenario

You are the network administrator for a small corporation. You are planning a migration to a three-layer hierarchical design using OSPF and VLANs. At the core layer, your router will provide access to the Internet. At the distribution layer, you will use one router for access to your public Web servers (DIST-A), one router for access to the enterprise server farm (DIST-B), and one router for routing VLANs (DIST-C). At the access layer, you will trunk two switches with VLAN implementation. In addition, you will completely redesign your addressing scheme using VLSM.

Design Considerations

You can use any five routers at your disposal. However, DIST-C must be a 1700 or 2600 series router that will support routing VLANs. The server LANs off of ISP, DIST-A, and DIST-B can be simulated with loopback interfaces.

Task 1: Lab Setup

Step 1.   Cable the lab with available equipment in the configuration shown in Figure D-3.

Step 2.   Label Figure D-3 with the appropriate interface names (such as S0, S0/0, E0, Fa0, and so on).

Step 3.   Label serial interfaces with the appropriate DTE or DCE designation.

Task 2: Addressing Scheme

Design an appropriate VLSM addressing scheme using the following method to assign subnets and interface addresses. Maximize the number of host addresses at each level of subnetting.

Step 1.   **VLSM Level 1:** Subnet the given address space 172.16.0.0/16 to provide enough addresses for 1000 hosts and assign subnet zero to VLAN 10.

Step 2.   **VLSM Level 2:** Using subnet 1 left over from VLSM Level 1, subnet it to provide enough addresses for 500 hosts and assign subnet 0 to VLAN 20.

Step 3.   **VLSM Level 3:** Using subnet 1 left over from VLSM Level 2, subnet it to provide enough addresses for 250 hosts and assign subnet 0 to VLAN 30.

Step 4.   **VLSM Level 4:** Using subnet 1 left over from VLSM Level 3, subnet it to provide enough addresses for 60 hosts and assign subnet 0 to the server farm.

Step 5.   **VLSM Level 5:** Using subnet 1 left over from VLSM Level 4, subnet it to provide enough addresses for three hosts. Assign subnet 0 to the CORE LAN (three hosts) and subnet 1 to VLAN 1 (three hosts).

Step 6.   **VLSM Level 6:** Using subnet 2 left over from VLSM Level 5, subnet it to provide enough addresses for the remaining two WAN links. Assign subnet 0 to the WAN link between DIST-A and DIST-C and subnet 1 to the WAN link between DIST-B and DIST-C.

Step 7.   Fill in Table D-1 with your addressing design and label the topology with the assigned subnets.

Step 8.   On the topology in Figure D-3, label each interface with the last two octets of the interface's IP address.

Task 3: Basic Router and Switch Configuration

Erase the stored configuration on all routers and switches and reload without saving changes. Configure each with the following basic configurations:

- Hostnames
- Passwords
- Host table
- Console line and Telnet lines
- Interface addresses

Task 4: Configure OSPF, Static, and Default Routing

Step 1.   Configure OSPF to advertise all inside routes:

- **The ISP router is not to participate in OSPF.**
- **CORE is not to advertise the WAN link it shares with ISP.**
- **Make sure DIST-A advertises the inside public web server.**

Figure D-3   CCNA 3 Comprehensive Skills-Based Assessment (Answer)

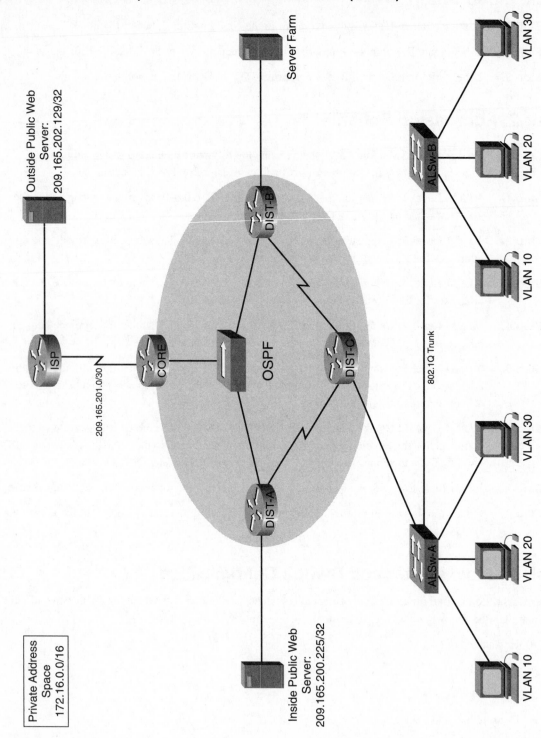

Step 2.   CORE must never be DR and DIST-A must always be DR.

Step 3.   Configure a 5-second hello interval on OSPF enabled routers.

Step 4.   Configure OSPF routers to use MD5 authentication.

Step 5.   Set the LAN interface on DIST-C to passive so that OSPF updates do not get sent out to ALSw-A.

Step 6.   Configure CORE with a default static route to ISP.

Step 7.   Advertise the default route to the rest of the inside routers.

Step 8.   Configure ISP with a static route to the 172.16.0.0/16 address space and a static route to the inside web server at 209.165.200.225/32.

Step 9.   Verify that inside routers can now ping the outside web server.

Task 5: Spanning Tree and Port Security

Step 1.   Configure ALSw-A to be the STP root bridge for VLAN 1 and VLAN 10.

Step 2.   Configure ALSw-B to be the STP root bridge for VLAN 20 and VLAN 30.

Step 3.   On both switches, configure the following on all access ports:

- **Set the ports to access mode.**
- **Enable port security.**
- **Enable the first MAC address to stick to the configuration.**
- **Enable port shutdown if there is a security violation.**

Step 4.   If necessary for your switch platform, configure the switch trunk links to use IEEE 802.1Q.

Task 6: VLAN and VTP Configuration

Step 1.   Configure ALSw-A to be the VTP server in the VTP domain CCNA3 with an appropriate password.

Step 2.   Configure ALSw-B to be a VTP client in the VTP domain CCNA3 with the correct password.

Step 3.   Configure the VTP server with the following VLANs:

- **VLAN 10: Finance**
- **VLAN 20: Sales**
- **VLAN 30: Purchasing**

Step 4.   Choose the ports to assign to each VLAN. It is not necessary to configure every port with a VLAN.

Task 7: Verify Configurations and Gather Documentation

Step 1.   You should now have full connectivity from any host on the network to any other host. Verify end-to-end connectivity.

Step 2.   When satisfied with your configurations, gather documentation for future reference. On all five routers, capture the following output:

- **show run**
- **show ip route**
- **show ip interface brief**

- **show ip ospf neighbors**

Step 3.   On the two switches, capture the following output:

- **show run**
- **show vlan brief**
- **show vtp status**

ISP

```
ISP#show run
Building configuration...


hostname ISP
!
enable secret class
!
no ip domain-lookup
ip host DA 172.16.7.66 172.16.7.81
ip host DB 172.16.7.67 172.16.7.85
ip host DC 172.16.7.82 172.16.7.86
ip host CORE 209.165.201.2
ip host SA 172.16.7.74
ip host SB 172.16.7.75
!
interface Loopback0
 description Simulated Outside Public Web Server
 ip address 209.165.202.129 255.255.255.255
!
interface Serial0
 description Link to Enterprise
 ip address 200.20.2.1 255.255.255.252
 clockrate 64000
 no shutdown
!
ip route 209.165.200.225 255.255.255.255 Serial0
ip route 172.16.0.0 255.255.0.0 Serial0
!
!
!
line con 0
 exec-timeout 0 0
 password cisco
 logging synchronous
 login
line aux 0
 exec-timeout 0 0
```

```
  password cisco
  logging synchronous
  login
line vty 0 4
  exec-timeout 0 0
  password cisco
  logging synchronous
  login
!
end
```

```
ISP#show ip interface brief
Interface                IP-Address       OK? Method Status                Protocol
Ethernet0                unassigned       YES unset  administratively down down
Loopback0                209.165.202.129 YES manual  up                         up
Serial0                  200.20.2.1       YES manual  up                         up
Serial1                  unassigned       YES unset  administratively down down
```

```
ISP#show ip route
Codes: C - connected, S - static, I - IGRP, R - RIP, M - mobile, B - BGP
       D - EIGRP, EX - EIGRP external, O - OSPF, IA - OSPF inter area
       N1 - OSPF NSSA external type 1, N2 - OSPF NSSA external type 2
       E1 - OSPF external type 1, E2 - OSPF external type 2, E - EGP
       i - IS-IS, L1 - IS-IS level-1, L2 - IS-IS level-2, ia - IS-IS inter area
       * - candidate default, U - per-user static route, o - ODR
       P - periodic downloaded static route


     209.165.201.0/30 is subnetted, 1 subnets
C       209.165.201.0 is directly connected, Serial0
S     172.16.0.0/16 is directly connected, Serial0
     209.165.200.0/32 is subnetted, 1 subnets
S       209.165.200.225 is directly connected, Serial0
     209.165.202.0/32 is subnetted, 1 subnets
C       209.165.202.129 is directly connected, Loopback0
```

```
ISP#show version
Cisco Internetwork Operating System Software
IOS (tm) 2500 Software (C2500-JS-L), Version 12.2(13b), RELEASE SOFTWARE (fc1)
Copyright (c) 1986-2003 by cisco Systems, Inc.
Compiled Thu 20-Feb-03 14:09 by pwade
Image text-base: 0x0307C780, data-base: 0x00001000


ROM: System Bootstrap, Version 11.0(10c), SOFTWARE
BOOTLDR: 3000 Bootstrap Software (IGS-BOOT-R), Version 11.0(10c), RELEASE SOFTWARE (fc1)


ISP uptime is 6 days, 2 hours, 55 minutes
```

```
System returned to ROM by reload
System image file is "flash:c2500-js-1.122-13b.bin"

cisco 2500 (68030) processor (revision N) with 14336K/2048K bytes of memory.
Processor board ID 18423267, with hardware revision 00000000
Bridging software.
X.25 software, Version 3.0.0.
SuperLAT software (copyright 1990 by Meridian Technology Corp).
TN3270 Emulation software.
1 Ethernet/IEEE 802.3 interface(s)
2 Serial network interface(s)
32K bytes of non-volatile configuration memory.
16384K bytes of processor board System flash (Read ONLY)

Configuration register is 0x2102
```

CORE

```
CORE#show run
Building configuration...

hostname CORE
!
enable secret class
!
ip subnet-zero
no ip domain-lookup
ip host SB 172.16.7.75
ip host SA 172.16.7.74
ip host ISP 209.165.201.2
ip host DC 172.16.7.82 172.16.7.86
ip host DB 172.16.7.67 172.16.7.85
ip host DA 172.16.7.66 172.16.7.81
ip host WEB 209.165.202.129
!
interface Ethernet0
 description Link to Distribution Layer
 ip address 172.16.7.65 255.255.255.248
 ip ospf priority 0
 ip ospf message-digest-key 1 md5 allrouters
 ip ospf hello-interval 5
 no shutdown
!
interface Serial0
 description Link to ISP
 ip address 209.165.201.2 255.255.255.252
```

```
 no shutdown
!
router ospf 1
 network 172.16.7.64 0.0.0.7 area 0
 area 0 authentication message-digest
 default-information originate
!
ip route 0.0.0.0 0.0.0.0 Serial0
!
!
line con 0
 exec-timeout 0 0
 password cisco
 logging synchronous
 login
line aux 0
 exec-timeout 0 0
 password cisco
 logging synchronous
 login
line vty 0 4
 exec-timeout 0 0
 password cisco
 logging synchronous
 login
!
end


CORE#show ip interface brief
Interface                IP-Address      OK? Method Status                 Protocol
Ethernet0                172.16.7.65     YES NVRAM  up                      up
Serial0                  209.165.201.2   YES NVRAM  up                      up
Serial1                  unassigned      YES NVRAM  administratively down down


CORE#show ip route
Codes: C - connected, S - static, I - IGRP, R - RIP, M - mobile, B - BGP
       D - EIGRP, EX - EIGRP external, O - OSPF, IA - OSPF inter area
       N1 - OSPF NSSA external type 1, N2 - OSPF NSSA external type 2
       E1 - OSPF external type 1, E2 - OSPF external type 2, E - EGP
       i - IS-IS, L1 - IS-IS level-1, L2 - IS-IS level-2, ia - IS-IS inter area
       * - candidate default, U - per-user static route, o - ODR
       P - periodic downloaded static route


Gateway of last resort is 0.0.0.0 to network 0.0.0.0

     209.165.201.2/30 is subnetted, 1 subnets
```

```
C         209.165.201.0 is directly connected, Serial0
        172.16.0.0/16 is variably subnetted, 8 subnets, 6 masks
O         172.16.4.0/23 [110/75] via 172.16.7.67, 1d21h, Ethernet0
                         [110/75] via 172.16.7.66, 1d21h, Ethernet0
O         172.16.7.1/32 [110/11] via 172.16.7.67, 1d21h, Ethernet0
O         172.16.6.0/24 [110/75] via 172.16.7.67, 1d21h, Ethernet0
                         [110/75] via 172.16.7.66, 1d21h, Ethernet0
O         172.16.0.0/22 [110/75] via 172.16.7.67, 1d21h, Ethernet0
                         [110/75] via 172.16.7.66, 1d21h, Ethernet0
O         172.16.7.80/30 [110/74] via 172.16.7.66, 1d21h, Ethernet0
O         172.16.7.84/30 [110/74] via 172.16.7.67, 1d21h, Ethernet0
O         172.16.7.72/29 [110/75] via 172.16.7.67, 1d21h, Ethernet0
                          [110/75] via 172.16.7.66, 1d21h, Ethernet0
C         172.16.7.64/29 is directly connected, Ethernet0
        209.165.200.0/32 is subnetted, 1 subnets
O         209.165.200.255 [110/11] via 172.16.7.66, 1d21h, Ethernet0
S*    0.0.0.0/0 is directly connected, Serial0


CORE#show ip ospf 1
 Routing Process "ospf 1" with ID 209.165.201.0
 Supports only single TOS(TOS0) routes
 Supports opaque LSA
 It is an autonomous system boundary router
 Redistributing External Routes from,
 SPF schedule delay 5 secs, Hold time between two SPFs 10 secs
 Minimum LSA interval 5 secs. Minimum LSA arrival 1 secs
 Number of external LSA 1. Checksum Sum 0x00C4B6
 Number of opaque AS LSA 0. Checksum Sum 0x000000
 Number of DCbitless external and opaque AS LSA 0
 Number of DoNotAge external and opaque AS LSA 0
 Number of areas in this router is 1. 1 normal 0 stub 0 nssa
 External flood list length 0
    Area BACKBONE(0)
    Number of interfaces in this area is 1
    Area has no authentication
    SPF algorithm executed 14 times
    Area ranges are
    Number of LSA 5. Checksum Sum 0x01DCA5
    Number of opaque link LSA 0. Checksum Sum 0x000000
    Number of DCbitless LSA 0
    Number of indication LSA 0
    Number of DoNotAge LSA 0
    Flood list length 0
```

```
CORE#
CORE#show version
Cisco Internetwork Operating System Software
IOS (tm) 2500 Software (C2500-JS-L), Version 12.2(13b), RELEASE SOFTWARE (fc1)
Copyright (c) 1986-2003 by cisco Systems, Inc.
Compiled Thu 20-Feb-03 14:09 by pwade
Image text-base: 0x0307C780, data-base: 0x00001000


ROM: System Bootstrap, Version 11.0(10c), SOFTWARE
BOOTLDR: 3000 Bootstrap Software (IGS-BOOT-R), Version 11.0(10c), RELEASE SOFTWARE (fc1)


CORE uptime is 2 days, 34 minutes
System returned to ROM by power-on
System image file is "flash:/c2500-js-l.122-13b.bin"


cisco 2500 (68030) processor (revision N) with 14336K/2048K bytes of memory.
Processor board ID 18423246, with hardware revision 00000000
Bridging software.
X.25 software, Version 3.0.0.
SuperLAT software (copyright 1990 by Meridian Technology Corp).
TN3270 Emulation software.
1 Ethernet/IEEE 802.3 interface(s)
2 Serial network interface(s)
32K bytes of non-volatile configuration memory.
16384K bytes of processor board System flash (Read ONLY)


Configuration register is 0x2102
```

DIST-A

```
DIST-A#show run
Building configuration...

hostname DIST-A
!
enable secret class
!
no ip domain-lookup
ip host CORE 172.16.7.65
ip host WEB 209.165.202.129
ip host DB 172.16.7.67 172.16.7.85
ip host DC 172.16.7.82 172.16.7.86
ip host ISP 209.165.201.1
ip host SA 172.16.7.74
ip host SB 172.16.7.75
!
```

```
interface Loopback0
 description Simulated Inside Public Web Server
 ip address 145.46.47.48 255.255.255.255
!
interface Ethernet0
 description Link to CORE and DIST-B
 ip address 172.16.7.66 255.255.255.248
 ip ospf message-digest-key 1 md5 allrouters
 ip ospf hello-interval 5
 ip ospf priority 2
!
interface Serial0
 description Link to DIST-C
 ip address 172.16.7.81 255.255.255.252
 ip ospf message-digest-key 1 md5 allrouters
 ip ospf hello-interval 5
 clockrate 64000
!
router ospf 1
 area 0 authentication message-digest
 network 145.46.47.48 0.0.0.0 area 0
 network 172.16.7.64 0.0.0.7 area 0
 network 172.16.7.80 0.0.0.3 area 0
!
line con 0
 exec-timeout 0 0
 password cisco
 logging synchronous
 login
line aux 0
 exec-timeout 0 0
 password cisco
 logging synchronous
 login
line vty 0 4
 exec-timeout 0 0
 password cisco
 logging synchronous
 login
!
end


DIST-A#show ip interface brief
Interface               IP-Address      OK? Method Status              Protocol
Ethernet0               172.16.7.66     YES manual up                  up
Loopback0               145.46.47.48    YES manual up                  up
```

```
Serial0                      172.16.7.81     YES manual up                        up
Serial1                      unassigned      YES unset  administratively down down


DIST-A#show ip route
Codes: C - connected, S - static, I - IGRP, R - RIP, M - mobile, B - BGP
       D - EIGRP, EX - EIGRP external, O - OSPF, IA - OSPF inter area
       N1 - OSPF NSSA external type 1, N2 - OSPF NSSA external type 2
       E1 - OSPF external type 1, E2 - OSPF external type 2, E - EGP
       i - IS-IS, L1 - IS-IS level-1, L2 - IS-IS level-2, ia - IS-IS inter area
       * - candidate default, U - per-user static route, o - ODR
       P - periodic downloaded static route


Gateway of last resort is 172.16.7.65 to network 0.0.0.0


     172.16.0.0/16 is variably subnetted, 8 subnets, 6 masks
O       172.16.4.0/23 [110/65] via 172.16.7.82, 1d21h, Serial0
O       172.16.7.1/32 [110/11] via 172.16.7.67, 1d21h, Ethernet0
O       172.16.6.0/24 [110/65] via 172.16.7.82, 1d21h, Serial0
O       172.16.0.0/22 [110/65] via 172.16.7.82, 1d21h, Serial0
C       172.16.7.80/30 is directly connected, Serial0
O       172.16.7.84/30 [110/74] via 172.16.7.67, 1d21h, Ethernet0
O       172.16.7.72/29 [110/65] via 172.16.7.82, 1d21h, Serial0
C       172.16.7.64/29 is directly connected, Ethernet0
     209.165.200.0/32 is subnetted, 1 subnets
C       209.165.200.225 is directly connected, Loopback0
O*E2 0.0.0.0/0 [110/1] via 172.16.7.65, 1d21h, Ethernet0


DIST-A#show ip ospf neighbor

Neighbor ID      Pri   State          Dead Time   Address        Interface
209.165.201.2     0    FULL/DROTHER   00:00:35    172.16.7.65    Ethernet0
172.16.7.67       1    FULL/BDR       00:00:34    172.16.7.67    Ethernet0
172.16.7.82       1    FULL/  -       00:00:36    172.16.7.82    Serial0


DIST-A#show ip ospf 1
 Routing Process "ospf 1" with ID 172.16.7.81
 Supports only single TOS(TOS0) routes
 Supports opaque LSA
 SPF schedule delay 5 secs, Hold time between two SPFs 10 secs
 Minimum LSA interval 5 secs. Minimum LSA arrival 1 secs
 Number of external LSA 1. Checksum Sum 0x00C4B6
 Number of opaque AS LSA 0. Checksum Sum 0x000000
 Number of DCbitless external and opaque AS LSA 0
 Number of DoNotAge external and opaque AS LSA 0
 Number of areas in this router is 1. 1 normal 0 stub 0 nssa
```

```
  External flood list length 0
    Area BACKBONE(0)
    Number of interfaces in this area is 3
    Area has no authentication
    SPF algorithm executed 36 times
    Area ranges are
    Number of LSA 5. Checksum Sum 0x01DCA5
    Number of opaque link LSA 0. Checksum Sum 0x000000
    Number of DCbitless LSA 0
    Number of indication LSA 0
    Number of DoNotAge LSA 0
    Flood list length 0
```

```
DIST-A#show version
Cisco Internetwork Operating System Software
IOS (tm) 2500 Software (C2500-JS-L), Version 12.2(13b), RELEASE SOFTWARE (fc1)
Copyright (c) 1986-2003 by cisco Systems, Inc.
Compiled Thu 20-Feb-03 14:09 by pwade
Image text-base: 0x0307C780, data-base: 0x00001000

ROM: System Bootstrap, Version 11.0(10c), SOFTWARE
BOOTLDR: 3000 Bootstrap Software (IGS-BOOT-R), Version 11.0(10c), RELEASE SOFTWARE (fc1)

DIST-A uptime is 6 days, 3 hours, 3 minutes
System returned to ROM by reload
System image file is "flash:/c2500-js-l.122-13b.bin"

cisco 2500 (68030) processor (revision N) with 14336K/2048K bytes of memory.
Processor board ID 18424578, with hardware revision 00000000
Bridging software.
X.25 software, Version 3.0.0.
SuperLAT software (copyright 1990 by Meridian Technology Corp).
TN3270 Emulation software.
1 Ethernet/IEEE 802.3 interface(s)
2 Serial network interface(s)
32K bytes of non-volatile configuration memory.
16384K bytes of processor board System flash (Read ONLY)

Configuration register is 0x2102
```

DIST-B

```
DIST-B#show run
Building configuration...

hostname DIST-B
!
```

```
enable secret class
!
ip subnet-zero
no ip domain-lookup
ip host CORE 172.16.7.65
ip host DC 172.16.7.82 172.16.7.86
ip host WEB 209.165.202.129
ip host DA 172.16.7.66 172.16.7.81
ip host ISP 209.165.201.1
ip host SA 172.16.7.74
ip host SB 172.16.7.75
!
!
interface Loopback0
 description Link to Simulated Enterprise Server Farm
 ip address 172.16.7.1 255.255.255.192
!
interface Ethernet0
 description Link to CORE and DIST-A
 ip address 172.16.7.67 255.255.255.248
 ip ospf message-digest-key 1 md5 allrouters
 ip ospf hello-interval 5
 no shutdown
!
interface Serial0
 description Link to DIST-C
 ip address 172.16.7.85 255.255.255.252
 ip ospf message-digest-key 1 md5 allrouters
 ip ospf hello-interval 5
 no shutdown
!
router ospf 1
 area 0 authentication message-digest
 network 172.16.7.0 0.0.0.63 area 0
 network 172.16.7.64 0.0.0.7 area 0
 network 172.16.7.84 0.0.0.3 area 0
!
line con 0
 exec-timeout 0 0
 password cisco
 logging synchronous
 login
line aux 0
 exec-timeout 0 0
 password cisco
 logging synchronous
```

```
   login
 line vty 0 4
  exec-timeout 0 0
  password cisco
  logging synchronous
  login
 !
 end
```

```
DIST-B#show ip interface brief
Interface               IP-Address      OK? Method Status                 Protocol
Ethernet0               172.16.7.67     YES manual up                          up
Ethernet1               unassigned      YES unset  administratively down down
Loopback0               172.16.7.1      YES manual up                          up
Serial0                 172.16.7.85     YES manual up                          up
Serial1                 unassigned      YES unset  administratively down down
```

```
DIST-B#show ip route
Codes: C - connected, S - static, I - IGRP, R - RIP, M - mobile, B - BGP
       D - EIGRP, EX - EIGRP external, O - OSPF, IA - OSPF inter area
       N1 - OSPF NSSA external type 1, N2 - OSPF NSSA external type 2
       E1 - OSPF external type 1, E2 - OSPF external type 2, E - EGP
       i - IS-IS, L1 - IS-IS level-1, L2 - IS-IS level-2, ia - IS-IS inter area
       * - candidate default, U - per-user static route, o - ODR
       P - periodic downloaded static route


Gateway of last resort is 172.16.7.65 to network 0.0.0.0


     172.16.0.0/16 is variably subnetted, 8 subnets, 6 masks
O       172.16.4.0/23 [110/65] via 172.16.7.86, 1d21h, Serial0
O       172.16.6.0/24 [110/65] via 172.16.7.86, 1d21h, Serial0
C       172.16.7.0/26 is directly connected, Loopback0
O       172.16.0.0/22 [110/65] via 172.16.7.86, 1d21h, Serial0
O       172.16.7.80/30 [110/74] via 172.16.7.66, 1d21h, Ethernet0
C       172.16.7.84/30 is directly connected, Serial0
O       172.16.7.72/29 [110/65] via 172.16.7.86, 1d21h, Serial0
C       172.16.7.64/29 is directly connected, Ethernet0
     209.165.200.0/32 is subnetted, 1 subnets
O       209.165.200.225 [110/11] via 172.16.7.66, 1d21h, Ethernet0
O*E2 0.0.0.0/0 [110/1] via 172.16.7.65, 1d21h, Ethernet0
```

```
DIST-B#show ip ospf neighbor

Neighbor ID      Pri   State         Dead Time    Address         Interface
172.16.7.82       1    FULL/  -      00:00:39     172.16.7.86     Serial0
```

```
200.20.2.2         0    FULL/DROTHER    00:00:38    172.16.7.65    Ethernet0
172.16.7.81        2    FULL/DR         00:00:35    172.16.7.66    Ethernet0


DIST-B# show ip ospf 1
 Routing Process "ospf 1" with ID 172.16.7.67
 Supports only single TOS(TOS0) routes
 Supports opaque LSA
 SPF schedule delay 5 secs, Hold time between two SPFs 10 secs
 Minimum LSA interval 5 secs. Minimum LSA arrival 1 secs
 Number of external LSA 1. Checksum Sum 0x00C4B6
 Number of opaque AS LSA 0. Checksum Sum 0x000000
 Number of DCbitless external and opaque AS LSA 0
 Number of DoNotAge external and opaque AS LSA 0
 Number of areas in this router is 1. 1 normal 0 stub 0 nssa
 External flood list length 0
    Area BACKBONE(0)
    Number of interfaces in this area is 3
    Area has no authentication
    SPF algorithm executed 36 times
    Area ranges are
    Number of LSA 5. Checksum Sum 0x01DCA5
    Number of opaque link LSA 0. Checksum Sum 0x000000
    Number of DCbitless LSA 0
    Number of indication LSA 0
    Number of DoNotAge LSA 0
    Flood list length 0


DIST-B#show version
Cisco Internetwork Operating System Software
IOS (tm) 2500 Software (C2500-JS-L), Version 12.2(13b), RELEASE SOFTWARE (fc1)
Copyright (c) 1986-2003 by cisco Systems, Inc.
Compiled Thu 20-Feb-03 14:09 by pwade
Image text-base: 0x0307C780, data-base: 0x00001000


ROM: System Bootstrap, Version 11.0(10c)XB2, PLATFORM SPECIFIC RELEASE SOFTWARE (fc1)
BOOTLDR: 3000 Bootstrap Software (IGS-BOOT-R), Version 11.0(10c)XB2, PLATFORM SPECIFIC
RELEASE SOFTWARE (fc1)


DIST-B uptime is 6 days, 2 hours, 57 minutes
System returned to ROM by reload
System image file is "flash:c2500-js-l.122-13b.bin"


cisco 2500 (68030) processor (revision L) with 14336K/2048K bytes of memory.
Processor board ID 19482472, with hardware revision 00000000
Bridging software.
X.25 software, Version 3.0.0.
SuperLAT software (copyright 1990 by Meridian Technology Corp).
```

```
TN3270 Emulation software.
2 Ethernet/IEEE 802.3 interface(s)
2 Serial network interface(s)
32K bytes of non-volatile configuration memory.
16384K bytes of processor board System flash (Read ONLY)

Configuration register is 0x2102
```

DIST-C

```
DIST-C#show run
Building configuration...

hostname DIST-C
!
enable secret class
!
ip subnet-zero
no ip domain-lookup
ip host CORE 172.16.7.65
ip host WEB 183.84.85.86
ip host DB 172.16.7.85 172.16.7.67
ip host DA 172.16.7.81 172.16.7.66
ip host ISP 200.20.2.1
ip host SA 172.16.7.74
ip host SB 172.16.7.75
!
!------------------------------------------------
!Although DHCP is not taught until Module 1
!in CCNA4, it is useful in this Super Lab.
!So the configuration is provided for instructors
!------------------------------------------------
ip dhcp excluded-address 172.16.0.1 172.16.0.10
ip dhcp excluded-address 172.16.4.1 172.16.4.10
ip dhcp excluded-address 172.16.6.1 172.16.6.10
!
ip dhcp pool VLAN10
   network 172.16.0.0 255.255.252.0
   default-router 172.16.0.1
!
ip dhcp pool VLAN20
   network 172.16.4.0 255.255.254.0
   default-router 172.16.4.1
!
ip dhcp pool VLAN30
   network 172.16.6.0 255.255.255.0
   default-router 172.16.6.1
```

```
!------------------------------------------------
!
interface FastEthernet0
 no shutdown
!
interface FastEthernet0.1
 description Management VLAN 1
 encapsulation dot1Q 1 native
 ip address 172.16.7.73 255.255.255.248
!
interface FastEthernet0.10
 description FINANCE subnet VLAN 10
 encapsulation dot1Q 10
 ip address 172.16.0.1 255.255.252.0
!
interface FastEthernet0.20
 description SALES subnet VLAN 20
 encapsulation dot1Q 20
 ip address 172.16.4.1 255.255.254.0
 ip access-group SALES_TRAFFIC in
!
interface FastEthernet0.30
 description PURCHASING subnet VLAN 30
 encapsulation dot1Q 30
 ip address 172.16.6.1 255.255.255.0
 ip access-group PURCHASING_TRAFFIC in
!
interface Serial0
 description Link to DIST-B
 ip ospf message-digest-key 1 md5 allrouters
 ip ospf hello-interval 5
 ip address 172.16.7.82 255.255.255.252
 no shutdown
!
interface Serial1
 description Link to DIST-A
 ip ospf message-digest-key 1 md5 allrouters
 ip ospf hello-interval 5
 ip address 172.16.7.86 255.255.255.252
 clock rate 64000
 no shutdown
!
router ospf 1
 area 0 authentication message-digest
 network 172.16.0.0 0.0.3.255 area 0
```

```
 network 172.16.4.0 0.0.0.1 area 0
 network 172.16.6.0 0.0.0.255 area 0
 network 172.16.7.72 0.0.0.7 area 0
 network 172.16.7.80 0.0.0.3 area 0
 network 172.16.7.84 0.0.0.3 area 0
 passive-interface FastEthernet 0
!
line con 0
 exec-timeout 0 0
 password cisco
 logging synchronous
 login
line aux 0
 exec-timeout 0 0
 password cisco
 logging synchronous
 login
line vty 0 4
 exec-timeout 0 0
 password cisco
 logging synchronous
 login
!
no scheduler allocate
end
```

```
DIST-C#show ip interface brief
Interface               IP-Address      OK? Method Status              Protocol
FastEthernet0           unassigned      YES unset  up                  up
FastEthernet0.1         172.16.7.73     YES manual up                  up
FastEthernet0.10        172.16.0.1      YES manual up                  up
FastEthernet0.20        172.16.4.1      YES manual up                  up
FastEthernet0.30        172.16.6.1      YES manual up                  up
Serial0                 172.16.7.82     YES manual up                  up
Serial1                 172.16.7.86     YES manual up                  up
```

```
DIST-C#show ip route
Codes: C - connected, S - static, I - IGRP, R - RIP, M - mobile, B - BGP
       D - EIGRP, EX - EIGRP external, O - OSPF, IA - OSPF inter area
       N1 - OSPF NSSA external type 1, N2 - OSPF NSSA external type 2
       E1 - OSPF external type 1, E2 - OSPF external type 2, E - EGP
       i - IS-IS, L1 - IS-IS level-1, L2 - IS-IS level-2, ia - IS-IS inter area
       * - candidate default, U - per-user static route, o - ODR
       P - periodic downloaded static route

Gateway of last resort is 172.16.7.85 to network 0.0.0.0
```

```
       172.16.0.0/16 is variably subnetted, 8 subnets, 6 masks
C        172.16.4.0/23 is directly connected, FastEthernet0.20
C        172.16.6.0/24 is directly connected, FastEthernet0.30
O        172.16.7.1/32 [110/782] via 172.16.7.85, 1d21h, Serial1
C        172.16.0.0/22 is directly connected, FastEthernet0.10
C        172.16.7.80/30 is directly connected, Serial0
C        172.16.7.84/30 is directly connected, Serial1
C        172.16.7.72/29 is directly connected, FastEthernet0.1
O        172.16.7.64/29 [110/791] via 172.16.7.81, 1d21h, Serial0
                        [110/791] via 172.16.7.85, 1d21h, Serial1
       209.165.200.0/32 is subnetted, 1 subnets
O        209.165.200.225 [110/782] via 172.16.7.81, 1d21h, Serial0
O*E2 0.0.0.0/0 [110/1] via 172.16.7.85, 1d21h, Serial1
                        [110/1] via 172.16.7.81, 1d21h, Serial0


DIST-C#show ip ospf 1
 Routing Process "ospf 1" with ID 172.16.7.82
 Supports only single TOS(TOS0) routes
 Supports opaque LSA
 SPF schedule delay 5 secs, Hold time between two SPFs 10 secs
 Minimum LSA interval 5 secs. Minimum LSA arrival 1 secs
 LSA group pacing timer 240 secs
 Interface flood pacing timer 33 msecs
 Retransmission pacing timer 66 msecs
 Number of external LSA 1. Checksum Sum 0xC4B6
 Number of opaque AS LSA 0. Checksum Sum 0x0
 Number of DCbitless external and opaque AS LSA 0
 Number of DoNotAge external and opaque AS LSA 0
 Number of areas in this router is 1. 1 normal 0 stub 0 nssa
 External flood list length 0
    Area BACKBONE(0)
    Number of interfaces in this area is 6
    Area has no authentication
    SPF algorithm executed 26 times
    Area ranges are
    Number of LSA 5. Checksum Sum 0x1DCA5
    Number of opaque link LSA 0. Checksum Sum 0x0
    Number of DCbitless LSA 0
    Number of indication LSA 0
    Number of DoNotAge LSA 0
    Flood list length 0
```

```
DIST-C#show ip ospf neighbors


Neighbor ID      Pri   State          Dead Time   Address        Interface
172.16.7.67        1   FULL/  -       00:00:31    172.16.7.85    Serial1
172.16.7.81        1   FULL/  -       00:00:30    172.16.7.81    Serial0


DIST-C#show version
Cisco Internetwork Operating System Software
IOS (tm) C1700 Software (C1700-Y-M), Version 12.2(4)YB, EARLY DEPLOYMENT RELEASE SOFT-
WARE (fc1)
Synched to technology version 12.2(6.8)T2
TAC Support: http://www.cisco.com/tac
Copyright (c) 1986-2002 by cisco Systems, Inc.
Compiled Fri 15-Mar-02 20:32 by ealyon
Image text-base: 0x80008124, data-base: 0x807D8744


ROM: System Bootstrap, Version 12.2(7r)XM1, RELEASE SOFTWARE (fc1)
ROM: C1700 Software (C1700-Y-M), Version 12.2(4)YB, EARLY DEPLOYMENT RELEASE SOFTWARE
(fc1)


DIST-C uptime is 6 days, 31 minutes
System returned to ROM by power-on
System image file is "flash:c1700-y-mz.122-4.YB.bin"


cisco 1721 (MPC860P) processor (revision 0x100) with 29492K/3276K bytes of memory.
Processor board ID FOC07190RE7 (3108345534), with hardware revision 0000
MPC860P processor: part number 5, mask 2
Bridging software.
X.25 software, Version 3.0.0.
1 FastEthernet/IEEE 802.3 interface(s)
2 Low-speed serial(sync/async) network interface(s)
32K bytes of non-volatile configuration memory.
16384K bytes of processor board System flash (Read/Write)


Configuration register is 0x2102
```

ALSw-A

```
ALSw-A#show run
Building configuration...


hostname ALSw-A
!
enable secret class
!
no ip domain-lookup
ip host CORE 172.16.7.65
```

```
ip host WEB 209.165.202.129
ip host DC 172.16.7.73
ip host DB 172.16.7.85 172.16.7.67
ip host DA 172.16.7.81 172.16.7.66
ip host ISP 209.165.201.1
ip host SB 172.16.7.75
!
!
spanning-tree vlan 1 priority 4096
spanning-tree vlan 10 priority 24576
!
!
interface FastEthernet0/1
 switchport mode trunk
!
interface FastEthernet0/2
 switchport mode trunk
!
interface range FastEthernet0/3 - 8
 switchport access vlan 10
 switchport mode access
 switchport port-security
 switchport port-security mac-address sticky
 switchport port-security maximum 1
 switchport port-security violation shutdown
!
interface range FastEthernet0/9 - 16
 switchport access vlan 20
 switchport mode access
 switchport port-security
 switchport port-security mac-address sticky
 switchport port-security maximum 1
 switchport port-security violation shutdown
!
interface range FastEthernet0/17 - 24
 switchport access vlan 30
 switchport mode access
 switchport port-security
 switchport port-security mac-address sticky
 switchport port-security maximum 1
 switchport port-security violation shutdown
!
interface Vlan1
 ip address 172.16.7.74 255.255.255.248
 no shutdown
!
```

```
ip default-gateway 172.16.7.73
!
!
line con 0
 exec-timeout 0 0
 password cisco
 logging synchronous
 login
line vty 0 4
 exec-timeout 0 0
 password cisco
 logging synchronous
 login
line vty 5 15
 exec-timeout 0 0
 password cisco
 logging synchronous
 login
!
end
```

ALSw-A#**show vlan brief**

```
VLAN Name                             Status    Ports
---- -------------------------------- --------- -------------------------------
1    default                          active
10   FINANCE                          active    Fa0/3, Fa0/4, Fa0/5, Fa0/6
                                                 Fa0/7, Fa0/8
20   SALES                            active    Fa0/9, Fa0/10, Fa0/11, Fa0/12
                                                 Fa0/13, Fa0/14, Fa0/15, Fa0/16
30   PURCHASING                       active    Fa0/17, Fa0/18, Fa0/19, Fa0/20
                                                 Fa0/21, Fa0/22, Fa0/23, Fa0/24
1002 fddi-default                     active
1003 token-ring-default               active
1004 fddinet-default                  active
1005 trnet-default                    active
```

ALSw-A#**show vtp status**

```
VTP Version                   : 2
Configuration Revision        : 1
Maximum VLANs supported locally : 64
Number of existing VLANs      : 8
VTP Operating Mode            : Server
VTP Domain Name               : CCNA3
VTP Pruning Mode              : Disabled
```

```
VTP V2 Mode                     : Disabled
VTP Traps Generation            : Disabled
MD5 digest                      : 0x3E 0x12 0x21 0x3C 0x7D 0x09 0xAB 0x97
Configuration last modified by 172.16.7.74 at 3-1-93 04:07:07
Local updater ID is 172.16.7.74 on interface Vl1 (lowest numbered VLAN interface found)
```

ALSw-B

```
ALSw-B#show run
Building configuration...

hostname ALSw-B
!
enable secret class
!
no ip domain-lookup
ip host CORE 172.16.7.65
ip host SA 172.16.7.74
ip host ISP 209.165.201.1
ip host DA 172.16.7.81 172.16.7.66
ip host DB 172.16.7.85 172.16.7.67
ip host DC 172.16.7.73
ip host WEB 209.165.202.129
!
!
spanning-tree vlan 20 priority 4096
spanning-tree vlan 30 priority 24576
!
!
interface FastEthernet0/1
 shutdown
!
interface FastEthernet0/2
 switchport mode trunk
!
interface range FastEthernet0/3 - 8
 switchport access vlan 10
 switchport mode access
 switchport port-security
 switchport port-security mac-address sticky
 switchport port-security maximum 1
 switchport port-security violation shutdown
!
interface range FastEthernet0/9 - 16
 switchport access vlan 20
 switchport mode access
```

```
  switchport port-security
  switchport port-security mac-address sticky
  switchport port-security maximum 1
  switchport port-security violation shutdown
!
interface range FastEthernet0/17 - 24
 switchport access vlan 30
 switchport mode access
 switchport port-security
 switchport port-security mac-address sticky
 switchport port-security maximum 1
 switchport port-security violation shutdown
!
!
interface Vlan1
 ip address 172.16.7.75 255.255.255.248
 no shutdwon
!
ip default-gateway 172.16.7.73
!
!
line con 0
 exec-timeout 0 0
 password cisco
 logging synchronous
 login
line vty 0 4
 exec-timeout 0 0
 password cisco
 logging synchronous
 login
line vty 5 15
 exec-timeout 0 0
 password cisco
 logging synchronous
 login
end


ALSw-B#show vlan brief
```

```
VLAN Name                             Status    Ports
---- --------------------------------  --------  -------------------------------
1    default                          active
10   FINANCE                          active    Fa0/2, Fa0/3, Fa0/4, Fa0/5
                                                Fa0/6, Fa0/7, Fa0/8

20   SALES                            active    Fa0/9, Fa0/10, Fa0/11, Fa0/12
                                                Fa0/13, Fa0/14, Fa0/15, Fa0/16

30   PURCHASING                       active    Fa0/17, Fa0/18, Fa0/19, Fa0/20
                                                Fa0/21, Fa0/22, Fa0/23, Fa0/24

1002 fddi-default                     active
1003 token-ring-default               active
1004 fddinet-default                  active
1005 trnet-default                    active


ALSw-B#show vtp status
VTP Version                   : 2
Configuration Revision        : 1
Maximum VLANs supported locally : 64
Number of existing VLANs      : 8
VTP Operating Mode           : Client
VTP Domain Name              : CCNA3
VTP Pruning Mode             : Disabled
VTP V2 Mode                  : Disabled
VTP Traps Generation         : Disabled
MD5 digest                   : 0x3E 0x12 0x21 0x3C 0x7D 0x09 0xAB 0x97
Configuration last modified by 172.16.7.74 at 3-1-93 04:07:07
```